S0-BXW-346

We soon reached Reading 3.
and went on board.

and sailed away up
The River Thames

We ancored for the night
at Goring - and Daddy
cooked -

while John watched
anxiously but all
was well.
Next morning it was
snowing - and looked
like Christmas.

we went shopping !

We have left the Thames and
went up the Oxford Canal
which was very narrow

but went through lovely fields
and we saw lots of
birds like you see
in St James
Park.
herons and ducks -
and every night we
stop and cook ourselves

---

a lovely supper. and
so to bed early.
and often we think of
you and Nanny.

and hope that you
are enjoy Ireland and
look forward to seeing
you very soon.
All love from both
Daddy + John

---

watched
...
x

very

Peter Thorneycroft

Stanley Crooks

Foreword by
The Rt Hon The Lord Carrington, KG, GCMG, CH, MC, PC

George Mann Publications

Published by
George Mann Publications
Easton, Winchester,
Hampshire SO21 1ES
01962 779944

Copyright © Stanley Crooks 2007
Copyright © George Mann Publications 2007
Illustrations copyright © as noted 2007

All rights reserved.
No part of this publication may
be reproduced, stored in a retrieval
system, or transmitted in any form or
by any means, electronic, mechanical,
photocopying, recording or otherwise,
without the prior permission
of the copyright holders.

A CIP catalogue record for this book
is available from the British Library

ISBN 9780955241550

Printed in England

George Mann Publications

This biography is dedicated
to the memory of
Carla Thorneycroft
who inspired the author to write it
but, sadly, did not live to see its publication

"Those who lead in Government should not only have first-class brains — that is always essential — but they must also have the ability to present their case in a competent manner. Mr Thorneycroft has a wonderful brain and a remarkable ability to present his case clearly. In addition he has courage and conviction, something which is needed to crown any public life with success."

Margaret Thatcher, 25th November 1960,
during a visit to Abergavenny in Thorneycroft's Monmouth constituency

1. The man and his image (*portrait of Peter Thorneycroft by Theodore Ramos*)

Letter of condolence sent to Lady Thorneycroft by the Rt Hon Enoch Powell

33 South Eaton Place,
London SW1W 9EN
4th June 1994

Dear Carly,

Much as he would, with characteristic self-depreciation, try to conceal it, Peter was a great man. I shall always be proud of having served under him and had some part in his courageous decision which will be long remembered with respect and gratitude.

His friendship, intertwined with yours, has been a continual support and encouragement to me, through all the years.

With all my love,

Enoch

The Thorneycroft Memorial Fund

The Thorneycroft Memorial Fund was established in May 1999 within Southampton University Development Trust, whose Trustees are advised as to the utilisation of the Fund by an Advisory Board nominated by The Lady Thorneycroft, DBE, composed initially of The Earl of Limerick, KBE, (who died in 2002), Sir Ronald Grierson and Dr Stanley Crooks. The Hon John Thorneycroft, LVO, joined the Advisory Board in 2001.

Thorneycroft Scholarships

The principal activity of the Fund has been to support a succession of Thorneycroft Scholars appointed to undertake research leading to doctoral degrees in the Department of Politics at the University of Southampton. The Scholars have been selected by a Panel formed of the Head of the Department and the Chairman of the Advisory Board from candidates invited by the Department to submit proposals for research in a field proposed by the candidate and approved by the Panel. The Thorneycroft Scholars so appointed and their fields of research have been:

Dates	Scholar	Research Topic	Degree Awarded
1999-2002	Kevin Hickson BA	The 1976 IMF Crisis and British Politics	PhD
1999-2004	Robert Frith BSc	The European Union as a Model of Transnational Democracy	PhD
2002-2003	Matt Beech MSc	The Politics of New Labour	PhD
2002-2006	Mary Morrison BSc	The Liberalisation of Agriculture as a pathway to development in Andhra Pradesh	PhD

Kevin Hickson and *Robert Frith* also received matching funding from the University of Southampton. *Matt Beech* was supported by the Fund for the final year of his research. *Mary Morrison's* research programme included a visit to Andhra Pradesh supported by the Fund.

Kevin Hickson and *Matt Beech* have subsequently published books based upon their research projects under the imprint of Tauris Academic Studies.

The Biography of Peter Thorneycroft

With the approval of Southampton University Development Trust, the Thorneycroft Memorial Fund has financed the printing and publication under the imprint of George Mann Publications of this biography of Peter Thorneycroft and the relevant work of a Research Assistant, John Webster. The author, Stanley Crooks, will receive no remuneration for his work. All proceeds from sales of the book will accrue to the Fund, which will continue to support suitable academic research projects for as long as it has funds available.

Contents

§ Foreword ix
§ Introduction x
§ Acknowledgements xiii

1   Preparing for Service 1

2   Politics 17
  MP for Stafford 1938-45 17
  Tory Reform Committee 1943-49 20
  MP for Monmouth 1945-66 31
  President of the Board of Trade 1951-57 45
  Chancellor of the Exchequer 1957-58 79

3   Gap years and World Tour 1958-60 103

4   Return to Politics 199
  Minister of Aviation 1960-62 204
  Minister of Defence 1962-64 216
  Secretary of State for Defence 1964 236
  Opposition 1964-66 238
  House of Lords 1967-94 251
  Conservative Party Chairman 1975-81 265

5   Business 279
  The Pirelli Group 280
  Pye of Cambridge 294
  Trusthouse Forte 302
  SITPRO 308

6   Painting 309

7   Retrospective 323

§ Notes 337
§ Bibliography 340
§ Index 341

Illustrations

Page

1. The man and his image (*portrait of Peter Thorneycroft by Theodore Ramos*) iii
2. Major Mervyn Thorneycroft DSO, Peter's father. (*photo: F A Swaine*) 1
3. Dorothy Thorneycroft, Peter's mother.(*photo: Hay Wrightson*) 2
4. Pollarded Tree (*charcoal Sketch by Peter's Mother, Dorothy (née Franklyn), aged 13, 1897*). .3
5. The Thorneycroft twins, Elizabeth and Peter ca 1913 (*photo: from family album*)..................4
6. Letter from Peter to his mother, 1917..5
7. Letter from Major Mervyn Thorneycroft to his children, Christmas 1917..................................6
8. Illustrated letter from Major Mervyn Thorneycroft to his children, 1917..................................8
9. Peter Thorneycroft at Eton ca 1925 (*photo: Hills Saunders*) 9
10. 2nd Lt. Peter Thorneycroft, RA, 1931(*photo: F A Swaine*) 10
11. Peter and his twin sister Elizabeth (*photo: from family album*). 11
12. Carla and Peter in Rome 'after the Vatican' (*photo: from family album*). 12
13. Peter Thorneycroft, Barrister, 1937 (*photo: Elliott & Fry*). 14
14. Big Ben (*from a watercolour sketch by Peter Thorneycroft*). 16
15. A Transit Camp, Deolali, India (*sketch by the author on his way to Burma, 1944*) 20
16. Thorneycroft's campaign poster Monmouth bye-election 1945..31
17. Wedding of Peter and Carla 2nd April 1949 (*photo: Keystone Press Agency*)........................39
18. Campaigning in Monmouth Constituency, 1950 (*photo: Burnicle Studios, Monmouth*) 40
19. Peter was in the King's Road painting (*from a watercolour sketch by Peter Thorneycroft*) 46
20. A delighted Victoria welcomes her parents home from Canada, 1954 (*photo: believed to be by Associated Press*)..59
21. Punch's view of Peter Thorneycroft and the Monopolies Commission 70
22. Letter to Peter Thorneycroft from Anthony Eden, 16th January 1957 77
23. Chelsea Reach (*from a watercolour sketch by Peter Thorneycroft*) 78
24. Horse Guards, Whitehall (*from a watercolour sketch by Peter Thorneycroft*) 80
25. Chequers (*from a watercolour sketch by Peter Thorneycroft*) 83
26. Carla and Peter Thorneycroft on Budget Day, 1957 86
27. Eaton Square: The drawing room..101
28. Eaton Square: The balcony 101
29. Thorneycroft meets Prime Minister Kassim of Iraq..122
30. Thorneycroft talking to an apprentice at the Training Centre of Bahrain Petroleum.............140
31. Peter's catch of fish..176
32. Preparing to move in the same direction (*sketch by Peter Thorneycroft*)............................213
33. Thorneycroft's introduction to the House of Lords 251
34. An example of Thorneycroft's notes for a major speech...253
35. The Thorneycrofts with the Fortes at the Café Royal 1984 (The occasion was an exhibition of Peter Thorneycroft's paintings.) (*photo: from the family albums*) 306
36. A page from Peter's sketchbooks..311
37. One of John Thorneycroft's early architectural fantasies 313
38. Peter the Captain Boating on the Fens (*photo: from the family albums*) 314
39. Boating on the Fens: Victoria in the galley (*sketch by Peter Thorneycroft*)..........................315
40. Venetian Sketch, PeterThorneycroft, 1955 317
41. Peter and Victoria sketching together (*photo: Terence Daum*)...318
42. Mona Monkey (*from a painting by Victoria Nathanson*) 319

43. Peter's 80th Birthday Celebration Northbourne Court, Kent. Carla (who had almost lost her voice) wishes Peter a Happy Birthday (*photo: from the family albums*) 320
44. Prime Minister Margaret Thatcher's Tribute to Peter (*photo: from the family albums*) 320
45. Peter responds (*photo: from the family albums*) 321
46. Peter sketching in Venice 1989 (*photo: from the family albums*) 322

Colour Plates

1 Illustrated letter from Peter Thorneycroft to his daughter, Victoria.......................................113
2 Illustrated letter from Peter Thorneycroft to his grandson, Richard - page 1 114
3 Illustrated letter from Peter Thorneycroft to his grandson, Richard - page 2 115
4 a. One of Peter's early works - St Paul's (1955) 116
   b. Market in Venice
5 a. Bath - a corner of the Royal Crescent..117
   b. Bryanston Square from the Nuffield Hospital
6 a. 'Wind at Garnath 118
   b. Kentish Landscape
7 a. Beach scene, Barbados 119
   b. Grenada (during a stay at the Calabash Hotel)
8 Development of a painting - Calle Bastion, Venice 120
9 Drawing Room, Eaton Square 281
10 Venetian Doorway, Rio degli Ognissanti, Venice 282
11 a. An Industrial Scene 283
   b. Industrial Landscape near Leeds
12 a. Chrysanthemums in a black vase...284
   b. Still life
13 Venice..285
   a. Canal bridge
   b. Traghetto
   c. Isola San Giorgio
14 a. Peter Pieman...286
   b. Peter with his grandsons, Alexander and Daniel
15 a. Carla and Peter with their grandchildren at Northbourne Court 287
   b. John Ward with the Thorneycrofts and grandchildren at Northbourne Court
16 a. Peter continued to paint until close to the end of his long life..288
   b. ... even when he had to rely on a wheel chair

Endpapers

Front: Images from Peter's illustrated letter to Victoria
Back: Illustrated letter from John and Alison Ward to Carla Thorneycroft (1994)

Cover

Front: Peter Thorneycroft, Chairman of the Conservative Party, 1975
Back: Beach Hats and Towels: watercolour by Peter Thorneycroft

Foreword

By The Rt Hon The Lord Carrington, KG, GCMG, CH, MC, PC

It is sad, but true, how quickly those who have been in the public eye and have made a real contribution to British national life, are forgotten. So it is all the more important that Stanley Crooks has written this book.

Over a great many years, Peter Thorneycroft played a notable part in the Government and Conservative politics. I remember just before the war how, as a young barrister, newly elected as a Member of Parliament, he was already making his presence felt in the House of Commons. More particularly, in the last days of the war, he was a leading light in the Tory Reform Committee, which was charged with devising a rethinking Conservative Party policy in the aftermath of war and the overwhelming defeat in the election of 1945.

In the middle years of Peter's career, after a very successful period as President of the Board of Trade, he was appointed Chancellor of the Exchequer. Not long after, he resigned on a point of principle and concern for the country's economic future. This, at a time when he was thought of as a future leader of the party, was a high-minded and selfless decision. It says much for Peter that he remained entirely loyal to the Government during his period in exile and much, too, for Harold Macmillan, who had the good sense to bring him back into the Government, first as Minister of Aviation and then as Minister of Defence. The diary that he kept during his trips abroad and which form an important part of this book, and the roll call of those he saw in so many different countries, show how his reputation had preceded him and that he was regarded as a prominent international figure.

He was a formidable debater in the House of Commons, as those who heard him will testify, and the most loyal friend and supporter of his subordinates. It is very largely due to Peter Thorneycroft that the Ministry of Defence, as it is now, came into being. He was the first Secretary of State for Defence and was responsible for uniting the three Defence Services into one cohesive whole, with tact and authority. His most little known success was his appointment as Chairman of the Conservative Party by Margaret Thatcher on her being elected leader of the Party. His was the wise advice, the experienced judgement, that was in no small measure responsible for the election victory in 1979.

Those of us who knew both him and Carly, in the happiest of marriages, remember them both with affection and admiration, and welcome this overdue account of a full and productive life.

Peter Carrington
London, December 2006

Introduction

Peter Thorneycroft (The Rt Hon Baron Thorneycroft of Dunston, CH) died in June 1994, and it is a mark both of his own modesty and of the reticence of his widow, Carla, that so many years have passed before the biography so well merited by his life of service to his country comes to be written.

During his lifetime, Thorneycroft resolutely refused to consider writing an autobiography, arguing that anyone active in public life who writes about himself is bound to present a biased view, dwelling on his achievements, doing his best to sweep failures under the carpet and, moreover, even if unintentionally, almost inevitably hurting the feelings or casting doubt upon the reputation of some other public figure with whom he has been closely associated (often a friend).

A biographer need not entertain such scruples but, whilst he should do his best to avoid the error of hagiography, it does seem right to respect the moral standards of his subject. Peter Thorneycroft was a man of deep personal integrity and of warm humanity, not without sin, but with such a small ration of it in his make-up that none but the most intimate of his acquaintances could possibly detect it. If in the rough world of politics he made any enemies, there were few who were not won over (or back) to friendship once the immediate occasion of conflict was past. When he recognised fine qualities in a political opponent he had no hesitation in saying so.

For many people, the big questions about Thorneycroft the politician are whether he was right, in 1958, to resign from his post as Chancellor of the Exchequer and whether, had he not done so, he might have succeeded Harold Macmillan as Prime Minister and changed the course of British history by bringing forward by two decades or so the stiffening of monetary and budgetary discipline the country so desperately needed in the 1960s, and which was not to be implemented until Margaret Thatcher came to power in 1979. The resignation was, and remains, a rare example of a politician – and one moreover at the height of his powers – putting his career in jeopardy in defence of a matter of principle which he was profoundly convinced was right.

However, unusual though the event was in the annals of British politics, it would be quite wrong to accord Thorneycroft a place in political history merely as a principled resigner. Right at the beginning of his career, as the leading light of the Tory Reform Committee in the 1940s, he had stirred up a soporific Conservative Party with his imaginative, coherent and prescient proposals for policies which he urged the Party to adopt as its post-war programme. His performances after the sweeping Labour victory of 1945, first as opposition spokesman for transport, and later as President of the Board of Trade in Churchill's 'restoration' Cabinet of the early 1950s, ensured that his talent could not be either undervalued or overlooked in the wake of the resignation, and his stay in the political wilderness was short. After a brief spell at the Ministry of Aviation, he went on with great determination and skill, in harness with Earl Mountbatten, to overcome the resistance of the former separate service departments to their amalgamation into a united Ministry of Defence. Defeat at Monmouth in the General Election of 1966 prevented him from seeing this project through to the end, but the foundations he had laid for his successors to build upon were secure and solid.

Thorneycroft knew very well that electoral defeat is a necessary price that politicians pay to preserve the parliamentary democracy in which he so passionately believed. Although disappointed at losing the seat he had held for twenty years, rather than wait for the opportunity of a by-election to bring him back to the Commons, he decided to take up again some opportunities in the world of business which had been presented to him whilst he was briefly out of office following his resignation as Chancellor.

Nevertheless, there remained much for him to do in politics and, although he undoubtedly missed the excitement of feeling the levers of power directly within his grasp as a Cabinet minister, his elevation to the House of Lords by Harold Wilson in 1967 enabled him to exercise, skilfully and effectively, the new role of elder statesman on issues ranging from the defence of the realm to the importance of teaching the Christian ethic to schoolchildren. The part he played as Chairman of the Conservative Party in helping Margaret Thatcher to win her crucial first election as party leader in 1979 cannot be over-estimated.

The emphasis of this book is primarily on Peter's life of public service. His role as husband and father receives less attention than it deserves. For 45 years, his wife Carla brought her own considerable talents to play in her indefatigable support for Peter's constituency and party work, canvassing in the streets and villages of the wide-spread Monmouth constituency in election after election, organising social and fund-raising activities for the Conservative party and providing, in the intimate atmosphere of their successive London homes, hospitality for the many distinguished guests who came to talk, negotiate or submit their ideas to Peter's penetrating, but always friendly, scrutiny.

The author's approach to his task has been strongly influenced by a request from Carla that the book should be framed in a 'reader-friendly' fashion rather than as an academic treatise, and every effort has been made to satisfy this desire.

During most of the long political and business careers that would have more than satisfied the craving for action of most men, Peter Thorneycroft somehow found the time also to indulge a love of painting that sprang into life at the urging of his wife during a damp family holiday in the summer of 1951. In his book, *The Amateur*, published in 1986, he told the story of his devotion to painting, of his experiments in different media, learning his new trade at the feet of some of the great artists of his day, and of the pleasure he derived from watching the talent of his beloved daughter Victoria flourish as she set up her easel and painted beside him.

Age brought its frustrating physical problems and more than a fair share of pain, but his mental agility, wisdom and sense of curiosity remained unimpaired to the end. Only a few weeks before he died he was discussing with the author the relative merits of the contenders for leadership of the Labour Party: (he 'rather thought' that Mr Blair might be the best choice for them to make), and emphasising how important it was for the health of our parliamentary democracy that we should always have an opposition competent enough to be capable of acceding to government whenever the electorate should decide that the time for a change had arrived.

Stanley Crooks
Twyford, Winchester
May 2007

Acknowledgements

Peter Thorneycroft kept few records relating to his career, except for a diary of the sixteen weeks of his sabbatical 'Journey to the East' from November 1958 to February 1959. The preparation of this book has depended heavily on albums of press cuttings and photographs which his wife Carla kept meticulously up-to-date for most of her husband's active political life, enriched by her recollections of the incidents recorded therein. I am deeply indebted to Carla and to her daughter Victoria and her step-son John for adding flavour to this material. The press reports have served the biographer as pointers to the principal events of Peter's career, and I acknowledge my debt to those lobby correspondents who, for almost the whole period of Peter's active political career, maintained a very high standard of reporting of Parliamentary debates. Except where I have specifically said so, I have not relied upon the press reports, but on the official records – usually Hansard or the Conservative Party archives – to ensure that quotations are accurate and that, where I have interpreted views or situations, I have done so with the available relevant facts clearly in mind. Parliamentary material is reproduced with the permission of the Controller of HMSO on behalf of Parliament.

I am deeply indebted to John Webster, who had hoped himself to produce a biography of Peter Thorneycroft, and had already done a substantial amount of work when he discovered that I had anticipated him. I had been looking for some time for a Research Assistant, and John willingly agreed to take on that role, which he has carried out with great efficiency.

Both John Webster and I have admired the professional competence of Dr Chris Woolgar, Head of Special Collections at the Hartley Library at the University of Southampton, to whose care the Thorneycroft Papers were committed by Lady Thorneycroft and the Hon John Thorneycroft in 1997. We thank him and his colleagues for facilitating our access not only to the Thorneycroft Papers but also to documents in the Mountbatten Archive, also in the care of the Hartley Library, relevant to the reorganisation of the Ministry of Defence.

John and I are grateful also for the most efficient and kindly support we received from Jeremy McIlwaine, the Conservative Party Archivist at the Bodleian Library in Oxford, and from Sheridan Westlake at Conservative Central Office in locating and allowing us to use material from the Conservative Party archives, especially that relevant to Peter Thorneycroft's Chairmanship of the Conservative Party from 1975 – 1981. I found especially kind the assistance which Bernard Horrocks of the National Portrait Gallery gave me in finding my way through the labyrinth of copyright claims relating to photographs, especially when the most diligent of due diligence had not succeeded in locating the heirs of photographers long dead. In such cases, I have indicated the name of the photographer and crave the forgiveness of any heirs whose copyright I may have failed to acknowledge.

My dear friend and colleague, Desmond Pollock, who was Company Secretary of all the Pirelli companies in the UK for twenty years, patiently checked my work for errors with his customary diligence, and I am confident that very few will have escaped his scrutiny. For any that have, I take full responsibility. Jasmine Boxall, who was the Personal Assistant of Peter's successor as Chairman of Pirelli UK plc, the Earl of Limerick, was a great help in converting an old type-script account of Peter's 'Journey to the East' into computer format, saving me hours of my clumsy typing.

Many individuals, friends, colleagues (and some former political opponents) of Peter have shared with me their memories of him, sometimes asking that they should not be directly quoted, and I acknowledge my debt to them. I am obliged to Marco Tronchetti Provera for his advice on the Pirelli chapter, and I thank Gordon Bussey and Sir Jack Stewart-Clark for the contributions they made to the chapter on Pye of Cambridge, and George Proctor for kindly checking the chapter on Forte.

I am especially grateful to Lord Carrington who agreed with such evident pleasure to write the Foreword to the book.

Baroness Thatcher has most kindly approved the many references to her in this book, in particular the extract from her speech in Monmouth constituency in 1960, the references to her in the chapters on 'Chancellor of the Exchequer' and 'Conservative Party Chairman' and the paraphrase of her speech on the occasion of Peter Thorneycroft's 80th birthday party in 1989.

A special tribute is due to my publisher, George Mann, not just for his competence and creativity, but also for the firm, but always kindly, guidance he has given me throughout the past two years. It was George who introduced me to Brynja Maughan, the quality of whose photographic expertise emerges clearly from the reproductions of some of Peter Thorneycroft's paintings which she photographed for the colour plate sections of the book.

~ 1 ~
Preparing for Service

Childhood

Peter Thorneycroft was the only son of Major Mervyn Thorneycroft DSO of Dunston Hall, near Stafford, and Dorothy Franklyn, daughter of Sir William Franklyn KCB. Peter and his twin sister, Elizabeth, were born at Dunston Hall on 26th July 1909.

2. Major Mervyn Thorneycroft DSO, Peter's father.
(*photo: F A Swaine*)

Mervyn Thorneycroft served with distinction in the Great War in the Royal Horse Artillery. At the beginning of the war, he was Adjutant of the Berkshire RHA in Egypt and Aden, a tour of duty which included the Battle of Sheikh Othman in July 1915. After a short posting as Staff Captain RA at the Canal Defence HQ of 2nd Mounted Division, he was given command of 'L' Battery RHA in 29 Division, taking part in the evacuation from Gallipoli in January 1916, the battles of the Somme in July that year and of Arras in April 1917. He finished the war as Brigade Major RA of 39 Division which was engaged in the Third Battle of Ypres in July 1917 before the 5th Army retreat in March 1918 and the final push forward in the last three months of the war. In the last battle in which he was engaged, he was blown up and buried by a mine. His men rushed forward, dug him out and saved his life, but he lost the use of his legs and, for the rest of his life, had to use a bath chair. After the war, he served a further year as GSO2 RA of III Corps before retiring at the end of 1919 to his wife and ten-year-old twins and to a civilian life as a landowner and farmer, still aged only 35, after what, even by Great War standards, had been an eventful military career.

The Thorneycrofts stemmed from a line of Staffordshire blacksmiths, who had prospered and become ironmasters. Peter once told the journalist Peter Howard that his great-great-grandfather was the last of the blacksmiths, his great-grandfather the last of the ironmasters, and his grandfather a squire. The great-great-grandfather he referred to was George Benjamin Thorneycroft, the first Mayor of Wolverhampton in 1831, and founder of the Thorneycroft Benefaction, a charity for the distribution of blankets to the poor of the town of which Peter was later to be a trustee. His great-grandfather was reputed to be a somewhat eccentric gentleman who invented an umbrella with a window – a most useful device, to ward off the rain and at the same time let you see where you were going. Much further back, in 1240 AD, there is a record of a Hamo de Thornicrofte in the village of Siddington, near Macclesfield, and Hamo is a name often to be found in the family annals: (Peter bestowed it as a second name on his own son John). There were other distinguished ancestors. His uncle, Major-General Alexander

3. Dorothy Thorneycroft, Peter's mother.
(*photo: Hay Wrightson*)

Whitelaw Thorneycroft of Tettenhall Towers, Wolverhampton (1879-1931), was a veteran of the fierce battle of Spion Kop during the Boer War and founded the Thorneycroft Light Horse Regiment. Dorothy Thorneycroft had shown as a child that she had the gene of artistic talent which, in later years, came to play such an important role in the life of her son.

A sketchbook dating from 1896-7, when she was 13 or 14 years' old, contains a remarkably wide range of her well-executed sketches in pencil, charcoal, water colour and sepia wash. One of them, a charcoal sketch of a pollarded tree, is reproduced here.

4. Pollarded Tree
Charcoal Sketch by Peter's Mother, Dorothy (née Franklyn), aged 13, 1897.

Little is known of Peter's childhood except that, from a very early age, he was fascinated by the activities of the local Otter Hounds and soon became an enthusiastic beagler and horse rider. There are a few photographs in the family archives that reveal first a well wrapped up, happily smiling toddler with his twin sister Elizabeth, and later a bright-eyed ten-year-old, a well-turned out and rather formal adolescent Etonian, and a young adult already showing the clear, slightly challenging gaze that many will remember of the mature man.

5. The Thorneycroft twins, Elizabeth and Peter ca 1913 (*photo: from the family albums*).

Three letters survive from 1917, one a brief birthday message from Peter to his "Mummy" dated December 1st:

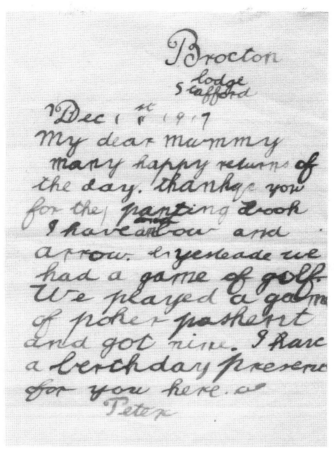

6. Letter from Peter to his mother, 1917.

The second, dated Christmas Eve, sent by Mervyn Thorneycroft from VIII Corps Headquarters in France to Peter and Elizabeth, hoping that they had had a very happy Christmas and not over eaten (and that the Germans would not have enough food and gradually die of hunger), exhorting them to give the pony plenty of work, and some hay if there was snow on the ground, and commiserating with them on the difficult History questions Miss Woodhouse had asked them in their recent exams. He urged them to learn French from Mademoiselle, if she had arrived, so that they would be able to ask for food when they came over to see him, and he sent them a picture of a town the Germans had shot to pieces, where he had been living (and making sure he got into a hole whenever they shot at it), and closing with a promise that, if the Germans didn't shoot him, he would

5

come home to see them in February. Mervyn clearly did not believe in hiding the realities of war from his offspring.

Christmas Eve.
Dec 24. 1917.
VIII Corps Hqrs.

My dear Peter & Elizabeth—

Thank you very much your your letters — I hope you have had a very happy Christmas and not over Eaten yourselves! and that you still have enough to eat, not too much. But I hope by now the Germans haven't got enough — and that they will gradually die of hunger.

How is the pony?— Mind you give him plenty of work — If the ground is covered into snow he will have to have some hay to eat — You must ask Salmon about that.

Mummy has sent me a book showing how well you have done your Examinations and what difficult History questions Miss Woodhouse asked you.

Now I expect it is the holidays and you have no lessons to do except

7. Letter from Major Mervyn Thorneycroft to his children, Christmas 1917.

perhaps a little French with
Mademoiselle, if she has arrived —
You must learn to talk French
as otherwise you wont be able to
ask for anything to eat when you
come over here to see me.
Besides Everybody can talk French
nearly now. —

This is a picture of a Town that
the Germans have been shooting at
for years, and they have nearly shot
it all away — Last year when you
were at Brocton I was living in it
but I was very careful to get into
a hole everytime they shot at it, near
were I lived, If the Germans don't
shoot me I shall come home again to
see you in February — Look after
mummy, keep her amused —
Soyez sages, mes infants.
Your affec DADDY.

7

The third letter, like the second sent from the trenches, is an early example of the Thorneycroft family's custom of illustrating their letters to each other, of which we shall see many other examples later in the book.

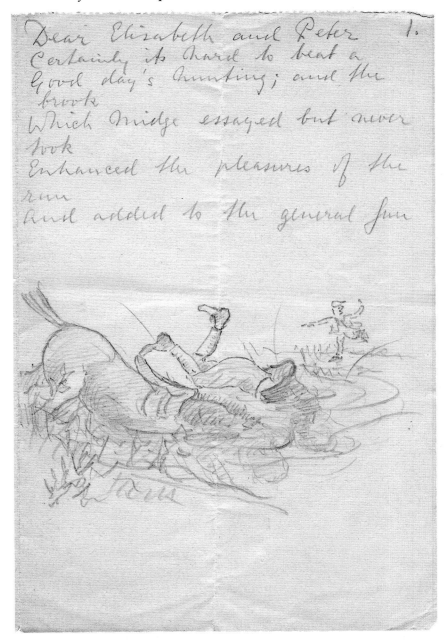

Dear Elizabeth and Peter 1.
Certainly its hard to beat a
Good day's hunting; and the
brook
Which Midge essayed but never
took
Enhanced the pleasures of the
run
And added to the general fun

8. Illustrated letter from Major Mervyn Thorneycroft to his children, 1917.

School

Peter was educated at Eton but we have been able to find little information about his time there. Simon Heffer in his entry on Thorneycroft in the *Dictionary of National Biography* says that he showed little academic ability, and his family recalls that he was not especially happy there. A photograph in the family album in Etonian dress shows a well turned-out young man with a confident gaze, and that is really all we know about him in his 'teens.

9. Peter Thorneycroft at Eton ca 1925 (*photo: Hills Saunders*)

Royal Artillery

Doubtless encouraged by his Gunner father, and perhaps also by his tutors at Eton who did not expect him easily to gain a place at university, Peter set his sights on entering the Royal Military Academy at Woolwich. His Record of Service (provided by the Army Personnel Centre in Glasgow) shows that on 12th

May 1927, his father wrote to the War Office asking that his son be accepted as a candidate for the Entrance Examination to the RMA next November, and asking also that he be considered for an 'Honorary King's Cadetship', explaining that he (Mervyn) had been obliged to retire from the Army in November 1923 on account of injuries received on active service. The young Thorneycroft needed the help of a crammer at the Army College in Farnham to get him through the entrance examination, but he succeeded, and entered the RMA in 1928. Two years later he was commissioned into the Royal Artillery, and posted to 3rd Field Brigade RA, serving for the next two years at Horsfield Barracks in Bristol and at Woolwich.

10. 2nd Lt. Peter Thorneycroft, RA, 1931
(*photo: F A Swaine*)

However, peacetime soldiering proved not to present enough of a challenge to a young man whose early years had already provided plenty of opportunities for the sort of manly physical activities and excitements open in those years to an army officer. True, the training of artillery cadets introduced them to some of the mysteries of mathematics and physics, and early signs of artistic ability no doubt won him good marks for the panoramic sketches of target areas that were expected of artillery officers but, on the whole, the Royal Military Academy and the Officers' Mess seem not to have provided the intellectual stimulus for which Thorneycroft was now ready.

There were other influences emerging at this time which were to exert profound effects on Thorneycroft's life. In the summer of 1930, his parents had invited friends they had met whilst on holiday in Capri to visit them at Dunston Hall and it was here, as Carla Thorneycroft later recalled, that she and Peter found themselves on opposite sides in a tennis match, and fell in love across the net. Carla was the vivacious and highly intelligent daughter of Count Guido and Countess Alexandra Malagola Cappi, 16 years old, and most attractive. She was later, after a long separation, to become his wife. Carla and Peter's twin sister Elizabeth had become firm friends, and they joined forces in urging Peter to make inquiries about the ways open to him to enter the legal profession, in which Elizabeth had recently decided that she would make her own career. Peter and his sister were already very close. They rowed together, they rode together, they discussed their plans together.

11. Peter and his twin sister Elizabeth (*photo: from the family albums*).

The combination of Elizabeth and Carla must have been irresistible. Elizabeth later had a brilliant career as a barrister and became an expert in international law, culminating in her appointment as a Don in International Law at Oxford, as well as becoming a gifted amateur astronomer.

Thorneycroft evidently had access to sound advice, and decided that he would get some hands-on experience of the judicial system before seeking a pupillage. Before he could do so, he had to resign his commission and, on 1st July 1931, the resignation of 2nd Lieutenant G E P Thorneycroft was recorded in the London Gazette. He was to return to the Royal Artillery on the outbreak of war in 1939. In the meantime, he devoted his attention to laying the foundations for the new career he had decided upon – and to strengthening the bonds that had developed so quickly after their first meeting between himself and the beguiling Italian girl he had met that sunny day on the tennis court.

The love between Peter and Carla was to endure until Peter's death in 1994

12. Carla and Peter in Rome 'after the Vatican' (*photo: from the family albums*).

and, indeed, beyond it, for Carla never really believed that Peter had gone from her life. It's course, however, was far from smooth. They became engaged in 1931, and a year later, during a visit to Carla's parents' house in Rome, the family album shows them together in formal attire, (with a jocular comment by Peter's mother underneath the photograph, "P and Carly after the Vatican (the under housemaid and the 3rd footman.)". However events conspired to separate them at a time when British relations with Italy were beginning to deteriorate. Their efforts to keep in touch by letter at that difficult time were not successful, and they lost contact, apparently irremediably. They were not to meet again until after the war but, throughout those years of separation, and until her death, Carla kept, in a little book of hand-written fragments of love poems by great poets - Shakespeare, Christina Rossetti and many others – a poem marked 'P.T. to C.M., 1932) which reveals the strength of Peter's love for her:

There is a Dawn

There is a dawn beyond our dearest dreams
And these our thoughts its fond first tender beams
Lighten our throbbing hearts as when the dim
Dark shadows creep away at hint of morning.
The silver grey of dew upon the slim
Straight blades of grass, the scents, the dawning
Colours, and all the hidden mystery of the earth,
All these are ours to take - was it not worth
One little hour of waiting by the gate?
Dear Heart, our hopes and all our dreaming
Will leap to life beneath the eyes of fate
However long the hour, thank God for deeming
Us brave to bear the pain, to win the prize,
We part to meet again - Hold me, dear eyes.

P.T to C.M., 1932

The law

Thorneycroft was able in 1933 to secure an appointment as marshal to Mr Justice Rowlatt on the Western Circuit, and spent several months accumulating practical knowledge of the way the courts functioned. One of the most respected mentors of aspiring barristers in those days was Mr Theobald Mathew, and it was the pupil room of his chambers in Inner Temple (affectionately known as 'the dog hole') that Thorneycroft entered in 1933.

A newspaper cutting (one of the thousands meticulously filed by his wife, Carla) written by the columnist 'Autolycus' in 1938, records an early example of Thorneycroft's methodical and painstaking approach:

> *"Once in his pupil days I went with him to the Old Bailey. We chanced*
> *upon a heavy commercial fraud case; an accountant was in the box being*
> *cross-examined by counsel on detail after detail of the prisoner's books.*
> *Thorneycroft went home thoughtfully; and the next week he was starting a*
> *correspondence course in accountancy."*

Thorneycroft, who had been awarded a Profumo prize in the Michaelmas Term of 1933, was called to the Bar of the Inner Temple in 1934, and quickly established a thriving practice in the Birmingham district. The same commentator observed that:

"Such unusually early success is due to his happy possession of two characteristics not often found together. There is a touch of fire in his nature that gives him inspiration in Court. And at the same time he is methodical and painstaking."

13. Peter Thorneycroft, Barrister, 1937 (*photo: Elliott & Fry*).

As a young man in the early nineteen-thirties, Peter often spent his summer holidays at Eishken, a hunting lodge on the Isle of Lewis owned by his Great-Aunt Eleanor. His cousin Audley Archdale, younger than Peter, recalled in a poem that he composed for Peter's 70th birthday an escapade one Sunday in 1937 - a fishing expedition (strictly forbidden on a Sabbath day) on Loch Shell, when they managed, lines baited with mussels, to land an enormous pile of haddock and:

Return to pier in modest triumph
quietly, though, it is the Sabbath.
But see there is upon the pier
a giant figure, quite severe,
looming o'er the happy cousins
knee deep in fish, piled up by dozens.
He takes the painter, holds the thwart,
we disembark, filled with the thought
that, in a trice, we're now disgraced
and all the fun is full displaced.
Murdo, silent, official greeter
Quietly, firmly, says "Mr Peter,
Miss Eleanor is wishing for you to see
in the gun-room, before your tea."
Kind cousin, you said in serious tone
"You'd better clear off while I face the Throne!"
So slink I away to my comfortable room,
changed my shoes and kept my 'heid doon'
until it was time for that afternoon tea,
and my turn to face the ignominy.
But all was quite quiet, not a word was being said
about boats nor fish nor rules that were shed,
just talk of the gales of the week before
and the certainty that there would be some more.

Peter had taken the blame for their sinful conduct, and young Audley escaped unscathed.

There is little doubt that Thorneycroft could have forged a highly successful and lucrative career for himself as a barrister. However, the death of Lord Harlech and the consequent elevation to the Lords of his son, W G A Ormsby-Gore, who had been MP for Stafford for twenty years, gave Thorneycroft the opportunity to contest his home constituency as a Conservative candidate at a bye-election on 9th June 1938. He was well known and liked locally and, young and inexperienced as he undoubtedly was, he was able to mobilise his supporters in determined canvassing on voters' doorsteps throughout the constituency. Foreign policy was the core issue of the election. Hitler's *Anschluss* of Austria had been perpetrated only three months earlier and Thorneycroft had found himself having to fight off a strong intervention in support of the Labour candidate, F G Lloyd, by the still formidable Liberal Lloyd George, who accused the Government of "*cringing before the dictators. British ships were being bombed off the coast of Spain, and we send twittering little protests ...... but not to Italy and Germany. We are afraid of them!"* But for some months past the mood of the country had been moving in favour of Chamberlain's policy of appeasement and Thorneycroft won the seat with a majority of 4,408. Turn-out was an impressive 78%.

Only four weeks earlier, on 11th May 1938, he had married Sheila Wells Page, a Staffordshire County hockey player of Tettenhall, whose parents were also hockey players, her father at international level, and her mother having been a reserve for England. The marriage service at St Michael and All Angels in Tettenhall had been conducted by the bride's uncle, Archdeacon Swindell. Politics was already invading the lives of the young couple. 600 members of Stafford Division Conservative and Unionist Association were taken in 17 coaches to view their candidate's wedding gifts at Tettenhall Towers, the home of Peter's Aunt Florence, and their honeymoon was curtailed by the election campaign.

Peter Thorneycroft was to dedicate the greater part of the next six decades serving his country as a Member of Parliament and, later, as a Peer in the Houses of Parliament. From the early nineteen-fifties, he began to sketch and paint, and his sketchbooks contain many images of scenes such as this in the vicinity of Westminster, drawn or painted when he found a little time to spare from politics.

14. Big Ben (*from a watercolour sketch by Peter Thorneycroft*).

~ 2 ~
Politics

MP for Stafford 1938-45

The new MP created a notable impression when he took up his seat in the Commons, marching to the Bar of the House, it was reported, with military precision, flanked by his sponsors Captain Margesson, a Hussar, and Captain Waterhouse of the Life Guards, all three faultlessly attired in morning dress.

His victory at the by-election had been seen as a clear affirmation of public support for Neville Chamberlain's policy of seeking to preserve peace through negotiation with the Germans, turning a tide which had been running against the Government in the early months of the year, when three by-election seats had gone to Labour. *"The rule of law must be substituted for the rule of war"*, said Thorneycroft during the campaign, but whilst expressing his belief that the League of Nations was the best way to achieve this in the future, he lamented that it was not yet ready for the task

Thorneycroft returned to this theme in his maiden speech in the debate on the Gracious Address on 10th November 1938, arguing that *"Millions of Germans today feel"*, he said, *"rightly or wrongly, that they have a mission in Central Europe"*, comparing this with Britain's belief that it had a mission to the English-speaking peoples of the world, and that, *"... we should try to understand them and that we should devote our enormous resources not to the building up of armaments but to increasing the prosperity of both peoples"*. He was not in favour of conscription, suggesting that men over military age were perfectly capable of manning anti-aircraft guns. He was, however, deeply concerned at the shortage of skilled men in British manufacturing industry, unlike Germany and Russia, where the training of young men for industry was one of the tenets of their faith.

Three months later, speaking to the 1912 Club at Bucklersbury in London, he cited the Munich Conference of the previous September as a classic example of the new diplomacy in action: contact between leading statesmen as opposed to the old technique of prolonged and careful approaches through 'diplomatic channels'. He went even further, suggesting that *"It was plain now that the real tragedy of Czecho-Slovakia lay not in the fact that frontier districts were ceded but that they had not been ceded long before."* On 24th February 1939 he hazarded a prediction that *"England will not be involved in a war this year, and there is every possibility of peace being maintained in 1940."*

But Hitler was to confound yet again those like Thorneycroft who were still prepared, against all the evidence, to trust him. In March 1939 his troops occupied the rump of Czechoslovakia left unclaimed by Germany at the Munich conference. Whether it had the character of appeasement, crass abasement or desperate playing for time, Chamberlain's policy was no longer sustainable. The reality of Hitler's aggressive intent could no longer be ignored or glossed over. It was time for heads to rule hearts.

The change of tone of Thorneycroft's increasingly confident speeches in the House during the Spring of 1939 is most marked. Conscription now had his full support but, drawing no doubt on his own experience of the Army's habits, he was concerned that conscripts should not waste their time on fatigues, but concentrate on their military training, and that former Territorial soldiers should not be obliged, when conscripted, to repeat training they had already mastered. In a debate on the Civil Defence Bill in June, the lawyer in him came to the fore, with a spirited attack on a proposal to take away a dependant's common law right to compensation on the death of a family's bread-winner.

With war now imminent, on 7th July 1939, Thorneycroft applied to rejoin the Royal Artillery Reserve and, on 30th August, he was recalled to the Colours as a Second Lieutenant, RA, with seniority backdated to 28th October 1937. On the day war was declared, 3rd September 1939, he was posted to Hartsbourne Manor near Watford as Intelligence Officer RA to Brigadier Price in 55 Division.

During the dangerous months of 1940 which saw the Germans sweep aside resistance in Poland, Belgium, Luxembourg, Holland, France, Denmark and Norway, the evacuation of British troops from Dunkirk, the Italian invasion of France and the air Battle of Britain, Thorneycroft was engaged in staff duties, increasingly frustrated by examples he judged to be of incompetence in the direction of the war effort. From August 1940 onwards he sent a monthly news letter to his constituents in Stafford and, in his October 1940 letter, his frustration boiled over in a fierce criticism of the disaster at Dakar, which he attributed to failure of the services to work together, in the absence of a single commander of all three services capable of making a decision and sticking to it. He argued that co-ordinating committees do not make decisions – they reach compromises.

His frankness did not stand in the way of promotion. Just before Christmas 1940 (a few days after his son, John Hamo, cut his first tooth) he was appointed Brigade Major RA in HQRA 12 Corps. His stay there was short. On 11th March 1941 he was instructed to join forthwith HQRA 10 Corps, for duty as Assistant CBO (Counter Battery Officer), in which capacity he was, for a short time, in command of the enormous gun at Dover which used to shoot a round or two into France every now and again (mainly, he thought, for the edification of visiting top brass). However, within days he was moved to the post of Brigade Major RA, Northumberland Division.

A constituency letter in September 1941 reveals his anxiety that those responsible for directing the war effort were getting their priorities wrong. Miners, who should have been extracting desperately needed coal from the pits, were being conscripted into the armed forces; fit young servicemen were doing jobs which could be done just as well by women; A1 soldiers were serving in anti-aircraft batteries, searchlight and balloon barrage units, and fit airmen in ground duties in the RAF. As well as making sure that all these young and healthy men were moved to front-line assignments, Thorneycroft advocated asking the Dominions to provide reinforcements.

Perhaps all this signalled in an indirect way a desire for a more active role for himself, but an active service appointment still eluded him. In March 1942, he was sent to join Junior War Course No 8 at the Staff College in Camberley and, from there, was posted in July as DAQMG in GS (P) at the War Office. Just before moving to the War Office, he made his first speech in the Commons for two years, in a tense debate on 'the Central Direction of the War', during which he repeated in the House many of the criticisms he had made elsewhere. He was beginning to be noticed and listened to. In November he was chosen by Churchill to second for the Government the motion to receive the Gracious Address and, the evening before at a dinner in 10 Downing Street, he was placed between Churchill and General Smuts. He noted as 'very memorable' a discussion with Smuts on the tactics adopted by his Uncle Alex (Major-General Alexander Whitelaw Thorneycroft) during the Boer War.

In January 1943, Thorneycroft asked to be released from the Army for three months to attend to his Parliamentary duties, and his release was approved with effect from 1st February. His leave of absence was subsequently extended every three months and he did not return to the Army for the rest of the war.

Tory Reform Committee 1943-49

Now began one of the most fruitful periods in the development of Thorneycroft's political philosophy. That he had already begun to think deeply about post-war politics is evidenced by his brief membership of the 1941 Committee, formed by J B Priestley, which in December 1941 proposed public control of railways, mines and docks and a national wages policy, and in 1942 urged formation of works councils and preparation of post-war plans for free education and full employment, although we have been able to find no evidence that he took any active role in the Committee's deliberations. (Richard Acland, also a member, later formed the short-lived Common Wealth Party).

At the beginning of March 1943, Thorneycroft was appointed Joint Honorary Secretary (with Hugh Molson) of a new Tory Reform Committee (TRC), chaired by Lord Hinchingbrooke, with 36 members of the Conservative Party, whose role was to be the preparation of a series of proposals on the policies for a post-war Conservative government. The TRC originated as a pressure group whose initial objective was to press the wartime Coalition Government to prepare a firm plan to implement as soon as possible the proposals of the Beveridge Report of 1942, *Social Insurance and Allied Services,* and the Scott and Uthwatt Reports on Physical Planning. In their book, *"Hinch" – A Celebration of Viscount Hinchingbrooke, MP,* published by the Mapperton Estate in 1997, Andrew Best and John Sandwich record that Hinchingbrooke told them that the object of TRC was to break the perceived link of the Party to a 'devil take the hindmost' attitude.

Many of those who served during the Second World War will recall how the periods of inaction – the lulls in fighting, the perilous (but often tedious) journeys in troop ships, the waiting in transit camps – were so often filled with political argument, often heated, between individuals thrown together from so many different backgrounds,

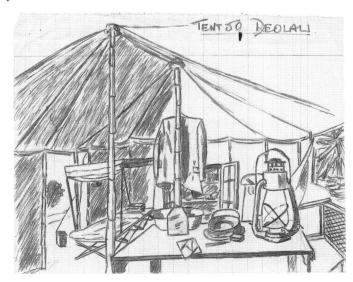

15. A Transit Camp, Deolali, India
(*sketch by the author on his way to Burma, 1944*)

public school boys and barrow boys, scholars and skivers, religious and irreligious, who, often for the first time, were learning something of how others lived and felt about their lives.

The many MPs, like Thorneycroft, who also served in the Forces must have been especially sensitive to the political signals that emerged from discussions like these and it is, perhaps, not surprising that more than a third of the members of the TRC had a military service background; nor that the first object of their attention was the Beveridge Report, which had generated such a tremendous surge of interest in the country and, not least, in the armed forces as soon as it was published. For years after the war, when he appeared on a television programme, Peter Thorneycroft would wear his Royal Artillery tie, knowing that its zig-zag red stripe on a blue background would be recognised immediately by thousands of viewers who had served in the artillery and who would be saying to themselves, "He's one of us! Once a Gunner, always a Gunner."

The Beveridge Report

The Beveridge Report (1942) was the first major policy document presented during the war which looked forward to the shape of post-war Britain, and the TRC recognised how important it was for the Conservative Party to formulate its own response to the issues Beveridge had raised. The TRC's assessment of the Report's proposals was wholly positive. However, they did not wish to leave the matter merely at the level of intellectual agreement on principles, but to point out the practical measures which would have to be put in place to ensure that those principles would be acted upon. The Beveridge Report had, in fact, received a laudably rapid response from the Coalition Government. It was reviewed by a committee chaired by Sir Thomas Phillips as early as December 1942–January 1943, and accepted by the Committee on Reconstruction Problems headed by Sir William Jowitt which, during the following months produced a blueprint for implementation of the main proposals. Implementation of the principal elements of the Beveridge Report was therefore already assured, and the TRC confined itself to considering whether further legislation was needed in the specific areas of 'Industrial Assurance', Approved Societies and Death Grants. These issues were important at the time, but need not detain us here. Their report, *Industrial Assurances, Approved Societies and Death Grants*, written by six of its members (who on this occasion did not include Thorneycroft) was published in January 1944. Far and away the most important conclusion of the Conservative Party – of the 'establishment', as well as the liberal-conservative modernisers of the TRC – was the unequivocal endorsement of the principle of a national system of social security.

Forward - By the Right

The TRC's concerns went beyond Beveridge. Their deliberations soon broadened into a general examination of how Conservative policy ought to evolve in readiness for the extremely difficult situation in which a Britain drained of its economic wealth by the war would find itself. The collective title they chose for their series of policy bulletins was *Forward – By the Right*, a title with a somewhat military ring about it, and perhaps a little misleading for what was, after all, a manifesto of a clearly liberal wing of the party. These were 'one-nation Tories', heirs of Disraeli, politicians who were convinced that belief in conservative principles was not the preserve of what were still, in 1942, called 'the upper classes', but was widely spread across the whole of society, and that the Conservative Party was capable of offering solutions to social problems which many of the millions who suffered directly from those problems – unemployment, poverty, sickness, bad housing, poor educational opportunities - could well find much more appealing than those of the socialists.

To set the ball rolling, an introductory pamphlet under the banner *Forward – By the Right* was published in October 1943.

The TRC's publications tackled one by one each of the major social issues already confronting the nation that would clearly have to be dealt with in post-war Britain in spite of the damage inflicted upon the economy by war and its aftermath. Each paper was written by two or more of the members, but had the imprimatur of the whole committee. Over a two-year period in 1943 and 1944, a score of pamphlets and bulletins made their appearance, the longest of them having only 60 pages. By the standards of Gordon Brown's 1,800 page dissertation in June 2003 on the possible consequences of joining the Euro, their analyses could no doubt be regarded as somewhat superficial. These, however, were people committed to clarity, and not at all persuaded that clarity of conclusion depends upon complexity of argument, prolixity or pretentiously precise calculations, especially in economic and social matters where theories cannot be tested by controlled experiments in laboratories, but only in the real world of fickle human beings.

The TRC members were well aware that they would have to demonstrate that their proposals could be afforded and to identify credible sources of funds to finance them. Already by their fifth bulletin, they were outlining the foreseeable costs of their proposals and suggesting ways of funding them. There are clear pointers here to Thorneycroft's later insistence that the national books must balance over an economic cycle and that, ideally, only capital investment should be funded by debt (principles rediscovered by New Labour more than 50 years later).

The specific proposals of the TRC were directed, of course, to solving the problems of their time and are now inevitably dated. There is scope for a lengthy and learned treatise examining in detail how the concepts they developed, which were valid approaches in the latter years of the war to the then foreseeable problems of the immediate post-war period, were subsequently moulded and refined as the problems themselves changed with the passage of time. Here, however, we wish to concentrate attention on those key elements of Peter Thorneycroft's early political thought which were later to form the kernel of his contribution to the politics of his party and of his country.

Propaganda

We have become used in recent years to living with British Governments expert in the manipulation of the information they release to the public, to the extent of having to add a new meaning to the ancient verb 'to spin'. Knowing rather well how effectively the flow of news to the public was being managed in time of war, the TRC was convinced, in 1944, that there would be no place for a Ministry of Information within the country in peacetime. They believed that the Government should pass their messages to the professional media, leaving columnists and editors at liberty to support or to criticise Government policies as they saw fit. They insisted that freedom from censorship was of higher value than any possible harm that could result from its abuse, and that the British Press would not be so wanting in responsibility as to jeopardise the public interest in a critical situation. The subject matter of national publicity should be, quite simply, the truth.

They recognised, nevertheless, in *Telling the World* (Bulletin No 3), that there would be a need for an information service directed outwards to the rest of the world because, if international relations were to be governed in future by law rather than by force, it was essential to foster mutual understanding between nations. It was clear that there were bound to be points of disagreement on major issues between, for example, the USA, the USSR and Britain, but at least their policies and actions should be intelligible to each other. They argued that, if the rest of the world was to have confidence in British policy, they must first have confidence in the character and institutions of the British people and that, to promote that confidence, Britain should keep the world constantly informed of its thinking not only on matters of direct international significance, but also on the cultural and social developments and influences which shaped its approach.

The TRC envisaged the newly created Central Statistical Office as the proper collector of information and, by implication, guarantor of its accuracy, and suggested that the CSO, alongside a National Publicity Office as disseminator, could well develop as specialist branches of the Cabinet Secretariat, accountable to the members of the Cabinet individually and collectively. To ensure co-ordination in the field, it was felt that overseas publicity staff of Government departments should report to their Headquarters office, but work closely with the Ambassador who, in case of doubt, should exercise control until any difference of opinion was resolved by departmental agreement or, if necessary, by Cabinet. They insisted, however, that they did not wish to be dogmatic about the machinery. Indeed, they seem not to have been in the least interested in any form of Government publicity organisation specifically aimed at the domestic audience, indicating somewhat dismissively that the Government must make its case to the electorate by what they called the ordinary means of persuasion open to its own supporters and to the opposition alike.

Their concern, then, was to ensure that the British point of view and values were understood by the rest of the world, and that the domestic audience who had no need for such schooling were given unvarnished facts, guaranteed to be accurate by the professionals of the national statistical agency.

Control of Land Use

In 1937, so the Scott Report of 1941 tells us, the population was stable at around 41 million, yet enough land had been designated for housing to accommodate 300 million people. It is little wonder that so much attention was being paid in the early 1940s to the immensely complicated problems of land values: the way they were affected by planning decisions; questions of whether, how and when land owners should be compensated for loss of value caused by planning proposals; whether any increase in value resulting from permitted development should belong to the land owner or to the public, or shared between them; how often planners' decisions on land use were being influenced more by the desire to minimise a local authority's compensation liability rather than to achieve the best use in the public interest.

Three of the Tory Reform Committee's bulletins were devoted to these issues. The thrust of their argument was that the primary and legitimate objective of securing optimum use of the nation's land was in danger of being obscured and seriously delayed by the search for a perfect, incontestable valuation method as a basis for compensation. This, in their judgement would result only in procrastination, because perfection was unattainable.

They recognised that at any point in time the market value of a parcel of land for which development was in prospect would include a 'floating value' above its undeveloped value, and that this element of 'betterment' would disappear if development was eventually refused. They felt that calculation of a specific value of the betterment element for each separate piece of land, as the Government was proposing, would be too cumbersome and that it would be sufficient (and fair enough) to assume that the market value of any land for which development was refused included a betterment element equal to a national average, which only needed to be ascertained once by the Government. The Uthwatt Committee (1942) had, in fact, already estimated that this national average was about half the market value in 1939. Compensation to the landowner if development were refused should, it was proposed, be half this amount, the other half being ascribed to the public. Correspondingly, if land was developed, the State would levy a betterment charge, to be used to build up a national Betterment Fund from which all compensation would be paid.

This was generally in line with Government thinking, but the TRC was not happy with the Treasury's cautious view that compensation payments should be delayed until the Betterment Fund had been built up for several years. They felt that such an approach would inhibit development, and that a time limit should be imposed on the payment of compensation, whereas the betterment levy should be payable for ever, giving the Treasury the assurance they wanted that, ultimately, income from the levy would exceed compensation payments.

There is no hint in any of the TRC's discussions of Land Use Policy of any doubt in their minds about the need to plan land use: indeed Bulletin No 4, *Government Policy for the Rebuilding of Urban Areas* (1944), written by Peter Thorneycroft and Hugh Molson, accepted the need, provided for in the Town and Country Planning Bill then before Parliament, for stronger planning authorities armed with compulsory purchasing powers not only to deal with reconstruction of bomb-damaged 'blitzed' areas, but also for redesign and renewal of 'blighted' areas (those with bad layout and obsolescent buildings and infrastructure). Nor did they question the fairness of the State exacting a levy for the benefit of the public on the value created by development. These most modern of Tories in 1944 regarded consent to develop land as a benefit, separate from the right of ownership, conferred on the landowner by the State, acting on behalf of the public. They urged that desirable development of land should be permitted, and that the State should share in its benefits in a fair, easily understood, way.

Employment

The bitter experience of the British people throughout almost all of the period between the two World Wars was too recent to be forgotten by any politician pondering what to do about employment after the Second World War. Even those who had escaped unemployment, or had suffered only short spells of it, had been unable to escape the fear that it might strike at any moment. War had given a respite from these anxieties. Millions were serving in the armed forces: almost all the rest of the population was engaged in supplying them with war material and keeping the rest of the economy going as well as could be managed with the limited resources available. But even under the pressure of war, many of the restrictive practices adopted by the pre-war labour force had survived, even if only kept in reserve for use another day. The fear remained that high unemployment would return. It was the crippling effect that this fear could have on the industrial economy that exercised the TRC, who saw the risk that restrictive practices devised to protect employment might instead strangle productivity.

Thorneycroft and his colleagues were keenly aware that it was not only from the restrictive practices of labour that the danger arose. Employers had developed their own protective schemes. If electricians were not allowed by their union to do any mechanical work or boiler makers to tighten a wood screw, manufacturers might for their part agree among themselves which firm was to be allowed to supply what quantity to which customer, or refuse to allow dealers to sell their products except at a mandatory price. The TRC pointed out that apart from the enormous damage to productivity of all these measures, almost none of them achieved the aim they had in view. Protection of a market share or a price level actually reduced the size of the market available to share. Higher labour costs resulting from demarcation practices made exports uncompetitive. Far from maintaining full employment, they promoted further unemployment.

The TRC concluded that if the root cause was fear of unemployment, the duty of Government must be to remove that fear by pursuing the policy of full employment in a free society that Beveridge had recommended.

Population

In their pamphlet, *To-morrow's Children,* published in October 1944, the TRC tackled the sensitive subject of the country's declining birthrate. The authors this time were J A Cecil Wright, Nancy Astor, Violet Apsley and Robert Grant-Ferris, and their report has something of a missionary tone. Right at the beginning, in the Foreword, they made the alarming prediction that the population of Britain would shrink, by a quarter in about fifty years, by a half before the present generation's grandchildren had grown old, unless action was taken immediately. A higher birthrate, they averred, was necessary to provide social security and opportunity. Otherwise, Beveridge would be so much moonshine with a declining population and more and more pensioners. It would also provide greater security against war.

The TRC were not worried that the world might get too full: "*… science continually adds to the margin by which man lives over nature ….*" They did acknowledge that the future was unpredictable and that present trends might be reversed. However, they pointed out that net immigration had been running at 50,000 a year and. if this went on, the problem would no longer be one of births, but of absorption. They noted that, after the war, many young people from Eastern Europe might wish to settle in Britain. Although insisting that their aim was to put the situation frankly before the public, they also suggested some solutions, especially fostering and strengthening family life and removing the economic barriers to early marriage, with tax reliefs and allowances for large families. They were in favour of encouraging immigration, from Italy, Bulgaria, Poland and the Soviet Union, as well as from the East. They claimed that they were not judging, as the Nazis had, between the value of one race and another. Their point was that immigration could help to offset the ageing of the population, and so facilitate economic growth.

In the 21st Century, the British public appears to be no longer much bothered about the birth rate, seeming to assume that if it seems too high it can be reduced by contraception, and if too low by IVF treatment and by taking a relaxed view of promiscuity. However, the TRC's comments on ageing of the population and on the absorption of immigrants still resonate strongly with current preoccupations.

Coal

Britain's output of coal, the nation's principal source of energy for heating, electricity generation and rail transport, had fallen steadily since the beginning of the Second World War from just over 200 million tons per annum (which was just enough to cope with domestic demand after export markets were closed by the German occupation of most of Europe in 1940) to around 195 million tons. By the summer of 1944 stocks were exhausted. By then, also, the occupation of Italy and the imminent liberation of France were to restore some of the demand for exports to those countries, whose own mining industries had suffered severe damage. Security of supply was in serious jeopardy, and was to remain precarious for a long time after the war ended, in large measure due to the poor state of industrial relations in the industry. Even during some of the most perilous periods of the war, strikes, absenteeism and low productivity of a discontented and often badly managed work force had caused serious disruption to industry and added to the sufferings of ordinary people.

The TRC's concern was to find a way for the industry to boost production in preparation for the burgeoning demand for coal in a post-war Britain faced with a massive programme of rebuilding its bomb-damaged manufacturing industry, towns and cities and, at the same time, aid the recovery of its European allies.

In March 1944, they published their report, *A National Policy for Coal*, a careful analysis of the state of the industry with reasoned proposals for its future development. The authors were Quintin Hogg, C G Lancaster and Peter Thorneycroft, and their message was forward looking rather then critical of the past. Although the TRC rejected as inherently unsound the nationalisation of the industry fervently desired by the trade unions, the plan they proposed was very far from a competitive market solution. They seem to have believed that the pressure for nationalisation could be staved off if the Unions were presented with a plan, short of nationalisation, which would give their members security of employment and decent wages in place of the hardships they had suffered between the wars. The TRC saw the highly fragmented ownership of the industry as the principal cause of its failure to achieve an overall balance of supply with demand. Too many owners of too many mines had been incapable of finding enough capital for modernisation, so that productivity had lagged a long way behind the more highly mechanised American, German and French industries. Most mine owners had tried to solve the resulting lack of competitiveness by cost cutting measures, dismissing large numbers of miners and squeezing the pay of those they continued to employ. The solution proposed by the TRC was to make use of the existing wartime organisation of a Ministry of Fuel and Power, a Coal Commission owning all coal deposits as a national asset, and Regional Controllers supervising the mining process. Although they warned of the dangers inherent in allowing Government to intrude into management, they nevertheless recommended that assessment of domestic and export demand should be the responsibility of an appropriate Government agency. To guard against distortion of trade by foreign government subsidies, the Government was advised to press for creation of an International Coal Council and to negotiate trade agreements.

These ideas were never put to the test. Although similar proposals were included in the Conservative Party's Manifesto for the 1945 General Election, that Election was won by Labour who, not at all persuaded that Governments should not intrude in management, nationalised the industry on 1st January 1947. Thorneycroft took many opportunities to argue later in his career that the TRC's warning had been well justified by the poor performance of the nationalised coal, transport and steel industries.

Agriculture

Few people in wartime Britain harboured any doubts about the importance of the British agricultural industry. Without it, the nation would have starved, as the ships attempting to deliver food imports suffered appalling losses from U-boat attacks. A grateful people accepted with little reservation that to maintain the industry, financial support by the State would be needed. The TRC had no need to argue the case: it was already won. In their pamphlet, *"The Husbandman Waiteth"*, published in March 1944, they took this as read. The authors, Ronald Tree, J S Wedderburn and Christopher York, wished to look further ahead, as a recent international conference at Hot Springs, Arkansas, had done. At Hot Springs 44 nations, including Britain and all other members of the Commonwealth except India, had committed themselves to formulating a long-term policy for their agricultural industries aimed at maintaining soil fertility, protection of crops from disease and promoting steady employment through the seasons – and undertaking to do this by adopting rotational mixed farming. The TRC was in full agreement with this, but was not satisfied that the Government had a clear plan for implementing its commitments. They recommended adoption of rotational mixed farming in most parts of the country, encouraged by a price structure set by the Government in consultation with the industry, with production quantities settled for long periods, and Government control of imports. Whilst accepting without question that Government had a key role to play, they rejected the idea of nationalisation of land and recommended, perhaps a little optimistically "a minimum interference with individual freedom, but [insistence] on a high standard of ownership and cultivation".

Sixty years on, the nations of the world have not yet been weaned from the notion that agriculture, unlike any other business, cannot be expected to operate without protection in one form or another from the uncertainties of the market place.

Air Transport

The TRC discussed post-war policy for Air Transport in a succinct Bulletin, *Air Transport Policy*, written by Ronald Tree and J A Cecil Wright and published in July 1944. The principal issues they considered were:

✧ which Department of State should have the responsibility for air transport. (They urged that it should not, on any account, be an Armed Services Ministry, but one concerned with trade – e.g. the Board of Trade or a new Ministry of Transport and Communications);

✧ should BOAC (British Overseas Airways Corporation) have a monopoly of all overseas air transport and, if not, should it have the power to control entry of competitors? Their clear answer was 'No'. *"Each operating concern should be free to develop … within the limits set by the standards of aeronautical practice which will surely have to be laid down by international authority". "Operators of Air Transport routes, including BOAC, should derive their authority to operate from a Public Board. It is probably unnecessary to look further than to the US Civil Aeronautics Board for a model." "BOAC should only operate one trunk route and should devote its remaining activities to --- the development of 'infant' air routes which, while desirable in the interests of imperial communications, are not yet capable of paying their way."* [International talks were already planned, but had been delayed as the war entered the critical phase of the invasion and liberation of France];

✧ the urgent need to release design and production resources of the British aircraft industry then tied up entirely for military purposes, so that a start could be made on designing a range of civilian aircraft. [Two committees chaired by Lord Brabazon had recently recommended construction of seven aircraft types for different applications].

Throughout this Bulletin, the TRC accepted without debate the notion of competing private businesses managing their affairs under the supervision of a national authority in accordance with a national plan for their industry, although they also noted that the future uses of Air Transport could not be foreseen.

It is clear that the work of the TRC on all of the issues they tackled was a combined effort of its members, who spread the load of preparing the bulletins and pamphlets between them according to their interests and their expertise. The role of Thorneycroft, first as a Secretary and then as Chairman of the Committee, was to guide and co-ordinate the work of the active members and to ensure that each declaration of policy had the full agreement of all members. To what extent he was an originator of all or any of the policies cannot be assessed from the published documents, but there is no doubt that he was a major contributor to TRC's agenda and deliberations and that, taken as a whole, *Forward - By the Right* was a statement of his own beliefs at that time.

The first Government appointment

As the war drew towards its close, Thorneycroft's mastery of parliamentary debate and the fecundity of his political imagination had won the respect of Winston Churchill and when, in anticipation of the first post-war election, the wartime Coalition Government was dissolved, freeing the parties to prepare for return to the normal democratic process, Churchill gave Thorneycroft his first opportunity of office, appointing him as Parliamentary Secretary in the Ministry of War Transport. This assignment lasted all too short a time but, because the Minister was a peer, Lord Leathers, it gave Thorneycroft valuable experience in presenting and defending a Government Department's case in the House of Commons.

At the General Election on 5th July 1945 Labour, with massive support from men and women of the armed forces, swept aside the Conservatives and, with them, the nation's wartime leader, Winston Churchill. In a battle of captains at Stafford, Captain Peter Thorneycroft, RA, was defeated by the Labour candidate Captain Stephen Swingler, RAC. Armour, temporarily at least, resisted the cannonade.

MP for Monmouth 1945-66

Defeat in his home constituency of Stafford was, of course, a blow, but Thorneycroft was already too valuable a colleague for the Tory party to lose sight of, and too firmly committed to his political career to be daunted for long by the setback. The death of L R Pym in September 1945 resulted in a by-election at Monmouth and on 30th October, in a straight fight with the Liberal, A B Lloyd Oakley, Thorneycroft won the seat he was to hold for twenty-one years.

16. Thorneycroft's campaign poster Monmouth bye-election 1945

He at once threw all his energy into a determined attack on what he perceived as a potentially tragic failure throughout the nation to comprehend the dangers posed by the massive Socialist majority and the consequent ability of the Labour party to impose sweeping reforms of the country's institutions. He was desperately concerned that the international Communist movement, led by a Soviet Union proudly flaunting its military prowess in Eastern Europe, might succeed in infiltrating, and so gaining control of, the Socialist parties of Western European countries. Building upon the good relations he had established with a number of members of the Liberal Party who had contributed actively to the concepts expounded in *Forward - By the Right,* he sought to attract the Liberals into a united front against Socialism. *Forward - By the Right* may have been an apt rallying cry in a time of war, but his aim now was to win the support of a much broader constituency in a fight against what he saw as the Socialists' mania for control of people's lives in the minutest detail. It was to be a fight for freedom, and it was a series of booklets under the title *Design for Freedom* that eventually emerged in 1948, endorsed by a hundred or so supporters, parliamentary candidates as well as Members of Parliament, more or less equally divided between Liberals of various hues and Conservatives. *Design for Freedom* was not just a statement of principles, but a reasoned analysis of how those principles hung together, and could be applied to the solution of the specific problems facing the nation, whether in the field of economics, physical infrastructure or social welfare. The most important of the statements of policy published under the *Design for Freedom* banner were *Design for Europe, Design for Recovery* and *Design for Wages,* and these were followed in 1949 by Thorneycroft's book *Design for Living.*

As was the case with *Forward - By the Right*, many of the policies put forward in *Design for Freedom* dealt with issues of the day which no longer have the same relevance. We shall try here to identify those which may have some significance for modern Tory reformers.

Trade

The TRC was unequivocally in favour of multilateral free trade, arguing that *"we cannot buy security behind a tariff wall designed simply to exclude an inconvenient import"*. A consequence of this was that the system of Imperial Preference would have to be gradually dismantled, in parallel with a progressive reduction by the United States of its many subsidies and protective tariffs, to implement the free trade principle they had preached to the rest of the world during the war. Bilateral agreements were firmly rejected on the ground that one of the two nations engaged in bilateral trading or barter of this kind would almost certainly have to make up the balance by accepting something not really wanted – or selling something which it could ill afford to spare – and because the stronger partner could use its strength as an economic whip.

Wages

The role of trade unions to negotiate wages on behalf of their members was not only recognised in *Design for Wages*, but considered to be irreplaceable. The concept of any form of statutory wage policy being acceptable in a free society was firmly dismissed as impossible to sustain without complementary control of prices, production and import quotas, rationing of consumption and other measures that only a totalitarian régime would wish to impose upon its citizens. Appeals to employees and employers for voluntary restraint in wage demands or price adjustments were similarly bound to be ineffective. The task of Government was not to intervene in wage bargaining between employers and employees: it was to eliminate inflation and keep taxation under control.

Europe

The Europe discussed in *Design for Europe* did not include the United Kingdom. It comprised those countries, war-damaged and often still starving, on the mainland of the Continent of Europe over which the Soviet Union had not imposed its rule. Britain was friendly to them, but not one of them, although content to see them trying to get together in some form of European union as Winston Churchill had recommended at Zurich in 1946. Britain's role, accepting realistically its economic dependence on America, was seen as that of working alongside the USA in containing the ambitions of a Soviet Union which had chosen, unhappily, not to join the endeavour to make the new United Nations Organisation an effective guarantor of world peace but instead wished to impose its tyrannical ideology on the nations which believed in freedom.

Design for Europe's prescription for a Europe which was certainly no less dependent than Britain on American aid, was the preparation of an Economic Plan for the restoration of war-damaged industrial and trading capacity which must include adherence to the principles of the proposed International Trade Organisation, albeit with those exemptions which could be shown to be necessary for realisation of the Economic Plan, but nevertheless aiming at the progressive dismantling of tariff barriers both between the European states themselves and between them and the rest of the world. The Plan should provide for *"a right of innocent passage"* over Europe's railways and waterways allowing goods to travel in bond from one country to another. A supranational organisation was envisaged to administer the loans for reconstruction that America was promising to make available under the Marshall Plan. It was recognised that democratic governments would have a difficult task persuading their people to accept the sacrifices involved and, in a rather unfortunate turn of phrase, it was suggested that, *"The people must be led slowly and unconsciously into the abandonment of their traditional economic defences, not asked, in advance of having received any of the benefits which will accrue to them from the Plan, to make changes of which they may not at first recognise the advantages to themselves as well as to the rest of the world."*: a realistic tactic, perhaps, but with a flavour of a confidence trick, however well-intentioned.

Relations with the USA

There was realism too in the concern expressed in *Design for Europe* that the European nations, remembering the long delays before the Americans came to their aid in the two world wars, would need an assurance of rapid and effective

American (and British) military support should the Soviets react with force to their collaboration with the Americans. Given the Russian 'sabotage' of the United Nations, the solution proposed was the creation of an international organisation in which the free nations of the world could pursue the objectives for which UNO had been founded, but was prevented from achieving. This organisation would require a very close association, with some surrender of sovereignty, between the USA and the British Commonwealth, overcoming the mutual suspicions still alive on both sides of the Atlantic – in America, annoyance that Britain seemed unwilling to accept that it no longer had the economic strength to stand alone, and was taking advantage of American aid to set up welfare schemes that it could not afford; and in Europe the fear that the American political system might result in Congress refusing to ratify agreements reached by the Administration. *"It would be disastrous, not only to Britain, but to Europe and America as well, if the US Congress should overindulge its sense of superiority and its desire for economy by imposing too humiliating conditions upon the applicants for a fresh loan under the Marshall offer."*

The Conservative Party Conference in Blackpool in October 1947 gave Thorneycroft a platform for a masterly speech in which he pilloried the leadership for believing that the Tories could win back power by *'wearing all the colours of the rainbow in our buttonholes'* instead of telling the electorate exactly where the party stood on each of the great issues of the day. There was, he said, no substitute for policy. The speech generated enthusiastic support from the rank and file attending the Conference and, later, from the Conservative media, but there was little sign either in the formal Conference resolutions or from their subsequent actions that the leadership had taken the message on board.

Thorneycroft looked for other vehicles to disseminate his message and to lay out for public scrutiny the detailed policies he was proposing. He chose the Press, selecting popular publications which would convey his ideas to the broadest possible readership. Already in 1944, he had found *Picture Post* an admirable channel for an article on his *Forward - By the Right* campaign. Now he found that *Everybody's* had the sort of readership that he wanted to reach.

In an *Everybody's* article in March 1948, nationalisation was his target: the delusory dream that nationalisation of an industry could release a pool of profits to augment the workers' pay packets; the failure of the Labour Party to foresee the extremely difficult problems that the process of nationalisation involved; the creation of *'lazy, oppressive'* monopoly suppliers and elimination of consumer choice; the loss of the freedom of workers, unhappy for whatever reason with their employer, to find in other firms alternative jobs in the trades for which they had been trained; the illusion that a vast industry can be managed efficiently by a centralised bureaucracy. Thorneycroft did not propose denationalisation at that time: he did not believe that it would be sensible or responsible to impose yet another major disruption on key industries. Instead, he urged that management should be devolved as far as possible; that competition should be preserved, for example between road and rail, and not stifled by raising prices in one nationalised industry to protect the inefficiency of another. He saw no reason why the regions of the National Coal Board should not compete with each other. He wanted Parliament to accept that a debating chamber was not an appropriate instrument for monitoring the day-to-day management of State controlled industries, and suggested appointing committees of the House to take on this role.

Another article in the same magazine in October 1948 reveals a highly effective opposition politician scathingly dissecting the ruling party's policy document, *Labour Believes in Britain*, prepared for the forthcoming Party Conference; the product, said Thorneycroft, of *'tired men with tired ideas'*, proposing the nationalisation of still more industries in the full knowledge that those they had already nationalised were a long way from working well.

For most of those years in opposition, Thorneycroft bore the responsibility for shadowing the Minister of Transport. He very quickly mastered his brief, and Hansard records many a battle on the floor of the House between the well-informed young Tory and the obstinate Labour stalwart Alfred Barnes from which, more often than not, Thorneycroft emerged with colours bravely flying. However, not many rail or bus passengers read Hansard and, in November 1950, Thorneycroft again used *Everybody's* for a savage attack on the Government's policies for road transport: the progressive compulsory acquisition of successful road hauliers who carried goods more than 25 miles; the rapid descent into heavy losses of the State haulier which took over these firms; the 'corrective' measures of discriminatory taxation and price manipulation in an attempt to reduce those losses, driving goods traffic off the roads and onto rail, where the Government wanted it to be, whether this would be economically viable or not.

Design for Living

Hansard's records of his speeches in the House, the reports of the lobby correspondents (who did not fail to notice Thorneycroft's fine performances in debate) and his own occasional articles in popular magazines were not enough to get his message across to his satisfaction. In a little book, *Design for Living*, published in 1949, Thorneycroft set out, with the succinct clarity characteristic of all his political writings and speeches, his analysis of the dangers the country faced and a pragmatic programme for squaring up to them. He began by insisting that whilst politicians could provide an institutional framework, they could not control the way individuals behave within that framework. However much politicians tended to delude themselves (and tried to delude us) that they could, they really were not able to deliver happiness. *"Free men show a remarkable facility for making not only themselves but a lot of other people indescribably unhappy"*. The job of politics then, was to provide a framework, and the real political choice open to the electorate was between different designs of framework. What happens within the chosen framework is determined by the people who act within it, not by the politicians who have designed it.

Thorneycroft nevertheless supported strongly the role of political parties in a democracy of free individuals, in providing nuclei around which people of differing views could unite to provide both a stable government, and a consistent and effective opposition whose principal role was to ensure that the majority governed with proper safeguards for the rights of the minority. (An Italian friend of Thorneycroft and of the author was once heard to ask, the day after a Conservative election victory, whether Thorneycroft could please arrange the export to Italy of Britain's 'spare government'). He rejected the notion of an effective centrist party (or 'third way'), arguing that when faced with the need to decide on an important issue, the centre will usually split, those who are left-leaning tending to support the larger party of the left, and *vice versa.*

In a scathing passage, Thorneycroft showed how the Labour Party in power, forced to deal with real issues of government, had found Socialist teaching inadequate: the slogans, 'higher wages', 'shorter hours' and 'away with the wicked capitalist', simply did not fit the needs of the times. Labour's ascetic Chancellor of the Exchequer, Sir Stafford Cripps, had found himself obliged to point out to the TUC Conference in 1948 the unpalatable truth that even if the whole of the net profit after tax available to the nation's businesses (about £300 million) were to be diverted into the pockets of employees it would be nothing like enough to satisfy the demands for higher earnings of wage and salary earners whose total income was £4,500 million, fifteen times as much. The call for shorter hours had given way to the much less appealing slogan 'Work or Want'. The only Socialist principle that had been applied with any rigour half-way through Labour's first post-war government was the nationalisation of key industries, and the most obvious consequence of that had been a substantial increase in the prices of their products and services. Thorneycroft's cutting remark, *"Bereft of nationalisation as a slogan, [the Socialists] would have little left except an antipathy to blood sports and a hatred of the Tories."* might just as aptly have been tossed across the floor of the House by a Tory leader half a century later.

An Archbishop of Canterbury, struggling to give a lead to the Anglican Church in the 21st Century, might do well to ponder a parable used by Thorneycroft to illustrate the dilemma faced by Socialists in the late 1940s who wanted so ardently to believe that their creed of Socialism was the only effective alternative the British working class had to the savage Soviet Communist version. *"This"*, said Thorneycroft, *"was rather as if a priest were to say, 'I know that my congregation do quite a lot of sinning, and many of them, alas, seem rather to enjoy it. It really is no good spending the whole of my sermon attacking evil. I must speak the same language as my congregation. I will compromise with sin a little. I will speak at least in part the same language as the Devil. In no circumstances will I fall into the error of these simple fellows who spend their whole time pointing out that there is a difference between right and wrong."*

However, *Design for Living* was not meant to be a facile attack on Socialism. It was a serious attempt to outline, in terms which voters could understand, a Conservative programme as a viable alternative. Thorneycroft insisted that, before attempting to formulate any policy, one had to decide what the policy was for and on what principles it was to be based.

His first principle was that *'the State is the most imperfect guardian of the public interest'*.

British history, he observed, had been a long struggle to protect the individual against central authority, devising one check after another to this end. The House of Commons was there to check the Government, in the last resort by refusing to vote it money; the House of Lords to check the House of Commons (more powerful than any other elected assembly in the world); the legal system to hold the scales of justice evenly between the Crown and the individual. It was in the Socialists' attack upon and erosion of these constitutional principles that the real threat to individual freedom lay, even more than in the excess of vexatious controls they had continued to impose since 1945.

Secondly, since no one man could enjoy more than a certain amount of wisdom, experience and knowledge *'it was necessary, in politics as elsewhere, to delegate responsibility'*. A man could only listen to a limited number of questions every day, let alone provide an answer to each of them. The time factor alone ruled out effective control from the centre. It was better to run the risk of a small proportion of bad decisions being made locally than the much greater risk of a colossal blunder on a major issue by a central authority. Decentralisation was preferable not only for reasons of efficiency, but also because it was good for people to make up their own minds and take their own decisions.

Thirdly, *'it was better to try, and encourage others to try, a diversity of methods, to judge cases on their merits and avoid adopting a doctrinaire approach'*.

He warned against assuming that democracy could be maintained simply by exercising a vote for a political party every few years, or that a democratically elected assembly was, of itself, a sufficient guarantee of freedom. *"True freedom demands that at every point in his existence a man should be influencing the conduct of the world about him."*

Freedom of the individual and his readiness actively to defend his freedom were at the core of Thorneycroft's message. His was a classic argument for a free market in which priorities were determined by consumer demand and the price mechanism, the very antithesis of Socialism, which wanted to decide centrally what it called 'the Social Priorities' – what was a necessity and what a luxury; what traffic should go by road and what by rail; what was to be manufactured and where it should be made. *"No Government"*, he averred, *"has any idea of what people want."* Even industrialists whose whole future depends on getting it right frequently made bad judgements. If they consequently failed, they went bankrupt, and their employees lost their jobs: those who suffered were those directly involved. But if a Government, centrally, made the wrong decisions, the whole nation suffered. A shortage of supply resulted in rationing: if food subsidies were too generous, taxes on cigarettes or beer were raised to cover up the mistake.

Thorneycroft accepted that capitalism was not perfect; it tended to create monopolies and to engage in restrictive practices: but to reject capitalism on these grounds would be to deprive consumers of the enormous benefits of the freedom of choice that only capitalism can provide. Its defects were controllable and it was, of course, the duty of Government to monitor and control them.

Clement Attlee's Socialist Governments of 1945-51 had massively reduced the battlefield on which capitalist competitors could fight, and *Design for Living* devoted two chapters to combating the arguments for nationalisation in general and for the nationalisation of transport in particular. Thorneycroft wanted to confront the practical issues which a new Conservative Government would have to face on taking office. It was right, he argued, to devote a lot of effort whilst in opposition to critical analysis and revision of a party's political theories and principles because, once in office, the job immediately became one of understanding and dealing with the realities of the country's situation, probably utterly different from what had been foreseen in the run-up to the election. He recognised that the enormous pressure to solve urgent problems placed upon Ministers once in office left little opportunity for quiet analysis of the problems that had to be faced every day.

Thorneycroft used nationalisation as a case study. What had been done could not easily be undone. The atmosphere would not be one *'in which British industry could be asked to start turning many further political somersaults'*. Labour had made many mistakes and it would take time, patience and sacrifices to correct them. But the principles for a Conservative government were clear:

- ✧ preservation of the dearly-won constitutional balance between and within the legislature, the executive and the courts;

- ✧ maximum freedom of individuals to make their own choices;

- ✧ delegation of Government decisions to the lowest practical level;

- ✧ balancing the national budget without burdening people with excessive taxation.

In the Spring of 1949 Thorneycroft's personal life changed dramatically. His marriage of May 1938 to Sheila Wells Page had ended in divorce, and he married the vivacious Italian girl, Carla, whom he had first met – and fallen in love with – in 1930. They had lost touch with each other as their countries moved further and further apart during the years leading up to the Second World War. During their separation, Carla had married Count Roberti, with whom she had two children, Piero and Francesca. Like Peter's, her marriage had ended in divorce and, soon after the end of the war, she had come to London where she had become the Fashion Editor of *Vogue*. She and Peter met again at a dinner party given by a mutual friend, and they married on 2nd April 1949, a marriage that was to last until Peter's death in June 1994, forty-five years of great happiness and devotion.

17. Wedding of Peter and Carla 2nd April 1949 (*photo: Keystone Press Agency*)

As a back-bencher in the House of Commons during this period Thorneycroft, although participating eloquently and cogently in debates on the kind of broad issues discussed in his writings, did not overlook some of the single issues calling for attention within the broader sweep of policy. In May, 1949, he presented a carefully researched Private Member's Bill to the House on Analgesia in Childbirth which was widely welcomed although, in the end, killed off by the Government who argued that the matter was adequately covered by existing or planned legislation. Carla was one of the first women to benefit from analgesia when, in 1951, she gave birth to her daughter, Victoria.

Seeking re-election

The massive majority enjoyed by Labour in its first period of office after the war was not to survive their first campaign for re-election, but the Conservatives' wait for a return to Government was not yet over. The election on 23rd February 1950 gave Labour victory, but with a tiny overall majority of only 7 seats. In Monmouth, Peter Thorneycroft almost doubled his majority after a well fought campaign against a competent Labour candidate, Graham Thomas, who had started the campaign completely unknown in the constituency.

18. Campaigning in Monmouth Constituency, 1950 (*photo: Burnicle Studios, Monmouth*)

Thorneycroft had concentrated his fire on a few, well-chosen issues: wasteful Government expenditure; Labour's failure to explain how the country was to manage when Marshall Aid ended in 1952; the Socialists' plan to nationalise still more industries when those already under State control were failing. The Conservative policies he emphasised were those aimed at reducing Government expenditure, freeing the country from dependence on foreign loans and so making it possible to reduce taxes. He urged a stop to further nationalisation unless and until it could be proved that the industries already nationalised had succeeded; pushed for more houses to be built and cheaper mortgage facilities to encourage home ownership; and, on the international front, underlined the need for unity in the Western world to resist the advance of Socialism and Communism.

Back in Parliament in March 1950, Thorneycroft resumed his role as Opposition spokesman on transport, lambasting the Government for allowing the Transport Commission to lose £50 a minute, £500,000 a week, of public money and raising rail fares to levels people could not afford to pay. He wanted to know which member of the Transport Commission had real commercial knowledge – he could not identify him. He found an unlikely ally in Ernest Marsden, a railway engine-driver from Ardsley who had told the *Yorkshire Evening Post, "Why am I glad to retire? I'll tell you why – it's because of this bloody Government."* - and found to his delight that he had been quoted in Parliament by Peter Thorneycroft. With such a small majority, the Government was skating on thin ice and, a few weeks later, in a debate on road haulage, Thorneycroft and his colleague Sir David Maxwell Fyfe, mounting a spirited attack on the policy of forcing private road hauliers out of business, were able to force a division which the Government survived only by relying on the casting vote of the Chairman of Ways and Means, Major Milner, to break a dead-heat of 278 votes for each side.

The summer of 1950 saw the first battles of the Korean War, and Thorneycroft's emergence as a forceful proponent of closer integration of the armed forces of Britain and the United States to meet the threat of further Communist aggression. In the House of Commons and in the country, Thorneycroft was winning increasing respect, not only with his mastery of his transport brief, but with his confident and pertinent contributions to debates on an increasingly wide range of issues. His performance earned him the honour of an invitation from Winston Churchill to move from the despatch box on 8th November 1950 a Conservative amendment to the Loyal Address on the highly contentious subject of perpetuation of wartime controls (over prices, building licences, trade and exchange rate) which the Government was proposing to exclude from annual reviews by giving them the force of statute in place of the previous procedure of regulation. [Having held office briefly in 1945, Thorneycroft could have claimed the right to sit on the Opposition front bench on his return to the House in February 1950, but he had chosen not to do so, preferring the greater freedom of a back-bencher to express views not always in line with his party's policies].

By the early months of 1951, the perilous situation in Korea, where the Chinese had thrown their military might against the United Nations' forces, was pushing domestic politics into the background. In a powerful speech in Stroud on 4th January,

Thorneycroft urged the parties to put on one side the political programmes they cherished so that the nation's resources could be devoted to rebuilding military strength, to confront a situation even more perilous than in 1940, when the English Channel was still a real defence. He berated those wishful thinkers who thought we could evade our responsibilities by blaming General MacArthur or the Americans for the events in Korea, or hoped that the Russians and the Chinese might begin to quarrel. He saw no disgrace in the Conservatives admitting the need for some controls, or in Labour postponing further nationalisation adventures. Country should come before party. Thorneycroft pressed home these arguments a few days later in a parliamentary debate on Defence, reminding the House that Communists already controlled most of Asia and a considerable part of Europe, and were already massing their forces on the borders of Yugoslavia. Korea was not an isolated event, but a symptom of much wider and deeper causes. The country needed a much stronger Regular Army, and should not have to rely on calling up reservists at short notice.

This was Thorneycroft the Statesman. But Thorneycroft the Party Politician lurked just below the surface, and burst into action when needed. He was adept at producing striking pieces of evidence, highly pertinent to the matter in hand, seemingly out of a hat. At a BBC 'Any Questions' session, when he was a panel member, he just 'happened to have in his pocket' a copy of a pensioner's budget to counter a question on how much a young couple needed to live. At a constituency meeting in Newport, he had at his finger tips the amount the Government's Gambia Egg Scheme had cost per egg ("£20 15s 7d of your money"), whilst £36 million had had to be written off because of the failure of their Groundnuts Scheme. The Labour candidate for Monmouth resigned in April 1951 because of the heavy strain of campaigning in such a wide and scattered constituency. By contrast, Thorneycroft and his wife had earned praise from their constituents a year before for taking the trouble to turn up at a garden fete at Llandogo, the smallest village in the division. In fact, they were both indefatigable in 'nursing' the constituency, always alert to the possibility that the Government, with its tenuous majority, might lose its control of the Commons at any moment, and be forced to call an early election.

Monday 25th June 1951 was a happy day - Carla Thorneycroft gave birth to their daughter, christened Victoria Elizabeth Anne three weeks later at St James's, Spanish Place.

Only a couple of weeks afterwards, the new father was opening yet another debate on transport while running a temperature of 103, having to go home to his wife and baby as soon as he had finished speaking. He seized the opportunity of the debate to outline the transport policy his party would pursue, abolishing the 'idiotic' 25 mile limit on private road hauliers, and reorganising the nationalised rail, road and canal industries in regional boards *"of a size which would give some reasonable hope of finding somebody big enough to run them"*. In the meantime, he urged his old adversary, Alfred Barnes, the Minister of Transport, to recognise the danger that the railway system could break down completely in the coming winter, and to do something to alleviate the acute shortages of both skilled manpower and coal.

The slender thread by which the Labour Government was holding on to power snapped at last, and a General Election was called for 25th October 1951. Labour had chosen Miss Josephine Richardson to fight Peter Thorneycroft for the Monmouth seat. She had been secretary to two Labour MPs, Ian Mikardo and John Freeman, and had recently been elected to Hornsey Borough Council. She had also been secretary to the 'Keep Left' Group of the Parliamentary Labour Party. A tough campaign was promised. John Freeman, with Harold Wilson, had joined Aneurin Bevan in resigning from the Cabinet in April 1951 in protest at Chancellor Hugh Gaitskell's decision, supported by the Prime Minister, to impose a charge of one shilling on National Health Service prescriptions, infringing for the first time the principle that the NHS should be free.

In his election statement, Thorneycroft argued that defence must take priority over everything else if the country was to have any chance of negotiating a just and lasting peace. He attributed rising prices to Labour's *'orgy of profligate extravagance'* and promised a ruthless pruning of both the great spending departments and the costly boards of the nationalised industries and encouragement, instead of elimination, of competition – and no more nationalisation. After defence, housing was to be the next priority. The trade unions would be fortified, and consulted about any legislation concerning them; (Thorneycroft had consistently argued that the unions had been seriously weakened by nationalisation). Finally, there was a call to keep and develop the Empire, to promote unity of purpose with the United States and, on that secure basis, to labour for a more united Europe.

Thorneycroft hammered home these themes in meetings all over the constituency, around fifty in all, including a very lively one for women only at Trellech, when he concentrated his opening fire on the rise in the cost of living under Labour and Aneurin Bevan's visceral opposition to house ownership. His opponent's links with the Bevanite camp presented Thorneycroft with a card that he played skilfully during the campaign. Bevan had become something of a Socialist bogeyman, whom Thorneycroft could justifiably categorise as the real, determinedly left-wing driving force within a Labour Party that the more moderate Attlee was having difficulty controlling. Bevan's resignation had, in fact, created a split in his party which was not to be healed for forty years and more. Whether Bevan's personal intervention during the campaign in support of Jo Richardson helped or hindered her cause is a matter of conjecture. In any case, the argument that won the day with the Monmouth electors was Thorneycroft's insistence that, in a dangerous world, Britain desperately needed to be strong, and that Labour was incapable of reaching agreement within its own divided ranks on policies that could achieve this. Thorneycroft was returned with a majority increased, albeit only slightly, from 4,251 to 4,523. The country at large was inclined towards the same conclusion, and the Conservatives and their allies returned to the Commons with an overall majority of 17, somewhat precarious, but at least better than the 7 that Labour had managed a year and a half earlier.

President of the Board of Trade 1951-57

L ooking back on his political career towards the end of his life, Thorneycroft told the author that the job he had enjoyed most was the relatively long time he had spent in the Board of Trade. It was a role in which, certainly in the 1950s, a politician could make a real difference to national performance by carefully shaping the environment in which business had to operate, and he had been given enough time to do so.

Churchill's decision following his election victory of 25th October 1951 to appoint this relatively untried young man to the Cabinet surprised few observers. Thorneycroft had put up many a brilliant performance in the Commons during the frustrating six years of opposition as the Conservatives' spokesman on transport. He had mastered his brief extraordinarily well and had given Alfred Barnes, the Labour Minister of Transport, a tough time in debates, castigating the Government for allowing the railways to be suffocated under a heavy burden of the overhead costs of a bloated central administration; for strangling the economy by maintaining for far too long an excessively tight rationing of fuel; and for squeezing private road haulage contractors out of business to protect the State-controlled British Road Services from the consequences of its inefficient operation. Thorneycroft seemed ideally suited to the Ministry of Transport, but it was the much more important post of President of the Board of Trade that Churchill chose for him. Carla Thorneycroft recalls taking a telephone call for Peter from 10 Downing Street and telling the caller that her husband was in the King's Road, painting. *"Do find him"*, said the caller. *"It is most important that he contacts us as soon as possible."* It was the Prime Minister who wanted to see him. *"I have the Board of Trade for you, my boy."* said Churchill, laying his hand on Thorneycroft's shoulder. Thorneycroft was to 'have' the Board of Trade for five years.

Promotion to the Cabinet brought little in the way of financial reward. One of Churchill's first acts was to order reductions of £1,000 per annum in the salaries of all Cabinet ministers, sharing their sacrifice by cutting his own salary from £10,000 to £7,000. The use of ministerial cars was also to be severely restricted. For Thorneycroft, these were secondary considerations. The Board of Trade would give him tremendous scope to broaden his experience nationally and internationally and to exercise his talents in finding solutions to the exceedingly difficult problems that Britain was facing right across the board as, having so recently emerged from an exhausting war, the country had somehow to find the means to re-arm without a ruinous impact on the economy.

The problems facing him were indeed formidable. The out-going Labour Government had accepted the obligation to re-arm as a junior, but politically

19. Peter was in the King's Road painting
(*From a watercolour sketch by Peter Thorneycroft*)

crucial, partner to the United States in the 'Peace Through Strength Initiative' that the Americans had devised to counter the military threat from the Soviet Union. They had not, however, willed the means to carry out that obligation, giving the impression for many months of hoping that, if they prevaricated long enough, the problem would go away.

It had not gone away.

Churchill and his new Government had as a matter of urgency to bring public spending under control to leave room for essential defence expenditure, and this at a time when gold and dollar reserves had been severely depleted, and output of the nation's most important fuel, coal, was totally inadequate. In spite of many attempts, even before the end of the war, to bring home to the British people how low our industrial productivity was compared with our international competitors, industry was still suffering from inadequate investment and from a virtually automatic resistance by employees and their trade unions whenever managements attempted to introduce better equipment or working practices to improve efficiency. Across the Channel, M. Schuman was pressing ahead with his plans to forge a new Europe based on tying Germany and France so closely together that conflict between them would never again disturb the Continental peace. Britain could not ignore this movement, which had won the strong support of the Americans, and was widely construed as proceeding organically from Churchill's own espousal of European unity in a speech he had made at Metz in 1946.

The problems of public spending and of restoring the nation's financial reserves and the health of sterling were within the remit of the new Chancellor of the Exchequer, R. A. Butler. Most of the others were for Thorneycroft and his Board of Trade to deal with, but they could only act within the constraints imposed by the dire financial situation.

Thorneycroft got down to business straight away. His first major speech in the House of Commons as President of the Board of Trade on 9th November 1951 was devoted to the pressing problem of ensuring that enough cotton of the right quality was imported to supply the Lancashire textile industry, which was expected to make an important contribution to the exports so desperately needed to improve the balance of payments. At the same time, he had to defend cuts in the imports of other materials regarded as less essential to the economy. The Conservatives were, in fact, caught in a dilemma. Their natural instincts were to re-establish as quickly as possible the free market institutions which had been suspended as a wartime measure, their functions having been assumed by Government departments. The Socialists had been delighted to maintain these arrangements as central mechanisms of a command economy. The reality the Conservatives now faced, and that Thorneycroft had now to defend in the House of Commons, was that those elaborate central mechanisms could not be dismantled without careful preparation and development of efficient replacements for them. Controls, anathema though they might be, could not be removed overnight. The Liverpool Cotton Exchange was just one example and one, moreover, whose independence Winston Churchill himself, no less, had promised to restore in his election statement. Churchill's pledge would be redeemed – but not yet.

Two weeks later, it was the trade aspects of the Peace Treaty with Japan that occupied his attention. Whilst recognising the inevitable growth of severe competition from Japanese industries in fields of great interest to Britain, such as textiles, machinery and ceramics, he firmly rejected the idea of imposing production restrictions on Japan as both impossible to monitor without a permanent and strong occupation force, and potentially damaging to our own interests and to international stability if Japan, as a result of economic weakness, became a fertile ground for Communist propaganda. Nevertheless, the trade risks could not be ignored. The contentious issues would have to be discussed by the British and Japanese industries concerned and, if it proved to be necessary, tariffs or quotas could be imposed on Japanese imports. Japan and Britain had to learn how to live in the world together.

A highly sensitive issue that Thorneycroft had to face at this time was to decide what action to take against cartels. He had set out his stall on this question in the Tory Reform Committee's manifesto, *Design for Freedom*, only two years earlier: *"Break them up!"* The issue had been brought to the surface by a report of the Monopolies Commission on the electric lamp cartel, on which one of his cabinet colleagues, Oliver Lyttelton, the Colonial Secretary, held diametrically opposite views. (Lyttelton had, until his Cabinet appointment, chaired Associated

Electrical Industries, one of the largest members of the cartel). Public suspicion that Lyttelton might unduly influence the Government response to the report was further fanned by the fact that Sir Lionel Heald, the Attorney-General, had been the King's Counsel responsible for presenting the cartel's arguments to the Commission.

Thorneycroft faced severe tests of his consistency and credibility on all these issues and, as Parliament rose for its eight-week recess in December 1951, he was subjected to some fierce press accusations of vacillation and indecision in his first weeks as a member of the Cabinet.

The early months of 1952 brought little to improve his public image. At the end of January he was obliged to confess that he had no proposals ready yet for relaxing the increasingly unpopular utility clothing scheme, although he was well aware that the textile industry was 'so tied up with purchase tax, utility and price controls that it could hardly move'. He had to admit that the far-reaching implications for Imperial Preference of restrictions imposed by the 1948 General Agreement on Tariffs and Trade had not yet been thoroughly analysed by his department, although consultations with Commonwealth governments were in hand. He was certainly not inclined to encourage exporters to ignore the European market, one of the few outside the Sterling Area free from the constant need for bilateral trade pacts. Defending himself against the charge of indecision on all these complex matters, Thorneycroft likened the evolution of Government policy to a painting: a sketch had been made in November; in January it was still only partly completed; the full panorama would not be revealed until the Budget in March. Thorneycroft was learning the hard way how prescient he had been when he wrote in *Design for Living* of how difficult it was for a minister of a newly elected Government to devote enough time to planning his work load for the long term, rather than reacting to the urgent realities of every day.

The range of subjects which fell within the remit of Peter Thorneycroft during his tenure of office at the Board of Trade was, indeed, dauntingly wide.

A single day, 13th March 1952, produced thirty-two Questions for Oral Answer by the President of the Board of Trade. Many of these covered the sort of arcane issues that in an over-regulated society distract leaders from their proper roles: how much leather footware was being imported from Eire? why don't we, like other countries, tax rayon as a silk product? what was the import quota for new potatoes? had a decision been made to allow a £2.5 million hotel to be built in London? will he abolish the tariff on imported fertilizers? will more nylon stockings be made available for the home market and did exports of these stockings reveal how the denier texture demanded by customers was changing? did he realise how much sub-standard clothing was being manufactured? what plans had he for developing the industrial estate at Kilwinning? and so on. Of course, there were also matters of real substance much more worthy of the attention of the nation's leaders: what had the National Research Development Corporation actually achieved; what progress had been made in the negotiations on a trade treaty with Germany; what action was he proposing to take on the recommendations of the Lloyd Jacob Committee on resale price maintenance: and there was a sly dig from Labour's Barbara Castle asking how many articles had been freed from price control since the Government took office.

It no doubt gave Thorneycroft not a little pleasure to tell Barbara Castle that same day of the abolition, except for furniture, of the wartime utility scheme and the related price controls. Quality would, in future, be monitored by the British Standards Institution, whose 'kite-mark' would be affixed to products which complied with its standards. Over a hundred Government orders and thousands of specifications would be torn up. However, the intricate web of interlocking controls meant that even this relatively straightforward first step towards freedom from regulation could not be taken without changing at the same time the rules governing purchase tax. Utility products had been exempt from this tax, and to ensure that the prices of all the freed articles did not rise immediately, a new and far from simple exemption arrangement had to be worked out.

This was a frustrating period for Thorneycroft. He knew very well what he wanted to do. He was a 'small government' politician. He believed in individual choice exercised through the marketplace, and that people must accept the consequences of the choices they made. He was convinced that decisions should be taken at the lowest possible level in the political structure to ensure that they were made by people who knew what the practical consequences of their decisions would be, and who would have to account for them to those directly affected by them. At the same time, he was a 'one-nation Tory', well aware that there were many people in society who needed protection from the unintended, but indisputable, negative aspects of a market economy: unemployment when a business failed; loss of income and extra expense for the individual when illness struck; denial of access to essentials of life such as decent housing, fuel, staple foods and clean water if market prices rose to an unaffordable level. He knew also that suppliers in a capitalist society tended to form protective cartels, and that these tendencies could usually be checked only by governments, since purchasers are in most cases more numerous and heterogeneous and so less able than suppliers to organise collective action.

The reality that faced him was that virtually the whole of the transport system had been organised by the Socialists into a State-owned monopoly, controlled by a department of state which had made a poor job of management. The quality, quantity and prices of a vast range of the goods available for consumers to buy were controlled in great detail through such measures as the Utility Scheme and the rationing arrangements still surviving from wartime. The trading systems of the whole world had been disrupted by six years of war, and only the first steps had been taken, especially through the General Agreement on Tariffs and Trade (GATT), to rejuvenate them. To get from where he was to where he wanted to be would require restoration of the nationalised industries to private ownership; the complete abolition of the Utility Scheme and all remaining rationing arrangements; and finding somehow the best achievable compromise for the British economy between defending the system of Imperial Preference and the unfettered free trade which was the ultimate aim of GATT.

Thorneycroft weighed his options pragmatically.

He knew that the process of nationalisation had placed an enormous burden on the people who had the unenviable task of managing the railways, the coal mines and the road transport enterprises, and that the reverse process of privatisation would impose a burden of similar gravity on those industries at a time when maximum effort was needed to get them operating efficiently. In the case of consumer goods a drastic, sudden abolition of controls would have led to chaos because of the intricacies of the network of controls which embraced not only product quality but supply of raw materials, manufacturing capacity and its correlation with import and export trading, and which involved also the tax system and therefore the nation's income and expenditure accounts. Implementation of the GATT provisions without seriously damaging relations with Commonwealth countries that had enjoyed the protection of Imperial Preference for so many years would require sensitive negotiations conducted with great diplomacy. The strategic goals could be achieved without serious disruption of the economy only by a series of very carefully planned and coherent tactical manoeuvres.

Painful though the decision was, Thorneycroft and his Cabinet colleagues had to accept that return to private ownership of the recently nationalised industries would have to wait. Instead, everything possible must be done to improve their efficiency.

A start could, however, be made to dismantle the controls on consumer goods, and the abolition of the Utility Scheme was a significant first step. This would not only restore real customer choice, but enable the politicians and civil servants of the Board of Trade to lift their eyes from the minutiae to the major issues confronting them.

GATT was one of those major issues and a much more intractable problem. Most of the comment in the media and on the back benches came from ardent supporters of Imperial Preference who were against GATT *tout court,* and wished that Britain had never signed the treaty. The preservation of trust between the members of the Commonwealth was certainly a major consideration for the British Government, but lurking in the background, weighing just as heavily with political leaders and senior civil servants, was the thorny question of trading relations with European countries.

GATT was a remarkable agreement. Its conception can be traced back to the Atlantic Charter of August 1941, drawn up with extraordinary faith by Winston Churchill and Franklin D Roosevelt as a blue-print for the principles that should guide the world when Nazism had been crushed – at that time no more than a devout hope. One of the eight principles expounded in the Charter was 'the enjoyment by all states of access on equal terms to the trade and raw materials of the world'. With every justification, the Americans considered that the system of Imperial Preference established by the Ottawa Agreement of 1932 was incompatible with this principle, and pressed for the Charter to include a provision for its progressive abolition. Churchill would only agree to this with the proviso that 'existing obligations' be respected. The American acceptance of this proviso effectively enshrined the principle that Imperial Preference was a permitted exception to the general 'most favoured nation' concept that underpinned most agreements, bilateral or multilateral, for freedom of trade. Nevertheless, the principle of free trade was kept alive in the Lend-Lease Agreement governing the supply by the USA of destroyers to Britain, which included in Article VII provision for *'agreed action directed to the elimination of all forms of discriminatory treatment in international commerce'*. When, in December 1945, a Britain impoverished by the war was forced to seek a loan from the USA, she was obliged also to sign the Anglo-American Financial and Commercial Agreement which carried an obligation on both governments to discuss agreed action to secure achievement of the Article VII objectives of four years earlier. This time, action followed quite quickly. The Americans drew up "Proposals for the Expansion of World Trade and Employment" which the British accepted as a basis for negotiation of concessions intended to result in progressive reduction or even elimination of preferences and duties, and the establishment of a mechanism – an International Trade Organisation – to oversee the process and monitor implementation of agreements reached. It took a further two years to organise a meeting but, in early 1947, twenty-three trading nations sent representatives to Geneva for what became the first round of a new multilateral agreement on reduction of duties, the 'General Agreement on Tariffs and Trade', or GATT, which was signed on 30th October 1947. One truly remarkable feature of GATT was that the detailed agreements reached at its meetings were applied provisionally with immediate effect, with the intention that they should be made definitive when the contracting parties had each ratified them in accordance with their national laws. But, in practice, ratification never happened. The agreed tariff changes nevertheless remained in force, with no member willing to challenge their implementation because the benefits were too valuable to lose.

By the time that Thorneycroft became directly involved in GATT affairs, further rounds had been held, at Annecy and Torquay. Each round resulted in tariff reductions, but the existing measures of Imperial Preference remained intact. No new preferential tariffs were permitted, but trade restrictions by imposing quotas were allowed if it could be shown that they were justified for balance of payments reasons.

Because the nation's foreign currency reserves were shrinking fast (ongoing commitments inherited from the previous Government had reduced them from $3.8 billion in June 1951 to $2.3 billion by December) urgent action had to be taken to stem the outflow of dollars. Imports from dollar-zone countries had to be reduced. Commenting on the import cuts in a speech to the Cotton Board Conference at Harrogate in October 1952, Thorneycroft asked the cotton manufacturers to judge them for what they were – *"ugly and temporary necessities for balance of payments reasons."* likening import cuts by quotas to *"splints that must be taken away as soon as the bone begins to knit together"* , and insisting that they should not *"regard them as a trade barrier behind whose fortuitous protection employers or trade unions can expect to enjoy a peaceful and untrammelled existence."* He reminded them of the intimate connection between these unpopular commercial policy decisions and the parallel, equally unpopular, monetary decisions of the Treasury, especially in raising the bank rate. The unpleasant effects had been to raise prices for consumers and the cost of money for businesses, but they had worked. The $1.5 billion drain from reserves of the second half of 1951 had been reduced to $650 million in the next half-year and to zero in the following quarter. He left the cotton men under no illusion that it was now up to them to take advantage of what the Government had achieved. The Government could not create trade for them.

For a few weeks at this sensitive time, from the end of November 1952 until mid-January 1953, life was made extremely difficult for Thorneycroft by a slipped disc that kept him flat on his back and confined to his bed for most of the time. It was a problem that was to trouble him for the rest of his life, making the long journeys by air that he could hardly avoid a painful experience. He was fortunate in having at the Board of Trade a highly competent Permanent Secretary in Sir Frank Lee, in whom he had complete confidence and, although guiding a department of state from one's bed cannot be easy, there seems to have been no hiatus in the programme of work.

An important question exercising minds in the trade ministries of members of GATT at this time was that of Japanese accession to the agreement. In Britain, the textile industry was viscerally opposed to allowing the Japanese in, and was a very powerful lobby. Here, Thorneycroft was faced with the dilemma of how to reconcile his conviction that an international regime of free trade brought long-term benefit to every nation, including his own, with the political need to cushion its impact on those individual industries – like the Lancashire textile industry - which had allowed themselves to become uncompetitive within the cocoon of a protectionist system. His response to this dilemma was to try to pacify the protectionist lobbies by opposing, at a GATT meeting in Geneva in September 1953, any early negotiations on Japanese accession on the grounds that this would lead, not to freer trade, but to intense pressure for protective tariff increases from many members (including Commonwealth countries) still fearful of Japanese competition, especially as the Japanese would find it virtually impossible to penetrate the highly protected American market and were therefore likely to concentrate their export efforts on European and other markets. At the same time he sought some minor concessions to the GATT rules to enable tariff increases in favour of a few British agricultural and horticultural products to be applied to imports from European countries, leaving those from Commonwealth countries exempt. He won his minor concessions, but found himself only weakly supported in the debate on Japan. The Japanese application for associate membership was endorsed not only by a United States desperately keen to tie Japan into the new international institutions as soon as possible, but by most of the other 32 members, including India, Pakistan, Ceylon and Indonesia. In a thoughtful and trenchant speech at the Geneva meeting, Thorneycroft laid great emphasis on the pressing need for the United States administration to change fundamentally its trading policies, which were effectively closing broad swathes of the American market to imports, not only with high tariffs, well over 50% in many cases, but also with devices such as artificially inflated Customs valuations of articles subject to duty, 'Buy American' legislation and onerous shipping restrictions, all measures wholly at variance with the GATT objectives. These concerns about US policy must have been shared by many other GATT members but, when it came to a vote, only Australia, New Zealand and France supported the British position, and Japan was admitted as an associate member, opening the way for negotiations to begin on the conditions for full membership.

The British opposition to welcoming the Japanese into the free trade agreement was certainly at variance with Thorneycroft's own views. It may be that his military training had taught him that strategic objectives are often best achieved by tactical manoeuvres that, on the surface, do not seem compatible with the strategy. He certainly knew very well how important it is before committing to an irrevocable action to make a cool appraisal of the likelihood that the action will have its intended effects, and what might be the consequences if it did not. (It is surprising how often this rather simple concept is overlooked. Was it, for example, applied by the US administration or the British Government before invading Iraq in 2003). In the case of Japanese entry into GATT, inevitable though it probably was because it enjoyed such strong political support from America, and consonant though it certainly was with his own principles, he believed that to press it forward in 1953 would be inimical, not helpful, to the objective of furthering the aim of free trade. He could not stop the process, but would have liked to delay it.

His failure in Geneva to put a stop to Japan's accession negotiations provoked some furious personal attacks in the Press, questioning his competence and even his sincerity as Britain's negotiator on these matters. Even the minor concessions he had secured were dismissed by his critics as worthless, especially because they had been granted on condition that the volume of imports from the Commonwealth of the exempted articles was not allowed to rise. He was not immune to criticism even from within his own party, whose Annual Conference was due to be held at Margate in October 1953 . One old warrior, Leo Amery, wanted Britain to turn the clock back and withdraw from GATT altogether, and there were other senior Tories arguing strongly for cancellation of those GATT rules which militated against Commonwealth Preference.

But Thorneycroft stuck to his guns. He wanted to leave no doubt in the minds of the leaders of industry that it was they, their managers and their workers who had to save themselves, by taking the steps needed to raise productivity, develop the necessary skills and modernise their equipment and designs to make themselves competitive in export markets. In a speech to the British Institute of Management in November, he pointed out that the British textile industry's share of world markets had fallen from its pre-war level of 29% to a mere 15%, and the reason was that they were no longer competitive. (The textile industries of Continental Europe had increased their share from 23% to 35% in the same period). He reminded his audience of the commercial strength of the USA, which was now the world's largest exporter of manufactured goods and Britain's main competitor. The need to improve productivity being so evident, he wondered why British manufacturers seemed so reluctant to embrace the idea of inter-firm comparisons to encourage the spread of best practice, a concept that had emerged from the work of the British Productivity Council but that had fallen on stony ground. He questioned whether enough was being done to train managers. He delivered much the same message to the textile manufacturers at a dinner in Leeds in January 1954, adding that Government could not save industries. Its role was to secure 'most favoured nation' treatment in export markets and ensure that quotas were used only for balance of payments purposes, and not for plain protective ends.

Thorneycroft's 'set-piece' speeches on occasions like these were always well-researched and persuasive. He proved to be adept also in the new medium of television. His first appearance was in February 1954 on the 'Press Conference' programme and Randolph Churchill who at the time was an occasional television critic wrote under the headline "Mr Thorneycroft finds it easy", *"What made last night's programme better than the usual was, I am sorry to say, not the Press. It was the extreme competence of Mr Peter Thorneycroft, President of the Board of Trade. He had the subject [of the Anglo-Japanese Trade Agreement] at his fingertips and disposed of the questions with overwhelming ease"*, adding, *"To read some newspapers, you would think that all politicians were stupider than all journalists. No one could have thought that who saw last night's programme".*

The Japanese press followed Thorneycroft's leadership of the British approach to trading with Japan with close interest. The *Asahi Evening News* reported at some length in February 1954 a debate in the House of Commons on a motion of censure on the Anglo-Japanese Payments Agreement, and Thorneycroft's defence of the decision to sign the agreement: *"From the first moment it was perfectly clear that we would face considerable political criticism: [but] it was in the interests of this country and the Commonwealth that we should sign it. The principles of this Agreement were not new; they were embodied in the earlier Agreement entered into by the Socialist Government. These principles were that trade should be conducted in sterling between this country and Japan, meaning that we must buy as well as sell – and that if there was an imbalance of trade, then one or other would have to buy more.* [If the Government had not signed,] *Japan would have bought less from the Sterling Area. That would not have been the best way to encourage Japan to come into the Western comity of nations. Commerce and foreign policies are not so divided as all that."* Thorneycroft believed that anxiety about unfair trading practices by the Japanese before the war was misplaced. Japan had given all the necessary undertakings in the Anglo-Japanese Peace Treaty, and had also signed the Madrid Convention on indications of origin and the Convention on industrial property rights. *"This is not free trade. It is a deliberate decision to choose an expansionist rather than a restrictionist policy."*

There were some significant departures in that speech from the line taken earlier – not only in the last two sentences, but in the reference to encouraging Japan to join the Western comity of nations, which had been one of the arguments used by the Americans at Geneva in 1952 in pressing, against British opposition, for negotiations to start on Japanese entry into GATT. The decision to conduct trade between the two countries in sterling was itself a departure from free trade principles, since it implied an intention to aim at balanced trade between the two countries and therefore a form of quota fixing to the exclusion of others. It was a pragmatic response to the reality that the US market which should have been a major outlet for Japanese exporters was still heavily protected, making it imprudent for other nations to abide faithfully by the principles of multilateral free trade.

Although GATT, and Japan in particular, occupied a great deal of the Board of Trade's attention, other major issues were being handled throughout this period, apart from the abolition of the Utility Scheme mentioned earlier.

In 1953, a Merchandise Marks Act outlawing false and misleading description of goods received parliamentary approval. This was a very important measure for the protection of consumers, placing the onus clearly on suppliers to ensure that their goods were properly described. It replaced the system of governmental control through the discarded Utility Scheme, with its bureaucracy and its undoubted, if unintended, effect of stifling innovation in product design and quality.

Early in 1954, following the death of Stalin in March 1953, a number of western countries including the United Kingdom were anxious to strengthen trade ties with the Soviet Union, now governed by a triumvirate – Malenkov, Khruschev and Bulganin. This was another of those important issues on which the United States and Britain, although broadly in agreement on key principles, differed on not unimportant details. It was clear that development of trade in civilian goods was highly desirable, and that trade in military goods must be controlled. These were governed by an agreement between all 15 members of NATO (except Iceland) together with Japan and West Germany, which placed an absolute embargo on exports to the Soviet bloc of arms and ammunition, and quota restrictions on a list of goods of lesser strategic importance. The argument was about the definition of which military goods were unacceptably risky to supply. The USA favoured a tight and extensive embargo list embracing not only armaments, but any equipment that could be used to manufacture arms: Britain took a rather more relaxed view of what the list should contain. It seems remarkable fifty years later that the only other country the Americans and the British thought it necessary to involve in direct consultations at this stage was France. Germany, the only major Western trading nation having a land frontier with the Soviet countries, was not invited to take part. It was therefore the trade ministers of Britain, France and the USA - Peter Thorneycroft, Maurice Schumann and Harold Stassen - who met in London at the end of March 1954 but, after two days of hard bargaining, little progress was made. The matter was referred back to a committee of the international group of 16 nations, who were asked to prepare firm proposals. The need was clear for consensus of all the interested parties if the deal was to have any chance of success, with no maverick states breaking the rules.

Thorneycroft now embarked upon a series of visits to discuss commercial policies, including trade with the Soviets, with a number of friendly nations. The first, in April 1954, was to Italy, to meet his opposite number Mario Martinelli. He praised Italy for the efforts it had made to free many products from trading controls, but had to submit to Martinelli's complaint that measures taken by the UK in coping with the economic crisis of late 1951 and early 1952 had severely restricted Italian imports in spite of Italy's own efforts to stimulate trade. It was later the same day, when he gave a talk at the Istituto per lo Studio della Politica Internazionale (ISPI), that he first met Dr Alberto Pirelli, who was President of

ISPI, the beginning of a relationship that was later to result in Thorneycroft serving for more than twenty years as Chairman of the Pirelli companies in Britain.

In May he was at the receiving end of a visit from the Argentine Foreign Minister, Jeronimo Remorino, who came to London accompanied by his colleague, Dr Alfredo Gomez Morales, Minister of Economic affairs, to negotiate a trade agreement. Not everyone in Britain thought that this was a good idea – Argentina had not been particularly helpful to Britain during the hard years immediately after the war.

A few days later Thorneycroft, accompanied by his wife Carla, left for Canada in a Super Constellation aircraft of Trans Canada Airlines to begin a three week visit which was to take in seven cities across the Dominion. (The Constellation had a bit of a reputation amongst seasoned travellers for rarely reaching the other side of the Atlantic with all four engines still running – but Flight 533 seems not to have suffered any such indignity on this occasion). After a brief stop in Ottawa to meet the Prime Minister, St Laurent, Thorneycroft went to Toronto where, on 31st May 1954, he opened an International Trade Fair and met C D Howe, the Trade Minister, for discussions on trade between Britain and Canada. Tendering was in progress for contracts to build the St Lawrence Seaway, designed to bring ocean-going vessels right down to Toronto and the Great Lakes, and Thorneycroft pressed the claims of British construction companies to participate in the business. He also urged Howe not to raise tariffs on wool fabrics, arguing that this would cause great hardship to the British textile industry. He was at pains to insist that he was not threatening reprisals, but pointed out that Britain had recently freed grain from controls, to Canada's considerable advantage.

From Toronto, Thorneycroft flew to the West Coast, first to Victoria, (where his twin sister Elizabeth had worked during the mid-1940s with the law firm R S Stuart Yates) to meet the Lieutenant Governor of British Columbia, Clarence Wallace, and then to Vancouver, where he explained the approach being taken by the UK to trade with Russia. He admitted that others had different views on what could safely be sold or bartered (for some goods, barter deals were preferred at the time to straightforward purchase contracts), but the UK wanted to have a clear, short-list to be drawn up of items agreed by all parties to be strategically dangerous, and for that list then to be rigorously enforced. *The Vancouver News* was interested in a reply to a question about the wisdom of trading with ex-enemy Germany, that *"it would be most unfair and unwise not to let Germany trade in the markets of the world"* and another, a robust defence of Britain's financial role, *"Britain is still the banker for half the world. Half the world's trade is still done in sterling."*

The *News* also took an interest in some of the members of Thorneycroft's entourage, recording that he was accompanied by his Parliamentary Private Secretary, F W Glaves-Smith and his personal secretary, Miss Irene White (who served him faithfully for the rest of his political career).

A short break at Banff Springs was followed by an address to a convention of the Canadian Manufacturers Association in Jasper, ramming home the message that if Canadians would buy British goods, Britons would buy theirs, and drawing attention to the inventiveness of British engineers who had developed, for example, highly efficient gas turbines which ought to be of interest to Canadian industry. Via Edmonton, then, to open new UK Trade Mission offices, to Toronto where the former soldier and member of the war-time Joint Planning Staff gave a talk to the Empire Club of Canada on Combined Operations, suggesting that *"The constant theme of foreign policies of all countries must be to pierce the curtain now between them"*.

The final leg of this long journey took the Thorneycrofts to Quebec – first to the ancient capital, Quebec City, where they stayed with the Lieutenant-Governor Gaspard Fauteux at his residence, Le Bois de Coulonge, and then to Montreal for a meeting with the Premier of Quebec, Duplessis, a luncheon with the Mayor Wilfrid Hamel, and a speech to the Rotary Club of Montreal, concluding with a long final press conference at which Thorneycroft summed up his impressions of Canada and dealt at some length with the complex issue of currency convertibility. On both issues he impressed his audience with his firm grasp of essential detail. He was very happy that British millers were buying two-thirds of the grain they needed from Canada, because it was a good quality, hard grain that milled well, as well being competitively priced. (The remaining third came mainly from Australia and Argentina). He had been very impressed at the Toronto Fair by the growing competition in world markets, with goods coming from many countries, including Japan and Germany. He emphasised that his visit had been a fact-finding mission. There had been no official negotiations, but he had met a lot of people and a wide range of topics had been discussed. He saw many opportunities for British participation in the development of mining, oil and other Canadian industries through investment of capital and supply of machinery and equipment. On convertibility of sterling into dollars, he knew of no solution other than to achieve a sound balance of trade. During the war, there had been a forced switch to North/South trading in North America, making Canada and the USA more dependent upon each other, and leaving Canada with a big trade deficit with America. If there was something basically wrong with the balance of trade, convertibility was not possible. He pressed home the argument he had deployed everywhere he had been, of the need for Canada to buy more from the UK to balance Britain's large trade in dollar goods, pointing out that a shift to Britain of only 7% of Canada's purchases from the USA would bring all three countries closer to a balanced pattern of trading.

This had been a marathon journey for Thorneycroft and his wife. They had covered almost 10,000 miles in two weeks, by rail, air and car, including a mad dash of a hundred miles on a rail engineer's trolley when fierce storms had washed out road and rail links outside Jasper, to get to the main line in time for a connection to Edmonton: in fact the weather had been wet for much of the fortnight. Although not untypical of a travelling politician's hectic schedule, it must have been gruelling for a man who, only a few months before, had been prostrate for several weeks with back trouble. Although Thorneycroft had enjoyed the support of his wife during the trip, their little daughter Victoria was never far from their thoughts, and there is a charming picture of Victoria greeting them on their arrival at Heathrow.

20. A delighted Victoria welcomes her parents home from Canada, 1954
(*photo: believed to be by Associated Press*)

Carla Thorneycroft had not forgotten her earlier experience as Fashion Editor of the London '*Vogue*' magazine, and noticed that the extensive use in Canadian houses of central heating in the winter (not yet in general use in Britain) and air-conditioning in the summer (almost unknown in Britain) presented design and market opportunities for the British fashion industry which, she suggested, should offer confections in lightweight wool and worsted for Canadian winters, and cottons for the summer – and she thought that cocktail and short evening dresses would find a ready clientele. She was very friendly with Lady Pamela

Berry, President of the British Incorporated Society of Fashion Designers, and was able to convey this message at a soirée for the Society at Lancaster House later that summer.

Less than three weeks after his return from Canada, Thorneycroft was back in North America at the beginning of July, for more talks with Harold Stassen, head of the US Foreign Operations Administration, on control of strategic exports to Communist countries. The London meeting in March between Stassen, Thorneycroft and Schumann had not resolved the differences between the USA and European countries. Britain was still pressing for a significant relaxation of restrictions on goods which would not strengthen Communist war potential, although it was clear that there was no question of lifting any restrictions on trade with Communist China and North Korea until a peace treaty had been signed. The continued disagreement had, for several months, prevented the international committee charged with preparing new lists of embargoed and restricted goods from making any progress. To try to break the stalemate, President Eisenhower had invited Prime Minister Sir Winston Churchill to Washington, and the visit had taken place at the end of June, Churchill having urged President Eisenhower to make a strong effort to promote a spirit of co-existence with the Soviet Union and do nothing that might increase the risk of a ruinous conflict between East and West. The further Thorneycroft/Stassen talks had been arranged at short notice as an outcome of those discussions. Thorneycroft's persistence paid off. Britain and the USA would now support a proposal to cut the list of embargoed goods by about a third, and reduce the list of goods subject to quantity limitations from 90 to 20 – a very substantial relaxation closely in line with the earlier British proposal. It was also agreed that policing of the agreement would be considerably tightened.

His absences abroad had left Thorneycroft with a heavy backlog of work, forcing him to delay a much needed holiday with his family, who had to leave for Italy without him. He caught up with them in Venice at the end of August and was able, with his wife, to indulge their love of art with visits to 'Venezia Viva', an exhibition at the Centro Internazionale delle Arti e del Costume, and to a retrospective show of a sculptor friend, Renato Signorini, as well as spending some time painting at Tellaro.

In September, he used the opportunity of an engagement with the Glasgow Chamber of Commerce to explain the opportunities for British industry opened up by the international agreement on exports to the Communist bloc. Locomotives and other railway rolling stock, agricultural machinery and a wide range of machine tools and other industrial goods could now be sold to the Communist countries, and the Clydeside shipyards, in particular, would benefit from pending decisions by the Admiralty to license construction of a limited number of merchant ships, tugs, dredgers and fishing vessels. These were all industrial sectors where Britain still, in 1954, had considerable strengths, and the markets of the Soviet bloc were of great interest to manufacturers. He was also able to point out that since the Conservative victory in the 1951 election, improvement in the national reserves had permitted a start to be made in paying off the country's debts, accumulated during the war and in the few years of Labour government afterwards. Industrial production was rising and exports were strong. A single firm, Vickers Armstrong had sold enough Viscount aircraft to earn £32 million of foreign exchange, a figure that also happened to be the amount earned by British industry as a whole every four days during the month of July. He could claim, with good reason, that the nation was doing pretty well under a Conservative government.

The national debate about GATT had quietened down somewhat during the summer while media attention had been upon the more exciting arguments about trading with the Communists. Nevertheless there remained, not only in the Press but within the Conservative Party itself, an unrepentant faction still hankering after the full restoration of Imperial Preference, and able to see only damage to British trading interests from the commitments to GATT, and especially from the clause prohibiting any new preferential tariffs. Thorneycroft, with strong support from the Chancellor of the Exchequer, R.A. Butler, decided to confront the issue head-on at the Party Conference in Blackpool in October 1954. They had prepared the ground well. At a recent meeting of the International Monetary Fund in Washington, Butler had sought the views of the Commonwealth finance ministers present, who all confirmed their enthusiastic support for GATT. Thorneycroft reminded Conference that UK imports from Commonwealth countries had risen to 54% of the total, from 39% before the war. Exports to the Commonwealth had also risen, from 49% to 53%. Nobody could claim that either Britain or the Commonwealth had been damaged by GATT – quite the contrary. *"We did not remain in GATT for sentimental reasons"*, said Thorneycroft, *"but because it paid us to do so."* He insisted that GATT was an essential pre-condition for any future agreement to make sterling a convertible currency. (The incorrigible Sir Victor Raikes did not see this as an advantage. *"Convertibility"* he said, *"would sweep away all defences of the Empire against being flooded by foreign goods."*). When the issue was put to the vote, the Imperial Preference faction led by Leo Amery was comprehensively routed. Reporting the debate the following day, 8th October, the *Manchester Guardian* wrote, *"The final debate of the day on the Commonwealth and world trade started as an unhappy attempt to mix Colonial policy proper and the General Agreement on Tariffs and Trade, but ended as a serious and unrelieved discussion on GATT and a triumph for Mr G E P Thorneycroft, President of the Board of Trade. For the first time at the conference, a subject was sternly debated and argument rather than sentiment clinched the issue."* The following day, the Chancellor of the Exchequer, referring to GATT in his own speech to Conference, which was interpreted in some quarters as hinting at a slight rift between himself and Thorneycroft, said that at the forthcoming GATT meeting in Geneva, Britain would be pressing for a review of individual preferences to allay the worries of Australia about its wheat trade, and the decline in value of some preferences since they were first negotiated, as well as seeking 'fair and proper' measures in the interests of the Lancashire textile industry regarding unfair practices of the Japanese. Given the big vote in favour of GATT the day before, it was perhaps unwise to lift, even slightly, the lid of a Pandora's box of old worries, but the issues that Butler mentioned were, in fact, on the GATT agenda, although perhaps more as a sop to the textile industry than with any expectation of them getting any support.

Thorneycroft did not shirk taking on the textile lobby more directly. A few days after the Party Conference, he attended the annual meeting of the Cotton Board in Harrogate and, rather than deliver to them a prepared speech, he laid himself open to questions from the floor, announcing in advance that he was going to do this so as to give his audience time to prepare their attack: he was in no doubt that it *would* be an attack! And attack they did. He was peppered with shot on all of the issues he had expected - and briefed himself to parry. There was the problem – a real and actual one - of imports of cheap Indian cloth while India imposed a tariff of 60% on British textiles; then the industry's fear that cut-price Japanese imports must inevitably follow Japan's entry into GATT; and worst of all the Government's careless neglect of the industry. Who had started the rumour that the Government has written off the textile industry? Thorneycroft asked: it wasn't true. India had been given the right to tariff-free entry into Britain as long ago as the Ottawa Agreement in 1932: the only measure available to us was the imposition of quotas, but if we did that, others would impose quotas against us to our great disadvantage. In fact the Government had recently persuaded India to lift its own quotas against UK imports, and rely only on its tariffs. And why be so afraid of Japan? Unlike India, Japan was not a member of the Commonwealth, and had no right to preference in trading with us. The most he might consider would be to re-instate disused measures such as countervailing duties or anti-dumping measures if unfair pricing should develop, but no Government could give an industry complete protection against imports. Why, he asked, had they such touching faith in politicians' ability to help them out of their difficulties? They should be begging Government to keep out of their affairs, not to interfere in them. Thorneycroft probably made few friends among the cotton men in this encounter, but he had shown that, when battle had to be joined, he was the better shot, although many of his victims would survive to take him on another day.

That other day was not delayed for too long. In February 1955, the Government accepted a Monopolies Commission recommendation that certain restrictive practices of the calico printing industry should be banned. This was the trigger for the Opposition to table a censure motion criticising the Government for not having taken more decisive action against monopolies and restrictive practices. The Monopolies Commission was, at the time, engaged in a broad investigation of a number of such practices and was due to report within weeks. Harold Wilson led the Socialists' attack, arguing that there was no need to wait for the report before taking action. There is no doubt that restrictive practices of many varieties were rife in British industry. They ranged from price-fixing agreements to allocations of quotas to members of cartels and restrictions on supplies to distributors. The Conservatives, with few exceptions – and Thorneycroft was certainly not an exception - were just as anxious to get rid of them as the Socialists. They were, however, intricately woven into the industrial fabric of the country. In the Commons debate, Thorneycroft insisted that it would be foolish to take action without a prior thorough investigation of each case on it merits, to determine exactly what action was appropriate to the particular case. He reminded the Socialists that in their six years in office, they had referred six cases to the Monopolies Commission and had acted on the Commission's report in only one of them whereas, in his three years at the Board of Trade, not only had the Commission been strengthened, but action had been taken in six cases, he was currently considering two further reports and expected to receive five more during the year. In the specific case relating to calico printing, the Government was generally in favour of the Commission's recommendations, but had felt it right to consult the industry and the Cotton Board before taking action. The Commission's procedures were being examined by the law officers and they had assured him that they appeared to be appropriate and fair. He was convinced that the careful, empirical approach that had been pursued by all Governments in the past ten years was still the right one. He went on to urge industrialists themselves to look closely at their arrangements and consider whether their established practices were still appropriate, without waiting for the Monopolies Commission to pass judgement on them. They should understand that, if their practices were shown after a full and fair inquiry to be against the public interest, they would be got rid of. Wilson was in good form, but so was Thorneycroft, and the censure motion was defeated by 300 votes to 267, Wilson easing the way for his own defeat by making a rather uncharacteristic tactical error in pressing the Government, during the debate, not to prohibit the Calico Industry's price-fixing scheme, but to let it go on subject to Board of Trade approval; not exactly the robust condemnation of restrictive practices that the censure motion was ostensibly intended to achieve. As *Punch* put it in their 'Impressions of Parliament' column, the Government, in supporting the Commission's recommendations, were *"decking themselves in a white sheet of purity that showed up the Opposition's garments as decidedly maculate"*.

On 5th April 1955, Sir Winston Churchill asked the Queen to accept his resignation from the office of Prime Minister and, the following day, Her Majesty asked Sir Anthony Eden to form an administration. The new Prime Minister made a number of changes in his ministerial team, but Thorneycroft's position was not among them. He was invited to continue his successful incumbency at the Board of Trade, and was delighted to do so. He was enjoying himself in this office, confident that he had mastered his brief very well and could continue to make an important impact upon the industrial and trading affairs of the country. The only change in his own team at the Board of Trade was that his Parliamentary Secretary, H. Strauss, was replaced by D. Kaberry. R.A. Butler remained Chancellor of the Exchequer and, in his Budget of 18th April, cut Purchase Tax on household textiles from 50% to 25%, a reduction dismissed by Hugh Gaitskell as 'miserably inadequate'. Thorneycroft may well have agreed with him in principle, but it was a big step in the right direction.

The respite did not last long. Eden decided to call a General Election on 26th May 1955, and Thorneycroft threw himself straight away into his campaign to keep his seat as Member for Monmouth and contribute to the national debate that had to be won to keep his party in power. He had a good story to tell. In an interview reported in the *Western Mail and South Wales News* on 9th May he quoted a recent article in the American magazine *Life* which, after recalling that in 1951 Britain was close to bankruptcy, went on *"The British people enjoy a prosperity unknown in their history: they have come nearer than any other people to exiling poverty from their land."* Thorneycroft argued that this dramatic recovery had been made possible by setting industry free from the crippling economic controls of the previous Socialist Government. Industrial production and consumption had risen and were still rising, public expenditure had been reduced, and yet two and a half million people no longer had to pay income tax. Business had certainly benefited, and been able to raise profits by 4% since 1951, but wage rates had risen more than four times as fast, and personal savings had multiplied seven times. The Conservative Party was now planning the most comprehensive programme of national development ever devised, covering atomic energy, railways, roads, steel, coal, electricity and gas and hospitals.

Fifty years later, so many of these themes still resonate: the economic resurgence that follows liberation from controls; how wages benefit when business prospers; the need to invest in the nation's infrastructure while keeping taxation under control.

Thorneycroft's campaign speeches were not concerned only with economic matters. He ranged over the whole field of policy. Peace, he argued, would best be assured by negotiating to achieve co-existence and settlement of disputes without recourse to war: the Korean and Indo-Chinese wars had been settled, in the end, by negotiation; Austria's independence had been assured by agreement between the West and Russia. He had high hopes of the forthcoming four-power conference if Britain continued to be led by Sir Anthony Eden. Who could the Socialists possibly find to act as Foreign Secretary, he asked: the Socialist party was split from top to bottom on foreign policy. Negotiations for peace would only be successful if backed by military strength. The Socialists had been right to build the atom bomb, and the Conservatives were now right to build the hydrogen bomb. Military strength meant having all of the weapons of modern warfare. The cost of providing this defence was high, but had to be borne, and unfortunately this meant that the Conservative plan to reduce taxes could only be implemented carefully and gradually.

Thorneycroft retained his seat with an increased majority and his party remained in control with a majority of 65 over Labour and of 59 overall. His tenure at the Board of Trade was to go on a little longer.

In July 1955, the Monopolies Commission produced its report on restrictive trade practices, with a declaration that many price-fixing arrangements operated against the public interest, as did most agreements to restrict supplies of goods to retailers, and that they should be banned. The declaration was clear enough, but it was supported by only seven of the ten commissioners, and the others insisted that their views be recorded in a minority report. When he presented the report to Parliament a few days later, Thorneycroft was not ready to say what action the Government would take on the Commission's recommendations. He wanted to examine both the majority and minority reports; these were complex matters on which intelligent men might well hold different opinions, and he would value the views of the House. The opposition and the left-leaning organs of the media had a field day, accusing Thorneycroft of dithering and of betraying his own principles by delaying a decision, when he had promised as recently as February that if the Commission found that any practices were against the public interest, they would be got rid of. "Pottering Peter", one newspaper called him. Pottering Peter pointed out that the Socialists had done practically nothing about restrictive practices in six years of office. He had asked for the Commission to report, had given them the time to examine the problems properly, and now intended to give himself enough time to consider thoroughly their majority recommendations and the views of the minority group before taking well thought out action.

While his officials were working on that, he got on with other tasks. At the end of September, there was an important British Exhibition to attend in Denmark. This was a splendid show, opened by King Frederick who was greeted by bagpipes of the Argyll and Sutherland Highlanders and the Punjab Regiment on his arrival and by the bands of the Life Guards and the Gordon Highlanders inside the Copenhagen Town Hall where the opening ceremony was held. Every newspaper in Copenhagen led with articles in English to greet their British visitors – some even devoting their front pages to the world news in English. A week later, Admiral Sir Michael Denny, C-in-C of the Home Fleet in HMS *Apollo* sailed into Copenhagen harbour accompanied by an aircraft carrier and three other ships of the Royal Navy and, towards the end of the exhibition, the Duke of Edinburgh arrived in the Royal Yacht *Britannia* to visit the trade show at the Tivoli and he later took the salute at the final performance of a Military Tattoo in the grounds of Rosenborg Castle in which 850 British and Danish troops had taken part. Throughout the fortnight, the warmth of the public's welcome was quite remarkable. The Danish people seemed to have forgotten the wounds that Lord Nelson had inflicted upon them long ago and remembered mainly Britain's lonely stand against the German armies in the darkest days of the recent war. Scandinavia, Thorneycroft reminded his hosts, now bought as much from Britain as did Australia, our best customer, and Britain was a major customer for Danish agricultural products, but he also had to admit that British industry was not performing anything like as well as Germany in selling cars and light engineering goods to Denmark. Official luncheons, dinners, talks with commercial organisations, speeches and visits naturally took up a great deal of time, during his short visit but Thorneycroft also held discussions with Danish ministers on a number of issues, including the highly sensitive one of supplies of British coal to Denmark, which had been seriously and suddenly curtailed as a result of the coal shortage in the British home market, leaving the Danes in a difficult situation. Indeed, the Danish Prime Minister, Mr H C Hansen had made a direct and caustic reference to the problem at one of the official banquets. *"An exhibition booth where we could have bought coal to our heart's desire would undoubtedly have been a major attraction.",* he said. *"Above all I should not fail to mention the warm and comfortable British textile goods for which there will certainly be a scramble if the coal supply is cut off."* The best that Thorneycroft could promise in reply was to maintain deliveries at the same level as in the previous year while Denmark tried to find alternative supplies which, realistically, could only come from America or Poland: an uncomfortable message for a Trade Minister to have to give on the occasion of an exhibition aimed at increasing trade between the two countries. Nevertheless, the Exhibition, which attracted thousands of trade visitors from all the Scandinavian countries and from West Germany, was counted, overall, a great success.

Thorneycroft returned from Denmark to attend the 1955 Conservative Party Conference in Bournemouth on 6th October. GATT was still a raw issue with some of the delegates, and Thorneycroft wanted to be sure that the Chancellor of the Exchequer would give no hostages to fortune when he addressed the Conference on economic policy. On 27th September, before leaving for Copenhagen, he had written to R.A.Butler, urging him to *"keep the temperature low on GATT, a battle fought and won last year! GATT, IMF and OEEC are clearly interlocked and indispensable to the policies you and I are pursuing.*

"It has been a long and arduous task to persuade the Conservative Party to support these policies. I am anxious that nothing should be said or done which could change that attitude. I share your view that the US have behaved badly in their recent decisions on commercial policy. It would, however, do real damage to the larger causes which we both have at heart if these US actions were to be used as an excuse to start back-pedalling ourselves. As to textiles, the import side is not a GATT problem. It arises from our Commonwealth trade policy. .... Textiles are a powerful protective lobby and will seize any opportunity to detect the slightest difference of view or even emphasis within the Government."

In the event, the matter passed without a stir, perhaps because the delegates were more excited by the announcement of the impending retirement of Lord Woolton as Chairman of the Party. Anthony Eden had chosen as Woolton's successor Oliver Poole, then a little-known ex-MP who had preferred, in 1950, to leave Parliament and return to merchant banking, although he had since given good service to the Party as its Treasurer. He was to have as a Vice-Chairman Donald Kaberry, who would have to resign from his appointment as Thorneycroft's Parliamentary Secretary at the Board of Trade.

Thorneycroft's next important engagement – becoming an annual event – was to speak at the Conference of the Cotton Board in Harrogate on 14th October 1955. As a year before, he faced a hostile audience. His message to them could not have been clearer. Their industry was in recession, but it was also in secular decline and no Government could cure the decline. People could not be stopped from buying cheap coarse cloth from Asian countries which had lower wages. The question was not whether the Lancashire industry could compete with Asians in coarse cloths, but whether they could compete in efficiency, designs and aggressive selling with European industries whose wages were similar to ours, and with Americans whose labour costs were much higher. He cited some successes such as recent imaginative innovations in man-made fibres and in selling industrial cloths. The doughty cotton-man Mr Cyril Lord was not impressed. If Thorneycroft persisted in his policy of allowing duty-free imports of cotton from the Commonwealth he would go down in history as the hangman of Lancashire. Thorneycroft gave him a blunt reply. It was the cotton industry that was depressed, not the whole of Lancashire. If jobs were being lost in cotton, other industries in the north-west had 50,000 vacancies. It was the industry that had to decide what to do about it. The Government had no plan for cotton. *"In truth"*, he said, *"it is not within the province of the Government to propound, or even within their capacity to carry out, this kind of policy for any industry, unless, perhaps, they own it."* Mr Lord wanted 100% protection: he would not get it. Thorneycroft acknowledged that current uncertainty about the disposal of surplus American cotton stocks was damaging almost every textile industry in the world, and the sooner the Americans sorted out this problem, the better it would be.

Cotton was not the only industry clamouring for attention. Across the Channel, the politicians of continental Europe had, since 1948, been taking cautious steps along the road towards economic and, eventually, political collaboration. In 1951, the European Coal and Steel Community had been constituted with France, Germany, Italy and the Benelux countries as the founding members, the first concrete emanation of a plan proposed in 1950 by Robert Schuman, the French Foreign Minister, who had envisaged not only an organisation to co-ordinate the iron and steel industry, but also a European army. The army proposal had stalled – effectively frozen by British suspicion of French intentions and, in the end, vetoed by General de Gaulle – but a sufficient consensus had existed to justify launching the economic project for iron and steel, whose real aim was to ensure that neither the Germans nor the French could, in future, exploit for military purposes their national industrial strengths in these two key industries. Britain had not joined, still unwilling to accept that her future lay with Europe, and nourishing the hope that the new European venture would fail. It had not done so and, having failed to participate in the early success of ECSC, Britain had now agreed to join a Council of Association, whose first meeting was held in Luxembourg in November 1955 under the chairmanship of René Mayer, the President of the High Authority of ECSC. Thorneycroft led the British Delegation which also included Geoffrey Lloyd, the Minister of Fuel and Power, Sir Archibald Forbes, President of the Iron and Steel Board and Sir Hubert Houldsworth, President of the National Coal Board. It was decided to set up three committees, for coal, steel and trade relations respectively, but otherwise the meeting seems to have done little more than talk about coal, the ECSC side stressing their achievements since 1951, reaching annual production levels of 50 million tons of steel and 240 million tons of coal, whereas the British had to defend their need to restrict exports of coal to the member countries of the Community which, in fact, were expected to fall from 5.5 million tons in 1954 to probably less than two million in 1956. As in Denmark earlier in the year, the President of the Board of Trade had an embarrassing story to tell of Britain's inability to foster coal exports because the National Coal Board could not produce enough even to supply domestic consumption.

Just before Christmas, Sir Anthony Eden announced a major reshuffle of his Cabinet. R.A. Butler, who had guided the country's economic recovery as Chancellor of the Exchequer, was to become Lord Privy Seal, handing over the Treasury to Harold Macmillan. Butler's move could be (and was, in some quarters) seen as a promotion which would enable him to bring his gifts of clear-headed political guidance to bear on all the departments of state. Others believed that it was a moderately subtle way for Eden to indicate that it was Macmillan, not Butler, whom he regarded as his most likely successor. Some of the other Cabinet changes brought younger men to the fore, including Nigel Birch, who went to the Air Ministry, and Iain Macleod (Minister of Labour). Selwyn Lloyd became Foreign Secretary and Sir Walter Monckton moved from Labour to Defence. Thorneycroft, himself still a young member of the team at 46 after four years in post, remained at the Board of Trade, happy to do so because many of the issues he was handling could only be pressed forward at speeds determined by the need to secure international agreement. He was, in fact, the only senior minister allowed the luxury of continuity in the same office. Macmillan had held the office of Foreign Secretary for only eight months and there were some commentators persuaded that Eden, who still thought of himself as the fount of all foreign policy wisdom, had found him too independent. There had been rapid change also at the Ministry of Defence, where Monckton would be the third Minister in just over a year. In the weeks following the reshuffle, the Press was full of reports that Eden himself had lost the support of his party, reports that were not stifled by a rather clumsy public denial by Eden that he was thinking of resigning and a rather more subtle statement of loyal support for his leader from Butler, who famously described Eden as 'the best Prime Minister we have'. (Butler was later to be described as 'the best Prime Minister we never had'.)

Thorneycroft got on with his job. In January 1956, he went to the Potteries to hear something of the pottery industry's problems from local manufacturers, their trade association and the trade union, the National Society of Pottery Workers. They seem to have given him a fairly easy ride. They would have liked their industry to be exempt from the Purchase Tax regime. There was no chance of that: so would every other industry. They would have liked the Government to stimulate demand for their products: he gave the same response that he had given to the cotton manufacturers – that this was a job for themselves, not for the Government. He recognised, warmly, the industry's achievement in exporting such a high proportion (over 70%) of their output and had no difficulty in agreeing with their argument that a strong export performance required a strong domestic market in which to test new designs and provide a platform on which exports could be built: he had never doubted it. The potters did not ask, as the cotton men had done, for a Government policy for their industry, but they did draw attention to a recent case of some manufacturers being accorded export quotas for the Australian market which they had not previously entered, and suggested that the Government ought to make sure that the market share of established exporters was protected against newcomers. Thorneycroft's reply to this was not reported, but it seems unlikely that he would have been very sympathetic. There were visits also to Manchester, for talks with the Manchester Engineering

Council, to the Renolds Chain factory in Coventry, to a Nylon Trade Fair at the Albert Hall and to a Factory Equipment Exhibition at Earls Court where Audrey Lambert and Jane Geoffreys showed him how they protected themselves at work from dust and metal particles.

21. Punch's view of Peter Thorneycroft and the Monopolies Commission (*cartoon: copyright Punch Library*)

The most important business for the new session of Parliament was to bring before the House legislation to deal with restrictive trade practices, on which the Monopolies Commission had reported in July 1955. Thorneycroft's initial response to the report, which was not unanimous, had been cautious. He had made it clear that he wished to consider the recommendations of both the majority and the minority – an approach that most objective observers recognised as wise, given the complexity of the matter, but that had inevitably laid him open to accusations of indecision. He had now decided. All restrictive trade practices were to be presumed to be against the public interest unless the industries concerned could prove that they were not. In presenting his Bill to the Commons, Thorneycroft rejected the claim that this amounted to a reversal of the time-honoured principle of innocence until guilt is proved. This was not, he argued, comparable to a criminal case in which an individual is charged with a specific offence. An industry could only be brought before the Restrictive Trade Practices Court if its practices had already been registered with the Court, so that the facts were already established and admitted. Furthermore, the proceedings were civil, not criminal, not concerned with innocence or guilt, but with deciding whether the admitted practices were or were not against the public interest, when tested against criteria which were laid down in the Bill. If they were, the practices would be prohibited: if not, they would be allowed to continue as long as they could satisfy conditions that would enable them to pass through a limited number of 'gateways', also defined in the Bill. The Labour Party argued that all restrictive trade practices should be prohibited, *tout court,* as criminal offences. Thorneycroft's policy was much more pragmatic. He insisted that Labour's policy (which they had not attempted to implement during five years in power) would cause immense damage to industries whose business practices, developed over many decades during which they were perfectly legal, could not be reformed overnight. He warned the Socialists not to argue too strongly for making these practices criminal offences: it might lead to a demand to treat some trade union practices in a similar way. His approach would ensure that each case was examined on its merits, and he pointed out that the mere publication of the Bill had already led to some industries looking closely at their current trading arrangements. The first practices required to register would be common pricing, level tendering and collective discrimination in the supply of goods. Sole agency arrangements, such as the 'tied garage' systems developed in recent years by the oil companies, were specifically exempted from registration, although Thorneycroft made it clear later, when the Bill reached the Committee stage, that such arrangements, even if not classed as restrictive practices, might still be referred to the Monopolies Commission if they were found unduly to limit competition. The debate on the Second Reading of the Bill was widely reported as a resounding success for both Thorneycroft and his newly appointed Parliamentary Secretary, Derek Walker-Smith. As on so many previous occasions when opening for the Government, Thorneycroft had mastered his brief well, enabling him to run rings around a somewhat pedestrian Douglas Jay, who seemed not to have understood the admittedly difficult subject sufficiently well for him to present cogent arguments. The House at large, indeed, seemed content to listen in awed silence to the competent presentations of Thorneycroft and of Walker-Smith, who wound up the debate. Walker-Smith won not only a pat on the back from his own leader, Sir Anthony Eden, but also the congratulations of Harold Wilson, Leader of the Opposition, himself an ex-President of the Board of Trade.

Eden's lacklustre performance as Prime Minister remained under debilitating attack at this time, not only from the Opposition and the Press, but also from within his own party. Now, at the end of July, 1956, he found himself confronted by the crisis in the Middle East that eventually put paid to his political career, when Colonel Abdel Gamal Nasser, President of Egypt, seized control of the Suez Canal. The Board of Trade was not directly involved in the evolution of this affair: it was a Foreign Office matter. However, the possibility of interruption to the shortest shipping route between Europe and the East and to Britain's oil supplies was a matter of great concern. Thorneycroft decided that he must cancel a family holiday in Capri to ensure that he would be on hand if needed. Much of the criticism of Eden's performance centred upon his recent handling of foreign policy issues, and the support of his party, or even of all members of his Cabinet, could by no means be taken for granted in this new situation, and Thorneycroft's voice would be of importance should Eden find it difficult to hold his Cabinet together. The aggressive manner in which Nasser executed his coup certainly helped to damp down some of the internal criticism that would otherwise have erupted from those who saw little moral difference between nationalising an Egyptian canal and a British railway system. It certainly helped in the early stages of the crisis in bringing the leaders of the Labour Party solidly behind the Government in condemning Nasser's arrogant flouting of international law and practice.

The threat to oil supplies was one of the issues raised by Thorneycroft when he visited Canada in September 1956 on his way to attend the International Monetary Fund and the World Bank in Washington. Canada had substantial reserves of oil in the Athabaska tar sands of Alberta. This oil was difficult and costly to extract and, moreover, would have to be paid for in dollars from Britain's already strained hard currency reserves, but might provide a source of supply of last resort if the Suez crisis were to drag on.

This was, in a way, a distraction from the main agenda for the visit, which was to hear the views of the Canadians on Britain's contemplation of steps to strengthen trading links with Europe, which were seen by many as tending inevitably to weaken still further the traditional commercial relations between Commonwealth members. Thorneycroft argued that development of the European economy must, in the long term, be to the benefit of Canada. He accepted that the new OEEC (Organisation for European Economic Co-operation) might be considered a discriminatory bloc, but pointed out that it was provided for in the GATT agreement and that, although internal tariffs between OEEC members would eventually be removed, the Commonwealth's preferential system would not be affected. At the worst, some Canadian imports into the British market might have to compete on equal terms with European products no longer burdened by tariffs. The discussion with the Canadians was a useful trial run for the presentation by Macmillan and Thorneycroft a few days later to the Commonwealth Finance Ministers assembled in Washington. Here the debate ranged more widely, touching upon the risk that the 'Six' European nations in conference at Messina (France, Germany, Italy, the Netherlands, Belgium and Luxemburg) might agree to establish a customs union from which Britain would be completely excluded. The British position was that a broader trading zone than the territories of the Six would be much more beneficial to the economic health of Europe than one confined to the Six. There seemed to be a consensus that agricultural products would have to be excluded from such a free trade area to protect the interests of Commonwealth countries: indeed the Europeans would have to accept this as a condition for Commonwealth co-operation. The discussion in Washington was constructive, but the finance ministers of the Commonwealth countries reserved their formal judgement of the British negotiating stance. There was no doubt about the American reaction. John Foster Dulles, the Secretary of State, had for a long time been a fervent proponent of a more integrated Europe: he envisaged a United Europe capable of becoming a world power ranking third behind the United States and the Soviet Union, although not in any sense a buffer or a mediator between the Americans and the Russians: a vision not very different from the sort of Europe that Winston Churchill had in mind. Neither China, nor India nor Brazil had yet claimed the attention of world leaders as potential economic forces.

On the other side of the Atlantic, the French and the Germans were about to heal a festering sore that had poisoned their relations for decades: they had agreed that the Saar was to be transferred from France to Germany. A meeting between the German Chancellor Adenauer and the French Prime Minister Jean Monnet was held in Bonn on 30th September 1956 to confirm that this historic decision would be implemented on 1st January 1957, and then move on to review the progress of the proposals for a Customs Union. The mood of the meeting was marred by a bizarre incident. Monnet had arranged to travel by air, and Adenauer was to greet him at Wahn airport, near Cologne, which was still controlled by the Royal Air Force. Somehow or other the flight plan of Monnet's aircraft was not conveyed to the RAF who, at the time he was due to arrive, were engaged in a jet fighter exercise. The jets had insufficient fuel to stay in the air long enough for landing priority safely to be given to Monnet, who was obliged to circle the airport in decidedly unpleasant weather until the jets had landed, much to his discomfort and to the irritation of Adenauer, not at all pleased to be kept waiting in the rain on the ground while the British occupiers of his country completed their aerial manoeuvres. The meeting between the two statesmen that had been intended to celebrate their rapprochement degenerated into an irritable and tetchy discussion between an annoyed Monnet and a discomfited Adenauer. The mood was not improved when Adenauer, who had studied the British ideas for a broader Free Trade Area, declared that he had found them, to Monnet's resentment, more promising than the French inspired proposal for an arrangement restricted to the Six. The meeting ended with an appeal from both countries for Britain to play a more active role in building Europe by making better use of the existing organisations of the Council of Europe, OEEC and the Western European Union, as well as developing a common market, with explicit references to establishing a European arms pool and activating Euratom.

Thorneycroft's thoughts on these momentous issues are summarised well in a memorandum (Thorneycroft Papers, University of Southampton) that he had prepared in May 1956 in anticipation of the discussions planned for that summer:

'Initiative in Europe'

A five-page memorandum by Thorneycroft dated 25.05.56

The following is a summary of this cogently argued document.

The Nature of the decisions to be taken

1) Existing policy

    a) we subscribe to GATT

    b) the structure of Imperial Preference is retained (Ottawa 1932)

2) Imperial Preference is under attack: from Australia (our largest single market) and New Zealand, because access to the UK market no longer as reliable; from UK manufacturers (especially cotton textiles) who resent free importation of Indian grey cloth. Current policy is to hang on to Imperial Preference, but recognising danger of erosion.

3) Trade with Europe depends on most-favoured nation rules which would be forbidden by the Messina powers (the Six). Western Europe plans have a <u>political</u> content – to tie West Germany to the West (supported by Eisenhower and Dulles) 'as a first step towards that European integration for which they yearn.' The Foreign Secretary should express an opinion on the political aspects. Do they provide a method – an indispensable method – of tying Germany to the West? If yes, can we afford to see them fail? If no, should we challenge it and use our influence to get it dropped? Messina might collapse – weakness and volatility of France. If it succeeds, a powerful bloc discriminating against us and dominated by the Germans. If it fails, we shall be blamed, and it will leave a sorry and rather embittered European scene behind. The truth may be that we cannot afford to let it succeed or fail without us.

The Courses open to us

1) The most tempting course, to do nothing, 'may be the most difficult and dangerous of the lot!' If we can contrive a policy, we can justly expound and defend it. If we do nothing, we forfeit any claims to leadership in Europe: in the Commonwealth, we may find ourselves 'clinging to the remnants of Imperial Preference. Unless we can agree on our broad strategic concept, smaller tactical arrangements may be not only ineffectual but really dangerous!'

2) Reference to working paper under Treasury leadership:

a) co-operation in OEEC

b) linking OEEC with Council of Europe

c) tariff negotiations on primarily European goods

d) FTA for steel in Europe

e) FTA generally in Europe

f) Euro/Commonwealth preference scheme

Thorneycroft's Comments:

a) and b) respectable & a great deal to be said for d). b) however outside the Spaak framework and to give a political dimension to OEEC before we have framed our own policy might lead us to a policy we did not want being thrust upon us.

Re d): our relations with the Iron & Steel Community are governed by Treaty and developing (perhaps too) slowly.

Re c): Geneva Round recently completed. How could we justify starting on a further round so soon? Also, reduction of tariffs on a m-f-n basis not what Messina proposes. Further tariff reductions not set in a wider strategic concept likely to infuriate industry and irritate C/W without making any real contribution to our problems.

Re f): 'Strasbourg Plan' has drawbacks. Whole idea runs contrary to policy of freer trade and payments; i.e., it depends on pledges to keep tariffs up against America, as well as lower them inside Europe: it is essentially a two-world concept, obnoxious to US and Canada. Risk of making a present of our preferences to Europe and then see Europe lower tariffs between them and discriminating against us.

Re e): FTA with Europe has powerful attractions, but implies abandoning all C/W preferences.

3) We need to find a method of taking the lead in Europe and securing advantages of the fullest possible commercial opportunities in that Continent, while holding the maximum we can of our preferential system and carrying public opinion with us at home.

4) I believe that the clue to securing the right balance may lie in going for a FTA with Europe, but excluding from the outset the whole of agriculture and horticulture. The Agricultural countries in Europe know from experience that agriculture has never fitted happily into a system of multilateral trading and non-discrimination. Importers use tariffs and quotas to protect their domestic industry, or develop costly and complex subsidy arrangements as in the UK. Exporters seek to build up monopoly practices to bolster up world prices, while the US does almost all these things at once.

A survey of its members conducted by the Federation of British Industries and delivered to Thorneycroft at the beginning of November 1956 revealed a broad measure of support for negotiations aimed at British participation in a free trade area, provided that safeguards could be agreed in some key areas: Imperial Preference must be preserved; discriminatory trade practices such as quotas, subsidies, dumping of products and currency manipulation must be prohibited as must non-tariff barriers such as restrictive national product specifications; and a few industries, among them dyestuffs and watches, would need special attention if they were not to be severely damaged. The exclusion of agricultural (food, drink and tobacco) products was generally supported, although a few of the trade associations concerned with these products, including the chocolate manufacturers, saw some merit in their inclusion. There were, inevitably, some trade associations opposed to any negotiations.

In the meantime, the crisis triggered by Nasser's nationalisation of the Suez Canal had escalated. On 31st October 1956 the British and French Governments in collusion with the Israeli Government, launched an attack on Egypt, Eden having ignored the clear advice of President Eisenhower not to do it. Within days, the pound came under attack on the exchange markets, the flow of oil from the Middle East to the West was disrupted, enormous damage had been done to Britain's relations with the USA - and Russia invaded Hungary. By Christmas, Britain had suffered the humiliation of having to obey an American injunction to withdraw all its troops from Egypt. British influence in Middle Eastern affairs virtually disappeared, leaving a vacuum that Nasser lost no time in trying to fill. That Thorneycroft gave his loyal support to Eden throughout the Suez affair is evident from a letter (reproduced on the following page) that Eden sent to him on 16th January 1957, after his eventual resignation, physically worn out and politically discredited by the crisis.

Thorneycroft's tenure at the Board of Trade was not to last much longer. On 10th January 1957, Harold Macmillan succeeded the broken Anthony Eden as Prime Minister, inheriting responsibility for a country and a Conservative Party riven by discord in the aftermath of the Suez affair. Thorneycroft was the first person to be called to 10 Downing Street that morning, to be told that he was to be appointed as Chancellor of the Exchequer.

From
Anthony Eden

CHEQUERS
BUTLER'S CROSS · AYLESBURY
BUCKS

Personal   16th January 1957.

My dear Peter,

    Thank you so much for your letter.   I want
first to try to thank you for all the splendid
help you have given me through these difficult
years.

    As you know, I share your conviction about
our Suez efforts.   I think it is still touch and
go whether the Russians' Syrian activities can be
scotched.   But certainly there would have been no
hope for all that area had we not acted.   I shall
never forget your loyalty and courage through all
this.

    Now I send you every possible good wish for
your new duties.   If I may say so, I warmly
applaud the selection.

Good luck & every
happy wish to you both,
yours ever
Anthony

The Rt. Hon. Peter Thorneycroft, M.P.

22. Letter to Peter Thorneycroft from Anthony Eden, 16th January 1957

Thorneycroft had worked very hard at the Board of Trade, but senior politicians do not devote the whole of their attention to their department's business. Apart from doing their best, with considerable difficulty, to spend some time with their families and with their constituents, they are called upon to dine with distinguished foreign visitors, participate in great State occasions and attend a succession of public and private events. During the period of Thorneycroft's long tenure at the Board of Trade, his schedule included the funerals of King George VI and of the King's mother Queen Mary; the Coronation of Queen Elizabeth II; State visits of the Shahanshah of Persia with Queen Soraya (to please whom he delegated to his chauffeur, Richard Drew - who was a dog-fancier - the delicate task of finding a bulldog puppy (named John Bull) for the royal visitor) and of Khruschev and Bulganin shortly after their assumption of power in the Soviet Union having shunted Malenkov off to a power station in Siberia and disposed of Beria. He had to decline, because of pressure of departmental business, an invitation to the marriage in Portugal of Princess Maria Pia of Savoy to Prince Alexander of Jugoslavia, but was represented by his wife, Carla. On 7th November 1956, he attended the unveiling of a memorial statue to Field Marshal Jan Christian Smuts by the sculptor Jacob Epstein: unfortunately Sir Winston Churchill was not well enough to perform the unveiling ceremony as had been intended: it was carried out instead by Mr Speaker, William Morrison.

All through this intensely busy period - indeed for the rest of his life - Thorneycroft dedicated some time, in the evenings, at weekends and during holidays, to improving his painting skills, setting up his easel in those parts of London which attracted him and were within easy reach, or making rapid pencil sketches which he would later turn into watercolours. Some typical examples of his work are reproduced throughout this book. Their purpose is to emphasise how the politician and, later, businessman, created for himself oases of calm in the frenetic world of his chosen career.

23. Chelsea Reach (*from a watercolour sketch by Peter Thorneycroft*)

Chancellor of the Exchequer 1957-58

Not everyone was lost in admiration for the way in which Macmillan had secured his appointment as Prime Minister. Nevertheless, he speedily demonstrated that the political skill that had brought him to power could also be deployed to win him the support in Government of those few able men who had been far from captivated by his merciless elimination of Rab Butler from the competition for succession, but whom he needed as key members of his administration. Perhaps the most striking case was that of Enoch Powell, who disliked Macmillan intensely, but was ideally suited to the post he was given as Financial Secretary to the Treasury, where his remarkable intellect could be brought to bear on the perennial and teasing problem of getting the right balance in the allocation of funds to the fiercely competitive departments of state. The second member of the Treasury team was Nigel Birch, moved from the Air Ministry to become Economic Secretary, well qualified for the job by his earlier active and successful experience in the City, and wholly in tune with Powell's insistent call for sound management of money. The leader of the team, Peter Thorneycroft, had during his highly competent leadership of the Board of Trade since Churchill sent him there in 1951 acquired an impressive grasp of the complexities of a wide range of economic issues in a period of international tension as the European nations drew closer together and the ties of Commonwealth loosened. Willie Whitelaw, who was a cousin of Thorneycroft, was to be the Parliamentary Private Secretary to the Chancellor.

Thorneycroft felt himself to be well prepared for his new role and delighted to have the support of Powell and Birch, on whom he knew he could rely for frank advice based on informed understanding of the problems they had to face – problems that he had studied deeply himself when he had been the guiding spirit of the Tory Reform Committee at the end of the war. He was less happy with the Permanent Secretary allocated to him. He had forged with Sir Frank Lee at the Board of Trade a relationship of sincere mutual trust that had been most effective. It is not often that a politician earns the unstinted admiration of his civil servants. A remarkable letter from Sir Frank, delivered to Thorneycroft at his Chester Square home the day after his appointment as Chancellor, conveys vividly the respect he had earned from his staff, speaking of: *'your gay courage, your resilience in the face of difficulties, the unfailing quickness of your mind, serenity of temper (especially when confronted by our failings), triumphs in the House and elsewhere, also above all to have wide ranging, easy, uncommitted discussions on every problem that has come before us'.*

However, Macmillan would not allow Thorneycroft to take Lee with him to the Treasury. Towards the end of his own tenure of the Chancellorship, Macmillan had brought his colleague and friend of the war years, Sir Roger Makins, from the Embassy in Washington to the Treasury as Permanent Secretary and, when he chose his Treasury team in 1957, he was determined to keep his man there. It was an odd appointment. Makins was a Foreign Office man to the core, with scant knowledge of economic affairs and, it was to emerge, lacking the ability (or the will) to learn what he needed to know to discharge his duties effectively as the Treasury's top civil servant. The appointment was to prove not merely odd, but fatal to the ambitious programme his new political masters were determined to pursue.

The change of job also involved a change of residence. The Thorneycrofts had been very happy at 68 Chester Square, an attractive house that Carla Thorneycroft had made an elegant and comfortable home. Tucked into one of the albums of press cuttings is a sheet of paper explaining the 'house rules' of 11 Downing Street to the new occupants. The Treasury evidently busied itself with much more than the balance of payments and the Bank Rate. The economy of No 11 and the example to be set to the nation by the Chancellor by making prudent use of the facilities at his disposal were also of great concern. They had determined that whilst central heating and hot water would be provided free of charge to the new Chancellor, he would have to pay for any use of electricity in the private rooms in excess of £200 per annum, and that the Treasury cleaners would only look after the official rooms on the ground and first floors. There was a garage – a double one – available for private use, but it was on the other side of Whitehall in Richmond Terrace Mews. A doorkeeper would be on duty at No 11 during the day (on week days only) but at other times, only the front door of No 10 would be guarded, covering both houses. However, the Chancellor would be given a set of latch keys to No 11 so that he could let himself in after hours. The Prime Minister would allow the Chancellor and his family to use the garden (which belonged to No 10) but this privilege ought to be exercised with restraint, bearing in mind that it was only a small garden and the windows of the Cabinet Room overlooked it directly. The garden gate did, the Chancellor was advised, serve the useful purpose of providing a discreet exit or entrance in case of need.

With these domestic arrangements happily settled, it only remained to reassure five year old Victoria Thorneycroft that her dolls, Julia and Rosebud Thorneycroft, would have proper accommodation when they moved to No 11. She was very pleased to find that there was a marvellous dolls' house all ready for them in the nursery on the top floor and that, if they woke up early enough, she, Julia and Rosebud would have a splendid view of the Household Cavalry getting ready for their daily ceremonial duties on Horse Guards Parade.

The new Chancellor had three months to prepare what was to prove to be not just

24. Horse Guards, Whitehall
(*from a watercolour sketch by Peter Thorneycroft*)

his first, but his only Budget, which was to be presented on 9th April 1957. However, he was already committed to an important engagement on the first day of his new office, to meet Paul-Henri Spaak, the Foreign Minister of Belgium and Secretary-General Designate of NATO, for a discussion on the British proposals for a Free Trade Area linked to the Common Market on which the 'Six' were almost ready to sign an agreement. The new Cabinet in which two of the most powerful British proponents of working with Europe, Macmillan and Thorneycroft, held the key positions of Prime Minister and Chancellor of the Exchequer, was warmly welcomed in both Europe and America as a sign that Britain was serious about its commitment to Europe. The appointment of Thorneycroft to succeed Macmillan as Chairman of the Council of Ministers of the OEEC was equally well received. The Council was due to meet on 12th February, with Thorneycroft in the chair for the first time, to consider the British proposals, and the discussion with Spaak was in preparation for the Council meeting. The meeting itself was short. (It might have been even shorter had a zealous official at Le Bourget airport not relented from his initial refusal to allow Thorneycroft into France with an out of date passport). No firm conclusion was reached. The new President of the Board of Trade, Sir David Eccles, outlined the British proposal, emphasising his Government's insistence that agricultural products must be excluded. Spaak reported that the Six expected to sign their Common Market treaty within a few weeks, and the Austrian representative, Herr Sigl, declared that Austria would be willing to accept a free trade area which included agricultural goods. The Americans re-affirmed their support for closer integration in Europe and the elimination of Customs barriers to trade. To keep matters moving, it was agreed that the proposals should be studied by a group of experts who would report back to the Council in July.

By the time he had been in office for a month, Thorneycroft had judged that the state of the UK economy called for a relaxation of interest rates. Mainly because of concerns about inflationary pressures, Bank Rate had been raised by 1% on

16th February 1956 to 5½%. Now, on 7th February 1957, it was to be reduced to 5%. Thorneycroft made it clear, however, that this was not to be interpreted by lenders or by consumers as an indication that control of credit could be relaxed. It was still necessary to restrain both public and private expenditure and also lending, so as to conserve resources for exports and investment. Two weeks later, Thorneycroft revealed to the House of Commons his estimates for public expenditure (indicative only in the case of defence) which would form the basis for his budget in April, underlining the strict control that he intended to maintain. To loud clamour from the Opposition benches the Chancellor announced some of the sacrifices that would have to be made to keep total expenditure within bounds. The price to be charged for welfare milk issued to children and expectant mothers would be increased from 2½d to 4d a pint, still only half of the retail price, whilst the price of school meals would rise from 10d to 1/-. ('Tory Scrooge', the *Daily Worker* called him next day).These savings, and increases in National Insurance contributions (10d for an adult male employee with a corresponding increase in the employer's contribution) would leave room for an increase of £110m in total expenditure from the 1956/7 level, including £64m more for education, £69m for the NHS and £31m for atomic energy, offset by some reductions elsewhere. Thorneycroft insisted that, without the increased charges, it would have been necessary to cut back some services.

There was a small flurry of excitement at the end of February when, in an off-the-cuff remark during the Second Reading in the Commons of the Cinematograph Film Bill, the President of the Board of Trade, Sir David Eccles, implied that the Chancellor had told him that he would be reducing entertainment tax in his forthcoming Budget to take account of the effects of a new levy on exhibitors provided for in the Bill. Sir David had committed a gaffe, giving the Opposition and the media an opportunity that they did not fail to exploit to allege that he had leaked a Budget secret – a cardinal sin that not so long ago had cost Hugh Dalton his job as Labour's first post-war Chancellor. Thorneycroft quickly pointed out that he had said only that he would take the levy and other considerations into account, with no mention of how he would do so, and, on that, he had not yet made up his mind. After the initial fuss had died down it seemed to be generally accepted that Sir David had been *'inelegant and maladroit'*, as the *Evening Standard* put it, in saying what he did, but that no leak had been committed and Macmillan quickly quashed any suggestion that the hapless Minister should resign. After all, he said, a leak was a disclosure to the outside world, not a comment to Parliament itself. It was one of those occasions when Parliament tends to waste time on trivia that would be better devoted to more important matters. On this occasion, even the media was inclined to question the judgement of the Opposition in not dropping the matter.

Much more important in the run-up to the Budget was a meeting convened by the Prime Minister at Chequers during the weekend of 24th February 1957, attended by the Marquess of Salisbury, Butler, Thorneycroft, Selwyn Lloyd and Duncan Sandys and Lord Home, to discuss a defence paper prepared by Duncan Sandys and its budgetary implications. The discussion was not formally minuted, but papers marked TOP SECRET (PREM 11/1768) in the National Archives indicate that the Minister of Defence and the Chancellor of the Exchequer were instructed to reduce the defence budget to £1,450 million for 1957/8 and that Thorneycroft reported to the Prime Minister on 12th March 1957 that they had been able to get it down to £1,475 million, compared with expenditure of £1,598.7 million in 1956/7. Two days later, he told the Prime Minister that defence research and development expenditure was not only costing too much money, but was straining scientific and technological resource, and should be cut. He recommended a review as a matter of urgency.

25. Chequers
(During a much later visit to Chequers, in 1980, when he was Party Chairman, Thorneycroft found time to make a watercolour sketch of the house)

The foundations on which Thorneycroft had to build his budget had been considerably strengthened by the efforts of his two predecessors, Butler and Macmillan, but the Suez operations of the previous year had saddled the country with a burden of additional costs, and had resulted also in a severe drain on reserves.

The impact on trade had been less than feared, but it had been necessary to boost dollar reserves by drawing dollars to the equivalent of £200 million from the IMF in December. Dollar reserves had begun to rise again in the early months of 1957 without further recourse to stand-by facilities. Nevertheless, the Chancellor was under strong pressure from the Bank of England to bring monetary policy firmly and speedily under control. He had no difficulty in embracing this objective and he had wasted no time in preparing the country to accept that sacrifices would have to be made. In an interview at the end of his first week as Chancellor, he had set out three ways in which he looked for support from the public: save more than last year; don't criticise the Government when it tries to cut expenditure; and don't ask the Government to spend more, even on your favourite scheme.

It is customary for the Chancellor of the Exchequer to present his budget proposals to the Monarch on the Monday evening before Tuesday's Budget, but on this occasion the audience with the Queen had to be brought forward by a day because Her Majesty was about to depart on a State Visit to France. Thorneycroft's meeting with the Queen on a Sunday evening was, said the Lord's Day Observance Society, a serious breach of the Sabbath which would cause deep grief to those who believed that political and State affairs should not be allowed to intrude upon this sacred day – a little unfair to a Chancellor who was a committed Christian and had, as usual, attended morning service at St Michael's in Chester Square that morning. *"Ah yes"*, said the LDOS, *"but he could have called upon the Queen on Saturday."* The path that a politician must tread is strewn with such rocks.

Introducing his Budget in the House of Commons, Thorneycroft underlined the continued need for restraint in public expenditure, in provision of credit and in wage settlements. However he was also determined to begin building what he called 'an Opportunity State', based on competition, incentives and investment, and he judged – and Enoch Powell supported his judgement – that the country's financial situation, although tight, was not desperate, and that there was no reason for him to forgo a modest step in the direction he was determined to take of reducing the tax burden as an incentive to individuals to seize opportunities and save to invest. The Chancellor's choice of beneficiaries for his restrained tax cuts was controversial, but consistent with this policy. First, there was to be relief for surtax payers, Thorneycroft arguing that the small number of people with incomes high enough to incur surtax had been ignored for thirty years, and that the amount of tax relief involved was too little to make any worthwhile difference to the many more taxpayers with lower incomes. (Surtax at the time was levied on incomes as low as £2,000 pa, and the total of income and surtax reached the swingeing rate of 18s 6d in the pound for the highest earners). Secondly, companies registered in the UK but trading entirely overseas would no longer have to pay UK income or profits tax on trading profits earned abroad: their tax liabilities would thus be the same as those of their competitors registered locally in the trading territory. The Chancellor also confirmed that he would honour a commitment made by his predecessor a year earlier to review the structure of duty on entertainments (the subject of Sir David Eccles' earlier gaffe). His solution was to free live theatre and sport from duty altogether and to reduce significantly the duty paid by cinemas. The loss of revenue due to these measures would be partially recouped by a new levy on combined TV and radio licences, which would have the effect of increasing the cost of a licence from £3 to £4. Purchase Tax was still within Thorneycroft's sights, and he now took the further step of reducing by half, from 30% to 15%, the tax on domestic kitchen and tableware and on furniture still subject to the 30% rate. These changes were aimed primarily at helping people on low incomes, and were reinforced by measures to raise the tax exemption limit for old people and to increase child allowances for older children, recognising that children cost more as they grow older. A supplementary duty on petrol of 1s a gallon imposed during the Suez crisis was also removed, even though the flow of fuel had not yet returned to its pre-crisis level.

Of all these measures, perhaps the most important was the easing of surtax. For the first time in many years, here was a Chancellor willing to declare publicly his belief that the people whose incomes made them liable to surtax were those 'whose activities and decisions do most to determine our rate of economic expansion' and that 'a tax system which offers the minimum inducement to those with the maximum responsibility' was inconsistent with the objective of opportunity and expansion. The level of salary that triggered liability to surtax had, in fact, remained the same at £2,000 since 1920. It was a small step that Thorneycroft took, moving the threshold up by only £100, but it broke an attitudinal log-jam that had lasted nearly forty years.

The Budget was well received by most of the media analysts. "A sound basis for expansion", said the *Daily Telegraph*. The *Evening Standard* rated it "a cheer-up Budget". Writing in the *News Chronicle*, Alan Wood counted it *"on the whole, a good Tory Budget, not a bad Tory Budget of the Butler kind. Butler bought popularity by giving income-tax reliefs to everyone. Thorneycroft picked and chose. He helped parents and young married couples, and he helped those who worked particularly hard. He helped minorities instead of chasing votes."* It was, Wood said, praise that he would gladly bestow on any politician who acts on his principles. There were dissenting voices of course. Not unexpectedly, the *Daily Worker* saw it as a "rich man's Budget – for Top Dogs Only", and the *Sunday Pictorial* lamented the Chancellor's unwillingness to organise cheap mortgages. A French journalist wondered whether the Chancellor of the Exchequer might not give some tips to the French Minister of Finance : (*'le chancelier de l'Echiquier ne pourrait-il pas donner quelques tuyaux à notre ministre des Finances ?'*).

26. Carla and Peter Thorneycroft on Budget Day, 1957

Missing from the Budget speech, however, was any immediate comfort for the Governor of the Bank of England that the Government was ready to bring monetary policy under control. Instead, the Chancellor announced the appointment of a Commission under the leadership of Lord Radcliffe charged with examining what policy options were available to achieve the best possible system of money and credit whilst complying with international obligations. The Commission would report its findings to Parliament in due course. It seems a little odd, 50 years later, not only that a Treasury team with the intellectual brilliance of Enoch Powell, the financial experience of Nigel Birch and the proven ability of Peter Thorneycroft to achieve rapid mastery of the most complex and politically sensitive matters should have found it necessary to procrastinate on this critical issue, but also that there was so little criticism of the delay by the Opposition or in the Press. It was, of course, only three months since Thorneycroft's accession to the Treasury with his two colleagues – too short a time, it seems, for the three very able politicians to win over the civil servants whose own views on monetary policy were cast in concrete. During the debate on the Finance Bill later in the month, Thorneycroft set out his commitment to continue the movement towards lower taxes that he had initiated in the Budget, saying that everyone in the country was over-taxed: Purchase Tax was too high; taxes on incomes were too high. Responding to Socialist claims that his talk of incentives was 'claptrap' he opined that men did not jump out of bed every morning and rush to work for fun. The majority worked for a living and, when they had worked hard and long, it was not unreasonable that they should want to keep a fair proportion of what they earn: he rejected completely the notion espoused by Harold Wilson that a Chancellor 'gives' money to the taxpayer when he refrains from taking it away. He repeated his consistent warnings that social services could only be sustained by the productivity and wealth of people producing things. The success of those people must be rewarded. Europe, the

US and even Russia rewarded success. Why not Britain? Why not indeed?, asked some of the Press, and if this was the right way to go, why did Thorneycroft not go a lot further down the road in his Budget? (His tax reductions had amounted to only £100m out of a total revenue of £5bn – 2%). The debates on the Finance Bill dragged on, as usual, well into the Summer. At one point, in early July, he had to field questions about the revenue from duties on cigarettes, and what he would do if the recent scare stories about lung cancer should cause the consumption of cigarettes to fall dramatically. He had no difficulty in confirming that the yield of tobacco duty was £698 million, and that cigarettes accounted for 90% of this, but he was not inclined to forecast how this might be affected by health worries, nor to anticipate what he might do in future budgets. He certainly saw no reason to rush into alternative sources of tax revenue.

With the Budget out of the way, Thorneycroft and his wife could find the time to complete their move from Chester Square to Downing Street. Carla Thorneycroft was happy to find that she could take most of her favourite furniture with her so that in No 11 she could reproduce the same comfortable and elegant home on which she had lavished so much care and flair during the past few years.

A few days after the Budget, the protracted discussion on Free Trade came alive again on 7th May, when Thorneycroft invited M. Maurice Faure, the French Minister of State responsible for conducting the European Economic Community negotiations, to visit London for discussions with himself and his successor at the Board of Trade, Sir David Eccles. The Treaty of Rome creating the EEC had been signed on 25th March 1957 and was awaiting ratification by the signatories. The discussions were cordial, and centred upon assuring the French and their co-signatories that rumours recently circulating that Britain wished to scupper the Rome Treaty were quite wrong – that, on the contrary, the venture had the full backing of the British Government whose aim was now to complete as soon as possible the negotiations within OEEC for the establishment of a Free Trade Area in association with the Community, to ensure that there would be no division of the European nations into separate camps, the Six and the rest. However, there remained the obstacles of the unwillingness of the Six to accept the British insistence that food products be excluded from the Free Trade area and unease with what was seen as excessive rigidity in the operating procedures of the EEC. These obstacles were not overcome at the London meeting. Instead, as seems to be an abiding norm in trade negotiations, they were referred to forthcoming meetings of officials for further consideration and recommendations.

5th June 1957 was the 10th Anniversary of the launch of the American Marshall Plan, which had played such a crucial role in the economic recovery of the European nations after the Second World War. The event was celebrated by ceremonies and broadcasts in the USA and throughout Europe. In Britain, it was

Thorneycroft who led the tributes to General George C Marshall and the American Government in a radio programme, underlining in his speech that the financial generosity of the USA in making gifts and loans under the European Recovery Programme totalling more than $13 billion had been the catalyst for a remarkable common effort of the European recipient countries, culminating in the formation with the United States of the OEEC, the recent signing of the Treaty of Rome and the Free Trade Area negotiations currently in progress. As a result, Europe was now the second wealthiest economy in the world.

Europe had certainly benefited mightily from the Marshall Plan, but the United Kingdom had not learnt, from the Americans or anyone else, how to achieve anything like the level of productivity of its workforce which had given the Americans the wealth which had made the Marshall Plan possible. July and August 1957 saw Thorneycroft engaged in a frontal assault on inflation castigating, in speeches to the National Production Advisory Council for Industry and at a ceremony when he opened a new headquarters of the United Kingdom Provident Institution, wage and salary increases not linked to higher productivity. The nation, he averred, had paid itself 7% more during the past year for doing no more work and this was bound to lead to inflation. The purchasing power of the pound sterling had fallen by 20% since 1951. He refused to attack the problem by tax increases or controls on consumption or by restraining particular industries. *"We are seeking"*, he said, *"full employment in a free society – and it would be a sorry reflection on society if we could only find stable prices by throwing away full employment or a free society."* Instead, he insisted that Government spending must be held down by taking the difficult decisions on where the axe must fall; investment must be planned to match savings; and the credit squeeze, exercised by pressure on the banks, must continue. He wanted the borrowing of money to be as difficult as the shortage of resources made necessary. In two areas where the Government had some control over borrowing, he took action, raising the interest rate charged on loans to local councils and to nationalised industries. But he was not arguing – it was no part of his political philosophy – that Government should interfere in wage bargaining. He wanted employers and trade unions to recognise that it was they who must stop deliberately creating inflation. Government's job was to drive home this message in the clearest possible terms. *"If inflation is to be checked, the first essential is to have a country which really wants to check it, and is prepared to accept the discomforts of any cure that may be involved."*

How stark those discomforts were to be was dramatically underscored on 19th September 1957, when Thorneycroft, resolved to check yet another speculative attack on the pound and to show the Government's determination to defend the exchange rate at $2.80, by raising Bank Rate from 5% to 7%, its highest level since 1920. The immediate effect was a sharp fall in share and gilts prices on the Stock

Exchange. The announcement was followed immediately by a statement that capital investment was to be severely curtailed, with major cuts in programmes of railway modernisation, school and hospital building and new road construction. Explaining his action, Thorneycroft rammed home his message: *"It will not be possible to check the rising cost of living and to maintain the worth of sterling if we try to spend more or live better than our resources allow or our production justifies. We must control the money supply."* The message was being directed more and more firmly at his colleagues in Government. Employers and Trade Unions had their responsibilities, as he had so insistently pointed out, but prices and incomes were only part of the story: the supply of money could only be controlled by the Government.

The pound strengthened, albeit only slightly.

The next day, Thorneycroft flew to Washington to attend the annual meetings of the World Bank and the International Monetary Fund. One of his first acts was to announce his decision to draw down a $500 million 'stand-by' facility arranged with the US Export-Import Bank at the time of the Suez crisis. Boosted by this reinforcement of Britain's dollar reserves the pound continued to strengthen, against the D-mark as well as against the dollar, and stocks and shares also regained some of the early losses they had suffered. These positive developments were somewhat attenuated, although not halted, by an accusation of the Shadow Chancellor, Harold Wilson, on 24th September that heavy selling of gilts before the announcement of the Bank Rate increase could only be explained by a prior leakage of information about the impending rise. Wilson demanded an inquiry, speedily rejected in the Chancellor's absence by Enoch Powell, who had seen no evidence to suggest that there had been a leak.

By now, Thorneycroft had left Washington to attend the Commonwealth Finance Ministers' Conference in Canada, at Mont Tremblant, where he and Sir David Eccles, the President of the Board of Trade, were generating considerable excitement with a proposal to move steadily towards completely free trade between Britain and Canada. This seemed to capture the interest of the Canadian Government, but the Dominion's manufacturers were quick to protest that, deprived of tariff protection, they would not be able to compete with British firms tendering for Canadian Government contracts.

With the Chancellor engaged across the Atlantic, Wilson stepped up his campaign about an alleged leak claiming, in a letter addressed to Enoch Powell at the Treasury, to have evidence of ministerial misconduct. Powell was in his constituency and unable to deal with the matter, and the Prime Minister decided to respond with an offer to ask the Lord Chancellor, Lord Kilmuir, to examine any evidence put before him. This did not satisfy Wilson, and the Leader of the Opposition, Hugh Gaitskell, now threw his weight behind the demand for a public inquiry into the issue. Wilson's case rested on the knowledge that there had been a meeting at the Treasury the evening before the Bank Rate announcement between the Chancellor and a small group of editors, and on reports of significant dealing in Government securities later that evening, after the closure of the Stock Exchange.

Back home again, Thorneycroft felt that he had more pressing matters to attend to than entering into the fray over Wilson's allegations. On 8th October, there was the Lord Mayor's Banquet, at which he had to make a major speech. Two days later, the Tories assembled at Brighton for their Annual Conference, with another important speech from the Chancellor. On 29th October, when Parliament resumed after the Summer Recess, Thorneycroft made a speech adjudged by seasoned observers to be the best speech made by a Chancellor of the Exchequer for a very long time. He was blunt and clear: inflation must be checked; it could only be checked if the whole country – the general public, employers, trades unions – were prepared to accept the necessary sacrifices; inefficiencies in the State-controlled industries must be corrected; public expenditure had to be balanced against public income (and taxes must not be increased to achieve this, because taxation was already too high for the country's economic health). The Government had no intention of interfering in collective bargaining, but those who asked for wage increases, those who granted wage increases, and those who adjudicated on wage increases should bear in mind that increases going beyond the growth in real wealth were the greatest danger we had to face, and we would be deceiving ourselves if we believed otherwise. It was the Government's duty to give this warning and, as a major employer, to act upon it. (It is a frequently underrated consequence of the nationalisation of important industries that it gives governments not merely influence upon, but also direct responsibility for, the wage settlements of large swathes of employees).

Macmillan continued to put up strong resistance to the increasingly strident calls for an inquiry into the Bank Rate leak allegations, but the problem would not go away. A turning point was reached when the Deputy Chairman of the Conservative Party, Oliver Poole, was accused in the Commons under the protection of Parliamentary privilege of being personally involved. Poole now requested an inquiry to clear his name and Thorneycroft, whose honour was also, by implication, impugned, urged the Prime Minister to agree. Macmillan did so most reluctantly, opening his statement in the House setting up a tribunal with a strong attack on Wilson who had made the allegations but had produced no evidence to support them, even before the Lord Chancellor, and yet had gone on to impugn the honour of an individual who was unable to defend himself in the House. *"Parliamentary privilege"*, he said, *"was intended to be the buttress of liberty. It should not be used as a protection for defamation."* These were strong words, and provoked Hugh Gaitskell to accuse the Prime Minister of prejudging the verdict of the tribunal even before it was established. However, established it was on 13th November, under Lord Justice Parker and, as is the way with so many politically inspired public inquiries, diverted scores of senior politicians, civil servants and business people from their affairs for several weeks, only to conclude that there had been no misconduct whatever on the part of the individuals accused, although turning up enough evidence of low level, minor incompetence to provide a headline or two for a disappointed Press Corps.

There had been some diverting passages in the course of the Inquiry.

One unhappy lady, Mrs Beatrice Hicks-Beach, was brought before the Tribunal because she had dined one evening with a friend, Mrs Dorothy Campbell, who had the unfortunate habit of claiming to have knowledge of important matters (in this case, prior knowledge of the Bank Rate increase) to impress her friends at cocktail parties. Mrs Hicks-Beach thought it rather tiresome to have to come before the Tribunal for such a trivial reason (and Lord Justice Parker quite agreed!).

On a more serious note, Thorneycroft explained to the Tribunal with his customary clarity why he had found it necessary to brief a few carefully selected members of the Press immediately before his major policy statement to ensure that they understood not only what he was doing, but why. He emphasised the severity of the crisis: a quarter of the country's reserves had drained away in a few weeks as a result of speculation against Sterling following the devaluation of the French franc. If his measures in defence of the pound were to have any chance of success, it was vital that they should be properly understood, and the role of responsible organs of the Press was crucial to secure that understanding. The select group had comprised Lord Drogheda (Financial Times), Sir William Haley (Times), Mr Tyerman (Economist), Mr Bareau (News Chronicle), Mr McLachlan (Daily Telegraph) and Mr Gampel (Reuters); Mr Fry (Manchester Guardian) had been seen separately the following morning. They were selected because they were recognised authorities in the field of financial journalism, and all could be trusted to understand the message and make responsible use of the information they were given – which did _not_ include any reference to the Bank Rate. It was not the first time that such a briefing had taken place. Some earlier examples had been the abandonment of the Gold Standard in September 1931, the White Paper on personal incomes, costs and prices in February 1948, and the Economic Surveys of March 1949 and April 1951.

The Inquiry had been an annoying distraction for the Treasury team. With a second budget approaching, their primary concern was now to keep hammering home their key message, that if inflation was to be conquered, the nation had to learn to live within its means and not indulge itself by spending more than it could afford. Conviction of the nation would come at the end of the race: the first hurdle was to convince their Cabinet colleagues that their ambitions for their departmental budgets must be reined in. The Radcliffe Commission on Monetary Policy was not due to report for several months but, without waiting for Radcliffe, the three Treasury ministers were beginning to feel their way towards a deeper understanding of the influence of money supply on inflation and a realisation that it was Government itself that held the key to its control. The Prime Minister himself was given advance warning by Thorneycroft before the 1957 Summer recess of the impending battle that would have to be fought to keep public expenditure from rising in the 1958-9 financial year.

Macmillan did not relish the prospect of such a battle. His political instinct was to avoid spelling out unpopular messages too clearly. Elections, after all, had to be won, and the electorate was surely better disposed to having its cake and eating it than to having slices of the cake taken off the plate. The rigorous approach of the three Treasury ministers was already provoking opposition from the civil servants. An important group who had been in the Treasury for a long time, led by Sir Robert Hall, were Keynesians to a man. Macmillan's protégé Sir Roger Makins ought, as a non-specialist in the traditional mould of British Permanent Secretaries, to have been able to stand back and weigh the relative merits of the arguments put forward by his political masters against those of the experts so as to be able to give impartial advice to his ministers. Unfortunately Makins had little interest in and little understanding of economics. The damaging rift between the leading politicians and civil servants of the Treasury was widening unchecked. It came to the surface when it was decided to establish a committee to consider whether any useful action could be taken to monitor or control prices, incomes and productivity. The Ministers wanted to appoint the economist Lionel Robbins to chair the new committee – a choice that horrified Sir Robert Hall and his colleagues. They saw Robbins, justifiably, as an arch enemy of Keynesian doctrine – precisely why the ministers wanted him.

Thorneycroft had been accustomed, in the Board of Trade, to work closely and productively with his civil servants in a spirit of mutual trust. Now he found himself with a team of civil servants obstinately convinced that they knew best, led by a Permanent Secretary he regarded as ill equipped for the post who nevertheless was in the strong position of knowing that he had the ear of the Prime Minister. The ministers Macmillan had appointed to the Treasury were, perhaps, the most economically literate trio of all his colleagues, but they were also precocious converts to the principles of monetarism. Macmillan had, wittingly or not, set the stage for the first major contest in Britain between Keynesians and politically active monetarists.

The story of the efforts of the Treasury team during November and December 1957 to convince their Cabinet colleagues of the need to stand and fight on the principle of curbing public expenditure has been told with exemplary clarity by Simon Heffer in his biography of Enoch Powell, *"Like the Roman"*. The proposal they presented for approval was a simple one – total public expenditure in 1958-9 must not be greater than in 1957-8. They left no room for misunderstanding. They were beaten in the end by the duplicity of Harold Macmillan, politically more cunning, but arguably without that finishing coat of wisdom and conviction that distinguishes a true statesman from an able politician. Macmillan portrayed the affair as a marginal difference of opinion about the trivial sum of £50 million, a mere 1% of GNP, which separated the Chancellor's proposals from what the Cabinet as a whole was prepared to accept. For Thorneycroft and his colleagues it was a question of readiness to accept or crass refusal to acknowledge that the time had come to cure, once and for all, the disease of inflation that threatened the economic viability and therefore the welfare of the whole nation.

Heffer is somewhat inclined to the view that of the three protagonists, it was Enoch Powell who was the driving force who wrote the Chancellor's script for him and goaded him to stick to it through thick and thin. This seems questionable. Thorneycroft was a person of impressive intellect. The policies he expounded in 1957 had their roots in his period of political exploration in the middle to late 1940s, and may be found clearly and succinctly expressed in *Forward - By the Right* and *Design for Freedom*. Of course they had developed as he gained experience of office, especially in the Board of Trade, and of course he found Enoch Powell a formidable and persuasive adviser. But throughout his life, Thorneycroft's method of analysis of complex problems was first to gain a broad understanding of the facts and draw a tentative conclusion from them; then to listen carefully to others he knew to have studied the same problem and on whose wisdom he believed he could rely; and so to reach a firm conclusion on which he would act in the confidence that he knew not only what had to be done, but why it was the right thing to do.

The Thorneycroft who stood his ground with Macmillan had no doubt whatever that his cause was one that had to be fought, and fought at that time, when the electorate was better prepared than at any time since the war, after the crisis of the previous summer, to accept a little economic pain.

In his autobiography, *The Course of my Life,* Edward Heath describes how, at a series of meetings during the Christmas/New Year period of 1957-8, the positions of the Treasury Ministers and of their Cabinet colleagues responsible for the spending departments became increasingly entrenched. (In Heath's version, it was only the Treasury Ministers who had *'dug into their positions'*). Anyway, by the beginning of January, the positions had become irreconcilable. Prime Minister Macmillan who had dithered, refusing to come down in favour of one side or the other, now had to make up his mind. He was due to leave on a long and important tour of

Commonwealth countries on 7th January and could not leave the matter unresolved. A Cabinet meeting on Sunday, 5th January 1958 was adjourned without settling the issue. According to Heath, during the break, Macmillan asked for his opinion, and Heath told him that *"there was no hope of keeping the Chancellor except by meeting his demands in full"*, and, when they returned to the Cabinet, Macmillan told his colleagues that he had not been able to resolve the differences and was afraid that some might feel that *"it was not possible to remain as a member of the team"*.

On 6th January 1958 Thorneycroft resigned. He did not reach his painful decision in splendid isolation. He was strongly supported by his two colleagues Enoch Powell and Nigel Birch who were absolutely insistent that that they must go with their leader. Powell was unquestionably one of the outstanding politicians of the post-war generation; Birch a lesser figure but nevertheless a man of considerable ability. They both believed as strongly as Thorneycroft that the Cabinet were courting disaster for the nation in refusing to accept how precarious the economic situation was and that now was the time to stop the rot.

Thorneycroft's resignation letter to the Prime Minister was succinct and pointed:

Dear Prime Minister,

I write to ask you to accept my resignation from the office of Chancellor of the Exchequer. My reason can be shortly stated. I am not prepared to approve estimates for the Government's current expenditure next year at a total higher than the sum that will be spent this year.

Your proposed departure from this country on January 7 has made it essential that a decision of principle on this matter be taken now. It is clear that in this proposal I do not have your support or that of a number of our colleagues. In the circumstances and since the level of Government expenditure is central to my responsibility as Chancellor of the Exchequer resignation is the only course open to me.

In the sterling crisis of last summer restrictions were placed in money terms on the level of public investment and of bank advances. The Government itself must, in my view, accept the same measure of financial discipline that it seeks to impose on others.

I recognise that to achieve my aim some combination of politically unpopular courses would have been necessary. I nevertheless regard the limitation of Government expenditure as a prerequisite to the stability of the pound, the stabilisation of prices and the prestige and standing of our country in the world.

    Yours sincerely

      Peter Thorneycroft

Macmillan replied:

> *My dear Thorneycroft*
>
> *I was sorry to receive your letter this morning offering your resignation as Chancellor of the Exchequer. I particularly regret that you think it necessary to take this step when the difference between you and the rest of the Cabinet is such a narrow one.*
>
> *The policy on which we are all resolutely determined is to check inflation and to maintain the stability of sterling. In this context, the limitation of Government expenditure is certainly of the greatest importance. But we must regard the policy as a whole.*
>
> *We have two objectives, one to restrain the supply of money, the other to hold back pressure for more rewards, including wages and salaries. You say that the Estimates for the next year must be the exact equivalent of the sum spent this year.*
>
> *The rigid application of this formula, to be carried out immediately and without regard to any other consideration, would do more harm than good. For, as became clear in our discussions, to apply it literally must involve cuts in vital services, including those affecting certain aspects of family life – and this without any regard to the effect on the industrial front and on the task of those who have the responsibility of working for wage restraint.*
>
> *This is not a matter of popularity. We have never shrunk from unpopular measures. This is a matter of good judgment.*
>
> *In view of the terms of your letter, I feel it necessary to put on record that, throughout the 12 months in which this Government has been in office you have had the full support of the Cabinet in the financial and economic policies which we have worked out together.*
>
> *When, only a few days ago, the Estimates were put before us, the Cabinet decided to pursue by every possible means the policy of keeping Government expenditure substantially the same as last year. We were faced initially with Estimates which, as they were first presented, were considerably higher.*
>
> *Many of the increases were unavoidable partly because of the larger number of children at school, the expansion of secondary and university education; and partly because of the provision that has to be made for the increasing number of old people.*
>
> *Nevertheless, as a result of our work together, the Cabinet was able to reduce this excess to something less than 1 per cent of the total of current Government expenditure. Moreover, we agreed to review our policy during*

the coming year to provide a greater measure of control over expenditure in certain sectors on the civil side which can only be dealt with as a longer term problem.

I therefore cannot accept that there is any difference of principle between the rest of the Cabinet and yourself. Resignation is always a difficult decision.

It is, in my view, justified only on matters of principle. I must add that your resignation at the present time cannot help to sustain and may damage the interests that we have all been trying to preserve.

The economic and financial measures which we adopted during the past year are, I believe, beginning to bear fruit. The Government are united in their determination to pursue them resolutely to the end. I am therefore sorry that you have chosen this moment to leave us.

> *Yours sincerely*
>
> *Harold Macmillan*

In his own letter to the Prime Minister, Nigel Birch gave as his reason for resigning that, *"Ever since the war, expenditure has been running at a very high level. Our motives have been good, but we have tried to do more than our resources allow. The result has been recurring foreign exchange crises and rising prices. I believe that the Chancellor's demands for reductions in expenditure were the minimum necessary. These reductions are certainly painful and distasteful, but the electorate is more likely to forgive us for taking painful and distasteful measures which they will know in their hearts are right, than for lacking courage and clear thinking"*. The implication was, clearly, that the Cabinet did not share this view, and had not accepted the reductions demanded. Birch left no doubt that this was his opinion in a comment the following day, *"The Treasury Ministers were out to win the battle of inflation, the others were not."*

The immediate reactions of politicians and the Press were mainly negative, tinged with puzzlement, real or feigned. Macmillan famously labelled the resignation 'a little local difficulty', and would not accept that a difference of opinion about a mere £50 million could be regarded as a matter of principle such as to justify a resignation – though he went on, somewhat inconsistently, to argue that failure to provide this tiny extra sum would result in cuts in 'vital' services. Thorneycroft's successor, Derick Heathcoat Amory, insisted that the change of Chancellor meant no change in economic or financial policy. Lord Hailsham, Chairman of the Conservative Party, called the resignation a misguided decision, and was at a loss to see why Thorneycroft found it necessary. In a message to party area chairmen, he said, *"It might seem to you on reading the Chancellor's letter that the Government were not resolved to deal with inflation at home and to defend the pound by all possible means in their power. Nothing could be further than the truth"*. He judged it *"impracticable and unnecessary to make permanent alterations in the shape of social policy depend on the exact out-turn of a single year's estimates"*. Edward Heath, the Chief Whip, regarded Thorneycroft's action as treachery, *"a political challenge to Macmillan's leadership"*. Hugh Gaitskell, Leader of the Opposition, was happy to see the Tory Government 'visibly crumbling'. *The Daily Telegraph* commented, *"The truth is that, though financial policy is pervasive, there are limits to the field in which the opinion of the Chancellor of the Exchequer is sacrosanct. There are areas in which the views of his colleagues should prevail, particularly when those colleagues have not flinched, and show no sign of flinching, from accepting and applying the extremely rigorous consequences of his views. There must seem to be a touch of the prima donna about any more extensive claims to dictate Government policy"*. (These are sentiments that, 50 years later, Tony Blair might well have wished he had been able to impose from the beginning of his premiership upon his Chancellor. Certainly, Blair's failure to assert his primacy as First Lord of the Treasury over the Chancellor of the Exchequer enabled Gordon Brown to arrogate to himself a degree of control over Government policy unparalleled in recent times.)

Most commentators, then, saw the issue as a disagreement over a minor sum.

The three protagonists, on the contrary, believed that they had been engaged in a major dispute on an important matter of principle, the choice between effective government and surrender to political expediency. The Treasury team could have followed the herd. Instead they decided that it would have been dishonourable for them to remain members of a Government that was unwilling to take the same medicine that it was prescribing for everyone else.

The observers who agreed with them at the time were many fewer in number than the supporters of the Government, but they were those whose opinions were founded on objective analysis rather than on facile populism. The leader writer of *The Times* pointed out on 7th January that, for months past, the Government had consistently and insistently preached the message that, if inflation was to be beaten and the strength of sterling protected, the whole country, whether in the public or the private sector, must accept *'a standstill in monetary terms at the level of the current year. The Civil Service had been told that any increase in pay must be made good by a reduction in numbers. The railways had been told that they could expect no money from the Government to finance an increased deficit'*. It was implicit in this message that public expenditure must be subject to the same limits as those the private sector was asked to accept, but when Cabinet ministers had to face the test of their own commitment to this policy by holding the expenditure of their departments at the level of 1957, the majority of them had opted for surrender, excusing themselves by saying that they only wanted to overspend by 1% - a tiny amount of money – and that they simply could not accept that spending on social measures such as family allowances or school milk should be sacrificed.

A great deal was made by the Cabinet majority and their supporters of the argument that vulnerable groups should not have to suffer in the fight to protect sterling and conquer inflation, ignoring the obvious point that, if only a tiny sum was involved, it should surely have been possible for Government departments as a whole to find savings of a mere 1% without sacrificing any vital programme. The veteran commentator Harold Wincott, writing in the *Investors' Chronicle* on 10th January 1958, rubbed in this point, saying that, '*even if it were accepted [that a reduction of £50 million in social security payments would cause wage claims of greater amount] are we really to believe it impossible in a budget of £5,000 millions to save a sum equal to not much more than ½d a day per head of population?*' Indeed, opinion polls taken a few days after the resignations suggested that there was widespread public support for this view, albeit with a marked preference for cuts in the defence and atomic energy budgets rather than in health, housing or pensions. Wincott averred that '*at no time since 1951 had the Conservative Party provided a Government which consistently stood by the principles of real conservatism*', and that '*greatly to his credit, Mr Thorneycroft had at last made an honest attempt, incidentally in keeping with his record at the Board of Trade, to translate Conservative principles into practice. His budget last April was the first real attempt in the post-war era to provide worthwhile incentives to the striving classes in this country*'

It remains for us to consider whether, in the light of later knowledge, the principles for which Thorneycroft fought were sound, and whether his resignation was wise in the circumstances.

On the first point – principles - there can surely no longer be any doubt. Even the Socialists (if the adherents to New Labour are true Socialists) have, after nearly half a century of prevarication, formally adopted the principles that, as a matter of prudence, current public expenditure must not exceed current public revenue, and that borrowing must be resorted to only to fund capital investment, (although they have then left themselves plenty of room for manoeuvre by adding 'over a complete economic cycle', and then adjusting their definitions of what constitutes capital expenditure, moving important items of public expenditure off the Government's balance sheet altogether, and altering the length of an economic cycle *ad lib* so as to put the most favourable gloss on the statistics).

On the second point - the wisdom of resigning - even hindsight provides no clear answer. Very few politicians have resigned from a major office on a matter of principle. Fewer still, looking back on their decision, can feel entirely confident that they might not have been better advised to stay and fight; to accept the loss of a battle but to stay on the battlefield and try to win the next one and, eventually, the war.

Thorneycroft himself refused at the time to add anything to what he had written in his resignation letter. In a speech to his constituents in Monmouth a few days later, and again, taking part in a Parliamentary debate on 23rd January 1958 in a speech lasting only twelve minutes, he repeated the same simple message: that inflation is the greatest economic danger, that it can only be checked by tight control of the money supply and that sterling must not bear the brunt of inflation control. He reminded the House that for twelve years *"we have been attempting to do more than our resources could manage. We have sought to be a nuclear power, matching missile with missile and anti-missile with anti-missile, and with large conventional forces in the Far East, the Middle East and the Atlantic and, at the same time, to maintain a Welfare State at as high a level as that of the United States of America."* and this against the background that the country had *"to repay debt abroad during the next eight years of a total equal to the whole of our existing reserves"*. *"Those"*, he said, *"are not unworthy aims, but it has meant that over twelve years we have slithered from one crisis to another."*

Thorneycroft seems to have left no evidence in writing of his own retrospective judgement on his resignation, although late in his life he told the author that whilst he had no doubt at all that his insistence on the principle of keeping a tight rein on public spending was absolutely right, he sometimes felt that it might have been accepted sooner had he stayed in post and kept plugging away at the message.

What is certain is that a person who resigns can no longer influence directly the course of events, and can only hope that the psychological impact of his action on the future conduct of those who had not accepted his advice may lead them to reconsider their attitude and embrace his opinions.

For the man himself, the resignation was an enormous sacrifice. As Chancellor of the Exchequer, he had been one step away from the pinnacle of his profession. Now he faced the political wilderness.

For the nation the resignation was a disaster. The Government had squandered the opportunity they had created, courageously and wisely, the previous September to take the whole nation with them in getting rid once and for all of inflation and all its pernicious consequences. The electorate had understood at that time the simple message that this required tight control of all expenditure, public and private. The country was ready to accept the sacrifices. The Government lost its nerve, and the battle was lost.

In the wake of the resignation, the further pruning of Government expenditure that Thorneycroft and his colleagues had wanted was not carried out. It might therefore be argued that the immediate aftermath was exactly the same as it would have been had the three Ministers not resigned, but had ruefully accepted that they could not achieve the extra 1% reduction they wanted. To argue thus would, however, be to perpetuate the myth that the difference between the Treasury team and the rest was about a trivial 1% of planned Government expenditure. It was not. It was about the failure of the Government, fully aware of what it should have done, to do it.

Loosening of the firm control that Thorneycroft had exercised over expenditure did not take long to begin. The Budget introduced by Heathcoat Amory in April 1958 was based on an estimate for Government expenditure of £150 million more than the actual out-turn for the previous year and £260 million more than the comparable estimate for that year. Within a few weeks the 'tiny' excess of 1% had increased to 5%. Control was lost. By mid-May, the Government suddenly found that it could, after all, make £25 million available to the railways to ward off a threatened strike: the largesse was used to grant a more generous wage award than could have been afforded had permitted expenditure continued to be capped. Emboldened by this concession to the railway workers, the bus unions threatened a strike, and were given an award which compensated for the increased cost of living. The precedent was set in the public sector that wages should move at least in line with the cost of living, without regard to the productivity of the group of workers concerned.

The long term consequence was that for the next two decades the country continued to flounder from crisis to crisis – the reckless insouciance of George Brown's National Plan of 1964; Harold Wilson's desperate and draconian prices, incomes and investment freeze of July 1966; devaluation of sterling in 1967; the disastrous Heath/Barber loosening of monetary restraint and the galloping inflation that ensued; coal crisis in 1972 followed by another futile pay, prices and incomes freeze. All of these crises might have been avoided had the politicians of 1958 faced facts, seized their chance and persisted with the tough measures which they knew very well were needed to bring inflation firmly under control.

It was not until 1979 that another Chancellor, Geoffrey Howe, this time supported by a determined leader, Margaret Thatcher, began to apply to the nation's income and expenditure accounts and to monetary policy the strong measures that Thorneycroft knew were necessary in 1958. Inflation which, as measured by the Composite Price Index, had peaked at almost 25% in 1975, was still in double figures in 1979. Howe's measures brought inflation down to 4.5% by 1983, but this had been achieved only at the heavy cost of squeezing the economy to the brink of recession. Howe's successor, Nigel Lawson, let the reins slip through his fingers somewhat and, by 1990, inflation was back up to 9.5%. It was John Major, Norman Lamont and Kenneth Clark who eventually succeeded in getting inflation down to 3.1% in the healthily growing economy which they bequeathed in 1997 to New Labour. The tools they used were inflation targeting and reducing political influence on monetary policy decisions. Unfortunately, the institution they chose, the European Exchange Rate Mechanism, proved to be too politicised itself to do the impartial job they asked of it. Gordon Brown's later solution of an independent Monetary Policy Committee working to an inflation target set by the Treasury appears, so far at least, to be more robust.

Eaton Square

27. The drawing room

28. The balcony

The Thorneycroft's now had to find somewhere else to live. They chose an apartment in Eaton Square which was to be their home for the rest of their lives. Carla applied her interior decorating skills to designing rooms which were at the same time comfortable and elegant. Peter painted and sketched the drawing room and the balcony on which he was in turn painted by Theodore Ramos, whose portrait of him is the first illustration in this book. Here they gathered their family around them, and welcomed their friends and here Carla was hostess to Peter's colleagues and political guests who came to consult him or discuss with him affairs of business or of state.

~ 3 ~
Gap Years and World Tour 1958-60

If Thorneycroft did have any doubts about the wisdom of his resignation, he kept them to himself. He was very careful, in the weeks following the resignation, to take no action which might have made the task of the Government more difficult. (Edward Heath, in saying in his autobiography that *"I felt then* [in 1958], *and still do* [in 1988], *that the whole episode was ultimately a political challenge to Macmillan's leadership"*, seems not to have noticed this restraint).

Thorneycroft's immediate concern was to take stock of his new situation. He had to decide whether to change course, renouncing his political ambitions. He might, to his considerable pecuniary advantage, have returned to the Bar, although it was twenty years since he had last practised. He could have embarked on a completely new career for himself in business, seizing the opportunity of several offers of directorships made to him by the heads of important industrial groups who had encountered him and recognised his qualities, especially during his time at the Board of Trade.

Thorneycroft felt that he needed time for reflection, time to analyse all the options, time to recharge his batteries. His daughter, Victoria, has a vivid recollection of her father taking her for a walk just after his resignation, walking very briskly around St James's Park, holding hands but not speaking. During the next few months, from the back benches, he intervened in Commons' debates from time to time. He kept in regular touch with his constituents and occasionally spoke to, or wrote articles for, the Press.

There was one consolation – that he now had the time to let his inquisitive mind roam across the whole political landscape without the constraints imposed by responsibility for a single department of State. Addressing his Monmouth Constituency Association at the end of March 1958, he made a thoughtful and pertinent speech on relations between the West and the Russians. A 'Summit' meeting with Khruschev had been under consideration for some time. Thorneycroft argued that, whilst some good might come out of such a meeting, it would be wise to hold first a Summit of the Western Powers to iron out important differences between them before exposing themselves in an ill-prepared state to the Russians. He expressed great concern about the current tendency of British nuclear defence policy, saying that solvency and conventional arms were likely to be of greater benefit than flinging resources at trying to be a competitive manufacturer of nuclear missiles. He argued that the West needed unity and strength and that Britain could play a vital role to that end, but that our prestige would depend not on the bombs we made or the money we spent, but on the role we played together with the Commonwealth, Europe and the United States in achieving that aim. The relevance of the speech was underlined two days later when Kruschev unexpectedly announced that the Soviet Union was unilaterally suspending all nuclear tests. In an interview with T F Thomson of the *Daily Mail*, published on 1st April, Thorneycroft expanded upon his Monmouth speech, saying that we should accept that *"we have moved out of the age of nations and into the age of continents"*. How to react to the Soviet's act was a Western, not just an American problem and *"the machinery for joint action and decision is precarious"*.

On 14th July 1958, the young King Feisal of Iraq, head of the Arab Union of Iraq and Jordan, and his uncle, Crown Prince Abdul Illah, were assassinated in Baghdad by a group of young Iraqi army officers led by Brigadier Abdul Karim Kassim. Fearing that his country would be the next target of Arab revolutionaries, President Chamoun of the Lebanon, called upon the American, French and British Governments to prepare to send him military aid. King Hussein of Jordan followed suit. Writing in the *News of the World* on 20th July, in an article defending the rapid and positive response of the British and American Governments to these pleas for help, Thorneycroft demonstrated that exclusion from office had not weakened his understanding of the complexities of international politics. He described as naïve those who thought that reliance should have been placed on the United Nations Organisation to act. The Americans already had their Sixth Fleet cruising off the coast of the Lebanon, and Britain had been able to put troops on the ground in Jordan very quickly: the Russians had already vetoed any action by the United Nations. Thorneycroft pointed out that the world community was facing a new type of aggression – no longer the 'old-fashioned and obvious' invasion of one country by another, but infiltration of insurgents organised from outside to stoke up revolution from within, backed by a steady flow of propaganda. He commented scathingly on the Socialists' acceptance of American action in the Lebanon whilst at the same time condemning the British action in Jordan – *"the politics of bedlam"* as he put it.

He did not neglect either his more down-to-earth constituency affairs. In September 1958 he attended a conference in Pontypool discussing juvenile unemployment in Monmouthshire and, later in the month, took an active part in an enquiry by the Transport Users' Consultative Committee into a proposal to close the Chepstow-Monmouth-Ross railway lines, suggesting some practical measures which might help to keep the lines open.

But after seven years in high office, acting at a level that had enabled him to exercise a direct influence on national and international events, he found life on the back benches less than satisfying. He had, in those seven years, met many influential people from a wide range of countries, getting to know some of them well. When travelling abroad in the discharge of his duties, he had come to appreciate the personal qualities and the knowledge and experience of large numbers of British diplomats and civil servants. He wanted to keep those contacts alive, and to use them to expand his knowledge and understanding of international affairs and of the great issues of the day.

In October, 1958, Thorneycroft informed his constituents that he had been invited by the Royal Institute of International Affairs to attend an informal Conference of the Commonwealth which was to be held in Palmerston, New Zealand, in January 1959. Taking advantage of this opportunity, he proposed to visit some of the Middle Eastern countries, Pakistan, India, Ceylon, Singapore and Indonesia. His 'Journey to the East' was to last more than three months, from 2nd November 1958 until 23rd February 1959.

These were not to be the travels of a mere wanderer. Everywhere that Thorneycroft went he found friends, more often than not in high positions. He had the entrée to embassies, government ministries, bankers' offices and the homes of eminent citizens, and he recorded in a diary that he kept of his journey the warm welcome and the wide ranging conversations he was able to have with ambassadors, with presidents, with bankers, with aid workers and many others. He was absorbing information, forming impressions and making judgements which would prove to be of enormous value to him in the important roles with which he was to be entrusted in future years. As he went along, he was all the time making new friends, winning the respect of still more people of influence, adding to what would nowadays be called his 'network'.

Although the diary covers only sixteen weeks, a tiny part of his long political career, it gives in Thorneycroft's own words a clear and absorbing picture of the way his lively and perceptive mind reacted to the political and historical impressions that flooded in upon him, and reveals so much about the personality of the man and of the times during which he practised his craft, that it is reproduced here in full - an autobiographical fragment within the portrait.

Diary of the Journey to the East
2nd November 1958 - 23rd February 1959

Sunday, 2nd November

At London Airport I met the father-in-law of the present Ambassador to the Lebanon in London. He was there with his daughter and his son-in-law who had spent the last four months in England. We talked of what I might see in the Lebanon. They urged three things - Baalbeck, a refugee camp, the Cedars of Lebanon. "Don't," they said, "be disappointed in the Cedars. They look rather small and there are only 34 of them. But when you get closer they are very large and very beautiful." They spoke also of my journey and of Russia. It was not one Russia, they said, but many Russias, and interestingly they compared the situation to the Arab world. Not one Arab country but many Arab countries. Similar on some matters but also very different in others, in history and tradition.

It was all rain over England, rain over France until we got to the Alps. And then the sun came out and the snow came up to meet us. And Mont Blanc was shining below, 23,000 feet. Beyond that the fields of France, which I had noted only a few weeks ago, but brown now and with the grape harvest gathered in. A stop in Rome where I met the representative of the Middle-Eastern airline, a Mr. Jaboua whose wife is the daughter of a Mr Wilkes, the Manager of the British Bank of the Middle East in Kuwait, who also urged me to see the Cedars and told me that they looked better under snow and said there might be snow already in the mountains. As I am also told that the temperature in Beirut is between 90 and 100 degrees, it looks as though the resources of my 44 lbs. of luggage will be stretched to the full range of garments.

Athens in the dark and a cup of Turkish coffee. My neighbours explained to me the delights of the various nightclubs to be met in the Middle East, recommended two in Beirut and Teheran.

Later, over Cyprus, and far below the lights of Nicosia, and I thought of our friends, Hugh Foot, his wife, and others down below. So to Beirut in the rain.

The rain comes apparently with the sirocco which they have had here with a high temperature in recent days. The situation report on arriving around midnight in the Embassy, which is by the way delightful to look at inside but with no views - the situation report is calm.

Apparently the main difficulty is to get the people to hand in their arms.

Christians and Moslems alike hold them and neither of them would give them up for fear the others won't. The position of isolation of the Lebanon is obvious. If Iraq should go to Nasser, neither Lebanon or Jordan would be easily held. It appears at the moment that Iraq is holding out against the idea of Arab Union or at least union with Nasser. But the Communists support the separatist movement against the Arab Union. Our aim is to keep Communism out of the Middle East. We have to consider which danger is the worst. Politics in any part of the world are a complex business, but politics in the Middle East are certainly a very tangled affair.

Monday, 3rd November

I slept until 9.30. I was tired after the day's air travel. When I woke it was cooler after the rain, but still hot and steamy after England, and as I woke I had the smell of the Middle East, burnt oil, olives and garlic. Outside the bougainvilleas are in full bloom.

I had an interesting talk with Mr White, the Manager of the Eastern Bank. He said that Lebanon was really a series of accidents. The virtual closing of Haifa, since the Arabs wouldn't take goods through a Jewish port, has thrown the shipping into Beirut. Similarly, air difficulties at Cairo over the years have helped to develop Beirut as an international airport. Meanwhile, the revenue of the Arab world has been growing, particularly perhaps since the difficulties of Abadan. Money has been going into Arab pockets, and these rich Arabs want somewhere to spent it. They look first towards the Lebanon, as their summer resort where Arabic is spoken. They treat it rather as we would treat the Isle of Wight. As to the people of the Lebanon, they are by now tired of trouble. They have been through quite a bit. Moslem and Christian were abducted in turn into the other's quarters. They had, he thought, no wish to go on fighting. Few of them, if any, had so far handed in their arms. It was this question of the holding of arms by the populace which was providing the greatest difficulty. His belief was that the only way to get the arms would be to buy them. You had to buy most things here. The Lebanese economy was based on a credit pyramid, tilted on its apex. During the trouble a virtual moratorium had been declared. Nobody had paid the next man until he himself had been paid. Meanwhile, however, a vast real property boom was going on, of which I was to see more later.

I had lunch at the Embassy with the New Zealand Trade Mission, with Mr Sooly of the Ministry of Economic Affairs, and Mr Dada who is head of the Economic Section of the Lebanese Foreign Office. The New Zealanders have been trying to sell meat and dairy produce in the Middle East, not, I think, with much success. I saw, too, the Pakistani Charge d'Affaires. He has a brother-in-law, a constitutional lawyer, who is now being brought in by Ayub Khan as Foreign Minister in Karachi. I must try and see him when I get there. He says that Ayub Khan is trying to do with as few politicians as possible, as there are no politicians in Pakistan without considerable pasts.

In the afternoon I took a taxi and toured Beirut. It was interesting to go into a mosque for the first time. I was rather moved when I saw the young men washing their feet to go in and the devotions of the older ones. My taxi driver had taken advanced, but not, I think, very advanced English whilst he was at school. He showed me, however, something of the city and the vast amount of building that's going on at the present time, and I saw, too, the white vehicles of the UNO observers. It is difficult now and at this stage to assess the effect of the visit of the Sixth Fleet and the American marines. They arrived, and it may be that they stopped a situation developing, but it was a trump card and it has now been played. Those who looked for support from them did not get it. Those who resented their arrival realized that in practice they intended to do nothing. It will not be easy to play this card again, and meanwhile the job is left to the Lebanese.

Tuesday, 4th November

The end of the sirocco and the morning broke with the sun shining and the air fresh and cool. I went off with Moore Crosthwaite, the Ambassador, to Baalbek. We drove up the winding road which leads up the mountains of the Lebanon, and as we got higher it grew cooler. On the top or near the top were the new houses which the rich Lebanese had been building for their summer residences. On the far side we wound down into the fertile valley which lies widely between the Lebanon and the anti-Lebanon. There are still signs of road blocks and check points. Here the earth is red and they are growing vines, smaller and rather meaner than they grow in Italy, still producing quite tolerable wine. There are camels in the fields; Arabs are working there with their wives, their goats and their personal belongings. Baalbek has often been described in pictures and in prose, but it is a glorious representation of a past civilisation, of the Phoenicians, the Greeks and the Romans. The first and last picture one has of it is the tall columns of the Temple of Jupiter rising above the fertile green valley which lies below them. We walked through the ruins together, to the Temple of Jupiter, the Temple of Bacchus, and the Temple of Venus, now rechristened St Barbara, a Christian church, with the mosque close beside it. In these areas the mosques and the churches shoulder one another, and represent the Christian and Moslem diversity of the country.

We had taken a picnic lunch but were invited instead to lunch at the hotel with an Arab gentleman, the colonel of the local guard and a young officer who had been Captain of the President's Guard in the recent troubles which all referred to as "les evenements". French is the language which they speak and I seem to detect even now a love of things French. The educated Arab who was our host had drawn much of his culture and his learning from France, had been educated on French books and thought in a French way. He might indeed have been an educated Frenchman anywhere. His cousin was a distinguished Arab poet now aged 83 and living in Egypt. In the village the UNO observers were billeted and also in the villages round about. Very young, very nice - and very innocent.

As we motored back through the now peaceful countryside, it was hard to imagine the strife which simmered just below the surface, the arms still hidden in the houses.

One saving grace of the recent troubles was that the division was not on straight, religious grounds. There were many Christians who thought that the time had come for President Chamoun to go, and for another to take his place. Government changes are not secured quite so smoothly in the East as they are at Westminster.

This then remains the problem of the Lebanon. Inside deep division, including deep religious divisions, and outside - and partly inside - the smouldering passions of Arab nationalism.

Dined with the Norwichs where I met Maud Fargeallah, a cousin of my host at lunch, a friend of Chamoun's and also of General Chehab. Also Tuto Antonius, an ardent supporter of the Revolution, and MacQueen, the Manager of the British Bank.

Maud Fargeallah's uncle had been murdered by the Turks, and her family driven into exile. They had now returned and her family's estates lie north of Baalbeck. She enlarged on the feudal nature of the Lebanese allegiances. She spoke also of General Chehab, himself a Maronite Christian, which is necessary in the position of President. Tuto Antonius is an ardent Arab nationalist. She described herself as a professional Cassandra. She thought it was all too late. The Arab world would fall to the communists, Nasser would no longer be able to hold it. She would have wished to see an end to the Nasser/Western world quarrel and an Arab world united against the communists. It seems that some form of Arab nationalism is now basic to all Moslem hopes. I think this must be recorded as a fact of life.

What seemed to be needed was some solution which would render it possible to put a stop to the quarrel with Nasser and the Western world. Above all, something that would stop it on something less than Nasser's terms, and Iraq at any rate would want something much less than Nasser's terms as a basis of a policy.

The building of the Aswan Dam was regarded as a kind of symbol. Was it possible to go back to Square One, the European Consortium, American Aid, the International Bank? Does the larger amount of Russian aid affect the issue? The Arab world was not naturally inclined to Russia. They spoke English or spoke French, as an alternative to Arabic. Their culture came from France or England. It was a European culture. They didn't speak like Russians, and they didn't like communism. Some form of Arab nationalism was certain to come.

One does tend in Beirut to be entertained and entertained very well by the Christians and have their point of view put. It's interesting to hear from time to time the different views expressed by the other side.

Wednesday, 5th November

In the afternoon I visited Biblos with Mr and Mrs Scott. This is traditionally the oldest inhabited place in the world. It gave its name to the Bible and is traditionally associated with the invention of writing. It is a romantic spot with remains dating from the early Bronze Age, the Phoenicians, the Greeks, the Romans and the Crusaders, and a fine Crusader castle. During the day I again discussed with several people the future policy of the Middle East. It was plain that the crux of this policy was whether we should go on seeking to divide and perhaps, rather doubtfully, move to drive in a wedge wherever we could, or whether we should make what is really rather a sharp reversal of policy and face the fact that it would be good for us and for the world that the Arabs should or could with advantage draw closer together. Not all of them, probably not many of them would draw together on Nasser's terms, but some form of closer association, something which would probably inevitably develop, may be desirable. Most Moslems and many Christians here in the Lebanon think that policy should develop along those lines. They believe, too, that if it were once more possible for Britain to be solidly behind policies of this character, relations with her would run more smoothly.

I dined at the Embassy with Rashid Kharami, the Prime Minister. He is young and his father was deeply respected in this country. He is a Christian Arab, serious and sincere in what he says. He took the usual line with me about Israel and the UNO Resolutions. He was emphatic that the Arabs must get closer together. His policy in the Lebanon appears to be to restore calm here and peace between the Christians and the Moslems in order that they might not fear closer union. The West could help, in part by a reconciliation with Nasser, part by economic aid, and perhaps most by not opposing the idea of Arab Union. On the economic front he pointed out that bulk purchase by Russia was more attractive to the individual producer in the Lebanon than the perhaps more important, massive investment by the West.

Thursday, 6th November

I rose early and took the aircraft to Baghdad sweeping in over the Tigris in bright sunshine at about 11 o'clock in the morning. I was met by Patterson, the Commercial Counsellor. The atmosphere in Baghdad is something totally different from that which we found in Beirut. The Lebanon faces westward across the Mediterranean; Baghdad is Eastern. Not only this, but whereas in Beirut the atmosphere was calm so that one would never know that a revolution had been attempted or planned, the atmosphere here is much more electric. One has the sense that something might happen at any moment. Something generally does happen. A few days before my arrival, Arif had been arrested. He had been the Deputy Prime Minister and Minister of the Interior in Kassim's Government. He had been appointed Ambassador to Bonn but had come back, presumably to lead a revolutionary movement which had by his arrest been nipped in the bud.

His arrest and the rumoured arrest of others with him will undoubtedly strengthen the present Government.

I lunched at the Embassy with Michael and Esther, and saw what is left of it. Indeed it is a shell. It has been gutted by fire, its roof has gone. Later in the day I dined at the Iranian Embassy with the Ambassador, Mr Mahmoud Malery. I met and talked with the Indian Minister, the Pakistan Minister, and others, and also with Mr Baggi, the Swedish Minister. I talked with him of the prospects of the Free Trade Area.

It is not at all easy to assess the situation in Baghdad. The Government has been forced to take a position earlier than it might have wished to do with the arrest of Arif. I have no doubt they would have preferred to wait a little before taking this stand, in order to strengthen their own position. Their policy appears to be a move towards Arab union on their own terms and in their own time. They may yet be able to do this, but powerful forces surround them, in particular at the moment they are labouring along with Communist support. This is an embarrassment to them. It is indeed the only propaganda machine at their disposal. Such a machine may well distort or, as it has done in many other cases, in the long run control the propagandists.

Friday, 7th November

A day of rest in the Muslim world. It was cool and sunny and the weather is like a lovely June or July day in England. I spent the morning sketching the mosques across the Tigris from the Embassy garden, and then lunched at the Alwaya Club. I met there a number of the English businessmen. They urged the need to further trade in the Arab world. They pointed out that such actions as the sale of submarines to Israel announced by the BBC or even the Prime Minister's speech referring to our close friendship with Israel were not advantageous to this end. They also talked of the need to reconcile our position with Abdul Nasser, and to sort out the position in the Trucial States.

I dined with the Wrights and met the Sudanese Ambassador, Jamal Mohammed who talked of the problem of the Aswan Dam. In short term context it has raised a number of difficulties for the Sudan, but in the long run it would help. It would increase Egypt's self-confidence, or at any rate lessen her inferiority complex. At present, the Egyptians who used to be allowed into the Sudan freely were being replaced by West Africans and this raised difficult social problems. We discussed the Middle East and the Trucial States. These States look in part to the Saudis and in part to Nasser. As education was increasing so increasingly they would look with suspicion upon their leaders. If we put troops in to defend the leaders, it would again be represented as an attack upon the Arab world.

Saturday, 8th November

Went along and had a talk with Milton Gregg and his staff at UNO Headquarters. They described to me their programme of technical aid, modest but useful. We talked of other things as well. It is possible for Iraq to travel the middle road which we all believe that she would wish to follow? Or will she go to something like a union with Nasser a la Syria? Or to Communism? With the arrest of Arif who was an ardent pro-Nasserite, it looks as though the one road is for the time being at any rate closed. The question arises, what to do about the other?

Communism in the eyes of many is highly organised in this country, not least in Kurdistan. Some think that nothing can stop it, that no action can be taken which will halt its march. Others like the Finance Minister with whom I talked later, regard it more as a surface manifestation.

Peter Thorneycroft – artist and paterfamilias

Peter emulated his father in illustrating letters to his children …

My darling Victoria –
Mummy and I have arrived in Donegal – in the far North West of Ireland – it is very lovely – lots of mountains and lakes. and a charming house with lots and lots of pictures in it.

and we are having a wonderful time. Daddy has been Taking photographs and Trying to paint pictures.

and mummy is finishing her carpet and we are planning to go to all the lovely places round here. and in the evening it is very warm and cosy here and we have oil lamps and candles as there is no electricity.

and we are enjoying ourselves. Very soon we will come back & see you again and we send you all our love.

X   X   X   X

Daddy.

An illustrated letter from Peter Thorneycroft to his daughter Victoria

Plate 1

113

... and to his grandchildren - this one to John's son, Richard

Northbourne Court
April 8th 1990

Dear Richard –

I one am a letter and have a moment in the quiet here of Northbourne to write. We are spending a few days on our own here and will be sorry when we have to leave. It is such a lovely place not the old church and this lovely house which we have all enjoyed living in. You will I think always remember your days here with your friends and the lovely park.

I am getting rather old and can't paint as well as I used to but it is still fun to try. and it is something that you can do wherever you go – a sort of diary of your journeys and the places you remember. Here the old farm buildings which are mostly older than the house & often happier are worth recording.

I think you have been happy here with all your friends and particularly being with Christopher Northbourne who is such a good friend to all of us;

An illustrated letter from Peter Thorneycroft to his grandson Richard

and as you look back upon those days
you will remember the happy times – and
particularly the sailing with your own boat
which is something that will always

be with you –
and all that
you have learnt
both in & out
of school.
I know you have not been very
well but you will soon be as well as ever.
One recovers fast when young so work hard at
the things you can do & make the very best of
them you can. Remember that we all. I
love you and we are proud of you – I
remember when I was young I found many
things difficult but stick to them and in
time one finds things easier. One develops
slowly and you will grow and I can
see the good life that lies before you.
with all love from your
Grandfather.

Plate 3   115

Peter Thorneycroft's artistic range was wide.

STREET SCENE

a. One of Peter's early works - St Paul's (1955)

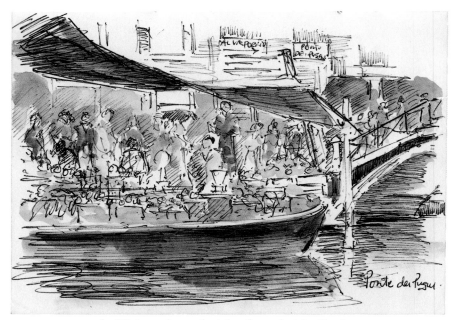

b. Watercolour sketch of market in Venice

Saturday 10th October. arrived in Bath to sketch. Wet + windy. Spent some time looking for subjects. Superb place could paint for years here. Probably best to treat it like Venice avoid the obvious popular + magnificent + paint the unconsidered corners + leave out the detail. will attempt it tomorrow

a. Bath - a corner of the Royal Crescent

b. Bryanston Square from the Nuffield Hospital (1977)
(Even when ill, Peter cheered himself up by painting)

Plate 5   117

LANDSCAPE

a. Watercolour 'Wind at Garnmath'

b. Kentish landscape painted by Peter with his great friend, Christopher Northbourne

Plate 6

SEASCAPE

a. Beach scene, Barbados

b.Grenada
(during a stay at
the Calabash Hotel)

Plate 7

119

An example of Peter Thorneycroft's development of a painting

Calle Bastion, Venice

Stage 1. Pen & ink sketch (*top left*)

Stage 2. Sepia wash (*bottom left*)

Stage 3. Watercolour

I went on to see Ibrahim Kubba, the Minister of Economics. He talked about oil. I asked him the direct question - whether he intended in the long run to nationalise the oil industry, and he assured me that nothing was further from his thoughts. What he wanted to do was to conclude the present negotiations and arrive at a settlement which might stand over the years.

Later in the morning I talked with the Finance Minister. I put to him the fact that while our relations behind the scenes with the Government were frank and cordial, this was not reflected in the press and the radio. I also raised the question of the destruction of the Embassy, and the need to reach a settlement on that matter. He was reasonably forthcoming on both these matters. We talked of the Sterling Area. He said he wished to diversify the holding of Iraq's reserves. On imports he said that though they would license them, they would do so on a non-discriminatory basis. And on investment, he looked to the mobilising of investment inside the country rather than seeking private or public investment from outside. I think this was a somewhat optimistic view of the probable requirements of Iraq in the years to come.

In the evening there was a Reception at the Ambassador's residence at which a number of the Iraqi Ministers arrived, the Foreign Secretary, the Minister of Finance and the Minister of Economics. It was the first time that they had attended a reception at the British Embassy since the troubles of July last. I also had a word or two with Sefton Delmer, of the Daily Express, and Sevewright of the Iraq Petroleum Company.

Sunday, 9th November

I had appointments in the morning with the Prime Minister, Kassim, with the Foreign Secretary, and with the Minister of Guidance. Of these, of course the most interesting was the interview with Kassim. I saw him at the Ministry of Defence, and I was swept up past the soldiers saluting and all looking very cheerful and seeming to enjoy running the country.

Ibrahim Kubba, Minister of Economics, had kindly come along to act as an interpreter for me. Kassim possesses a considerable amount of charm and a pleasant smile. He told me frankly enough that he and his Government did not yet represent the people. They were a small group of men. They wanted time to consolidate the country. They wanted an opportunity to bring peace to the nation. Above all, they wanted an opportunity to educate the nation along the right lines. They wanted to hold a middle-of-the-road position. He himself believed in Arab unity, but he wanted to move towards it in his own time, in his own way and at his own pace.

29. Thorneycroft meets Prime Minister Kassim of Iraq

Earlier, I had heard the Foreign Secretary deliver a diatribe against the Baghdad Pact, and he maintained that it was an unnatural alliance for the Iraqis and divided them from the rest of the Arab world. In some ways, Sanshal, the Minister of Guidance, gave me the most interesting interview. He has a more subtle mind than the others. He admitted, which the others had not done, the strength of the Communist organisation in Iraq, but, of course, he maintained on the usual lines that the strength of Communism had been due to the evil behaviour of the previous regime. He was, and admitted himself to be an even more ardent Arab nationalist than perhaps his colleagues. He described the land reforms which he intended to undertake and which he believed would damp down the strength of Communism in the country. He like nearly every other Arab I have met, in either the Lebanon or Iraq, emphasised the importance in their view of the West coming to terms with Nasser.

Later I lunched with Mr Crawford, the Minister, and met the Manager of the Ottoman Bank and others. We discussed the virtual collapse of the Development Board or at least its grave weakening since the new regime came in. Later on I dined quietly at the Embassy with the Ambassador, with Sevewright and his wife, and with Heneage from the Iraq Petroleum Company.

Monday, 10th November

I motored out in bright sunshine along the straight road which leads from Baghdad to the Airport Base at Habbaniyah. I was accompanied by Major Richmond, the Deputy Military Attaché and a Gunner Officer, and we talked about Glubb and the Arab Legion in which he had served.

Habbaniyah is a base for staging aircraft and 600 men are there, but there are no aircraft, no aerodrome and no opportunities for staging anything. Captain Stubbs was faced with a considerable problem to keep this team together and reasonably happy. Enclosed as they are within the compound, delightful though that compound is, and unable really to go into Baghdad at all. I thought he was doing a fine job. I visited with him the Technical Section, the Hospital, the Schools where some of the wives are volunteering as school teachers, the Canteen and the Officers' Mess.

Really, two problems confronted them. One was how to get their Christmas rations out of Basra Port, where they are virtually impounded waiting for import licences, and the second is to find out what are the future plans of the Government, will they always have to stay here, for a long time under these conditions, or is there a reasonable chance of them getting home.

At dusk I boarded a Middle Eastern Airways plane to fly back to Beirut en route for Amman. I passed over the desert in darkness and through a very considerable thunderstorm. It was pretty bumpy. Flashes of lightning lit up the whole sky and it was quite a spectacular affair. We arrived safely at Beirut. Nothing stays still for very long in the Arab world and I was greeted on arrival with news of the death sentences on Jemali and two of the other Arab leaders by the Military Tribunal in Iraq, and by further news that King Hussein seeking to fly his own aircraft over Syrian territory yesterday had been forced back by Mig fighters to his own territory.

I dined, and dined very well incidentally, with Louis Rocher at his residence, a lovely house which used to be occupied by the French High Commissioner, in Beirut. We talked together of the need to co-ordinate the policies of Europe and particularly those of France and England, in our relations with the Middle East, controversial though the issues were, and in any approach that we made to Colonel Nasser.

Tuesday, 11 November

A perfect day in Beirut. Charles Wheen and his wife came to see me at the Residence. They are just back from a visit to Ethiopia. We sat on the terrace in the sunshine, talking of painting, which they had taken up and which they very much enjoyed.

Then by Jordanese Airways, starting a little late, to Jerusalem and Amman. It was my first view of the Holy Land, of the Jordan Valley and the road from Jericho to Jerusalem.

Met at the Airport by Charles and Natasha. We motored through Amman. It was gayer and less derelict than Baghdad. It was also in holiday mood, celebrating the safe return of the King after being turned back by the Mig fighters over Syria.

It was interesting to compare the scenes in Baghdad and Amman. Like Baghdad the lorries were out full of young people and of soldiers, cheering and carrying branches as they carried them centuries ago. The soldiers were firing into the air, and the children were clamouring aloud to hold the guns, but were made to be content with fireworks instead. Everybody was enjoying themselves, and everybody appeared to be contented and happy.

No one quite knows the rights and the wrongs of the Syrian affair. It seems that somebody must have messed up the clearance of the King's plane over Syria, but what matter? The King is safe, Long Live the King! It is interesting to compare the demonstrations and the crowds in Baghdad and Amman. The same language, the same branches, the same clapping hands. Here perhaps it is a little calmer, they seem a more solid and serious people. But they cheer in the same way and crowds are fickle; they could change. In either place they could start shouting for someone else. They wave the branches as they waved them on Palm Sunday. They changed then - they might change again.

In the evening, there was a dinner at the Embassy which, incidentally, is a very charming one, to say goodbye to Senor David Careno, the Spanish Ambassador, the doyen of the Diplomatic Corps here, who is leaving. Charlie made a very good speech, partly in Spanish and partly in French.

After dinner I had a talk with Mr Said Jumah, who is the Permanent Under Secretary at the Foreign Office here. He is a Kurd, though settled for two generations, I think, in Jordan. He confirmed the views which I had heard expressed in other countries, that Communism was pretty highly organised in Kurdistan. He thought that the Russians might well do a good deal of mischief in that area. As to Jordan, he said that that was one of the few solid elements in the Arab world. It had become a symbol of Arab independence. Talk of Western reconciliation with Nasser was in part at any rate derived from talk on Radio Cairo. Arabs differed widely as between one national and another and anything like Arab integration was quite out of the question. Certain Arab integration with Nasser was out of the question for he was no Arab at all.

Wednesday, 12th November

I had a talk with the Prime Minister, who was quietly confident that Jordan could set an example of independence in the Arab world. Indeed he regarded Jordan as a symbol of such independence. The Arabs believed in Arab nationalism, and he did himself. The King was popular and never more popular than at this moment after the Syrian episode. He was popular throughout the country including those who lived on the West bank.

He said two things about the refugees which were perhaps not entirely consistent with each other. He said first of all that the refugees must be regarded as part of the political problem of Israel. Solve that and you solve the problem of refugees. He said, secondly, that the refugees were part of the economic problem of Jordan. If economic development took place, in Jordan, then the refugees as Jordanians would be absorbed into the new enterprises. The biggest of these enterprises would, of course, be the Jordan Valley Scheme, known as the Johnson Scheme. The difficulty about this Scheme is, however, that it involves Israel, Jordan and Syria. It has not been easy to reach agreement on it. Undoubtedly it would make the greatest contribution towards the economy of this area. Meanwhile, certain lesser schemes which formed a minor part of the major Johnson Scheme, were perhaps going forward. It didn't seem that he regarded Israel as a major military problem at the present time, though in the past, and perhaps rightly, she had been so regarded. So long as Jordan remained stable and united, it was probably unlikely that Israel would attack, though, of course, border incidents are going on all the time.

Later, I saw Wing Commander Dalgleish, the R.A.F. officer who had been flying the King at the time of the Syrian incident. It's pretty plain that the Syrians were anticipating the visit and that the Migs were in the sky. The evasion had been done by flying the Dove low rather in the way that a bird seeks to evade a hawk when it is attacking. The Migs had pursued them into Jordan but, of course, the frontier is very ill-defined at that point, and as soon as the main road had been reached, they broke off the attack. No shots were fired. I think perhaps two things emerged from that incident. First of all, the Syrians, at any rate from here, appear to have come very badly out of it. It has united Jordan as perhaps nothing else could do. Secondly, in the complexities of air clearance, while the flight plan had been cleared, it was obvious that if the matter were debated in some international organisation such as UNO, considerable confusion would arise on the clearance issue.

Later still I went with Charlie Johnston to the Diwan, and had an interview with the King. He was quietly confident that Jordan would remain stable, setting an example of independence. He talked to me about his escape from the Mig fighters. He felt himself that the economic development of Jordan was a high priority. He spoke favourably of the Johnson Scheme. He is, I think, a quietly spoken, sincere and certainly very courageous man.

I dined with Mr Whitfield of the Ottoman Bank, a leader of the British community here, and met a number of those interested in the banking, financial and commercial world. Unanimously they seemed to be against Nasser. They were anxious for news of Baghdad, as in Jordan at the moment they are more or less cut off from Iraqi contact. Their contacts with Syria inform them that the Syrians were becoming increasingly dissatisfied with the Nasser association. If Iraq held steady, and the country there became stable, Syria would become increasingly displeased. She would look on the one side to Jordan, somewhat to the Lebanon, and in these circumstances to Iraq as Arab countries which were independent of Egyptian control. Hopes here were clearly moving towards some arrangement whereby the Arab countries would move together but upon an independent basis. The kind of policies to which these men were feeling their way, was an acceptance of Arab nationalism, a moving together of the Arab world, a relaxed and perhaps formally correct attitude to Nasser, and Western aid to economic and industrial development.

Thursday, 13th November

A day of wind and cloud. I did no work on it, but spent the day visiting Jeraz. The road winds over the hills down into fertile valleys and I passed the flocks of goats and the people who were farming the land, and the women, some of them good looking, tall, proud Circassians. The children waved to me cheerfully as I passed; the soldiers saluted. It had the atmosphere of a happy, contented, and on the whole stable country.

Jeraz itself is a great Roman city. It's larger than Baalbeck; it has great streets which stretch across it, lined with columns, temples and churches. The Curator showed me round. He lives in a small house above the ruins, with his wife and nine children, and I don't think a great deal of pay. There is much more excavation that could be done. Some of the most interesting things are in the Museum. The mosaic floors of the churches, the pottery vases from the Greek tombs, and other items of interest.

I came back in time for lunch where I met Joe Alsop who also came in for dinner in the evening. He took on the whole a rather gloomy view of the Middle East, but seemed to have cheered up in the course of the afternoon. Jordan at any rate was a much more settled country than when he saw it a year ago. I had a fairly early bed, ready for what would be a long and fairly hard day tomorrow, when I go to Jerusalem and through the gate there into Israel.

Friday, 14th November

I started off by seeing Colonel Clarke of UNRRA, in charge of refugee camps. He told me that they have about 300,000 refugees on the West bank and about 200,000 on the East. The numbers are, however, difficult to check. The test of a refugee includes a test of needs. They're increasing at the rate of about 18,000 a year. In his view, if all the development possible took place in Jordan, they might at best absorb about 300,000 of them, and then they would be doing very well. But really it means that about half the refugee problem has to be dealt with in the long run outside the frontiers of Jordan, either in Iraq or Syria. Technical education was an expensive but effective method of approaching the problem. About half the refugees are under 16 or 17 years of age, and once they've been trained they are pretty easy to place.

After this, I went along with the Ambassador to sign the book at the Diwan. It was the King's birthday and there were scenes of very considerable excitement outside. Soldiers were dancing on the steps of the Palace, people were coming and going, guns were being fired and live ammunition as well.

We signed the book and I said goodbye to Charles at the Embassy and set off on my journey to Jerusalem.

I passed on the way some of the genuine Bedouin tribes, in their tents and with their camels as we moved down the new road which has only recently been opened, to the Dead Sea, up the other side, passing the road to Jericho on our right of which we had a distant view. I was in Jerusalem about mid-day.

Arrangements had been made for a guide and I walked for a little in the Old City and saw the Holy Sepulchre. I bought a small gold cross for Victoria. The Old City is picturesque inside its walls, with the women wearing the same costume as they are supposed to have worn in the time of Our Lord. Later I lunched with Stewart, the Consul General, and at 3 o'clock moved through the Gate into Israel.

I was staying at the King David Hotel in a comfortable room with a private bath, and they plan for me what I think will be a pretty strenuous three days.

In the afternoon I have been touring the New City and seeing something of the big building development that is taking place. The new flats that they've put up for the emigrants as they arrive; emigrants of all nations. To start with, they tried to mix them all up straight away, but now I'm told they tend to group them more according to their separate nationalities. My guide, Mr Charles Kariv, who comes from the Ministry of Foreign Affairs, told me, complete integration is going to take quite a number of years, but meanwhile it's all a great adventure.

As I'm dictating this, I can look out of my bedroom window across to the Old City of Jerusalem and the frontier only a bare quarter of a mile away, with the Mount of Olives on the left and the Hills of Moab on the right. Quite a romantic spectacle.

I dined with Mr and Mrs Harowitz and met Mr Eshkol, the Finance Minister. Like many people here, he originated in Russia. Many of the early settlers in Palestine are in fact Russians, Germans coming in later. These early settlers still provide the bulk of the leadership in Israel. The next generation are coming along but tend in the main to enter business and commerce rather than in politics where a void may be developing. Mr Eshkol told me that in effect he tried to achieve two Budgets - the Defence costs and the Social Services covered by current taxes, the Development Charges and other matters covered on a capital Budget. There was a trend towards inflation, augmented in the case of Israel by the fact that wages are linked to the cost of living.

Saturday, 15th November

I went in early to Tel Aviv, where I met the Prime Minister, Mr Ben Gurion. Like all the Jews here, he lives simply, almost austerely, and I saw him in his library. We were interrupted at one moment by his little grand-daughter who embraced him. He asked me about Baghdad and my tour in the Middle East, and then we talked of Israel. He has a capacity for simplifying great issues.

Israel was, he said, in a sense fortunate. They had to do things and because they had to do them, they achieved them. They fought because they had to fight in order to survive. They sacrificed much in order to develop the country because development was essential if they were to maintain that standard of life which they required. Emigration and Defence were the two great burdens which they had to carry. The emigrants were a burden but it was their policy to take them and to take them from all countries. The last remaining great source of supply was Russia, though emigrants were coming out of Rumania today.

I pursued my travels along the road to Nazareth. I saw the cave in which Joseph and Mary were supposed to live. I also saw the Arab Bazaar, bright with colours of various sort of grain and pepper, with a local Arab dignitary who ran the Probation Office, and he spoke wisely and well of the problems of youth in the Arab world coming into the towns, and coming out of the old Arab Patriarchal system. They are not allowed into the café, they have no clubs, they develop or tend to develop a certain Teddy-boy characteristic.

And so on past Cana where the water was turned into wine. The sun was warm and bright and the breeze was cool and the country looked not unlike Scotland on a very fine June day.

I reached the Lake of Galilee at sunset, stopped on the Galilee hills above it and looked across it and saw the reflection of the hills on the other side in the waters down below. It was a very beautiful sight.

I stayed the night at Tiberias and had dinner with General Igo Alam. He lives in what is called a kubuz which is a community centre run on early and idealistic Socialist lines, democratic and co-operative. They share their food, their clothes, their children's education. They run a common school, no wages are paid and all have to do something. Some of them working in the fields, and others at the fishing. There are about 250 in this particular kubuz. They tell me it does not work without difficulty, but it works and the boys and girls certainly like it very much indeed.

I have been asking questions about the Israeli defence system. Potentially the country is long and narrow and could be attacked from three sides at once. The defence is organised in depth; each village or kubuz is sited not only from a social but from the military and tactical point of view. The country is divided into three Commands, with a strong, armoured, mobile reserve. But to defend this long, narrow strip where obviously no early warning system could be worked, it is necessary to be prepared to strike first, to be ready to move in at any moment where the enemy are deployed, obviously for attack.

Sunday, 16th November

I resumed my travels. I got up early and had breakfast by the Lake of Gallilee and then moved off in the car towards the valley which lies at the head waters of the Jordan where the point of Israel runs up between the Lebanon and Syria. In this country they use every inch of ground they can. They have done here a very considerable reclamation scheme. Settlers had been put in and were working in the valley down below me.

Then we moved on and after a cup of coffee at the hill town of Safad, we went further along the road and attended a Christian Arab wedding, where we met my host of the night before, Brigadier Alum. We sat next door to the bride and bridegroom at the feast which followed the wedding. The whole sheep had been cooked and the Arab food was spread upon the table. It wasn't to tell the truth, very appetising. But we talked with many people including the Probation Officer I met at Nazareth the day before, and stood outside in the sunshine looking at the hills and watching the crowd down below. The whole village had turned up. It was the wedding of the son of a local notability. The Arab and the Jew mixed here at least in friendship.

And then on to Acre where I had an opportunity of seeing the massive defences which still stand there from the time of the Crusaders, and then Haifa, a modern, new, growing town, with a large harbour down below, and a great technical college where I had an opportunity of walking round. It's a very fine building, very modern architecture with 3,000 Israeli students. There's great competition to get into it. And so back to Tel Aviv where I am staying the night.

Monday, 17th November

I started south for Beersheba with Mr Goulan of the Ministry of Foreign Affairs. On the way we visited the Weizman Institute. It's beautifully laid out as a centre for scientific research in Israel, covering everything from electronics to nuclear research, physics and the rest. The design of the buildings and the generous layout is so arranged, they tell me, to attract scientists to Israel, and certainly they seem to live there in conditions which would compare very favourably with those anywhere else in the world.

Then on southwards through the orange groves until the country becomes drier and more desert appears. Then we reached Gath. When we were there I went in to see the Chief Engineer in charge of the water supply, Mr Gordon, who told me that he had once seen me in 1948 and we had had an argument at a meeting at King's College in London. He had served during the war with the Paratroopers and fought at Arnhem. He had given up what might be a good career as an engineer in England and settled down in Gath to look after the affairs there.

The area, like all other areas in Israel, is organised upon a defence basis. The community centres or settlements located in Strategic positions. Water is the key to Israel, or at any rate to the south of Israel, as it is to a great deal of the Middle Eastern world. The settlers come from many places, and quite a lot of them from North Africa where they are accustomed to a climate of this character. They start them off in settlements, and they start on the basis of day labour until they have got some experience in agriculture. After all, Jews outside Israel are not generally active in agricultural pursuits. Later on they are given an opportunity of farming land of their own, thus the place is organised for defence. The settlers are in position. As somebody said here, "You don't feel a place is really your own until you sit on it". Then on further south to Beersheba where the real desert begins. I didn't get right down to Negev, though I saw a good deal of the conditions in that area. Beersheba is now a new, modern town based principally upon industry. Chemicals, ceramics, agricultural machinery. It has grown from about 3,000 to about 40,000. Every now and then they think they will consolidate their position and then more emigrants appear. Here again, of course, water is the main element. They use every drop they can get including the effluent from their own sewage. They make attempts and sometimes successful attempts to grow trees in this desert area.

We met the sheikh of the local Bedouin tribe, for the Bedouins are thick in this part of the world. He was a calm, dignified man who said that he felt that these great developments about him were of help to the Bedouin in that area. All around in this part of Israel you see what appears to be sand, and then every now and then green oases where the settlers have taken root and the trees have begun to grow. In the older settlements of ten or fifteen years the trees are high and the green is very apparent. In the younger settlements, less so.

We went a little further south into the desert and saw the soldiers training. National Service here is something much tougher than what we see in England. I saw the soldiers, young men on National Service, stripped to the waist and doubling about in the hot sunshine. And so we came along the road back to Jerusalem in the evening light, stopping for a coffee at a café on the way through.

When I got back to Jerusalem, I had a bath and changed and went along to see Mrs Meir, the Foreign Secretary. We discussed Baghdad, Brigadier Kassim and the danger to him of the communist element in Iraq. She told me a story of an early Jewish community somewhere in Poland. Like many communities in the world it had one man who was perhaps not 100%. He thought that there were only three great men in the world - Napoleon, Moses and himself, and he thought he would never die. When people told him that after all Moses and Napoleon had died, he thought for a bit and said "Well, that was so, but one man might break through." The same with the men in this world who thought they could toy with communism and survive. We talked, too, of what Israel is doing to help the world. There was a kind of Afro-Asian Seminar on in Jerusalem at the present time, concentrating on agricultural development in hot and difficult areas. Sixty representatives were coming. They had catered originally for only thirty, but those who were coming included representatives from Ghana and from India.

She enlarged upon the help of this kind which Israel could give to the Arab world, especially to Jordan. After all, their problems were the same. The desert was the same divided only by a diplomatic line. We talked of Hussein. She had known his grandfather, Abdullah, and she last saw him as long ago as 1948. At that time she had crossed into Jordan dressed as an Arab woman because Abdullah, powerful as he was, had not dared tell the frontier posts and had to let her come at her own risk. He was a sad man that night. He saw that war was coming; the Iraqi levies were already in his country, and afterwards he was prepared to talk and to seek peace. If he had lived, she said, things might very well have been different.

She's a remarkable woman - rather like a female Ernie Bevin. I was sorry to leave Israel.

Tuesday, 18th November

I left Jerusalem at 1.30 a.m. for Lydda Airport, and boarded the Air France plane at 4 a.m. It was bound for Bangkok and Tokyo, but I was taking the short hop to Teheran. I didn't sleep much as we were flying into the sun and dawn broke early, and I reached Teheran at 11.15. It is high but much colder here and bright sunshine. I had lunch with the Harrisons and in the afternoon went to the Museum. They have a wonderful collection of prehistoric pottery. It is mostly 2,000 and 3,000 years before Christ, and wonderful in its skill and beauty. Strangely there is nothing much else between that date and the tenth century of our Lord, which shows how civilisations can come and then disappear for long periods.

After that I went into the Bazaar. The Bazaar itself is wonderfully built and constructed, rather like a Persian fairy tale, and inside it they sell things which are indistinguishable from Woolworths.

In the evening I dined with Persian friends of John's. One holds the Chair of Veterinary Research at the University of Teheran, and the other is a member of the last Royal House. We talked during dinner and later with John, about Iran. It is a strange country. It is not the Middle East or Europe or altogether Asia. It is part of the Caucasus. It has tigers and wolves, bears and mouflon, and jackals. A quarter of the country speak no recognisable form of Persian, one fifth of the country is tribal, and a lot of it is quite uninhabitable. We had a discussion of the Baghdad Pact. They were considering what the Russians would require in order to advance through Persia, and an American General rather caustically replied 'Boots'. Yet it may have a certain stability, if the Army remain loyal, as there is every indication, I understand, at the moment they intend to do. This country, too, has something of a Kurdish problem. Kurdistan includes bits of Syria, Turkey, Iraq and Persia. It does provide a wonderful field for the potential troublemaker.

Wednesday, 19th November

I visited what corresponds to St James's Palace. It was a strange mixture of old beauty and Victoriana. A clock with a peacock which flapped its wings given to one of the Shahs by Queen Victoria and on the floors the most wonderful carpets.

After lunch, up the hill with John where we saw the summer residence where the Ambassador can move to in the hot weather. Very pleasantly situated in a lovely garden. And then to one of the old villages. All the villages have the same kind of arrangements. The big house, the mosque, the bath house - communal bathing is their practice here, the men have it at one time and women another. The Moslem religion is, of course, closely associated with hygiene.

Dined with Mason in the evening, and met the Finance Minister and his wife, the Commercial Minister, the Minister for Industry and other members of the Government. Mrs Nasser is what I understand is a rare example in Persian womanhood of someone who believes in public works. She is very keen at the present time to establish a children's hospital. The Finance Minister's Budget difficulties seem to be the same as in any other country. Too much to spend on defence, on education and on health. His income comes as to £9,000,000 from oil, £11,000,000 from indirect taxation and the remainder from direct. The direct taxes raising about the same amount, £9,000,000 as in the case of oil.

Thursday, 20th November

Flew to Isfahan. It was clear sunshine and I flew in Iranian Airways, scraping over the top of the passes with the snowy peaks towering up above us. I walked round the Bazaar with a guide before lunch. The Bazaar here is a much more real place than in Teheran. As in all Persian Bazaars the various trades were grouped together, the metalworkers the shoemakers and so forth. But here in fact everybody was making something. Little children tapping away at silver and bronze, making various articles for sale.

In the evening I read a book by Girschman on Iran. It is remarkable how often this land has been the meeting place of East and West. They come round each side of the Caspian Sea and struggle for the area. Let us hope it does not happen again.

Friday, 21st November

I motored to Persepolis. I started early motoring through wide valleys with the mountain ranges standing up straight from the flat land below. In the distance we could see the snow upon the higher peaks. We had a puncture fairly early on after the first hour or so, and had it mended in an Arab village where I was the object of some interest to the small boys. We had lunch in the garden of a local hotel, but I did not try the local diet but stuck to the sandwiches that I had brought. I was approached by an English-speaking Turk who introduced me to two members of the Kashgi tribe who wanted a lift into Persepolis which we gave them.

After lunch the road climbs higher and, strangely enough, as it goes higher, more water is apparent. The arrangements which the Iranians make for water are three thousand years old and most ingenious. They tap the water in the lower parts of the mountain and channel it down with underground channels to the villages below. They dig these channels without instruments, by a process of long tradition, throwing up the earth above which looks as though great moles have been working along the hillside.

Then down through narrow, precipitous gorges where the land is changing and more green is appearing. So round the final bend where you see the pillars of Persepolis standing up in the evening sunshine. I took a stroll round them, took a few photographs, arranged for a guide for tomorrow morning, and plan an early bed.

Saturday, 22nd November

Sun and a cold wind. It is of course, about 4,000 feet up here. I started off by visiting the Tomb of Darius the Great. These empire builders certainly knew how to build upon the grand scale. Their tombs even are hewn out of the living rock. To get there, it's necessary to climb up the rock face. I haven't a very good head for heights, but I managed to conceal my trepidation from the Persian guide and got there. Inside it is, of course, disappointing. The Arabs have despoiled the Tomb, the gold coffins have been removed and the bodies have been burnt. Some say - at least the Persians say - that the Arabs are the locusts of the Middle East.

I went on to visit Persepolis itself. The Spring Palace of the Achacmenid Kings. Here it was that they rested during the spring months when all the country round about was green and gay with wild flowers. These kings were proud of their Empire. They were not ashamed of it. The great stone carvings show their thrones supported by men from India, and Assyria, from Egypt and Macedonia. They intended posterity to remember them, and memorials were cut deep, deep in the stones about them. *"I am Darius, the great King, King of Kings, King of many countries, son of Histaspes and Achamenion,"* said Darius, the King by the favour of Oramasda. *"These are the countries which I got into my possession along with this Persian folk which felt fear of me, and bore me tribute. Elam, Medea, Babylonia, Arabia, Assyria, Egypt, Armenia, Capadocia, Sardis, Ionia, who are of the mainland, and those who are by the sea and countries which are across the sea, Sagartia, Parthia, Dragiana, Aria, Bactria, Sobiana, Korasmir, Saggagihdr, Aracosia, Sind, Gandara, Synthians and Makr."* said Darius the King. *"If thus thou shalt think, may I not feel fear of any other. Protect this Persian people. If the Persian people shall be protected thereafter for the longest while, happiness will by Ora come down upon this Royal House."* And so they lived there amid these great halls and courts, and the beauties of the Queen's Palace where I saw what had obviously been a bathroom with a woman carved in stone carrying a towel and a bottle of scent looking rather like the bath essence of a great house today.

Persepolis backs on to the mountain with some tombs above. Its rear is thus protected and in front lies the great plain across which Alexander's armies advanced to its ultimate destruction.

After lunch I took the road westwards across this plain on the great journey which had been taken for centuries to the old Persian city of Shiraz. I slept at the Park Sahib Hotel. Rather a pleasant building built in the modern Persian style which is rather like American Colonial. It has a large pool in front of it with goldfish. I had a talk with a charming young Pakistani who is visiting here, a lawyer educated at Cambridge and the Middle Temple. He said that Pakistan was really ready to welcome military rule after the last Government under which a good deal of graft had taken place. Some of the lawyers were rather worried about the constitutional position, but two constitutional lawyers had been included in Ayub Khan's Government. It does seem that those who organised the Baghdad Pact managed to get some oddly-assorted bedfellows together. Pakistan and Persia are perhaps natural allies connected by race and tradition, but Turkey in this part of the world is regarded traditionally as the enemy of all, and the Arabs as the invaders. Pakistan is cut off from her natural ally, India, but she looks towards India a little enviously. India's policy of neutrality manages to get the best of both worlds, the East and the West. Pakistan would like to get the best of both worlds, too.

Yet though the defection of Iraq has clearly gravely weakened the Pact, there is something to be said for maintaining a northern crust with Turkey, Persia and Pakistan ahead. Behind this front it is just possible that the Arabs might have an opportunity to sort out their problems. This after all was really what Kassim was asking for in Baghdad.

Sunday, 23rd November, at Shiraz.

My Pakistani friend lent me Sachie Sitwell's book about this area, and I read the appropriate chapter. It was pleasant to read his witty and penetrating thoughts about many of the places like Teheran, Isfahan and Persepolis, which I also had visited. I went into the town and had a look at the Museum, which is small, and then the tombs of the two great Persian poets, Sa'adi and Hafiz. They are relatively modern but rather lovely and set in beautiful gardens. At one, one can go down steps to a kind of underground river where the trout rush forward when you throw bread to them, which is amusing. The town itself has the usual wide streets which one sees everywhere in these parts. The Persians are good town planners. All the shops are rather dusty and selling much the same things, headed by Colgate's Toothpaste. The well-dressed man wears pink-striped pyjamas and a striped blue cloth coat, and some kind of a semi-military hat.

I am taking an easy day, sitting in the garden, dictating these notes, watching the pigeons go overhead, enjoying the sunshine and the flowers, in preparation for the hard world of oil and commerce to which I shall return tomorrow as I approach the Gulf.

Monday, 24th November

I flew into Abadan from Shiraz. Travelling with me was an American, Mr Shindler, who is working with one of the American companies on a dam in the Province of Kurdistan. His wife had been ill and she was in hospital at Shiraz. It is, I believe, a first class hospital.

I was met by John Bennett, and we motored off the island of Abadan to his home at Koramshah. After lunch we took his launch up the Shatt-el-Arab River which is really the end of the Euphrates, and saw the Port of Koramshah. There are very considerable delays in this port, ships being held up for as much as thirty days. The reasons are various, but mostly mal-administration of the port. The Arab port workers are paid about 45 reals a day, something under 5/- for an eight-hour shift. But as in fact they can't live on this, most of them are working about seventeen hours a day for 8/-.

Then we turned downstream and went back towards Abadan Island. We saw the place where Cementation Ltd. were building a new bridge. I met Mr Beridge who was running the show and John Bennett says they're a very efficient concern.

The geography of Koramshah is interesting. The Iraqis are on the other side of the river, and the Arabs on both sides intermarry and trade together without very much regard to the Customs. The Iraqis also are immediately around north of the Persians in this area so that the main port of Persia is surrounded by the Iraqis and inhabited mostly by people of Arab birth. There are some 600,000 Arabs in this area and many of them speak no Persian.

At dinner that evening I met the Mayor of Koramshah who admitted the difficulty of the Arab problem. About a third of them are loyal from past association; about a third of them are loyal because of their financial interest, and a third of them are ardent supporters of a quick union with the United Arab Republic. He was troubled by the fact that the standard of living of the Arabs on the Iraqi side was higher than those on the Persian side. I met, too, the Governor of Kurzistan and his Swedish wife. He was rather more cagey about the Arab problem and tended to give me the stock and comforting answers. Also Mr Azari of the National Iranian Oil Company and his daughter. She was educated in England and trained as a nurse and was a niece of the man who ran the hospital in Shiraz. She was anxious to return to continue her training which had been interrupted by polio, and start an eye clinic in Koramshah.

Tuesday, 25ᵗʰ November

I got up early and saw the sun rising over the Shatt-El-Arab, which is very nearly as beautiful as the sunset. At 8.30 we were with Mr Koo who is the General Manager of the Consortium. He is a competent American and probably an expert on the technical side. I also saw the Persian Manager in charge of personnel, and we talked a fair amount about the problems of the Consortium in relation to the local Persian population.

The Consortium is well run and competent. It is putting £75 millions into the hands of the Persian Government. The relations between the Shah and the Government are good. The Consortium is run by a Dutchman from Indonesia whom I did not meet and who lives in Teheran. Nevertheless the Consortium faces some difficult political problems. It is running now at only 70% of capacity, and on this there is considerable criticism from the Persian side. There may be good reasons for them, but I don't know what they are. Apparently there is objection from the constituent members of the Consortium to running it at a higher rate. The degree of integration with the local population is not very great. No Persian, I understand, has been recruited from the universities of Persia for the past five years. The stores are bought almost exclusively from abroad rather than by local agents through the Bazaar. The contrast between the wealth of the Consortium and the poverty in the localities about it was considerable and obvious.

I carry away three problems with regard to my visit to Abadan. On the side of the Consortium there is the question of the run-through of oil and whether one can accept a 70% run through for very long, or rather whether the Persians will accept it. Secondly, whether the Consortium is really integrated sufficiently with the local population. And on this I may be able to judge better when I see what is happening at Kuwait and Bahrain. And thirdly with regard to the working of the Port and the delays there. John Bennett emphasised the importance of the International Bank insisting upon a proper administration before they extended loan assistance.

At 1 o'clock I took the plane for Kuwait. As a matter of fact I very nearly missed it and in fact it started five minutes early. I arrived at Kuwait, had lunch with the Halfords and a little rest. Then motored to the headquarters of the oil company, twenty five miles away, where I saw Mr Jordan, the Texan Manager. He is a competent, quiet, capable man. The oil company here integrates its purchasing arrangements more closely with the local population. Kuwait is full of money and big motor cars, and really is an enormous welfare state, with large parts of the oil revenue concentrated on a relatively small population. But it's a feudal state, run by the Sheikh and his family who hold all the Ministries. Relations between the Government and the people with the oil company are probably good and sounder than in Abadan. Nevertheless, it presents a picture of the sort of problem we are up against in the Gulf, with a feudal family running on autocratic lines, a population which is listening more and more to Nasser and Radio Cairo for its political information.

Dined at the Embassy with friends including a Dr Parry who has done a great job in that area, and took a relatively early bed.

Wednesday, 26ᵗʰ November

I boarded the Britannia for Bahrain. Bahrain, and you can see it immediately from the air, is a greener country than Kuwait. It is also relatively a poorer one. The oil income is not so great. Stayed with the Gorts. They have a modern, comfortable house by the sea with a pleasant garden. After lunch I walked round the Bazaar with the Commercial Officer. Crowded with people, the women wearing the face masks which I had not previously seen in the Middle East, and all of them more closely shrouded than in other places I had been to. The merchants in the Bazaar seem satisfied with the purchasing arrangements of the oil company and feel that they have a stake in its success.

Thursday, 27ᵗʰ November

I spent the morning with the oil company. They are an American company with mainly British employees. I saw their Training College where they are training young Bahrainis up and giving them a general education including Algebra to what seemed to me to be quite a high standard to administer to storekeepers. Training them in the practical work as well. Many of these young men go to the oil company afterwards, but others go to other posts in the Middle East. The public relations of the oil company here seem to be stronger, in part they are in paper, but in a large part they exist in the fact that the purchasing is done very largely through local sources and local agents, and not only big ones at that.

30. Thorneycroft talking to an apprentice at the Training Centre of Bahrain Petroleum

27th November 1958

In the evening I had a talk with three young Arabs. I might really have been talking to three Young Conservatives at home. They were young and intelligent and could see, or at any rate claimed that they could see both sides of an argument. They were certainly frustrated. They were troubled about a system in which the Government was very largely feudal. With regard to the administration of justice, they pointed out to me that it was in the hands of a man who could neither read nor write. These are not very easy arguments to answer. Indeed, these three young Arabs pinpoint the political problems of the Gulf, where we are committed one way or another to supporting Sheikhs on feudal systems, not very anxious to change, with all the Ministries in the hands of themselves or their families. At the moment our policy seems to be to edge them a very little bit at a time, very, very slowly along the road to a more liberal policy.

Friday, 28th November

I took the Britannia and flew to Karachi where I'm staying with the High Commissioner, Alec Symon. The atmosphere in Karachi is very British. You see the British influence everywhere, the police smartly dressed, wearing their scarlet head-dresses. In the evening I attended a reception at the Yugoslav Embassy. It was the Yugoslav National Day. The reception was held in the gardens, gaily decorated with lights, and it gave me an opportunity of meeting quite a number of the leading personalities. I had a talk with the Minister of Communications. Odd though it may be, the railways are one of the few things that are paying here. I also talked with the Secretary of the Cabinet. Later I went on and dined with Sir Walter Cawthorne and his wife. He is the dean of the Diplomatic Corps here. I sat next to Mr Zulficar Buto, the Minister of Commerce, and after dinner we talked a little of the main problems of Pakistan. The most urgent one appears to be the problem of the canal waters. I understand the position is that India has now got to a position where by turning a key she can switch the waters of the Punjab to her own uses and deprive Pakistan of this particular form of irrigation. The damage to Pakistan in these circumstances appears to be considerable but I am arranging to have a talk next day or so with someone who can inform me on the facts and figures. I also met Mr Condon, the Managing Director of the Pak-Petroleum Ltd. And his Austrian wife who is a cousin of Poupe Weikersheim, and they asked me to go along on Sunday to the beach with them.

Saturday, 29th November

I saw the Minister of Finance this morning, Mr Shaeb. He used to be in the International Bank and I met him there when I was in Washington. He is an intelligent, nervous, highly-strung man. In fact, he has every reason to be nervous. Pakistan is in the throes of a very considerable inflation. The problems and the arguments are not unfamiliar to me. Here, as elsewhere, the Government appears ready enough to deal or attempt to deal with the effects of the inflation, but somewhat nervous abut dealing with its causes. The Minister of Finance told me of his difficulties in cutting Government expenditure. Defence was more or less inviolate, though a little might be done by amalgamating Services. In the general field of public expenditure, commitments had been made far ahead, and it was difficult to cut these, and yet unless something was stopped it looked as if the inflation would go on. All this was familiar ground. The Pakistanis have introduced considerable rigidity of price control, and the Minister of Finance made it plain to me that while he recognised that some of it was necessary for the time being, the object should be to remove it as far as possible. It was doing almost as much harm as good.

He spoke, too, of the problem of remitting capital and income out of Pakistan. A number of British residents are complaining that if they amass more than £5,000 that is the limit that they can repatriate. The rest must be frozen here. Others who are earning reasonable incomes and have been remitting half of them home for their children's education, have now been told that this must be limited to 25%.

Mr Shaeb said that he was looking at these matters and contemplating whether a more flexible arrangement similar to Exchange Control which we have in England could not be adopted. The difficulty here is, he frankly told me, that they lack the necessary staff to administer Exchange Control on a discriminatory basis, but he is seeking to work along these lines.

I asked him about Bank Rate and was astonished to hear that here in Pakistan in the middle of an inflation it was as low as 3%. This is an obvious field in which he must tighten up if he is to get a grip of the situation.

Afterwards I drove round in the warm sunshine in Karachi and looked at the shops which are bright and modern and full of all the up-to-date appliances of modern civilisation. On the other hand I went and tried to get another spool for my Minifon and was told that they were out as Import Control was hitting hard at imports of this character. By contrast when I went to buy a pair of bathing pants and they hadn't got a size to fit me, they promptly said they would make them in two or three hours. Rather different from the attitude of the shopkeepers in England.

I had tea with Mr Quadir, the Minister for Foreign Affairs. He is intelligent and lucid, and in private life has been a constitutional lawyer. He talked to me at length about the problems of Kashmir and the Canal waters. I formed the clear opinion that a solution of the Canal waters problem was the most urgent of these problems. The attitude of Pakistan on this matter is that unless a satisfactory solution is reached, large parts of the country will go out of production. They have a difference with the Indians on this matter and on what ought to be done. For their part, they are quite prepared to accept the arbitration of a third party, either the International Bank or the Court of International Justice. Discussions on this subject start in Washington in the first week of December. It is hoped that a solution will be found, but the Indians according to the Pakistanis have so far proved intractable, and they are the people in possession of the head waters.

At seven o'clock I went along to see the President, Ayub Khan. He was sitting in the garden of his house, relaxed; he had just returned from the beach. We talked together for about half an hour. The revolution here is rather like a revolution conducted by the Commandant of Sandhurst on the landed gentry. He shoots with the land owners in the neighbourhood and yet has the responsibility of inflicting upon them a very radical land reform plan. He regards it, probably rightly, as essential. He knows he could never get it through any Parliamentary system. Opinions differ as to Ayub Khan's real power. Some say he is much under the influence of some of the young officers and has to toe the line according to their wishes. But he is a man of some presence. He was educated at Sandhurst and one might well have been sitting talking to any intelligent British officer. After we had talked a bit about my trip through Iraq, he showed great interest naturally in what was happening to General Kassim and also talked about some of the more urgent problems of Pakistan such as the Canal waters, and he referred to the wider problems of the East. He developed at some length the theme that the main problem of the East was too much population. If there were 60 million instead of 80 million in the country, it would be easier to run, and they were increasing at a very great pace.

I asked him if there were any religious or any other difficulties about family planning, or at any rate the advocacy of family planning, and he thought not. He was anxious to develop the education of the people and to instil into them the courses which in his view would lead to the greatest prosperity.

Later I went on to dine with the Leslies. He runs the Burma Oil Company in Karachi. The President came in, and we dined at separate tables, and I was at the table with the President and Mrs Leslie and others. We talked happily about shooting and other forms of sport. There are various stories and accounts current of the struggle between Ayub and Vinza but I don't think anybody really knows the truth. Clearly Ayub in the last resort had the majority support of the Army and certainly he's in charge today. The new dispensation appears, at any rate as viewed from Karachi, to be favoured by the people. It is significant that here as in the Sudan, the revolution appears to have gone over very peaceably. And here at any rate they have been at pains to keep the whole of their Civil Service so that they have a machine with which to govern.

Afterwards we went on to the Caledonian Ball and watched them dancing eightsome reels. The Scots are a hardy race and pursue their national customs including the haggis which we ate and the salmon which arrived from Japan, and the athelbrose which we drank after dinner. They will pursue these customs in any temperature.

Sunday, 30ᵗʰ November

A day of rest and I made it so. I went along with Mrs Condon - she is a cousin of Poupe Weikershim - and he runs the Pakistan Petroleum Company here, and I went with her and Mrs Drew and Mrs Dunn to the beach. It is a lovely one and about half an hour from Karachi. We bathed there, had lunch in a little hut, and laid down and had a siesta in the sun. Very peaceful and very restful.

When I came back I went along to the Minister of Commerce, and his wife. We had a further talk abut the problems of Pakistan, went over again some of the ground of the Canal waters. I asked him about his policies for Pakistan industry and whether he was being compelled to cut back in order to deal with the inflation. He said they were cutting back on some of the major schemes, but he himself was anxious to develop village and local industries. He had invited a Japanese team over to advise him on this particular aspect of commercial policy.

After tea with him and his wife, Lady Symon came and picked me up and took me along to the St Andrew's Day Service in the English Church here. Afterwards we dined at the Embassy.

It is not easy to judge Pakistan from a few days in Karachi. Like any other capital city, it possesses the intelligence of the sophisticated, international world. One impression that hits one here is the extent of the British influence. The smart, soldierly bearing of the police, the fact that the civil servants talk almost precisely the same as civil servants would in Whitehall, the attitude of mind to most subjects and the sense of humour are essentially British in their outlook. The Pakistanis I met have no doubt where they stood in foreign policy. Their attitude was that you had to make up your mind which side you were on and stick to your friends. It's difficult to resist these sentiments. At the same time, I suspect there may be a feeling underneath that India is gaining considerable advantages from a policy of neutrality, and there must be quite a lot of Pakistanis who would wish to see her gain the same advantages for herself.

Under partition Pakistan probably had the worst end of the deal. She got the fewest of the civil servants. With the Canal waters problem she is threatened with more difficulties with regard to her food supply. On top of this she has, or course, an enormous refugee problem, and among those refugees poverty is considerable. The policy they want to pursue is to develop their agricultural production, the only way of absorbing refugees on the scale which is now desirable; to hold back a little on the capital development in industry and to try and balance their Budget. But here the constant drain of defence expenditure on what they regard as the threat from India is likely to prove a difficult obstacle.

I had a final talk with the High Commissioner in preparation for my visit on to Delhi. There is in Pakistan eyes no doubt that India is conducting a considerable press campaign against her at the present time based on the fact that she is a republic-dictatorship and the theme that the resources of the world ought today to be concentrated on the last surviving example of democracy in India.

I look forward to my arrival in Delhi this afternoon.

Monday, 1ˢᵗ December

I flew from Karachi to Delhi in an Indian Airways Dakota which took five hours and its heating arrangements were strange. It was either ventilated by very hot air or very cold and we alternatively perspired and shivered. But it got there. We flew mainly over that great desert which really seems to stretch from Morocco along the north coast of Africa, through the Middle East as far as Delhi. When I arrived, I went along to the Embassy and stayed with Malcolm MacDonald and his wife, and Grantham from Hong Kong who has now got oil interests was staying there, too.

We discussed my programme in Delhi and some good arrangements seem to have been made for me while I am here. We also discussed what I had better do on my journey further East. He strongly supported the idea that I should spend a few days in Bali with James Pandy from whom, incidentally, I got a letter confirming the booking of my room when I arrived here. My present plan has been slightly altered inasmuch as I am going to fly to Colombo, if possible not through Karachi. I shall try and do it through either Bombay or Madras. Leave Colombo two days early and go straight through Singapore to spend a couple of nights in Kuala Lumpur. Then return to Singapore, spend two nights there and then go on to Djakarta.

Malcolm also spoke to me about the Canal Waters problem from the Indian angle. I shall discuss this further with Minister and permanent officials here. But from what he says it looks as though it may be settled. If it was settled, it would certainly get out of the way one of the main points of difference between India and Pakistan at the present time. I am also arranging to have an analysis of the Indian financial position prepared for me on a sheet of paper before I see Desai.

Tuesday, 2ⁿᵈ December

In the morning I went with Sir Alexander Grantham and did a rather lightning tour of Delhi with a young Indian who was a friend of his and had set up one of the first travel agencies in the city. It is a modern city, large, spacious, tree-lined, shady. Today it was flooded with sunshine. We passed the great houses; the Viceroy's house in which the President now lives, the great forts, the ruins of the old city on which the new Delhi has been built. We saw new temples built on the ruins of the old. The rebuilding here is on a vast scale, and Nehru will probably go down to history amongst other things for having built as much as any Viceroy of India.

We returned to the Residence before lunch and I strolled a little in the shady garden and the pleasant terraces. It is a very beautiful place though, not of course upon the scale of the old Viceroy's Residence. We went on to have lunch with Mr Nehru and Malcolm MacDonald, Sir Alexander Grantham and myself. He lives quite close to here in a long, low-built white house now covered with the bougainvillia. At this time of year in the Indian winter, it is possible to grow the English summer flowers, and they were growing them there. The lawns were green and carefully mown, and scarlet umbrellas were being put up in preparation for some lunch tomorrow.

Nehru himself seemed a little preoccupied when we first met him. He was as charming and courteous as ever. I daresay he has enough on his mind. He spoke during lunch of various things, including the Congress Party. The Opposition, he said, consisted mainly of Independents who sometimes worked together against the Government. The Communists were, of course, the most highly organised Opposition group. The situation differed from that in England. India was run on the basis of a federal government. As to the future he did not contemplate the Congress Party splitting. Some think it will divide; some even think that it would be wiser if it divided, if it could be done, into a Right and Left Group rather on the English model. But for his part, he saw it going on, at any rate for fifteen years. He plainly thought that it would see him out.

We spoke of Pakistan, and I told him of my meeting with Ayub and their preoccupation with the Canal Waters. He said that the discussion on the Canal Waters had now been going on for seven years. Happily it had now got down to the more practical details of how much money, and what type of engineering works and where, and he felt that practical details of that kind were perhaps easier to settle than the emotional ones. He made

146

the point, of course, that in India's view Pakistan was asking for too much, that if what she had wanted in her plan went through, it would have contemplated really the development of the whole of Pakistan. I had the impression, however, that a settlement of the Canal Waters problem was not impossible.

After lunch we went down with Nehru into the garden and he showed us the small pandas which he had as pets and which had to spend a good deal of their time up in the hills as they cannot stand the hot sun of the Delhi summer, and he fed them on dates. Afterwards we strolled beneath the shady trees and later returned back to the Residence.

In the afternoon I had a talk with Manubai Shah, the Minister of Industry. We met in his Ministry. He talked with fluency about India's industrial problems and the need for investment from the West. According to him the Indians adopted a pragmatic approach to Socialism. They had a public and a private sector, but their feeling was that advances in the public sector should be made entirely on their own merits. They didn't agree with the Gaitskell approach of an equity holding in the private sector. If they were going to own something they would like to control it.

In the evening I dined at the Embassy with Mr Roi, the Secretary to the Ministry of Finance, and with Mr Rangernathan, the Secretary to the Ministry of Commerce and Industry. We talked, as was inevitable, a bit about India's financial problems. Though on paper at least they seem to have got the situation rather more under control than it used to be. Then we had a wider conversation about the problems of India in general, and in particular the caste system on which they both spoke with great interest. Nehru had said that the caste system was declining in the social world but increasing in the political one. But from what these two officials said, the caste system was still heavily engrained in the Indian social arrangements. Nobody really married outside their caste or at most a bare 5%. Girls were still married under arrangements between the parents. One of these officials' daughter was married the other day and she had never seen her bridegroom until just before the wedding. Until a recent Act divorce was not allowed and even now was only allowed for new marriages taking place after the Act came into force. Women did not dance in public, nor indeed for that matter, in private. One of these officials was a Brahmin and the other not, but they said that caste was not a matter of one cast despising another. It was just something that was closely integrated into the Indian social life. It had weakened perhaps a little over the last thirty years. Thirty years ago if there was a wedding, the Brahmins were asked and came, but they sat down to food first, the others afterwards. Today, at any rate in Bengal, they tend to sit down together. Thirty years ago for that matter these two officials would not have been eating together at the same table.

From what they said, however, it looks as though the caste system was here to stay for a very long time. Nehru himself is perhaps its principal antagonist, and it is interesting to contemplate what may happen when he goes. It looks as though the caste system will go on strongly in Indian life for many years to come.

We talked, too, a little about India and Pakistan. The basis for reasonable arrangements between them is certainly to be found in the fact that most of the civil servants - particularly those in the old I.C.S. - know each other very well.

Wednesday, 3rd December

I rose early and went along to see Mr Desai at his house, for an appointment at 8.30 in the morning. He's an interesting man, a fine austere face. He's not unlike Mr Nehru to look at, a quiet penetrating and reflective mind. I talked with him a little about Indian relations with Pakistan. He said that Ayub had the reputation of being a fanatic and pleasure-seeking. The tragedy of Pakistan, he said, - and this might be said, too, of India - is that it was created out of hatred. Yet he thought that the Pakistani Revolution was inevitable. If Pakistan was prepared to accept a scheme for the Canal Waters, put up by the Bank, as far as he's concerned it looks as though that might provide a solution. We talked, too, about the Congress Party. It was in his view unfortunate that the Congress Party was the only democratic organised Party in the field. Yet if it had divided and split into two camps, these two political groups or parties would have been bidding against each other for political support and more harm might have been done to India.

His Five Year Plan would emphasise agriculture, but agriculture was not enough to raise the standard of Indian life from the very low level at which it was today. To raise that standard, it was necessary to have some industrial development. He said that the population problem was a great problem for all Asian countries, yet in the case of China when they had at one time talked of the need to limit it, they were now according to him advocating a larger birth rate. He did not think that the growth in population necessarily involved great difficulties with regard to the standard of life. If the new population could be harnessed to industrial production, if the producers could produce something more than their own immediate needs, the Western industrialised countries had started a bit ahead, they had so to speak got over the hump; if only India could get over the hump, too, the thing might run more smoothly.

He had met Enoch in London. He hadn't been able to see me as I was away at the time. He talked reflectively about life and office and emphasised that office was not the only thing to seek for. He thought that the Communist strength in India was considerable though not, of course, at the present time overwhelming. At the present time they held Kerala. It was in his view perhaps rather a good thing that they did as people could judge them not only by their words but now by their deeds. Democracy in his view was in any event something which should be sought for, for itself because it was good and not simply for the material rewards which it could bring.

Mr Desai is much spoken of here as a possible successor to Mr Nehru as Prime Minister. He is a mystic but he is a formidable, and in many ways, an admirable figure. He is likely to play a large part not only in Indian but in world affairs.

After a tour of the Old City, I returned to lunch at the Residence, with Malcolm, with Mr Pilai and with various other officials including Matai, the Secretary to the Prime Minister.

They asked me a great deal about what I thought of my visit to Pakistan, but they were extremely interested to hear what Ayub had said and in particular what Mr Quadir, the Foreign Minister of Pakistan, was thinking. Both Malcolm and I emphasised that there was an opportunity perhaps of reaching a settlement of the Canal Waters at the present time, and if it was taken, then the other difficulties might fall more easily into place. I think they were impressed by what we had to say, and I left feeling that perhaps things were nearer to a settlement than might have been thought a little time ago.

In the evening there was a cocktail party mainly for Harper's Bazaar who are over here doing a feature. They are going over to Agra to photograph where I shall meet them tomorrow evening.

Thursday, 4th December

I said goodbye to Malcolm MacDonald and his wife and took the road to Agra. It was a delightful journey through the Indian villages and the large expanses of water. Indeed, at one place the road was flooded and we had to make a detour through the fields. Indian roads are always full of incident. Brightly coloured birds, vultures, and every kind of life. Temples, camels, potters working at their wheels which they have used, or similar wheels, for centuries. We stopped for lunch at Secunda, the tomb of Akbar, and I walked through the great main gate across the lawns to the mosque, and had a look round it in the hot sunshine before having lunch under the shade of the trees. After lunch I went on to Lawrie's Hotel which is a long, low, rather pleasant building where I had a bit of a rest until half past three.

I then took the car, and motored along to the Taj Mahal. I stayed watching it until the light faded at about five o'clock. It's not possible to describe in words, or not possible for me to describe in words, that building, except to say that it is one of the buildings in the world that more than lives up to one's expectations. I left it and its gardens rather regretfully as the sun was setting and the light fading altogether. Alas, there was no moon so I was unable to see it as it should, I believe, be seen by moonlight, and I went back to Lawrie's Hotel where we had rather a European-type dinner, and afterwards we had a drink from the Residence's bottle of whisky with Harper's Bazaar and talked about the problems of French politics. The French team were filming over here.

Friday, 5th December

I took the car together with a Mr Bambani, the representative of Indian Airways, who has been most helpful to me during my stay in Agra, and we went over to the deserted city of Sikri. Built by Akbar, it was only inhabited for about fourteen years during his lifetime and abandoned shortly after his death, I understand principally because the water supply then ran out. It is a vast city, built of red sandstone, somewhat Chinese in form with the palaces for his various wives, some Hindu, some Muslim. It was his purpose to produce - and indeed, he did draw up - a universal religion, but it didn't last for very long. In one of the courtyards is a kind of chequer board where something like a game of chess used to be played, only using dancing girls instead of players. Where he used to have his afternoon siesta is an early example of air conditioning, he lying on a cool platform high up while the floor of the room was flooded with water from the neighbouring wells.

I had lunch with Mr Bambani at the Imperial Hotel, and incidentally had a very good and very hot curry, and then returned to Lawrie's Hotel for a siesta.

Later in the afternoon I toured again with Mr Bambani, and in the evening caught the night flight from Agra to Delhi. It was a bit late arriving; it had been delayed at Benares, and we had something of an adventure on the way home as one of the engines stopped twenty-five miles out of Delhi and the second engine faded out as soon as we throttled back to come in to land. However, we landed quite all right; and stayed rather helplessly on the far side of the airport and were towed ignominiously in. It meant that I was a bit late for dinner, with the British business men. Malcolm MacDonald had arranged for me to act as host to them. They seemed in good heart, and it was quite a cheerful dinner, and they all knew each other very well. India was a risk but it was a risk not to be in India at all.

Saturday, 6th December

I started early and caught the 7.30 plane to Bombay. There had been a slip in arrangements and Bombay, I found, hadn't been informed, but I arranged for them to be telephoned while I was in the course of my journey, and this they did.

On arrival at Bombay, however, the plane was a little early and there was no one to meet me, so I found an Indian friend who gave me a lift in. We motored along with him, with the wife of the last Governor of the Reserve Bank, and stopped for coffee at the Willingdon Club, a lovely shaded building, and we sat happily on the terrace there, and talked while I telephoned the High Commissioner. Mr Bailis of the Board of Trade is in fact here and the High Commissioner is in Poona at the moment.

Mr Challenjiva who works for Burma Oil and who was my Indian companion, took me along also to see the Sports Stadium, which corresponds rather to our M.C.C. Bombay is an impressive city with a vast bay as you approach it, with lovely green trees, beautiful buildings; it looks like any great, modern European capital.

I met Bailis at the Taj Hotel where I am staying, and after we had chatted a bit, we went along to see Mr Iengar the present Governor of the Reserve Bank. He is an intelligent and capable man. We met in the Reserve Bank and we talked for a time of politics. We referred to China and he pointed to the performance which they were putting up there and the political impact which it would certainly have upon India. In India it is not easy to have the sort of commune arrangements which they are at present practising in China, or to some extent for that matter, practise on a voluntary basis in Israel. The divisions within a village, their meal habits, the caste system and many other factors operate against it. Instead, Nehru was swinging to the opposite extreme to the Chinese. Whereas the Chinese were basing their policy on community life, in which perhaps 8000 or even 80,000 men were gathered together in a commune, Nehru was laying the emphasis on the individual, the responsibility of the villages, and of the people who lived in them to get on with the job for themselves.

This led on to a talk about the Third Plan. Iengar emphasised much more strongly than anyone in Delhi had that the emphasis of the Third Plan would be in line with this political thought. It would concentrate upon agriculture and the smaller unit. They in any event wouldn't be able to afford a large number of big new schemes; they would finish up those they had done, and then they would concentrate on the smaller units with particular emphasis on bringing water, irrigation or machinery to the village. It was, of course, a stage of planning which would make even greater administrative demands.

Progress was painfully slow in India, but it was taking place. He didn't spend all his time in the air-conditioned office in which we were sitting, he travelled far and wide. So far as he could see, the standard of living of the ordinary Indian was gradually creeping forward.

I went back to the Taj for lunch and in the afternoon went with Brook Bradley of the Commonwealth Relations Office in a launch over to Elephant Island on the other side of the Bay. It's famous for its rock carvings; they have, alas, been badly damaged. It's a pity that the antipathy which the Christians and the Muslims feel for graven images has made them smash up so much lovely carving in these parts of the world. The least damaged of these carvings is a huge triple-headed head of Shiva, executed with immense power and skill, moving in its dignity. It's odd that they did not smash this, yet perhaps any man who contemplated it would hesitate to smash it up.

The Island itself is rather a paradisal place. The local fishermen who live there earn their living with fishing and a little primitive agriculture which is being encouraged from Bombay. The heat of Bombay is tempered here with a pleasant breeze and no new building is allowed on the Island.

Afterwards we took the launch back and came in across the water to Bombay with the sun setting on the buildings making it look not unlike Venice as one comes in from the lagoon. As we edged in to the landing place, the Gate of India, huge Arab dhows sailed past us as they had been sailing in these waters for a thousand years or more.

After a bath and change, I went to have a drink with Bailis of the Board of Trade and a few English friends and then went on to dine with Iengar and his wife and a delegation from the International Monetary Fund. They have a charming, official home set in a garden, and we dined on the terraces. I talked afterwards with Mrs Iengar and Mrs Pundit's daughter. I ate a curry and even sought to eat, and in fact succeeded in eating some betel nut. It was a delightful evening.

I rose at 5.30 on Sunday, the 7th December and went in to the airport just as the dawn was breaking. The Bombay population was moving into work, the men in white, the women in their saris, looking in the half light as though they had come back from some great ball, and as we got to the airport, the sun was just rising. Many people in Bombay sleep out all night as there is a shortage of accommodation in this over-crowded island, and rather than sleep many to a room, the open air for much of the year is the best place.

We were airborne at 7.30 and stopped at Madras for 40 minutes. Madras was in the throes of the monsoon, hot and wet and at intervals raining. Then we were airborne again and flying over the Indian Ocean, moving in towards Ceylon, away from the coast of India and over seas studied with fishermen's boats and many curious shaped islands.

Ceylon itself looked green and lush as we flew in. I noticed that over the harbour a number of boats were standing off and I believe that there is a considerable delay in this port. When I landed at Colombo, it was hot - the hottest weather I had met so far - and I motored in to the Residence, constructed on modern lines by the Ministry of Works, and was greeted by Mr Morley, the High Commissioner. His wife is away at the present time.

After lunch and a siesta I went on to a carol service at a local Christian school. The lights had all failed when we went in. The boys sang in clear, treble voices 'When the snow lay round about, deep and crisp and even, Brightly shone the moon that night, though the frost was cruel'. And meanwhile, of course, we all drooped, Europeans and Cingalese alike. The temperature was somewhere near a 100. At intervals the light failed and they brought in candles in coloured shades. It was spectacular and really rather lovely, but increased somewhat the heat.

Back to the Residence for a much needed bath and change. A pleasant dinner with various friends from the British community and one or two Cingalese including the Rev. Lakdasademel, an intelligent Roman Catholic priest, and a friend of Elizabeth's. I gave him Elizabeth's address so that he can write. We discussed some of the problems of Ceylon, its 6 million Cingalese and 2 million Tamils and the resultant communal problem. It's a small island and everybody knows what everybody else is doing. The private lives of Ministers are freely commented upon; the Ministers themselves a little lax in the doctrines of Cabinet responsibility and criticise each other fairly freely in public.

Monday, 8th December

I went along and saw the Governor-General at 9.45. He lives in a lovely Dutch house and we sat upstairs in a big drawing room with the fans making a much-needed breath of air. We talked for an hour about my tour, about the problems of Asia, and he invited me to come and stay with him in Government House when I made my visit to Kandy. Later I went on and saw De Zoysa, the Minister of Finance whom, of course, I had met before in Washington. He told me of the difficulties of Cabinet Government here and the attacks which they launched upon each other. It was clearly his view that the sooner the Marxist side of the Cabinet was dropped, the better. We talked, too, a bit about the expenditure tax, and I urged upon him the caution with which the Labour Party at home were approaching a problem of this kind. He said that in effect people had rather got hold of the wrong end of the stick. His desire had been to lower the direct taxation further, but he had failed to secure the approval of his colleagues in the Cabinet, and he was prepared to make some adjustment in the tax proposals that he had outlined. Kaldor is expected here later this month.

Finally, at noon, I went along and had a talk with the Prime Minister, Mr Bandaranaike. He launched into the question of constitutional reform. He pointed to the fact that democracies had been somewhat on the way out in Asia, as indeed I knew from the area over which I had travelled. He thought that the fault lay not in the idea of democracy itself but in the organisation which was designed to put it into effect. Here in Ceylon it might be better if they had a system of representative committee, like the London County Council, as indeed they had when they were working the Donoughmore Report upon the constitution of Ceylon. In any event, he's Chairman of the constitutional committee which has been set up to study these matters, and I think he clearly has it in his mind to try and achieve some form of constitutional reform before Ceylon again goes to the polls. I think he may well find it difficult to get agreement of the other parties to these particular proposals.

Afterwards, he came on to lunch at the Residence with De Zoysa and a number of other officials and Ministers, and we talked of various matters. In particular, I had a talk with Mr Perera, the Leader of the Opposition, who is a Trotskyist and who officially or whose Party believes in leading Ceylon out of the Commonwealth, though I think he rather wistfully hopes that it may still stay in the sterling area. We talked of many subjects including the possibility of closer co-operation in South East Asia, between Pakistan, India, Ceylon, Burma and Malaya. Such co-operation might take the form of a common market, a free trade area, but some closer integration of economic effort was thought by many of them to be desirable. So far it had tended to break down always on Pakistan/Indian jealousies.

I took the afternoon off, sitting in a thin silk shirt and a pair of shorts in the garden, writing a few letters, enjoying myself watching the various birds which are gaily-coloured and rather fun, playing about me. And in the intervals I prepared a few notes for a talk I am giving to the European Association here at seven o'clock this evening.

I spoke to the European Association about my tour and afterwards they asked me a number of questions. It seems to me that they are bothered not so much about what the Government of Ceylon are doing at the present moment but about the uncertainty as to what they might do next. They're not alone in this.

I dined later at the Residence with Leslie Rowan's brother, and with others. There was a great deal of criticism of the Government. It was felt by Rowan that if we were to give Ceylon self-government, we ought to have started earlier to make them responsible. Instead we flung it at them before they were really ready or had the administration or the experience to undertake it. There is in all the quarters I have met so far very considerable criticism of the Government.

Tuesday, 9th December

I flew to Jaffna which is the Tamil country on the north western tongue of Ceylon. I went there with Sherman, the Security Officer, of the High Commission Office. As we flew over it I saw it again as I had seen it flying south from India. A green, lush country looking very lovely in what is called 'the rainy season'.

We were met at the airport by the Government representative and went round to see the cement works. Both Sherman and I had been a bit bothered as to how we would stand up to it in the temperature, but in the north of the island while it is probably just as hot as in Colombo, the air seems dryer and we seemed to manage even the hot bits of the cement works without any actual collapse. After our tour we went on to the Rest House with the Government Representative, had some excellent cold beer, some lunch, and a much-needed siesta.

In the afternoon we went on to see a big girls' school in the area. I was quite unprepared for the welcome. They gave us the full honours. I was garlanded with flowers and all the other appurtenances of a Hindu welcome. Then they danced for us. Very lovely the dancing was. First three girls dancing some classic dance and scattering flowers, and then three smaller ones doing the first movement of the classical dances with little movements of the head and arms. After that there was a gypsy dance which was supposed to describe the mountains and the valleys of the country in which she lived, and finally a girl who did one of the classic Hindu dances, reproduced in all the monuments throughout the country. Such dancing is really unlike anything that we see in the West. But it is striking in its discipline and its grace, and underlying it is a hint of the erotic which is never far separated from Hindu mysticism. It's only in very recent years really that dancing has become respectable for girls of good family. It is now a regular part of the curriculum in this school, and they also teach them not only academic studies but cooking and embroidery.

Then we went on and took a look at a very holy Hindu temple in Jaffna, and finally, to an old Dutch fort erected with the solid seriousness of the Dutch, very massive with a beautiful Dutch church in the middle and the tombs of many of the Dutchmen who lived there at the time. And then on to tea at the Government Representative's Residence which was incidentally built by a British civil servant out of his own funds many years ago. Standing in the midst of a beautiful park full of old trees, and there we met many of the local representatives and dignitaries including the Mayor and Judge who was on Circuit, and the Bishop of a local Protestant Church.

Finally, in the dusk we motored along with the Rev. Bunker and his wife, who was head of the American Mission here and with whom we are staying for the evening.

We had an informal supper with the teachers of the Mission where 1,700 students are trained, and I was prevailed upon to say a few words, so repeated more or less what I had said to the European Association the night before. The people here were very well informed about events in England. They knew all about Mr Harold Macmillan and what he was doing, and about my resignation, and asked me many interesting and intelligent questions about these topics.

I gained a number of impressions during the day in conversations that I had. The caste system is still strong; the system, however, of child marriage has gone, and widows do sometimes now remarry. The feeling between the Tamils and the Cingalese is still strong. Sherman tells me that in Colombo, for example, it is by no means easy to ask them to dinner together. During the recent communal strife a number of brutal murders took place, particularly in the south, at least one Hindu priest was burnt outside his temple, and in the north one of the Cingalese temples was ransacked, and the image desecrated. The general view here was that the politicians had not helped by playing up this particular form of communal strife. Everybody I spoke to deplored the weakness of the Government, though it doesn't seem to be the machinery of government that is at fault but rather the men. It's not a lack of brains because there are plenty of brains about, but rather lack of character, restraint and courage.

My final thought after a rather long, hot day is that we couldn't have had a kinder welcome in Jaffna and it was one which I much appreciated.

Wednesday, 10th December

We left the Bunkers at 8.15 and motored along the road to Kandy. We stopped once or twice on the way to see some of the local developments that were taking place and the efforts that were being made to settle the population of Jaffna in the jungle districts that surrounded it. It was a road through the jungle that we took with tall palm trees on either side and thick, dense undergrowth and bright flowers.

Our first main stop was at Anuradapura, which is one of the big jungle cities of Ceylon, dating back a thousand five hundred years or more. It has the remains of a vast city there; its temples and its streets and its houses and its monuments to the Hindu religion. Little of it has so far been excavated, but if it was excavated to the full, a remarkable spectacle would probably be revealed.

We went on from there for about another fifty miles to a place called Sigria, which is an enormous rock standing up amidst the surrounding jungle. On the top of it a palace has at one time been erected. We did not climb fully up to the palace, but we climbed about half way up and looked at some interesting frescoes on the rock. Round about this rock pleasure gardens had been designed and a surrounding moat, and a King of Ceylon had at one time established his headquarters there, and held out against invasion for a long time until he made the mistake of going out and fighting the armies in the plain. And so on to the King's Pavilion in Kandy, to which the Governor General had very kindly invited us. We dined there together and talked of the problems of Ceylon and the recent crisis of which he said that it did appear that every event that had started had been started by someone outside that particular area. Some master mind had been behind these things though it was difficult to identify which.

Thursday, 11th December

I got up and walked out into the sunshine and visited the Temple of the Tooth in Kandy. We walked up to the Sanctuary and saw all the worshippers coming in with their offerings of flowers. After that we went to the Botanical Gardens which has a wonderful display of orchids and of trees.

Lastly, we went to the University of Kandy which is laid out so that every student can live in it. There is a good deal of concern here as to what the official language is to be. Many of the professors there are anxious that English should be retained.

After lunch at Government House I went up to stay with Mr and Mrs Webber of the Fordyce Estate, near Dekoya. It started to rain during lunch and was pelting down as I drove up, climbing all the way first of all through the rubber-growing area in the foothills and then into the higher ground where the tea is grown. And as we went up we saw the girls picking the tea.

Arrived about 5 o'clock; it was still pouring with rain, and stayed there the night, dining with friends of the Webbers. There was a good deal of concern amongst the tea growers as to what the future in Ceylon may hold for them. They are happy in their work, they live under conditions which are considerably better than they would be living on a comparable income in England. The workers are mainly Tamils, but the Cingalese Government are pressing for a 50/50 sharing of new jobs with the Cingalese. As there is already a certain number of persons there who are under-employed, this looks as though considerable difficulties may arise.

Friday, 12th December

I started off at 8.15. The rain had disappeared overnight, the sun was shining. We were able to look round at the surrounding countryside and had breakfast on the terrace, and motored down through the sunshine past the green tea plants, the girls and men going to their work, and lower down to the rubber-growing area again, where one or two elephants were working, humping the timber. And as we went down, the flowers were very bright, the temperature rose steadily as we got into the lower regions and out into the plain which surrounds Colombo.

I had lunch at the Residence with Mr De Silva and an ex-Conservative Member of Parliament. The Government of Ceylon really carries no reputation for good in any quarter that I have met during my stay in Ceylon. This is a danger where communal disagreements and bitterness are only lying just below the surface. Yet the Island is rich and could be a happy one.

It was said at lunch that the recent report of a planned coup wasn't really a mare's nest, but that there had been a genuine plan to take over the Government, which had failed for lack of support. They also thought that if the Government was tough enough, it could ride over the problems of the Cingalese/Tamil dispute and do what was right and just by the Tamil minority. Toughness is not, however, a characteristic of the present Cingalese Government.

I drove to the airport at four o'clock and as the Britannia hadn't come in, motored on to Ngumbo which is a fishing port near the airport, and watched the fishermen sailing in their catamarans in the evening sunshine. We eventually took off for Singapore at about twenty minutes past six.

I arrived at Singapore at about midnight which is about 3 a.m. Singapore time.

On Saturday, 13th December I had a good night's sleep and in the morning got up and went out shopping, collecting some spools for my Minifon and buying a couple of shirts, and a little tobacco. It was hot - one of the hottest places I have met so far, but from what I have seen of it this morning, a well-built and lively town.

I took the plane to Kuala Lumpur at 2 p.m. where I am staying with Sir Geoffrey and Lady Tory, and I spent the weekend there. It was difficult to arrange anything at short notice as I had only laid on this Kuala Lumpur trip rather late, but in the evening I motored round the town which is more provincial than Singapore, full of Chinese, very bright and gay, with everybody looking very prosperous and very clean.

The Malayan Government is one of the strongest Governments of South East Asia, mainly through the personality of its Prime Minister, who doesn't hesitate to put any subversive elements in gaol. The Government seeks to secure a united Malayan nation, the population being split about fifty/fifty between the Malays and the Chinese with quite a sprinkling of Indians as well. It may be that the control of Chinese education will prove to be the key to this particular problem. The older Chinese are probably not communist; they're probably split between the Communist Chinese and the Formosa Government, but the younger ones look to China and are proud of what has been happening in their homeland. They attend school sometimes right up to the age of twenty-five and in these schools they form powerful groups to urge communist propaganda. It is thought that the Malays may hold Malaya against communism but perhaps not necessarily while still preserving a democratic regime. There's about one division of British troops here who have been engaged in clearing the communist terrorists out of the jungle, which incidentally must have been the most formidable operation. They are held here partly on strategic grounds under the Defence Agreement we had with Malaya. Just what they would do in the event of conflict in the Far East or where they would be reinforced from, I am not by any means clear. Singapore is, of course, our principal defence base here. It was chosen after the First World War at a time when the treaty arrangements didn't allow either America or ourselves to have bases nearer to Japan.

We talked at dinner, which included Humphrey, Secretary to the Treasury here, of the problems of South East Asia. The sad progress of events seems to be that we hand over to a man of goodwill who is reasonably tough, something then happens to him and he is succeeded by what might be described as the 'wet centre in politics'. Nothing very much happens; the Government gets weak and grows into contempt and then the Left take over. Occasionally this process is interrupted by a coup which may hold the position for a time. In all this and against this background, the Malays may stand a better chance than some. They have the clear threat of the communists from the North, and if Singapore were to go Left to the south of them, as may well happen, they would be surrounded and under threat - and as Ben Gurion said of Israel, 'A nation which is under threat can achieve a great deal more than one that isn't'.

Sunday, 14th December

I motored with Sir Geoffrey Tory to see a rubber estate, and we had a walk round it, seeing them tapping the trees, watched how the latex was collected, and brought to the factory and put through the rollers into the final form where it arrives at, say, the Pirelli factory in London.

On the way back we signed the book at the Prime Minister's house and found that he was in, and I was able to have a few words with him. He's a calm, confident, relaxed man and I should think that so long as he can retain the reins of office, Malaya will go along fairly happily. What will happen afterwards, no one can say.

In the evening I flew back to Singapore, rather a bumpy flight, and landed here in time for a bath and change before dinner. Dined at Government House with Sir Robert Scott, the Commissioner General, General Richard Howe, the C-in-C Far East, and Mr Shaw, the Governor's Secretary who is also Clerk to the Council of Ministers.

After dinner we discussed amongst other things the general strategical position. One can't help remembering as one's here the time when the Japanese swept through Malaya and Singapore fell without the firing of hardly a single shot.

Today there are four brigade groups in Malaya and Singapore is still our main strategic base in the Far East. One asks oneself the question 'how long Malaya is likely to remain a base in which British troops are acceptable.' Acceptable they are at the moment because they have been engaged in suppressing the Chinese terrorists. One asks oneself whether Singapore has still got its guns pointing in the wrong direction. I am going to spend tomorrow morning going round with the military looking at the installations here and it's early days to make up one's mind to the military situation. The thoughts that strike one, however, are that four brigade groups are precious thin for the defence of the Far East, and the hope that they will be reinforced by the all-red route through Africa seems slender - at any rate, it seems unlikely that they could be reinforced on any large scale.

As to Singapore itself, it is, of course, based upon a large Chinese population and the idea that it could be used as a base for operations in support of the Americans against China seems to be a little far-fetched. At the moment the theory seems to be that all this area should be equipped not only for very minor conventional operations which it seems fit to undertake, but for larger-scale operations as well. It does appear that enormous sums of money have been and will be spent for very little on the ground. I suppose the 64-dollar question is whether the Chiefs of Staff consider that we should be prepared to operate if necessary in nuclear warfare in this part of Asia or not. If the answer was 'not' of course considerably more forces might be spared upon a conventional basis. At the moment we seem to be backing both horses.

Monday, 15ᵗʰ December

I went down in the morning to have a talk with Mr Lim Yen Hook at the Legislative Assembly. He was as charming as ever and took me into the Smoking Room where I had an opportunity of chatting with a number of the Ministers whom I had seen before. He emphasised to me the importance of a united Malaya; that was why he was in favour of making Malay the official language. That policy was not only good in itself, he thought, but it was essential if they were to prevent the Chinese looking to China to the north of them for support, and Malayans looking to Indonesia to the south. In the longer term he wanted unity between Singapore and Malaya but did not seem to think he would get it very early.

At the present time, the Chinese were trying to get out of China in order to come to areas such as this and because of the pressure upon space it was necessary for him to put considerable checks upon immigration of that character. He did not think there was any strong movement amongst the Chinese here to link up with Communist China. They liked their way of life here; they certainly wouldn't wish to live in communes.

Later I attended the debate or part of the debate in the Legislative Assembly and it was interesting to see the rules of procedure, the need for a speaker to sit down when the Speaker of the House rose to his feet, the procedure with regard to amendments and so forth all handled on identical terms with the House of Commons in London.

I also talked with Mr Lee Quan Yeu, the Leader of the Opposition. He's a confident - some say, even a vain man. At any rate he's very confident about winning the next Election. He told me that there was nothing except the Communists to the Left of him, but he's perhaps not quite so extreme as he sounds. In fact he says there's very little Socialism that anybody could introduce into Singapore. Anybody who thought he could socialise Singapore would need his head looking at, according to Mr Lee Quan Yeu.

He told me that at the present time the communists in China were calling off the terrorist campaign; it had obviously been a major tactical error, and were instead supporting by legitimate means nationalism both in Malaya and Singapore. Though this was a good thing in the short term, the real danger was that in the longer term they might be able to develop nationalist communist parties in these countries.

During the morning I also saw the Mayor, Mr On Eng Yuan, who talked to me for some time about the City Council affairs of Singapore. He himself belongs to the Opposition Party, the P.A.P. He thought that the Chinese in Singapore were really divided into three classes; those who'd lived here for several generations who were really naturalised and looked upon themselves as, say, an American whose grandfather was English, and had settled in the United States; the second were the naturalised ones who had come here but only one generation and were regarded more or less as neutral, and the third were the pro-communists. He thought that more could be done to lean towards the natural aspirations of Chinese culture. At the moment there was a complete ban on all types of books from China coming in, only subversive literature should be kept out. There was also a ban on the import of Chinese textiles, mainly I think on an anti-dumping basis. This could be somewhat liberalised.

He was young and intelligent and he thought that the Party to which he belonged was likely to win at the next Election.

Tuesday, 16th December

I toured the military bases. General Howe picked me up in his car and took me to the military headquarters and described to me on the map the strategic situation in South East Asia, which I will not record here. I went on from there to the Air Force Base and saw where the new runway was to be constructed both for the purpose of taking the latest form of fighters and, if necessary, the V-bombers. I was then flown over in a Pembroke to the Transport Area of the R.A.F. on the other side of the Island and met by Admiral Gladstone in his barge and we proceeded up the Straits to the Naval Headquarters which he then proceeded to show me.

Very large numbers of the local population are, of course, employed on these bases, in repair work, in ship construction and maintenance and the like. As for the various roles which they could perform adequately, or should attempt to perform with the forces available, it is perhaps better to deal with these separately.

Wednesday, 17th December

I had a talk with Mr Steed who is the General Manager of the General Electric Company. In the afternoon I took the aircraft for Djakarta, Garuda Airways. We landed safely and I went along and had a quiet dinner with MacDermott and his wife.

The Indian President is paying a visit to Indonesia at this moment, and the motor cars are rushing up and down the streets, the guards following them and sirens wailing, rather on the system adopted in the United States of America and the Soviet Union. The visit is reported to have been a success but has entailed a great deal of wear and tear and sitting in the sunshine by the Corps Diplomatique.

Thursday, 18th December

In the morning I went with Mrs MacDermott out of Djakarta along the road to the Botanical Gardens which are very lovely. We saw the water lilies and sat in the shade and talked. Returned to lunch with the Ambassador, and met amongst others the Governor of the Bank of Indonesia. We discussed the problems of Indonesia. Dr Schacht once wrote a report about its economy in which he said that the real problem of Indonesia was political rather than economic, and it remains political today, though when Dr Schacht wrote it the problem was the Dutch; today it is the Indonesians themselves. The rebels are still holding out in large parts of central Sumatra. The struggle still goes on; the central authority holds on to the cities but is imperfectly in control in the agricultural areas. Yet as one motors along the road, as I did this morning, one sees the enormous natural wealth of the country. The rubber trees which grow virtually wild; the richness of the soil in which anything grows almost as soon as it is planted. As against this, the population has been soaring upwards, particularly in Java, where there are 60 million people crowded on the island, by far the largest concentration of population in the whole widely scattered area of Indonesia itself. They have been taking all there is out of the land and a recent report has suggested that they must put some fertilisers in.

In the evening dined with the Canadians. Met the Philippine representative who had been a friend of Elizabeth's at UNESCO, Analdi I think his name was, and the French Ambassador and his rather witty and charming wife, who gave me a spirited account of rich Americans arriving in Indonesia on a luxury tour, described in vivid detail the precise arrangements, sanitary and otherwise, they encountered as they went round.

Friday, 19th December

Had a talk with the Foreign Minister and the Finance Minister. The Foreign Minister said that there were some contacts with the rebels, but thought that a settlement in the immediate future was unlikely. He was not too keen on foreign capital. He was grateful for the Gannets which had recently been supplied but wanted some ships. The Finance Minister was the most forthright and comprehensible of the Ministers that I met. I talked with him and with the Governor of the Bank who had lunched with me the day before.

What was wanted in Indonesia, he said, in the order named was more skills, more organisation and more capital. He maintained that there were no contacts with the rebels; that contacts had been tried and conversations had always broken down. Yet it does not seem that Indonesia can start forward on a new future unless something can be done to reconcile its internal differences and these cannot be reconciled simply upon a military basis in an area as large and complicated as this. I talked here about oil and I think he would have settled the oil problem with the Shell if he could have carried a sensible solution through his colleagues. The difficulty is to carry anything through his colleagues!

I lunched with Wardle Smith and some of the British businessmen. The oil men there say that legislation is being prepared, has been approved by the inner Cabinet, but isn't likely to get through the full Cabinet, let alone through the House of Parliament. I attended earlier in the morning a meeting of the Assembly and saw something of their proceedings. Rather different from the House of Commons. They smoke, they read newspapers, and mostly they read their speeches, too. It was rather an uninspiring Assembly. But, of course, I only saw it for a short time.

It is said that Sukarno plays up the dangers of foreign intervention for political ends. It was upon the cry for independence that he got in and he wants to maintain the same theme in his public presentation of his policy. Yet we've got £200 to £300 millions invested in this country - comparable to the figure of Malaya and India. Clearly what we've got to do is to hang on and hope for the political situation to improve. The potential possibilities of Indonesia are immense, both as a market and as a producing area. The bulk of the rubber is produced in Sumatra, and is periodically raided by rebels where they burn down the factories. Quite polite to the planters but they don't want the Central Government to win any foreign exchange.

I spent the 20th to the 24th December in Bali, staying with Mr James Pandy at Sagara House, Sanur. I flew in by Garuda Airways passing over a giant volcano which rose up from the plain below, and the top of which was just showing through the clouds. The pilot very kindly flew all round it with one wing tip very nearly touching the crater so I had a good view. It was rather impressive with deep sulphur-coloured dust inside and mist and steam rising from it. Like many volcanoes in this area, it is semi-active.

Bali itself was a pleasant rest. I ate and sat by the sea. We went for a little trip round the island, or parts of it, through the villages, watched the people in the villages working away at their drawing and their carving which they do with some skill. I bathed in the mornings in the water inside the reef. It's dangerous to go out. You have to bathe early in these parts if you want the water to be cool. I think Balinese art is somewhat over-rated. It is of a touristy character. It's produced in very large quantities and the artists never seem to draw from the life but follow a rather pedantic, traditional role which makes all the drawings look flat and rather colourless. They work, too, in silver but it is a rather heavy type of work. Their wood carving is clever but stylised in a contemporary type. Pandy's studio contains some other paintings of a different type. Some of the Dutch ones were quite passable. Some by various artists, including some Balinese artists, were quite dreadful.

I watched, too, a little of the dancing which is mostly done by very young girls in beautiful, tight-fitting costumes. They do it with great skill and grace. It's drawn from the Indians. Little movements of the head, the hands, the eyes, a male dancer and then some masked plays. It was interesting to watch.

I also went and called on Madame Le Mayeur whose husband was a Belgian painter who married her when she was his model about twenty-six years ago, and he lived and painted in Bali during that time, and died last May in Belgium. His paintings are by far the most interesting that I saw on the island. They were painted originally rather in the Impressionist style, and taking a little after Turner, but during his period on the island his colours got brighter and brighter, until at the end he was painting with all the sunshine and the colour and the flowers. The woman in his paintings being invariably his wife. She is an attractive and interesting woman of middle age but full of dignity and charm. His paintings have, I think, considerable merit. They are a style which he has evolved himself; they don't derive much from other people, but painted with skill and courage. They certainly stand out amongst the rather drab, contemporary work which one sees in other parts.

On the 24th I made an early start from Denpaser where I had to wait about two hours at the airport, and flew to Djakarta. I went up and spent the Christmas Eve and Christmas Day with Mr and Mrs Newton, the Canadian Ambassador and his wife, in the hills above Bagor. It was pleasantly cool. On Christmas Day I had a swim before breakfast and then we went and had lunch with friends a little higher up the mountain with thick cloud. I came down in the evening, down past and through the tea gardens to the valley and the steamy heat of Djakarta, where I had supper with Mr and Mrs Senor, the Minister at the Embassy, and caught the night flight from Djakarta.

The airport was the scene of considerable Christmas activity, as they were holding a ball, and we went off amidst song and dance.

Our first port of call was Perth. We landed at 8.30 in the morning in a temperature of 80 degrees. Many people felt rather hot but as it was a dry heat I found it almost cool after the tropics. And then on across the dusty wastes of Australia, part of it desert and apparently a sort of black sand, parts thickly settled and cultivated, and landed at Melbourne in the evening light where it was quite cool, and then flew on and arrived at Sydney about half past ten in the evening. I was met by Mr Bruce, the High Commissioner, and a representative from Caltex, and they brought me into the Belvedere Hotel where I spent the night. I was ready for some sleep.

Saturday, 27th December

I rose fairly early and went out to do a little necessary shopping with Bruce who kindly drove me round Sydney, and I saw the famous Harbour

Bridge, and for lunch I went over that bridge and had a meal with Bob Menzies in a lively house which looks out across the harbour.

We had a long talk together about the problems of the world and he talked to me about my resignation. He had himself, he said, resigned three times in his life. He certainly doesn't seem to have suffered from it. He gave me a lot of good, wise and kind advice.

I dined in the evening with Angus Maude who has come out here as the Editor of the Sydney Morning Herald. This paper represents the Opposition group to the present Australian Government. And during the recent Election, Angus Maude and this paper weighed in pretty heavily on the Labour side and in some pretty savage attacks on Bob Menzies. I arranged with him to meet Mr Henderson, who is the General Manager of this newspaper group, on my way back from Canberra through Sydney.

Sunday, 28th December

I went off into the country, near Palm Beach, for lunch with friends of the Lennox Boyds' and we came back along the beaches and saw the thousands of people from Sydney, bathing there on the Sunday afternoon. It's like a very accessible and glorified Blackpool. With this amount of space to disport themselves, the Sydney population and particularly the young men, keep remarkably fit. I dined in the evening with Mary Hordern.

Monday, 29th December

I lunched with the Governor of the Commonwealth Bank and his Board. It was rather like a small-scale meeting with the Governor of the Bank of England his Board, and we talked together about sterling and other subjects. The Bank of England had just announced the assimilation of its external rates of exchange. We talked a little about that. We also talked about Indonesia, and the Board were rather of the opinion that it wouldn't serve the Australian purpose to trail along behind the Dutch.

In the evening I went over and had a drink with the Carringtons at Admiralty House, which is really the residence of the Governor General, but which is lent to the Carringtons for the time being. It's a lovely house with a beautiful view across the habour.

I arranged with Peter Carrington about coming to see them on my way from Melbourne to Sydney stopping at Canberra.

I went on from there to have dinner with Lady Lloyd-Jones, a charming lady, whose husband, a much respected man in Sydney, was quite something of an amateur painter, and many of his paintings as well as some quite good paintings by other men, including Matthew Smith, are disposed about the house. It was a very pleasant evening.

Tuesday, 30th December

I went to the Blue Mountains. I had been warned that if I went up there I'd be suffering from the heat and the flies, but in point of fact it was rather cold, and very quickly we got up into the fog and the clouds. I went there to have lunch with the Kamfners. Mrs Kamfner is Judy Cassab who painted my portrait. I was made very welcome and we had a lovely lunch with paprika, and then we went out afterwards and tried to see the view, but, of course, we only saw the clouds. However, we called in and saw their children who were lunching at another house, a couple of delightful boys.

Afterwards we went back and as we couldn't paint outside, we painted a still life at home. A gum tree and a guitar. And I much enjoyed with Judy Cassab's help attacking a large piece of paper with brushes and paints, palette knives and newspapers, and fingers, and anything else that came handy. The result was startling but not unattractive.

I had been lent a car for the day by the Rootes Group with a young man, McKechnie, who drove me there and back. On the way back he told me as he'd been touring earlier in the year for the Rootes Group in the country outback, that he had run over a wild boar and seeing that it was apparently dead, he and his companion had run back along the road to look at it. It suddenly came to life and charged. They raced back to the car, then climbed on to the roof. The boar missing them by inches, spent the next hour attacking the car, while they in the blazing heat tried to prevent their feet from getting too much burnt on the roof. After a time a Chevrolet came along and the driver produced a rifle and shot the boar and asked them how many days they'd been up there. This is the kind of active life that members of the Rootes Group have in Australia!

Wednesday, 31st December

I visited the Art Gallery in Sydney with Charles Lloyd-Jones. The pictures there are not outstanding but I had an opportunity of seeing something of the Australian painting of today and yesterday.

In the afternoon Mrs Livingstone had very kindly arranged with her son-in-law for us to go round the harbour in a speedboat. We did [this] in quite a considerable wind and shipping a certain amount of spray, but having a magnificent view of that great harbour. In and out of the various creeks and under that great bridge. On the way round we came across the

Livingstone brothers' yacht which had just been returned from the Hobart Race as it had sprung a leak. It's a magnificent ship and we saw the two Livingstone brothers, two rich bachelors who are keen on ocean yachting and are at the present time contemplating trying to build a boat capable of participating in the America's Cup.

I dined in the evening with Mary Hordern and met Frank Packer and his wife, who's the Daily Telegraph in Sydney. He is a broad tough man, very much concerned with the way in which self-government is being given to the Commonwealth - as he thinks - rather too fast.

When I got back to the hotel, the proprietor came up and handed me a huge bowl of fruit and half a bottle of champagne. They thought I was far from home and ought to be able to celebrate the New Year adequately, which I did.

Thursday, 1st January 1959

I flew to Melbourne with the Prime Minister in his special plane, dropping Dame Patty Menzies on the way. We arrived a little before twelve o'clock at the Melbourne Cricket Ground, which manages to seat something like 100,000 people. May and Cowdrey were batting and looked almost inseparable when we arrived. But after an hour or so, Mackniff came on with the new ball and took some wickets pretty quickly. The English tail didn't do much good. In the Australian innings Harvey started what was to be a magnificent innings of 167, 60 of which he completed that afternoon. It was certainly an interesting day's cricket.

In the evening I rang the Painters, Jean Patterson that was, and got them to come out and have dinner with me at the Windsor Hotel, and they motored me back to their home in East Brighton for a cup of coffee afterwards.

Friday, 2nd January

I motored down to Portsea where Mr Harold Holt lives. It's a lovely drive along the coast. The Australians are a gregarious people. Literally thousands of them are gathered on the coast at this time of year, many of them living in tents shoulder to shoulder. Portsea itself is a little less closely inhabited. I think a lot of the land round there is reserved by the Army. It's a beautiful place.

The Australians who have houses round Portsea certainly live a very comfortable life. Harold Holt himself, the Finance Minister, is much interested in skin-diving and we spent part of the day watching them do this though for my part I thought the water was far too cold to stay in. I talked a little with him about the financial situation. In fact the affairs of Australia are in fairly good shape, provided always that the terms of trade start to turn shortly in favour of that country and by implication against the United Kingdom.

I stayed on for dinner and motored back afterwards, sleeping in the back of the car after a long day in which I had got rather sunburnt.

Saturday, 3rd January

I motored in the morning to Berwick which is where Mr Dick Casey, the Foreign Minister, lives. It's a very different kind of country from Portsea, very English-looking; rather a high rainfall, fairly lush vegetation. When I arrived there I met him and his family, and some parachutes were dropping on his private airfield. He runs a couple of aircraft. We went down and watched the parachute jumping, and then came back and had lunch. We went round his farm where he runs 2,500 sheep and quite a lot of cattle. I saw the sheep-shearing shed and the various appurtenances of the farm.

Afterwards we talked of foreign policy. The problem he has of dealing with the Dutch over Indonesia. He wanted friendly terms with their neighbours to the north, but was not finding this particularly easy with India. I don't think Nehru and Bob Menzies get on particularly well. He asked me about convertibility; was rather anxious that we weren't going to plunge into it on the full scale.

It was a pleasant and relaxed afternoon, and we watched the children bathing and enjoyed ourselves. I motored back after tea and went out to dinner with Bob Menzies at the West Brighton Club. Rather a curious feature of Australian life are men's clubs with men of quite distinction - surgeons, businessmen, and the like - but they met together and sang and drank together, and Bob Menzies sat there and relaxed, a popular figure. He had brought two guests, Ian Johnson, one-time captain of the Australian cricket team, and myself, and at appropriate moments we all said a few words. Ian Johnson spoke well and my remarks were very well received. When I rose they sang "There'll always be an England". I made them laugh, and we had a very enjoyable evening. Later on we went on the way back to the Johnson's house and there talked cricket until midnight. Bob gave a spirited account of Jardine's Captaincy, of Larwood, the Leg Theory and the rest. He certainly fits in to the Australian background.

Sunday, 4th January

I lunched with Jack McEwen, Sir Robert Knox, a friend of Martin Lindsay, and Brian Harrison was there, also John Tinsdale of the Wheat Board, and Mr Dooley, the representative in Victoria of the Commonwealth Bank. We talked of trade and financial matters. Australia is worried about the increase in competition from Communist China, and Jack McEwen has been bargaining with various countries on the basis that they wouldn't accept dumped wheat, he wouldn't accept dumped tea or tin, and he'd had some fair success on this particular line. All of them were a bit worried about the trading practices of the French who are regarded as acting with considerable wrongness in their trading practices. They're also very much disturbed at the teeming millions to the north of them.

After lunch I visited the Art Gallery. They have some quite pleasant European pictures. They've also quite a good English collection, including John's rejected portrait of the Mayor of Liverpool and his attendant, and there's a fair selection of the Australian School, starting with the Victorians who made the Australian landscape look like a Scottish glen, and proceeding through Tom Roberts and others to the modern and contemporary school.

In the evening I flew to Canberra and arrived at Government House after dinner. Jack Slessor had arrived before me and Lord Inchcape.

Monday, 5th January

I shopped in Canberra and confirmed my ticket. I had lunch with the Carringtons and met the Venuzis; she is a sister of Dillie Marx. Afterwards we dined at Government House where the full traditions of curtseying to the Governor General as the Queen's Representative were preserved. The Australians are more adult, more prosperous, more pro-British than we are led to suppose in England.

Tuesday, 6th January

I flew to Sydney. Bruce met me and took me to the I.C.I. Building where I had a talk with Sir Daniel McVee. He's the head of the metal industries of Australia and from my point of view importantly of the power cables of Australia. He didn't think there was a very big market for power cables and the fact that two competing companies had set up meant that they had been over-capitalised in the past.

After leaving Sir Daniel McVee I went down and saw Judy Cassab in her studio in Sydney and looked at the paintings that she had for the show in London. I lunched with Angus Maude and Henderson, who is considered to be the power behind the throne in the Sydney Morning Herald. He described the criticism that he had of the Menzies' policy. In the main it seems that he thinks they tax the private sector too high and then spend the money too lavishly upon the public sector, causing inflation. I told him that it wasn't the only country in which these kind of things happen. Much hangs politically both in New Zealand and the United Kingdom upon which way the terms of trade change.

I bought a copy of Pringle's book "The Australian Accent" and read it as I flew that evening from Sydney to Auckland. We landed in the evening in pouring rain. On the way I talked with Professor Carrington who was with me on the plane. We discussed the Conference and thought that we might perhaps suggest that the Commonwealth themselves might take a greater interest in the Colonies which had not yet achieved self-government, and also about the possibility of a trade organisation for S.E. Asia.

As I said, it was raining when we landed at Auckland, and the roads in the rain and mist looked not unlike Monmouthshire; an impression which was confirmed to some extent when daylight broke.

On the 7th January I flew down to Wellington and it was pleasant to be met by George Mallaby and to stay with him and his wife. We had lunch there together rather late, a few people in to drinks, a quiet supper and early to bed.

Thursday, 8th January

I met the staff of the High Commissioner's office and gave them an account of my travels. I then went on to lunch at the Wellington Club with George which was exactly as though one had stepped out of Pall Mall. I found that I had booked for New Zealand a week longer than was necessary, and I rearranged my tickets or am attempting to do so, so as to spend rather longer in Tokyo and in Peking. I also arranged to spend a weekend fishing with Mr Pickard, George's No. 2 here; we are leaving tomorrow afternoon to go up to Lake Tarpo to catch on Saturday and Sunday a few rainbow trout before the Conference starts.

Friday, 9th January

George Mallaby left for Auckland as he's on his way to the Singapore Conference which they have each year for all the High Commissioners and representatives in South East Asia. I packed my suitcase and went off to lunch with the Prime Minister and Mrs Nash. Professor Carrington and Mr Pickard of the C.R.O. were there. Mr Nash and the Labour Party carry on a precarious Government here with a majority of 1 which must be rather a strain on the back benchers! At lunch he talked to me of his boyhood days in England. He knew and had bicycled in the Wye Valley and Monmouthshire considerably.

After lunch I left with Pickard in his car and we motored through the New Zealand countryside to Tai Appi where we stayed the night. We arrived there with what is considered in New Zealand a late dinner, which is about 7.45. The practice here is to eat about 6.30 or 7. However, everyone is very co-operative and will do anything one asks them to.

Saturday, 10th January

We made an early start from Tai Appi in the open car, but as soon as we climbed up to about 3,000 feet, on the so-called desert road south of Tarpo, we came near the snow-line and it began to get pretty cold and we had to put on our sweaters. We then went through this volcanic area down to the huge lake below.

We were met by Bob Biddle, a Government Ranger, and we had a day on the lake. It wasn't a very good day as far as fishing was concerned, rather calm and misty, and we had to take the fish trolling with a fly or with a spinner, but we each got one of about 3 lbs. And we were quite content.

Sunday, 11th January

Breakfast at 7.30 and we were on the lake by 8.30. It was cloudy but the sun came through. Mostly we trolled as it's the only way really at this time of year, or seems to be the only way to attract the fish. We got twelve fish between us, one of them which Pickard got up to 4 lbs. And all of them over 2 lbs. They were rainbow trout, and they fought very well and they were great fun. Bob Biddle lost one line striking at a fish, and I lost another immediately afterwards the backing breaking, but Bob let his own line fall in the water and sink down and by some kind of miracle collected mine back again.

For lunch we cleaned and cooked one of our own rainbow trout over a wood fire on the shores of the lake. I've seldom known a trout taste better.

It turned to drizzle in the evening as we went back across the lake, but there was a bit of a breeze and I hooked one, lost him, then hooked another good one, and then we came in and dined at the hotel.

Monday, 12th January

I made a 7.30 start for Palmerston. We went through drenching rain, so strong that one could hardly see the road, but we arrived abut 11.30 at the

Grand Hotel. It isn't a very grand hotel, but it's clean and much better than I'd expected, and I've got hot and cold water in my room.

The opening ceremony which was performed by the Governor General, was very good. He spoke well, and after lunch we had a speech by Mr Nash. It was too long but it was a good speech. He obviously knew what we were there for and felt something in his heart in favour of the Commonwealth. Later there was a Reception which should have been held in a garden and would have been lovely, but it was held in a huge room and the Air Force band in that sounded a little oppressive. Altogether we felt a bit battered with the opening ceremonies.

I had been made Chairman of the group dealing with the finance and economics. I've got two young men here, a Dr Soper from the United Kingdom, and Mr Holmes, who is a New Zealander, and both seem very helpful and rather knowledgeable on economic subjects. It should be quite fun.

Tuesday, 13th January

The Conference starts. I presided over the Economic Group throughout the morning and the afternoon. I will not record here all that took place. The day went well; we seemed to be getting on with each other quite well, and through a reasonable amount of work.

In the evening I went with Carrington out in a motor car which is available here, up a little ride into the hills. New Zealand is a very lovely country, and after the rain it was all smelling sweet, with the wild thyme and other herbs growing beneath one's feet as one walked up the hillside. Carrington said that nearly all the grass here and most of the vegetation generally has been imported from Europe. It has been quite an achievement and quite efficient farming must have been undertaken.

Wednesday, 14th January

We started out discussion in Group B on the Common market. I took the precaution of drafting a few conclusions before we started the debate. Black of Australia opened well on these lines. The alternatives were that we should either go into the Common Market or stay out and make the best of it or try a new approach. And it seemed to me that the general opinion of the Conference was that we should try a new approach on the basis of a united Commonwealth. At the end of the discussion I gave some draft conclusions to think over that night and during the next morning in preparation for the debate next day.

Thursday, 15th January

We resumed the debate on our attitude to the Common Market. India and Pakistan had changed their delegates as if they'd got wind that something important was happening, and they sent in Mata from India, an intelligent man who had been imprisoned many times by the English, but he's got a good mind and wasn't altogether unhelpful. We had a discussion then and later in the evening and after a tricky passage we got the conclusions through.

We had a discussion on the Sterling Area in which Callaghan spoke, raising on the general Shonfield line whether we ought to have a Sterling Area at all. He was very well answered by everybody including a Mr Shann from Australia, who is a farmer and a politician, but really dealt with him very well and the general feeling of the meeting was that we needed a Sterling Area and all to co-operate in order to keep it going.

Friday, 16th January

We had a debate on Commonwealth co-operation in trade and services. It was a good discussion. They're able men in the Committee and it was ably summed up by Professor Deutsch, and I am persuading him to open in the plenary discussion on this subject later.

In the afternoon we went into plenary discussion and after a report from the political side, which was mainly about language problems of a rather technical nature, we moved on to a discussion of the economic affairs. Black opened again as arranged on the Common market, and did it very well - a little bit long but he made his points clearly and soundly. We had on the whole a pretty good discussion, and at the end of it the matter was referred back, as requested, to us to draft our final conclusions.

Saturday and Sunday

I went up to Lake Tarpo with Pickard, and we had two lovely hot days up there, and we caught quite a few fish. They weren't at all easy.

On the Sunday morning I rose at five, went out, nominally to try and catch a few in the early hours as it was thought they would rise better, but they weren't rising, and we went up the river, and it was still and calm and you could hardly distinguish between the trees and their reflections in the water. And all the wild birds were there and the buzzards were flying and many rare birds of that kind.

31. Peter's catch of fish

During the weekend between us we caught between twenty and twenty-five fish which we divided equally and took back, myself to Palmerston, and Richard to Wellington.

On the Sunday Joe Begie, a New Zealander from Palmerston North - 53 Argyle Avenue - came out and fished with us and we had a very pleasant day together, cooking the trout for lunch as usual which we'd caught in the morning. He has a friend called Squadron Leader Cliff Cranford, who is coming to England and will look me up, and we shall try and do something about him.

Monday, 19th January

I returned to Palmerston starting again at 5.30. I'm getting rather used to early starts. It was still a rather lovely, clear day and we motored back, hampered occasionally by flocks of sheep and Army manoeuvres by the desert road, and arrived only about an hour late for the start of the Session.

They were discussing multi-racial affairs and disputes in the Commonwealth. They discussed it all day in the rather hot atmosphere there, and I don't think they came to any very useful conclusion.

But meanwhile at Tokarno I had drafted some final draft of the conclusions for the discussion on the Common Market which may turn out to be well. I got hold of Holmes of New Zealand, Black of Australia and Deutsche of Canada, and we agreed between us to try and sell them to the heads of the delegations.

Tuesday, 20th January

We spent another day on economics. In the morning Deutsch opened on the idea for attacking trade restrictions through regional organisations in the Colombo Plan and the Economic Commission for Africa. This was the proposal that I'd tried out in Group B and we agreed to give it a run in plenary. It went pretty well and we agreed on joint action to advocate these lines in these various organisations.

At the end of the morning we got agreement, too, for the conclusions on the Common Market which I had drafted at Tokarno. There was a bit of a last-minute hitch. I think people didn't quite realise what they had agreed to, and there was some doubt about it being published, the New Zealanders being a bit anxious, but this blew over and all was well.

In the afternoon we had a good debate on capital investment, and a good speech both from Robertson of South Africa, whom I'd got to open it, and Mata, the Indian. Callaghan plunged in after Robertson, attacking him, but the thing calmed down, and I wound up the debate and was complimented on what I'd said.

In the evening we had a steering committee and then went on and saw some New Zealand films - a rather lovely one in colour of farming in the high country in the South Island.

Wednesday, 21st January

We finished the debate on investment which went well and afterwards I drafted the conclusions with Robertson. All was plain sailing. In the afternoon we turned to strategic and international affairs with the military in the form of Jack Slessor and Archie Nye leading. Archie Nye made a good, objective speech, but there is no real agreement about strategy and international affairs in the Commonwealth. We are up against exactly the same difficulty as they meet at the Prime Minister's Conference.

Thursday, 22nd January

We resumed the debate which droned on all day. Jack Slessor drafted some conclusions, but there was not very much agreement about them and everybody's hedging and going off into various directions. Also on the political and cultural side they spent a good deal of time early on debating things like multi-racial problems, and now that they were up against the real things, we were under pressure. I think the truth is that if you are going to get any agreement on these sort of subjects, you have to separate defence pacts like NATO, SEATO and the rest of them, from foreign policy.

In the evening we had the New Zealand party which was held in Sir Matthew Oram's garden. He was until recently the Speaker in the New Zealand Parliament. It was a very lovely garden and a pleasant party. Afterwards, I returned to my hotel and dined with my friends.

Friday, 23rd January

We had a debate on Machinery and there was some disposition to amalgamate the Commonwealth Relations Office and the Colonial Office on the basis of making colonies associate members of the Commonwealth. We got some kind of agreement on bits of Slessor's draft, but it's rather milk and water stuff now.

And then we went on to lunch with Walter Nash, who spoke well, and the Conference was wound up.

In the afternoon, or starting at about 8 o'clock, I flew to Auckland and was met by Mr Banks, and taken to the Grand Hotel and tomorrow I plan to see the Auckland Bridge and the Races in the afternoon.

Saturday, 24th January

I met Sir John Allen in the morning and we went along to have a look at the Auckland Harbour bridge. I'd helped them in the earlier days to get the steel, and it is now nearing completion. The Harbour looked very lovely in the bright sunshine with the white sails of the yachts. The bridge is a clever piece of construction by Dorman Long. They had floated the centre section in; by building it on the beginnings of the bridge, taking it off and floating it on at high tide and letting it settle into place; quite an engineering feat. We went round it in the launch and afterwards took the launch round H.M.S. Albion, the aircraft carrier, and the old 'Cossack', Admiral Vian's destroyer, which were there on a visit from Singapore.

Afterwards I went on to the Auckland Races. They've got a lovely racecourse there, full of flowers and green lawns, and sometimes as much as 50,000 people come to watch the racing. I met there a Dr MacGregor Grant and a Mr Fisher, who is a youngish man and in a big way of business in Auckland. He makes refrigerating machinery and the like. I watched three or four of the races and then I went off with Fisher to a local gymkana of the Pony Club and watched the children riding. They rode very well, as they do in England, and they had some lovely ponies. And afterwards they got me to give away the prizes, and they were very happy when I said they rode as well as they did in England.

Afterwards I dined with the Fishers, cooking steak on their barbecue. The standard of life in New Zealand is very high. I think it's nearer to the American than to the English. But everyone cooks for themselves, and I don't think there are very many servants.

Sunday, 25th January

I flew to Sydney where I was met by Mr Bruce, the Trade Commissioner. We went to lunch at the Wentworth Hotel and ran into Jack McEwen and his wife, and also Malcolm McCorquodate was lunching there. He was over in Sydney on business. We talked of the Conference and what we had achieved there, and Jack McEwen was rather attracted by the idea of the Commonwealth negotiating jointly with the nations of the European Economic Community.

Afterwards I went round in the car and had a look at Bondi Beach with Bruce and then went on to have an omelette with the Bruces, before catching the evening plane to Darwin. There were quite a lot of friends on the plane - Micklewood of the B.E.A., Mr Hussein from Pakistan, and Dr Soper from the Conference, were all travelling. We ran into a big electrical storm on the way to Darwin. It was pretty rough, and I had some Bovril spilt over me, but no great harm was done. We landed in at about 4 a.m. and after some delay in getting the luggage off, I went along with Mr Marsh, the Assistant Government Agent, in charge there at the present time, and they took me to his house where I stayed the night.

Monday, 26th January

I woke in Mr Marsh's house, the Government House in Darwin, which is a large old-fashioned house with a big verandah running round and all the rooms opening out of it, and a view over the harbour. It's pretty hot in Darwin, it's quite unlike any other part of Australia. Here in the north it's really the tropics. By a coincidence Darwin was declared a city today, and this afternoon Mr Marsh is to read the official pronouncement. Meanwhile, he took me for a run round the city. The houses are all built on stilts to protect them from the white ants, and it is very widely scattered and the only central streets look very like a frontier town. I saw the harbour, the new jetty and the two 6" guns which with a 9.2 form the only defence of this continent against Asia.

Incidentally, Darwin was the only place that was attacked in Australia during the war. The Japanese came in and did a good deal of bombing. I also met Mrs Mackenzie who with her husband keeps some animals in a kind of zoo near there - a lot of crocodiles, and birds and eagles and the like. We ended up on the seafront where they go to bathe, and had a glass of beer, looking across the waves to Asia. The heat was tropical and the beer was very welcome. They said that the consumption of Australians in this area was one gallon per every person every week.

Lunched at Government House and afterwards went out with Marshall, the Administrator's Secretary, to have a look at the rice development which is taking place at a spot called Humptiedoo. They are trying to plant rice on a large scale with very little labour and doing it by machinery. I met a man called Mr Moir, who is the industrial research expert from the Australian Government. He told me about the scheme. It would make a tremendous difference to the Northern Territories if they could do it. There are great areas there which don't really need any clearing; there are no trees in them and if we could grow rice on them, it would be a great advance in great blocks of something like 5,000 acres. One of the menaces is large flocks of magpie geese which I saw as I was going round and took a photograph of. The track which leads down here goes on right through Alice Springs and right through the centre of Australia to Adelaide, and we travelled back along it in the evening and got time for a shower and a change before going on to see the official ceremony in which Darwin was declared the city. The Mayor did his part and Marsh was quiet and clear and referred to the four generations of Parliament who were there; the Mother of Parliaments represented by me, then the Commonwealth Parliament, the local Legislature and a representative of the Federal Parliament, and finally the local Council. Afterwards we had a few drinks and met some of the people I had met in the morning, and then back to dinner with friends at Government House. It was very friendly and gay, and we laughed and sang songs and they took me off to the airport at midnight, and I took the plane for Hong Kong.

Breakfast in the early morning of Tuesday, the 27th January in Manila, and as we flew out we saw some of the beaches where the Japanese made their landings in the Philippines during the war. And so on to Hong Kong. The mists were just beginning to clear and we flew in below the tops of the high mountains that surround it, in over the harbour full of life and landed on the airstrip which runs out into the sea. I was driven to Government House crossing the harbour by their launch, and had lunch with the Blacks. In the afternoon we visited housing. There are 2 ½ million Chinese living in Hong Kong, very much overcrowded, increasing at a considerable pace, not only from new births but from immigration from the mainland which is really impossible, so I understand, to stop.

I went up the stairs out of the streets and saw the long rooms divided into cubicle boxes in which the Chinese live in very overcrowded conditions, and later I went to see the new houses or blocks of flats which are being erected, some of them eleven storeys high. Even here the accommodation by European standards is not very high. Five and seven to a room but they have water and lavatories and washing accommodation. I dined in the evening with Van Helden of Blair &Co. who represent Pirelli Tyres out here. We dined at the Metropole Restaurant and had a Chinese dinner - not I think a very good one; it was rather a sloppy one towards the end. There were thirteen courses served and I wielded my chopsticks to the best advantage.

Wednesday, 28th January

Spent the morning visiting factories on the Hong Kong side of the harbour. I visited quite a number, making cameras and plastic bags and plastic toys. The workers show great ingenuity. The factories are faced with somewhat similar problems to the houses i.e. they have to go up and down rather than spread out, because of the shortness of space. They have, however, skilled men to work with. Several of them mentioned to me the difficulty of selling in S.E. Asia with the growth of import restrictions, and I think we were on to something in Palmerston when we drew attention to this point. We shall need to develop it in a larger sphere if anybody is to pay much attention.

In the evening an official dinner party at Government House with Mr Clegg, who is head of the Chamber of Commerce and whom I had met at lunch incidentally at the Chamber of Commerce during the day.

The Chamber of Commerce here is so organised that only the British can be on the Executive Committee though Chinese can be members of the Chamber. Apparently the Chinese Chamber of Commerce has gone completely Communist and similar difficulties followed, so I am informed, the admission of Chinese to the Chamber of Commerce in Singapore. However, they are thinking here of the possibility of trying to mix the Chinese and the business community a little closer at the top of this particular body. The business men here are concerned to keep selling their products and their eyes are particularly on the markets of the United Kingdom and the United States. They've just had to come to a bargain with the United Kingdom about the export of cotton textiles and

Mr Kearns from the United States Department of Commerce is arriving here in two or three days and hopes to settle in a day or two a similar arrangement for the United States. The business community are more doubtful as to whether he should have it.

Yet they are very cheap producers in Hong Kong, and while I think that they should continue to export to these markets in developed countries, I have no doubt whatever that they should be given an opportunity to develop markets in the teeming millions of S.E. Asia which, unless something is done about them, will all try and develop self-sufficient national economies.

Thursday, 29th January

Went out into the New Territories. The weather was warm for this time of year - 80 degrees and 99[%] humidity. I went out with General Brabazon and we saw the Tank Regiment and the 5th Field Regiment. I went up into an O.P. of the Field Regiment on a hill overlooking China. Below me was a peaceful river which marks the borderline between what we regard as freedom and bondage. The other side you could see the Chinese working in their commune. They arrived, several hundred of them, at a railway station, decanted on to the platform and were walking up to the hut where they were cleared before going off to work.

Some time ago I believe the British observers watched a public execution from this O.P., but normally the work is peaceful, agricultural work though now done in larger units than it was before. You no longer see the individual scattered about the countryside but groups working together.

After this I went on, had lunch at the Jockey Club with the General and other officers, and later motored back towards Kowloon. I was met and taken to the South Sea Cotton Mill owned by Mr. P.Y. Tang. It's an efficient mill. They do the spinning and the weaving of the yarn and make the grey cloth which from time to time has been such a trouble to Lancashire. They do it very efficiently, certainly they don't do it by sweated labour. The wages are, of course, lower than in England. I think a worker in the weaving shed where, by the way, he looks after 30 looms, of the automatic type, earns something like £15 a month. But if he's a bachelor he gets his lodgings in a hostel free, he gets education, he gets medical treatment. They're on the whole, well looked after and appear fairly happy and content. They're better off than many of their compatriots elsewhere. Mr Tang himself was a Chinese industrialist, came like many others of that type from Shanghai in 1948 when it was clear to them that trouble was developing upon the mainland of China.

Friday, 30ᵗʰ January

I went over to Kowloon to look at the resettlement area where literally thousands of immigrants from Communist China live. Some estimates are as high as 10,000 a month coming in. They are halted intermittently by the Chinese Communists on their side of the border, but they're really pretty free to filter through by junks and various other means. They squat in a huddle of wooden huts, 10, 15 or even 25 people in a hut. Oddly enough, disease is not rampant and the children look quite healthy, but not surprisingly tuberculosis is the principal complaint. They include little cottage industries, even a private enterprise school and shops. Last year a disastrous fire during the winter months broke out and burnt down a large section of the squatter area. I was taken round by one of the resettlement officers. They had just routed out a number of opium dens.

I went on from there to the Rehousing Settlement where they put the people from these squatter areas as fast as they can turn them out, but you have to run very fast here even to stand still. The new blocks if you saw them without seeing the squatter area first of all would look like Glasgow tenement slums - that is to say, a family of seven is given one room with communal washing arrangements further along - a paradise compared with the places from which the squatters came. I believe that Professor Abercrombie when he came refused to believe that people could live or plan to live on such a density, but when he saw the conditions, he realised that it was true. The rent for one of these rooms, by the way, is about $14 a month, about 5/- a week.

There are some private enterprise schools on the top for which I understand you pay $4 a month. And the children on the whole are well dressed.

As I was saying, there are some of the better-class flats which rent at about $40 Hong Kong a month. Judged by any European standards, these conditions are, of course, pretty bad, but judged by the conditions in which many people in this area are living, they are good. We talked of the riots which started in this area in 1956. It appears that they started on Nationalist Day when the Nationalist flags are allowed. Someone stuck a flag on a building and a housing representative told him not to stick it there as it would be difficult to get off. That started the show. The Triad Societies which are rather like the criminal societies of Chicago played a considerable part in the subsequent riots.

Saturday, 31st January

I left early on a blustery, rather squally day on which it was quite bumpy in the harbour, and started for Tokyo. We had a good flight in a Hong Kong airways Viscount, and the pilot let me come forward and stand behind him as we came in to land at Taipei in Formosa. We stopped for a few moments there only to refuel and then on to Tokyo, and I had a good view of Fuji standing up symmetrical and snow-capped. I am told that I was lucky to do so as for many months it is covered in cloud. However, I had a good view and also of Tokyo as we came down, and went off to dine informally with Harpham, the Minister here, in the evening.

Sunday, 1st February

I motored with the Harphams and Turpin who is the Economic Counsellor here and his wife to Hakone. It was clear and cold. The roads in Tokyo and indeed in Japan as a whole are abominable. Tokyo is a vast, unbeautiful city, rather like the wrong end of the Tottenham Court Road, However, we motored out, and about an hour and a half in the centre of Tokyo we came to the house of Mr Yoshida who had asked to see me, and we went in and had a talk with him. He has a charming house and a rather attractive Japanese garden where even now some of the blossom was out.

We talked about Japan and the Palmerston Conference, and any ideas I might have about trade in South East Asia. Mr Sato, the Minister of Finance, was there, who is a brother of the Prime Minister, though I think the Prime Minister was adopted by another family so they have different names which makes it rather confusing. His wife was there, too, but she waited until she was called in and sat discreetly in the background - as is the custom of Japanese wives.

Mr Yoshida at the end of our conversation said he wanted to give me a little memento of Japan, and produced a rather charming piece of Japanese silver dish.

We then motored on to Hakone, lunched on the way at a hotel where they have got springs and you can have a swim in them in the Pool of Dreams or of Perpetual Youth. However, we merely had lunch and didn't plunge into the Pools. When we got to Hakone where there's a lovely lake, we went for a walk along the lakeshore and had some delightful views of Fuji. Later we returned and had tea in the hotel, and then motored back to Tokyo which took us about two and a half hours. We all arrived a bit jaded and I stayed on and had supper with the Harphams and had an early bed.

Monday, 2nd February

I spent the morning with Brian Hitch, the Information Officer, and though on Mondays most things are closed in Tokyo, we managed to go along to a store, went up on the escalator to the top and walked down looking at the various goods that were on sale. They were cheap and rather attractive. All of it was very interesting, particularly the food counters, where every conceivable variety of Japanese, Oriental and European food seemed to be on sale. From there we went to the Meiji Shrine which is modern but graceful and has some charming gardens which must be lovely in the spring. I had lunch with the Cornargias and we moved over into that complete Italian atmosphere.

After lunch I sent on to see Mr Ishiyato who is the head of what corresponds roughly to the Federation of British Industries. Later I went to a cocktail party at the Harphams where I saw quite a lot of the Japanese in the Ministries of Commerce and Finance and the Foreign Office, including the Vice Minister for Foreign Affairs. Talked with them about the various problems of trade in South East Asia and so forth, and went on to dinner with Mr Butcher and his wife, who is the Manager of the Hong Kong and Shanghai Bank in Tokyo.

Tuesday, 3rd February

I visited the Diet which is semi-circular in shape, rather more like the Assembly of the United States of America. Afterwards we went into the Finance Committee where the Prime Minister was being cross-examined by a Socialist Member of the Opposition. Mr Sato was there and saw me and came and spoke to me. One of the main differences I noticed between Japan and England in this matter was the way the press took photographs and flashlights throughout the proceedings which made it all a little disturbing.

I went on and had lunch at the Embassy and saw some of the Heads of Missions including Boon who used to be with the Ministry of Commerce in Ottawa, whom I knew well in the old days and who is now Ambassador here. At 4 o'clock I went on and saw Mr Adachi, Head of the Chamber of Commerce, and a Mr Kano who is a kind of eminence grise in the political world and rather a controversial figure, but able and speaks English very fluently. They cross-examined me closely on a number of questions including convertibility and the Common Market and my ideas for expanding trade in South East Asia.

In the evening I dined with the Governor of the Bank of Japan. His name is Mr Masamichi Yamajiwa, and we had a Japanese dinner with feet under the table, chopsticks and girls waiting discreetly upon us. I don't think we talked of any very serious subjects, but it was interesting to be in a Japanese house. All the ceilings are very low, they're obviously built for people who are not the same height as the Europeans, but they're very careful of us and see we don't knock our heads on the ceilings, and the whole things of removing the shoes, walking to the house, going into the dining room where your feet hang down under the table and you sit on the floor, with no pictures or furniture, or very little, has an air of great simplicity and charm.

Wednesday, 4th February

I took the train up to Nikko and as I left Tokyo the sun was shining on the flat plains and paddy fields that lie about it. The trees are wrapped rather intriguingly in straw, presumably to keep them warm, which makes them look as though they had stockings on, and the Japanese countryside with the little Japanese houses looks exactly like one of those miniature Japanese gardens.

I arrived at the Kayana Hotel about 11 o'clock, had an early meal and as it was a lovely day I took the bus higher up into the mountains. It drives up through some really formidable hairpin bends on to a huge plateau lying some 5,000 feet up and containing Lake Chuzenji., It's a big lake, today shining blue in the sunshine and surrounded by snow-capped peaks. Walked along the lake shore in the snow and was rather glad of the overboots which I had borrowed from Bill Harpham, and slithering along I came to one of the well-known shrines there. It was really deserted so I took my footwear off and wandered round it. Then back to the lakeside hotel where I had a cup of coffee, a sandwich to sustain me on my way, and down to the waterfall. It must be a very formidable sight, that waterfall, when the snow is melting and the water is coming down, though today little water is coming over and much is frozen.

Then back to the bus stop and took the bus to the foot of the cable car and came back to a place called Umadeshi which was on the route I started, and I finally came back into Nikko. I spent a little time shopping in Nikko, buying some of those lacquer soup bowls for home before I returned to the hotel. I had dinner early and an early bed preparatory to another day here tomorrow.

Thursday, 5th February

I spent the morning looking at the temples and shrines about Nikko. They're very baroque, very ornate - but they were interesting to see, and I spent the morning wandering round them, watching the children and the people who were coming in, and later I went to the skating rink there and saw the children skating and playing games in that area.

I had lunch at the hotel and afterwards because I couldn't go up to one of the falls owing to the road being blocked with snow, I was advised to have a look at the Botanical Gardens. Actually, there were no flowers in the Botanical Gardens at this time of year but I had a delightful walk down by the river and watched one of the Japanese fishing there rather unsuccessfully. Returned to the hotel, had tea and then caught the 4.50 train to Tokyo.

I had a quiet evening with the Harphams and prepared my suitcase for leaving early the following morning for Hong Kong.

Friday, 6th February

I left early in the morning on the Hong Kong Airways flight to Hong Kong. It was a good flight but when we were over Taipei, the news from Hong Kong was pretty bad; there was fog coming in and I went up to the flight deck, had a talk with the pilot, and he let me listen in to the various conversations that were going on in that area. One of the Hong Kong Airways pilots did eventually break through the cloud layer and found it wasn't quite so bad below, and we managed to scrape in.

I was met by Mrs Barton and taken by launch over to their flat where we changed and I had a bath and went on to the St George's Ball. This is the great function of the year in Hong Kong and done with all the old ceremony. We had a big dinner and a speech was made by the President of the St George's Society, Mr Stoker, who was my host, and the candles and the roses were there, and everybody danced the Lancers, and I danced Sir Roger de Coverley. Altogether it was a very gay evening and I left with Mrs Barton about half past twelve, motored along the rather twisty road to Shek O where I was staying.

Saturday, 7th February

I stayed with the Bartons. The weather in Hong Kong changed. It was now hot and sticky, and raining, and after a rather wet morning in which I spent the time writing letters, at 12 o'clock I went round and had a drink with David Keswick. I had lunch with the Bartons and friends at their house at Shek O and in the afternoon I went out and played a round of golf.

In the evening we dined with Clement, the Sassoons and his Polish wife, and she gave me the name of her father in Warsaw so that if I go through there I might be able to make contact with him. During the day I'd had a message from the Foreign Secretary to say that owing to the visit of himself and the Prime Minister to Moscow, it wouldn't be possible to lay on a round of high-level visits, and would I like to rearrange the trip. I've asked him to try and cut my visit to Moscow short and arrange the time to be taken up in Warsaw.

Sunday, 8th February

I left the Bartons early and went down through Hong Kong to the train. The Chinese New Year was on, the crackers were going off everywhere in the streets, everybody was smiling and very cheerful and the children were playing and shouting.

At Kowloon I was met by the representative of the Chinese Travel Agency. There was quite a crowd there, rather like Bank Holiday at home, everybody wearing their best clothes - such as they were - and everybody gay and more people trying to get on at every station. We arrived at the frontier and I was seen through by the Hong Kong Police. On the other side of the frontier I met a German couple and an Indian who were also waiting to go into the Chinese Republic. The Customs were a bit fussy about a film of mine, but were content to have it sealed up so that I could show it to the Customs at Peking. The only other trouble I had was that I was carrying a copy of the Sunday Times which Hugh Barton had pressed into my hand on leaving. The Customs looked at this and said that they didn't think it was very nice, putting it down distastefully. However, no trouble was really caused.

I had lunch at the frontier restaurant which consisted of soup with vegetables in it - quite good - and tunny fish, which wasn't very pleasant, and then caught the train. The train proceeded along through the Chinese countryside with the radio blaring. This blaring radio is very much a feature of life in the Republic of China. We arrived at Canton about 4 p.m. I was met very efficiently by a tourist official who spoke French, and taken in a car to the hotel. I arranged with him to give me a little bit of a tour round the city afterwards, and this he did. I looked at the memorial to those killed in the 1927 Revolution and the memorial to Sun Yat Sen, and returned to the hotel for dinner and an early bed.

Monday, 9th February

I had a 6 a.m. start, escorted by a representative of the tourist agency who saw me off at the airport. I must say the tourist people are pretty good here. I got into the machine which was a Chinese one, two engines, mostly filled with cargo, and we flew out through morning mist and over a mountain range. There were three stops on the way to Peking. The first one was a long and cold one. I eventually ascertained that we were waiting for the weather to clear. The Chinese Airlines are very careful, but they will only fly when they can see visually as they haven't very many other aids, and sometimes one can wait in places for a long time. Had a good Chinese lunch at Hankow with a Chinese metallurgist whom I had met at Shangsha where we had stopped first, and we talked pleasantly about the various problems of metallurgy and on other non-political points.

Arrived at Peking and was met by the Wilsons and taken in to the Embassy.

Tuesday, 10th February

We went down in the morning to the Market where the New Year crowds were gathered. They looked very remarkable. The thing that impresses one about China is the very large number of people, but they were on holiday; they were cheerful, and though perhaps not very excitingly dressed, they all appeared to have adequate clothing and to be well fed.

Afterwards I visited the Forbidden City, part of which is under reconstruction and repair, but the sun was shining and took quite a lot of photographs.

In the afternoon we went to the Summer Palace and I climbed up the hill towards the top and took more photographs there and looked at the lake below, now covered with ice. In the evening the Indian Charge d'Affaires and his wife came to dinner.

Wednesday, 11th February

I went to the Great Wall with Mrs Maby and another wife from the Embassy. It was about thirty or forty miles out. It was bitterly cold when we arrived and we had to clamber up the steep slope, holding on to one another and endeavouring not to fall down. It's an impressive engineering feat; it climbs up far more over the contours of the hills than I had imagined. I was photographed there standing beside two of the Chinese soldiers.

Afterwards we came back to the valley where the Ming Tombs are. It's a very lovely valley with these Tombs scattered along it, all in the same state of architecture though not all in the same state of repair. We had a picnic there and then returned to the Embassy.

In the evening I dined with the Mabys, Mr Yang - who's a sort of Public Relations Officer of the Chinese Government - was there, and Mr Flatow, the Polish Ambassador. I think the only two things they said which were of interest was that the Chinese were likely to stop dumping in overseas markets, and that family life was really going to go on in the communes.

Thursday, 12th February

Shopped with Mrs Wilson in the morning and bought myself one of these fur hats which though curious in appearance is really necessary in these parts of the world. The shops are rather dark and drab but we found some lovely brocades there. I bought a little jacket and skirt for Victoria which I think she may like, and in the afternoon I visited Cotton Mill No. 2. I was met by a woman director, the Manager of it, and taken round by her aide and another woman. They employ about 6,000 men and women and are engaged in spinning and weaving grey cloth. Most of the workers have been trained in Shanghai as this is not so much a natural textile area. They are paid about $60 a month which is the equivalent of about £8 and they pay for their food, their education and their rent at a small rate out of that sum. It's an efficient and well-run show and I should think it would compare with a cotton mill anywhere.

There are kindergartens for the babies, primary schools; there are clinics and all the paraphernalia of a modern industry associated with it. And in this case many or most of the workers live on the factory site.

They sell the cloth that they make to the Government - 7 different varieties of it - at around, I think $90 a 100 metres. The price, they say, remains pretty stable. The profit is got by the Government selling on to the ultimate customers. About a third of their cloth goes for export.

In the evening I dined at the Embassy and had quite a talk with Dr Gie of the Overseas Trade Corporation and raised with him in a preliminary way two of the problems of dumping and the trade fair which the Federation of British Industries wish to run.

Friday, 13th February

I visited a commune. It was situated some five or six miles south east of the boundary of Peking. Rather well situated because its main task is growing vegetables for the food market in Peking. It was originally formed by the gathering together of four agricultural co-operatives and consists altogether of some 30,000 people. It's divided still into four separate stations and I went round with the Head of the station on which we found ourselves.

They were relaxed and happy and hospitable and very forthcoming in what they said. We went to look at the vegetables which at this time of year, of course, they were growing in hothouses, and they grow some quite nice flowers as well. In this particular case they had limited the industrial activity to those industries which are ancillary to agriculture, namely the making of pots for the flowers or processing the grain or repairing the equipment. The equipment, incidentally, is pretty simple. There is no great parade of expensive tractors and the like and most of the things they do are done with bits of wood and metal which they string together on their own. We asked them a lot of questions about how they paid tax, and they maintained that local farmers assumed production of a piece of land and then they paid out a fixed percentage of 15% or 16% in cash or kind on that production. But you get a different answer from almost everyone you ask about tax problems in China. They borrowed money from the Government when they wanted it at .4% and banked their own surplus when they wanted to with the Government at the same rate of interest.

As to the social side, husbands and wives live together. As the Station Commander said, 'Mr Dulles isn't right when he says we don't have any families in China'. The schools, the canteens, etc. are communal. They didn't attempt to say that everything was right, they laughed a bit at the blacksmiths who they maintained didn't know their job, but they seemed to be doing it reasonably well, and in one place where a canteen had been erected he said 'It looks crooked, but they haven't got any carpenters on this particular part and they're doing the best they can.'

The men are paid $43 a month, which is not a very high rate but out of that they pay for their clothes and for their medical attention. If they're skilled they get from $3 to $10 a month more.

Not everybody likes the communal feeding arrangements. As the Station Commander said, 'Bachelors who only get one meal out of it don't like it as much as families who get six free meals out of it.' So opinions differ, but looking at the food as it was prepared, it wasn't too bad, and looking at the conditions in which the Chinese were living before, this may be as sensible a way as any other of looking after 30,000 people, growing vegetables in a not very large area of ground.

Saturday, 14th February

I visited the technical university in Peking. 11,000 students are educated there. They get their training free and pay for their board and lodging though allowances are made for the poorer ones which include about 60%. They cover a wide range of technical subjects - engineering, construction, hydraulic engineering, electricity, chemicals and so forth.

I went on to have lunch with the Dutch Ambassador. Everyone here in the Foreign Embassies, I think, tends to be a bit shut off and far away, and I think that goes for the Russians as well as everybody else. It is a distant place in China, and their attitude is a little on the defensive and secretive. It's not easy to get to see anybody and I think that this atmosphere is noticeable as you move about it.

Having said that I must record that the same evening I was asked to go and see Mr Yay, the Minister for Foreign Trade, at 7 p.m. So I went along there by myself and found him in the Ministry in a room which was pretty chilly and with Mr Ming whom I had met earlier. We raised - after the usual drinking of tea and polite preliminaries which are a proper part of any interview in China - three main topics. The first was the question of dumping. I explained that throughout South East Asia where I had travelled I found a great number of complaints about this practice. I was told by Mr Yay that the reason was that the export corporations thinking that world prices were falling were anxious to get hold of the cash quickly in order to take advantage of purchasing on this falling market, and they had moved in a way which they thought best calculated to get it quick. But they were aware in the Chinese Government of the irritation that this had caused and instructions had gone out that it was not to be repeated.

With regard to the contracts for cotton waste and other products which had recently been broken with the British, we had rather a useful discussion on this. Mr Yay was quite frank - the Native Products Export Corporation had in fact, not for the first time, he said, made a mistake. It is rare for the Chinese to admit a mistake but they did so in this case and said that the selling of immature cotton in any form was contrary to the plan and the Export Corporation shouldn't have done it. However, he agreed that China had a reputation to preserve of keeping her contracts honourably, and in this case he was going to recommend that the licences should be issued. I reported this to Duncan Wilson afterwards and we agreed to inform London and urge them not to give any premature publicity.

The last subject that we talked about was the possibility of a trade fair in 1960 organised by the Federation of British Industries. It's agreed that there should be a Fair; it's agreed that the British traders should be welcomed, but there's a difficulty which has arisen because no one knows whether the Peking Exhibition Hall will in fact be occupied by a permanent exhibition of Chinese products or be available for demonstrations of this character. The most I could get was an assurance that every effort would be made to give an answer one way or another to the Federation of British Industries before the 31st March.

I left Dr Yay after what was, I think, a friendly and helpful interview, and he certainly treated me with great courtesy, and I went on to have a very good Chinese dinner with the Wilsons and the Burkes and the Morgans, and went on from there back to the Embassy, to get a fairly early bed before an early start tomorrow morning.

Sunday, 15th February

I left early from Peking; had a bit of trouble with the films which, though they let you take them in China, they rather take off you as you leave the frontier. However, they took them to develop and give back to the Embassy to post on to me. I flew in a Chinese plane as far as Ulan Bator which is the capital of Outer Mongolia. It was rather an impressive sight as we came in over the mountains down into the great snow plain under a clear blue sky with the capital city lying in the corner of the plain about 20 kilometres away.

We landed there about 12 noon. The only refreshment available was the inevitable glass of tea which serves both as a hand-warmer and as a refreshment in this part of the world. And then we took off again and presently were flying over Lake Bikar which is a huge lake about 250 miles long now thick with ice and showing the reflections of the mountains in it, until we arrived at Irkutsk, in Russia. This, I think, is really the right way to come in to Russia; you really feel you are coming home after Outer Mongolia and the air hostesses looked rather like Scots girls and smile and joke, and the whole thing is quite relaxing.

I landed in Irkutsk about 3.30 and I was told that really the meal I ought to be eating was breakfast, and so I had red caviar and fried fish, and it was pretty good, and I had a wash and brush up and felt better. Then I got into the Russian jet and we climbed up fast to start with - but not too fast or uncomfortably, and as we were getting to our maximum height or the height which we were going to fly at (around 24,000 feet) we saw another of these jets coming in towards us. I suppose we must have been going towards each other or away from each other at about 800 miles an hour, and it flew past us about a mile away leaving a long trail behind it. They are comfortable planes, oxygen is provided if you want it - there are two people who seemed to feel the effects of the height rather as we flew - and as far as Omsk there was something wrong with the heating apparatus. I think we were rather overheated. When we got out at Omsk it was certainly bitterly cold and I went into the canteen there or the restaurant and managed to have a glass of beer and an apple, and then came back and we flew on with the heating apparatus right by then, quite comfortably, as far as Moscow where we arrived at 8 p.m. in time for dinner. But, of course, it was about 1 a.m. Peking time.

I went in to the Embassy, past the new blocks of flats they are building on either side, had dinner and was pretty well ready for bed.

Monday, 16th February

I started my short stay in Moscow. My first appointment was to look round the Kremlin Museum. I did this and saw the coaches, one of them presented by Queen Elizabeth I to the Czar of Russia. A wonderful collection of English silver including some from the collection of Charles I, the Faberge jewellery and many other items of interest and beauty. It is a lavish and rich display, well set out, and it was being looked at by a number of Russians including some of the Young Communist League wearing scarlet ribbons round their necks. I also saw the 14th and 15th century churches. They are perhaps more beautiful outside than in. Outside they have this curious Eastern - almost Persian - form of architecture; inside they are heavily painted from the floor to the ceiling.

I had lunch at the Embassy with Lady Reilly and the Canadian Ambassador and afterwards I went on to see the French Impressionist paintings. I was lucky to see them; they had only just been reassembled, though the best collection is, of course, in Leningrad, but here in Moscow were some borrowed from the Hermitage in Leningrad. There was a really beautiful display of Monets, of Gauguins, of Matisse and others.

In the evening to complete what was really a cultural day I went with Martin and Ewer who, incidentally was a friend of Piero's, to 'Swan Lake' put on by the Stanislavsky Company with the second ballerina, Vlassava, dancing. It was a wonderful and spectacular display. In London I don't think they could have put it on quite like that with plastic swans swimming across the lake and a really spectacular scene at the end. They plunge into the lake; but despite its almost naïve presentation, the dancing was beautiful, and I thoroughly enjoyed the evening.

Tuesday, 17th February

I had my only really official engagement with members of the Parliamentary Group - the Soviet Congress. I was met by Mr Zotoff who was First Deputy Chairman of the State Planning Committee of the Council of Ministers known as GOSPLAN, and Mr Skukoff who is Chairman of the Commission of Soviet Control and a member of the Economic Commission of the Council of Nationalities.

I had an interesting talk with them and they were capable and able men. We discussed the trade side. Their import needs were really for capital goods and were not likely in the immediate or near future to consist of imports of consumer goods. There was no mention made of strategic controls which was interesting. Their exports were grain, timber, oil, and in the communist countries a good proportion of machinery.

I asked them about wages. They said that wages had in fact increased in money terms about 8% a year but prices had been going down. The increase in productivity, in other words, was higher and deliberately planned and kept higher than the increase in wages, and the margin was used as a reserve for capital purposes, pensions and the like. I cross-examined them fairly closely about this very favourable picture, and they cited examples to me where productivity had gone up, but they were mostly in the commodity fields, in butter, in grapes, in petroleum, in diamonds and in natural gas. When I pressed them as to whether increased productivity in textiles had really gone up by 8%, they really hedged the answer.

Nevertheless, the overall picture is about accurate, and the main success in this communist economy seems to be, not as they think, in the absence of competition, but in the power to contain their money incomes within their increase in production, and it is in this difference between the democratic and communist world that there may be some dangers in the future.

In the afternoon I went along to see the Russian paintings and particularly the paintings of Petroff who has been shown fairly widely in the recent exhibition in London and his picture of the Cossacks conferring on their reply to the Turks. The Russian paintings on the whole are representational, rather sad. They all have some political or social theme, and crowds of people were going round being lectured about them. Very different from the almost complete absence of people who have been looking at the French Impressionists.

Wednesday, 18th February

I went with Martin to the airport and got into the Polish aircraft for Warsaw. But after we had been flying for about an hour and a quarter, we heard that Warsaw was closed by fog and we put in to Minsk. There was only one other passenger on the aircraft, a Pole. He was called Jan Gogogovsky and he worked at the Petroleum Institute, Lubitz 25a, based on Cracow. He spoke a little French so it was just possible, but only just, for us to communicate, and the air hostess spoke a little French, too.

We stayed for a time in Minsk and then made another effort to reach Warsaw. We took off but after we had been flying for about twenty-five minutes, the pilot came through and said that Warsaw was again closed, so we turned back and landed in deteriorating weather at Minsk. The prospect of spending the rest of the evening - it was then about 5.30 or 5.45 - in the airport, was not a very pleasant one and I decided to try and see what I could of the town. I was told it would be very difficult, but I managed to get hold of someone from Intourist who came out, and though they couldn't cash Travellers Cheques, I cashed in the remainder of my dollars (about 5 or 6) and my last £ sterling and managed to get together 100 roubles, and with this I and my Polish friend went off in a car after supper to see the circus. It was really a magnificent display, better than any circus that I have seen in London. I believe they do these things very well in Russia and we had a most enjoyable evening, watching the various spectacles. We also had an opportunity of seeing something of the town of Minsk which is the capital of Byelo Russki or White Russia, and which has very largely been rebuilt since the war. The old Polish frontier used to run very close here and it was on the front line and largely destroyed during the last war. The new buildings are very Russian, that's to say, they are built on more grand, almost Victoria lines of copies of Roman architecture which is rather typical of the Russian building of today.

Got back to the airport about 11 o'clock, had a glass of beer downstairs and went up to my not particularly comfortable but perfectly clean room and managed to get a bit of sleep before starting the following morning.

Thursday, 19th February

We took off at 11.30 a.m. (9.30 Warsaw time), arrived in Warsaw and was met by Berthoud and someone else from the Embassy. He took me back to the Embassy which is on a modest scale and I had a rather welcome bath and change before lunch.

I went straight on after lunch and had an interview with Mr Dytrik, the Minister of Finance. It was an interesting but not particularly exciting one. Their standard of living in Poland, so they claim, again I think probably rightly, has increased about 30% over the last three years, that's in real terms, but here unlike Russia the prices have risen. Their economy is a more complex one. Still there has been a net gain. 60% of their trade is with the communist bloc, and 40% with us. To the communists they export capital goods, to us agricultural goods. They seem anxious to expand trade with us, but it is not easy to see how trade on this basis can be stepped up much further.

I had a drive then round the city which has been restored wonderfully at vast cost to exactly the original basis or much of it has.

Then in the evening I had a cocktail party at the Embassy which was very widely attended. The Russian and Chinese Ambassadors were there, Mr Gronvold, the Norwegian Ambassador, with whom I was to have dinner later, Mr Growa, the father of Mrs Clelland, who had asked me to see him when I was in Hong Kong, many other Ambassadors and a large number of Poles at Ministerial and official level. Relations here are clearly quite different from relations further East in the communist world; indeed things warm up considerably in relationship as one moved further west.

I dined with the Gronvolds and there was Mr Vineyvitch whom I had to meet tomorrow, the Vice Minister of Foreign Affairs, the Chef de Protocol and others. We had an interesting discussion after dinner on Polish and Russian art. The recent exhibition in Moscow where the Poles had put in a number of modern, and in one or two cases abstract paintings, had created quite an impression there. There is an attempt in the communist world to bend art to the social requirements of the day. They are anxious to do this even in Poland. The Chef de Protocol and I and Berthoud took the opposite line and said that you couldn't really force artists - at least not great artists - to paint other than what was in their hearts. But the truth is that there is, so to speak, an artistic underground and in Moscow particularly some of the abstract paintings of the young Russian painters are being sold on the black market for quite good prices and then resold in the Paris market.

Friday, 20th February

I went along and had a talk with Mr Vineyvitch, the Polish Vice Minister of Foreign Affairs. He spoke to me about the Rapacki Plan. He urged the advantages of disengagement and he thought that if some advance could be made on disengagement problems, even on a narrow front, it might ease things in other fields. The disadvantage of the Rapacki Plan, he said, was that it had come from the East and was, therefore, regarded with suspicion. And yet they had done their best to reconcile the differences between the East and West and any agreement which the East struck with the West would make it more difficult for the East to argue that the West was wicked, untrustworthy people. The Plan itself was of advantage to Poland.

I asked him how much the East really wished for disengagement on the grand scale and cited the obvious wish of China to keep the pressure against the United States high with propaganda and the like. He said that in the case of China they had been refused admission to UNO, they had felt that they had got to build up very rapidly the resources and strength of their country, and in order to sustain the immense effort required, they had whipped up a certain amount of antagonism inside China against the world outside.

He thought that Russia was really interested in disengagement and that Mr Kruschev's speech at the 21st Congress really bore this out. I pressed him on the possibility of the withdrawal of conventional forces and in response to some detailed questions which I repeated more than twice, he was emphatically of the view that if the West would withdraw in Germany, in particular if Germany did not become a nuclear power, Russia for her part would be prepared to withdraw the substantial or fairly substantial forces which she had in Eastern Germany and would withdraw from Poland too. At present all she really had in Poland were lines of communications.

I asked him what would happen in Poland in circumstances of this kind. He said he did not think that there was any prospect in Poland of having another Hungary. The situations were different. In Hungary there had been an internal revolution; in Poland all that happened was that the present Government had taken over the nationalised industries and other arrangements which had been really instituted by the Germans.

In any event, though I put the point very plainly to him and its difficulties, he was firmly of the opinion that the Russians would be prepared to withdraw from the Polish Eastern frontier in return for reciprocal arrangements in the West.

I had lunch with the United States Ambassador, the Vice Minister of Foreign Trade and representatives from the University were there, and we spoke with freedom about the problems of Poland, Russia and so forth. This is perhaps the only communist country where really free discussion is carried on upon a wide scale.

In the evening we went to a concert of Chopin and Liszt which was packed, at which by communist country standards the people were well dressed and which was extremely agreeable. Afterwards we all went on and had supper with Mr Roy, the Indian Ambassador.

Saturday, 21st February

I started for the airport at 7.20 with the intention of flying to Cracow but in fact when we arrived, the fog which had threatened to delay us the evening before had been dispersed, but we were told that owing to the high wind a definite decision had been taken that the flight would not take place. So I went for a walk in the morning just outside Warsaw, spent a quiet day in the Residence in preparation for tomorrow when after very nearly four months I shall fly back to England.

~ 4 ~

Return to Politics

Home again, Thorneycroft was soon immersed in Parliamentary affairs. While he had been away, the negotiations between the Transport Commission and the National Union of Railwaymen had been trundling along. At a meeting of the Conservative Party's 1922 Committee on 9th May 1959, Thorneycroft launched a scathing attack on the Government who, by conceding a 3% wage increase had, in his opinion, set a dangerous precedent which would lead inevitably to a similar increase for other industries, a *"breach in the dam which may open the way to what we have been fighting to avoid – renewed inflation"*.

September brought the announcement of a General Election, to take place on 8th October 1959. Thorneycroft, confined to bed with a high temperature, was unable to attend his adoption meeting in Monmouth on 17th September, and was represented by his wife, Carla, who delivered his adoption speech in his absence. This was not exactly a novelty for her. During his absence abroad, she had nursed his constituency assiduously and with great charm. In his election campaign leaflet Thorneycroft rehearsed the Government's economic and domestic achievements since 1951: exports at record levels and balance of payments positive to the tune of £1,600 million; taxes cut in seven budgets; 2 million new homes; almost 2 million new school places; a better health service; a modern pensions plan; the cost of living stabilised and full employment maintained. In speeches around the constituency that he made in spite of his fever, he reaffirmed without equivocation his belief that control of public expenditure was vital for control of inflation, and dismissed the notion that it would be sensible to divert funds from the £1,500 million spent on defence to increase old age pensions. His consistent defence of the principle for which he had resigned may not have endeared him to other senior members of his party, none of whom came to Monmouth to give him support during his campaign, but it went down very well in his constituency. Even his opponent recognised that a man who could give up such an important post on an issue of principle deserved respect. Thorneycroft was defending a majority of 5,797 votes, but boundary changes since the last election had brought part of the new town of Cwmbran into the Monmouth Division. The Labour candidate, Gordon Parry, was convinced that this would produce four thousand votes for him. Thorneycroft was not in the least bit worried. For him, Conservatism had as much appeal for the sort of people who lived in new towns as for anyone else.

Mr Parry, a local teacher, had replaced as candidate Miss Jo Richardson, who had fought Thorneycroft in the last two elections and, a little indiscreetly, Parry had let it be known that he thought her gender might have reduced her appeal to many traditional Labour supporters. Thorneycroft, on the other hand, had no doubt whatever that he enjoyed tremendous support from his wife, who was greatly admired for her energetic commitment to constituency affairs and activities.

Thorneycroft kept his seat, polling 25,422 votes against 22,970 in 1955, and securing an increased majority of 6,527. Parry received 19,165 votes, 2,000 more than Jo Richardson had won in 1955. It seems that the people of Cwmbran had shared their 4,000 or so votes more or less equally between the candidates. Nationally, the Conservatives won 363 seats, 22 more than before, Labour 258 (23 fewer) and the Liberals 5, losing one seat. Despite his record of loyal support for the Government, and his excellent performance during the election campaign, Thorneycroft was not invited to rejoin the Government. His colleague Enoch Powell who was offered a post refused to accept it.

Summing up in his constituency newsletter the lessons of the campaign for the country at large, Thorneycroft saw the result as a resounding rejection of Socialist policies. He pointed out, however, that the democratic system worked best when there was an effective opposition, and that an opposition could only be effective if it looked like an alternative Government. He wondered what the Labour Party could possibly do to make themselves effective in that sense *"when there was no body of men on the benches opposite who look like forming an alternative Government in any foreseeable future"*. He also sounded a note of caution for his own side, reminding his supporters that although Governments can plan to pass certain laws, it is events that shape the problems that confront them. A month later, in the wake of the Labour Party Conference at Blackpool, he was able to deduce that the Socialists had learnt nothing from the election. Having carefully avoided any reference to further nationalisation measures during the election, they now showed at their Conference that *"they clung obstinately"* to their old Socialist beliefs, and *"rejected the idea that they might become a liberal or radical opposition unconnected with Marxist philosophy.*

During the ensuing weeks, still confined to the back benches, Thorneycroft kept up his attack on the *"dreary annual round of wage claims demanding more money for less work"*, complaining that *"Sir Brian Robertson has just celebrated another thumping annual loss by the British Transport Commission with a promise to back-date an increased pay award."* He was proving himself to be an adept performer on television, and had become a frequent and popular participant in programmes like *Panorama* and *Who goes next?*, and used these appearances and letters to the Press to ram home his plea for economic discipline, for example, in February 1960, castigating the Government for agreeing, surrendering to the threat of a strike, to allow the railway workers a 5% wage increase, without regard to profitability and without even waiting for the report of the Guillebaud Committee which had been charged with reviewing that very matter. His solution for the railways was to run them as a normal commercial business at a profit, closing unprofitable branch lines, charging passengers economic fares, and getting rid of redundant staff. He argued the more general case for a contract of service for every employee, with a fair period of notice related to length of service and the right to engage in official strikes, but with unofficial stoppages condemned and demarcation and other disputes between union members referred to arbitration. In the House of Commons, on 23rd February, he joined Viscount Hinchingbrooke and the maverick Gerald Nabarro in questioning the practice of nodding through without debate the Estimates of public expenditure which would determine the amount of revenue that the Chancellor of the Exchequer would shortly be asking the House to approve in his Budget. Nabarro pointed out that the Estimates had increased by £360 million, including *"quite a number of items about which I am very doubtful"*, and Thorneycroft thought that *"the House might reasonably pause for a few moments before it passes on the nod a Vote on Account of £1,300 million."* Harold Wincott, in one of his shrewdly amusing and percipient 'conversations with his son' articles in the *Financial Times* on 1st March recalled that, when Mr Thorneycroft resigned in 1958, Madame Tussauds had *"melted him down to make Tommy Steele"*, and wondered whether holders of the gilt-edged stock the Government had issued to finance the increase in expenditure might be a bit tired of rocking and rolling and perhaps like Tommy Steele to be remodelled as Mr Thorneycroft.

In the international arena, he was troubled by the state of the discussions, still ongoing from the time of his tenure at the Board of Trade, between the Common Market, the members of the Free Trade Area and the Americans. He was especially critical of the Americans who seemed unable to decide whether to support or oppose a commercially stronger Europe. He was concerned that it was proving so difficult to build a bridge between the Common Market and the Free Trade nations, and the risk that this might result in the two trading blocs erecting high tariff barriers between them to the detriment of trade, splitting 'free' Europe in two. In his letter to his constituents in February 1960, he drew attention to the problems the French were facing in Algeria, where a million French settlers were not at all happy with De Gaulle's plan to grant a large measure of autonomy to the country, commenting that Algeria was not the only African country with large minorities of European settlers.

Thorneycroft's increasingly frank strictures were beginning to become uncomfortable for the Government, although he was very careful in the way he framed his criticisms. In an article in the *Financial Times* on 2nd March, he painted a positive picture of what had been achieved since 1957: balance of payments satisfactory; exports high and rising; upsurge in production; gold reserves £178 million higher; sterling strong; and prices stable. He recognised that some of the credit must go to the Chancellor of the Exchequer, but *"a substantial factor … had been the downward movement of the Terms of Trade from 106 in 1957 to 90 in 1959. To purchase cheap and sell relatively dear is as helpful to us as to any other shopkeeper. A return of the Terms of Trade to the levels of 1957 would have swift repercussions upon the cost structure of the whole of British industry."* Referring to a decision a few days before to *"pull the props out from under the gilt-edged market"* by refusing to buy back Government stocks, he urged that *"we make up our mind which road we are intending to travel and then for a time at least stick to it. At this moment we are putting the monetary brakes on, shouting warnings to the passengers, pressing on the accelerator of Government spending and wages; while wondering what to do about the Budget.* He urged *"that sensible and courageous man, the Chancellor of the Exchequer"* to try to get everything working in the same direction as soon as possible. The arrows found their mark, and the barbs hurt.

Thorneycroft's health was causing him some problems at this time. In the run up to the General Election the previous Autumn, he had contracted a chill which had developed into double pneumonia accompanied by a kidney condition. Convalescence in Morocco seemed to have put him right again but now, in the Spring of 1960, he was stricken by jaundice. He did not allow this to keep him out of action for long. On 20th March 1960 he returned, in an article in *The Sunday Times*, to his consistent theme of the importance of controlling Government expenditure, and his concern that Parliament was not discharging its responsibility to the nation of critically examining the spending proposals of the Government but was, instead, nonchalantly waving them through without debate. It was not, he averred, for lack of opportunity: *"there were numberless occasions when Civil and Military supply comes before the House"*. The problem was a lack of will. He was not arguing that *"the constant recurrence of overstrain in the economy arose through spending money on foolish things, but through spending too much on too many good things"*. He cited with approval a comment made by the Prime Minister a few days earlier, that *"we must count the bawbees and show a modicum of restraint"*. The Prime Minister was right, said Thorneycroft, but the counting must start in the Treasury, and the modicum of restraint around the Cabinet table. More than two years had elapsed since his resignation, and his message had not been understood. He and his colleagues, Powell and Birch, had done the counting in the Treasury, but his colleagues in the Cabinet had not shown restraint, then or subsequently. He returned to the charge in the Budget debate in the House of Commons on 6th April with a sharp warning to the Chancellor, Heathcoat Amory, that he must retain the confidence of the public if he did not wish to find himself out of office, and that meant not allowing the notion to gain ground that inflation was something that could be tolerated.

In January 1958, Thorneycroft believed not only that freezing public expenditure would have been the right thing to do, but also that the mood of the public had been well prepared for drastic action and that the freeze would have been accepted, however reluctantly. By the Summer of 1960, Heathcoat Amory, who had announced his intention to retire from the Cabinet, showed clear signs of being ready to embrace Thorneycroft's policy, but he now faced the difficulty that, having for two years relaxed the squeeze on credit that was an integral part of his predecessor's programme and allowed consumer spending to stimulate the economy, he now had to manage an economy with domestic production saturated, full employment, imports booming and all the signs that inflation was about to take off and sterling lose value on the exchanges. In his recent budget, having failed to cut public spending, he had been obliged to raise taxes. He had already lifted Bank Rate from 4 to 5% and then to 6%. But a public which was used to hearing from the Government that "they had never had it so good" was much less inclined than it had been two years earlier to accept that the time had come for austerity and sacrifice.

Thorneycroft had not only adhered firmly to his principles throughout the period of his exile from office, but had done so with no sign of disloyalty towards the Government. At the end of July, the Prime Minister put an end to several weeks of intense media speculation about an impending reshuffle by announcing a series of changes to his Cabinet, which included Peter Thorneycroft as Minister of Aviation and Enoch Powell as Minister of Health. It might be thought that Macmillan was making a rather clever move in placing two of the principal exponents of tight expenditure control in two of the highest spending departments.

Minister of Aviation 1960-62

The Ministry of Aviation may not have been Thorneycroft's first choice of ministry for his return to office and he hesitated briefly before accepting Macmillan's offer of the post. However, he knew that there were plenty of important issues on the aviation agenda, and it was a step back into Government. Like the other Cabinet members, he would receive a salary of £5,000 pa plus £750 of his salary as an MP, but had to relinquish the business appointments he had been allowed to accept as a backbencher.

The 1950s had been a period of earnest but frustratingly difficult search for technically viable and affordable systems for accurate delivery of nuclear weapons to their targets. For a number of years, Britain had relied upon its fleet of conventional bombers to drop free-fall bombs, but the development of rocket propelled anti-aircraft missiles had, by the latter years of the decade, made reliance on these relatively slow aeroplanes unsafe. The delivery vehicle itself would have to be much faster – and therefore rocket propelled - to evade enemy defences. Successive British Governments seem to have been determined to do everything possible to avoid having to rely on buying missiles from the USA. The British defence industry was confident that it had both the ideas and the technical capability to convert them into practical solutions, and Britain had access to the Australian Woomera firing range for development testing. What was lacking was the economic strength to support the costly development work needed to go it alone. Nevertheless, the Americans recognised the value of British expertise and, from the summer of 1954 onwards, the USA and Britain had been collaborating in missile development, the Americans concentrating on an Intercontinental Ballistic Missile (ICBM) whilst Britain, with American support, was to develop a Medium Range (MRBM) design. Developed from an earlier design, Black Knight, the new British missile was christened Blue Streak, and the contract to build it had been awarded to De Havilland in 1955, with an estimated cost of £50 million. By the time Thorneycroft became responsible for the programme in 1960, the estimate had already risen to £300 million and there was a dawning realisation that the missile was technically incapable of doing its job, mainly because the time needed to load its fuel exceeded the trajectory time from first warning to arrival on target of the enemy weapon it was supposed to intercept and destroy. For military purposes, Blue Streak was worthless. Thorneycroft therefore found Britain without a launch vehicle it could rely upon, and with nowhere to go for a replacement other than the USA.

The Americans, in the meantime, had decided to develop a missile to be launched from aircraft, believing that a mobile platform would be less vulnerable than a fixed launch site. Douglas Aircraft was to be the main contractor to develop

Skybolt. *Faute de mieux,* Britain had decided that Skybolt could be carried by its Vulcan bombers and Macmillan had reached agreement with Eisenhower in March 1960 for a purchase of 144 Skybolts for the Royal Air Force. If Blue Streak's failure as a military device was embarrassing, Skybolt was to prove to be an unmitigated disaster. The Americans began trials in April 1962 with no success whatever after five attempts. Eventually, on 19th December that year a successful launch was at last achieved but, by then, the Americans had decided that aircraft platforms were not such a brilliant idea after all and, on the very same day, abandonment of the Skybolt programme was announced, leaving Britain with nuclear weapons that were, for the time being, completely useless.

Something had to be done, and quickly. The only solution left was to abandon altogether the approach of airborne delivery and persuade the Americans to make available their Polaris submarine based missiles. Urgent talks were held between Macmillan and John F Kennedy which resulted in an agreement for sale of a number of Polaris missiles for three nuclear powered submarines. The Royal Navy took over from the Royal Air Force the main responsibility for Britain's nuclear deterrent.

Thorneycroft realised that, if any value was to be salvaged from the expenditure already incurred on Blue Streak, there remained only the possibility of using the rocket in civilian applications and doing everything possible to share the development cost burden with other friendly states. There were, of course, alternatives: the first, to abandon space projects altogether and save a lot of money; the second, for Britain to develop a communication satellite system alone, forgoing any financial contribution from others but reaping all of whatever the commercial benefits of the investment should prove to be. Both Hawker Siddeley and De Havilland had prepared quite convincing proposals for development of global communications satellite systems at a cost much lower than the £600 million the Government had already spent on developing Blue Streak for defence purposes and, moreover, promising a commercially attractive return on the investment. Thorneycroft, however, remained as firmly convinced as in his Treasury days that Britain could not afford to undertake on its own every promising-sounding project that was put forward. He also believed that it would be unwise to have to rely solely on the Americans either as developers or suppliers of rocket systems: they had on too many occasions shown themselves reluctant to share the benefits or the technical know-how of their developments with their allies. Thorneycroft saw another major advantage in the 'Space Club' concept. It offered the possibility of a collaborative, cost-sharing and potentially profitable European venture which would surmount not only national boundaries, but also the increasingly important boundary between the trading blocs of the European Free Trade Area and the European Common Market.

Thorneycroft therefore took on with enthusiasm the task of convincing Britain's European partners who had already, the previous November, agreed to join a European Space Research Organisation, to take the practical step of adopting the technology already developed by Britain and join in the further development of a heavy satellite launch vehicle to the mutual advantage of the participants. The British suggestion was that Blue Streak, already shown to be reliable for launching from a fixed platform, could form the first stage of a satellite launch vehicle, combined with Black Knight, also fully proven, as the second stage. A new rocket would have to be developed for the launch vehicle's third stage. The height of the launching gantries at Woomera would have to be raised and oxygen manufacturing facilities provided on the site, in both cases requiring the support of the Australian Government. It was envisaged that three orbiting satellites would provide enough capacity for a communications system with global reach for voice, data and television transmission.

Thorneycroft devoted a large part of September and October 1960 to intensive discussions with first the Australian and then the Canadian Governments seeking their backing for the programme, although it was already clear that the Canadians were committed to work with the USA on missile projects. Shortly after his return from Canberra and Ottawa, Thorneycroft went to Paris to present his 'Space Club' plan to the Prime Minister, M Debré and his colleagues. The French, as reluctant as the British to rely solely on allies' developments, pressed the claims of one of their own rockets, Véronique, for the second stage instead of Black Knight, and they did not want it to be forgotten that they had a rocket range in the Sahara that could easily be extended, and was much closer to home than Woomera. Thorneycroft held further bilateral talks with the West Germans, Danes, Norwegians, Swedes, Swiss and Italians in January 1961, those with Germany tackling also a wide range of other issues, including possible French and German collaboration with the British in development and eventual production of a supersonic air-liner, and of a vertical take off and landing jet fighter based on the Hawker P1127, as well as problems of air traffic control in the increasingly congested European airspace. The discussions were difficult: the cost was uncertain, though certainly high; the risks of technical failure were great; and political urges to satisfy national lobbies were strong and often irrational. At one point, there was talk of a feeling within the German Government that Britain's real aim was to save the Blue Streak project with other people's money. However, a small, but significant, outcome of the talks in Bonn was an agreement for the German Navy to buy 50 British Seacat sea-to-air missiles from Short Brothers for operational tests.

Thorneycroft's remarkable personal success in this intensive round of bilateral talks paved the way for a multi-lateral conference sponsored by France and Britain which was held at the end of January 1961 in Strasbourg, chaired by Thorneycroft. This was preceded by a visit of rocket experts from a number of European countries (Belgium, Denmark, Germany, Italy, Holland, Norway, Sweden and Switzerland) and from Canada, to Spadeadam in Cumberland, where the Blue Streak missile had been developed, concluding with a successful launch of a missile. Under Thorneycroft's chairmanship, the Conference even managed to reach a fairly broad consensus on a proposal for sharing the estimated cost of £68 million: Britain 26%, France 23%, Germany 19%, Italy 11%, Belgium 5%, Sweden 5%, Holland 4%, Switzerland 3%, Denmark 2% and Norway 2%. Technical discussions at the Strasbourg Conference ranged well beyond the use of the launch vehicle for communication satellites. Sir Harrie Massey, head of the British National Committee for Space Research, held out the prospect of launching also a 'general purpose' earth-orbiting satellite, an astronomy satellite able to pick up signals from stars that could not penetrate the earth's atmosphere, and a 'deep space' probe. Professor Auger, a leading supporter of the embryo European Space Research Organisation, emphasised that the ESRO would be a user of space vehicles, and would not itself engage in the launch vehicle project. The Conference achieved broad acceptance of the principles of the Anglo-French proposal which, by the end of the Conference had crystallised into a firm understanding that Blue Streak would be used for the first stage and a French rocket for the second, both Britain and France agreeing to make freely available the technology each had already developed. On the final day, Thorneycroft offered to increase the British financial contribution to one third of the cost of the first programme of development based on Blue Streak. The participants agreed to present the proposal to their Governments and were urged to aim at early commitment to the project.

One of the possible collaborative projects which had been touched upon during the round of bilateral talks concerned the development of a vertical take off and landing aircraft (VTOL). One variant of this, the SC1, was being developed by Short Brothers and Harland in Belfast, and it was to Belfast that Thorneycroft went on 17th February 1961, a few days after his return from Strasbourg. His first engagement there after landing at Nutt's Corner, the airport then serving Belfast, was to inspect with Lord Glentoran, the Minister of Commerce, the plans for converting an RAF station at Aldergrove so that it could function also as a civilian airport, replacing Nutt's Corner by the end of 1963. He had a private luncheon with Lord Brookeborough and then, although not quite recovered from a bout of influenza, devoted the afternoon to a visit to Bishopscourt, a radar station operated by the RAF which was one of four sites used for co-ordinating military and civilian air traffic over the UK. Visiting Short Brothers and Harland the following day, he confirmed that the Government intended to support the firm as an autonomous aircraft manufacturer, that he was actively seeking partners for development of the SC1 and that the Germans would be placing a trial order for fifty of Short's successful Seacat missile.

One of the consequences of Thorneycroft's decision to resign from the Treasury had been that he ceased to have any direct role in the slowly maturing debate within Government on Britain's relationship with Europe. However, the lengthy round of negotiations on missile collaboration had given him many opportunities for dealings with senior members of a number of European and Commonwealth governments, in which he performed very well. By June of 1961, the delicate issue of the effect on members of the Commonwealth and of the European Free Trade Area if Britain were to negotiate entry into the European Common Market could no longer be shelved, and a small team of three Cabinet ministers was formed to conduct the discussions with Commonwealth members. Duncan Sandys, the Secretary of State for Commonwealth Relations was the minister primarily responsible, and he would lead the team, but he was to be assisted by John Hare, the Minister of Labour, and Peter Thorneycroft. Sandys was to exchange views with the governments of New Zealand, Australia and Canada; Hare with the African members of the Commonwealth, Nigeria, Ghana, Sierra Leone and Rhodesia/Nyasaland; whilst Thorneycroft would go to India, Pakistan, Ceylon and Malaya. Macmillan's nomination of Hare was thought a little odd in some quarters, although he was, in fact, well qualified for the task allocated to him, as he had had experience of African affairs during his service at the Colonial Office five years earlier, and also knew the problems of the farming industry well from his stint as Minister of Agriculture. Thorneycroft's credentials for his part of the job were incontestable in view of his lengthy and successful experience at the Board of Trade. Corresponding discussions with the members of EFTA were to be conducted by Edward Heath, the Lord Privy Seal, and Reginald Maudling, then President of the Board of Trade. Both men were already committed to attend a meeting of the EFTA Council of Ministers at the end of June. (The members of EFTA were Austria, Britain, Denmark, Norway, Portugal, Sweden and Switzerland).

Heath and Maudling encountered a great deal of suspicion when, on 27th June 1961, they met the other members of EFTA, who feared that Britain was poised to abandon them in order to clear the way for British membership of the Common Market. After a fraught meeting culminating in an unplanned working dinner and an extra session next day organised in a hurry after the intended closing time of the meeting, they had to agree to a further meeting at the end of July when the team visiting the Commonwealth countries would have returned and reported the results of their mission.

Thorneycroft started his tour on 27th June, with an itinerary that would take him to Singapore, Kuala Lumpur, Colombo, Karachi and Delhi, returning to London on 17th July. After a briefing session with Lord Selkirk, High Commissioner in

Singapore and Commissioner-General for South-East Asia, his first discussion was with Lee Quan Yeu, Prime Minister of Singapore. He assured Mr Lee that Britain would take no decision to launch negotiations to enter the European Common Market until the consultation with members of the Commonwealth had been completed, and their points of view carefully considered. The key argument he put forward was that Britain needed the trading benefits to be gained from participation in the larger market of Europe, with a population of 150 million, much the same as the domestic American market, so as to make the most efficient use of modern production equipment. Sterling would be stronger as a result, and demand from the extended market for raw materials would bring great benefits to the Commonwealth countries able to supply them. He indicated that some other members of EFTA were likely to join the ECM, a welcome development for Britain, whose objective was a single, not a divided, Western Europe. There was no official statement from the Singapore Government, but the indications were that they were not worried about any adverse effect on their important exports of rubber, but they were concerned that some of their agricultural exports could be hit badly if the preferences currently granted to African territories of France were to be maintained and Commonwealth countries did not receive similar treatment. Similar concerns were expressed by the Malayan Government in Kuala Lumpur the following day, but they could see advantages if a broader market were opened up for their exports of tin and rubber. In Colombo, he found the Ceylonese Prime Minister, Mrs Bandaranaike, with views similar to those he had heard expressed in Singapore and Malaya, and looking in particular for protection of exports of tea and coconuts. However, her Minister of Trade and Commerce, Mr Ilangaratne, was reported to be actively considering what economic measures might be taken to protect Ceylon's interests should Britain decide to join the Common Market, and thinking of calling a conference of Asian and African states to examine the whole question. The Pakistani Minister of Commerce, Halfizur Rahman, saw no problems provided that his country's trade in cotton goods and jute, etc continued to receive preferential treatment. In India, Thorneycroft found greater suspicion – an undisguised fear that the Commonwealth was being asked to make important sacrifices so that Britain might benefit from joining the Common Market. Unlike Hong Kong and most of the African members of the Commonwealth, India was not a colony, and her foreign trade, especially in textiles and tea could be severely affected if the colonies were treated within the Common Market as the French dependencies were.

Back home, the Finance Bill was making its customarily deliberate way through the House of Commons. Three years after the dramatic resignation of Thorneycroft and his colleagues from the Treasury, Selwyn Lloyd had couched his Budget in terms that differed very little from those that Thorneycroft's Cabinet colleagues had refused to accept three years before. Now, commentators gave much greater credit to Thorneycroft. There was a growing and wide-spread recognition that the country was in an economic mess and that, if Macmillan had followed the advice of Thorneycroft and his Treasury colleagues in 1958, the electorate would have been much more willing to accept the sacrifices that the Government was now belatedly asking them to make. The mood of the trade unions was not improved by asking them to accept rigorous wage restraint for their members at the same time as Selwyn Lloyd in his Budget had given significant tax relief to surtax payers, raising the surtax threshold from £2,000 to £4,000 per annum.

On 31st July 1961, Macmillan announced in Parliament the long awaited decision that Britain would apply to join the European Common Market, with the promise that no agreement would be reached without the approval of the House of Commons, and after further discussions with Commonwealth members. From a position of cautious scepticism only five years earlier, Macmillan had moved to pragmatic realism. *"Our right place"*, he said, *"is in the vanguard of the movement towards the greater unity of the free world, and we can lead better from within than from without."* Hugh Gaitskell, the Labour leader, made one of his most brilliant and statesmanlike speeches in response to Macmillan's statement, recalling all the promises that had been made over the years to members of the Commonwealth to do nothing that would damage their trading relationships, and insisting that those promises should be kept. Macmillan's response was that it was *"wrong to regard Commonwealth and European interests as conflicting. Basically they must be complementary"*. Talking of agriculture, he remarked that the Common Market was at an early stage in the development of its policies and that Britain would only be able to shape those policies as a member. He averred also that the trading principle of the Common Market was to rely on tariffs, not on subsidies, and that Britain might have to change its system of farm support from one of payments from the Treasury to one dependent on the market giving farmers a fair return on their produce. He rejected any idea that the Common Market could develop into a federal state: the member countries were too old and diverse for that to happen, although a confederation might be a possibility in time.

For Thorneycroft, the policy of applying for entry to the Common Market presented no problems. Indeed, he felt himself well prepared to lead the negotiations – but this was not to be. Macmillan was to take a summer break, shooting grouse and pondering a major Cabinet reshuffle. Thorneycroft joined his wife and daughter in San Marino. On 17th August 1961, Macmillan announced that he had asked Edward Heath to take charge of the entry negotiations. Still Minister of Aviation, Thorneycroft told his constituents that this was one of the greatest decisions in the history of the country. It was a decision that Britain had to make. It posed three major problems: some loss of sovereignty was inevitable, but the Crown would remain; farmers' insistence on protection; and relations with the Commonwealth, where he warned that it was not possible to conceive of full approval by all Commonwealth members

In the meantime, the work of the Minister of Aviation went on. The annual Farnborough Air Show was due in September, and Hawker-Siddeley wanted to launch its Blue Streak rocket onto the market. Thorneycroft lifted the security embargo on the project so that information could be released to the media and to potential buyers. On 19th September, at Dunsfold Airfield, Thorneycroft experienced at first hand the excitement of breaking the sound barrier in a Hawker Hunter aircraft flown by Hawker's chief test pilot, Bill Bedford.

18th October saw Thorneycroft flying by Comet to Stavanger to see for himself the conditions in which a Viking aircraft of Cunard-Eagle Airways had crashed on 9th August, killing 34 schoolboys from Croydon, on which he was shortly to receive the report of the crash investigators. A few days later he was a Government representative at a Memorial Service for Dag Hammarskjöld, the Secretary General of the United Nations, who had been killed in an aircraft crash in Africa on 18th September. There had indeed been a rash of aircraft accidents in recent weeks, another, on 7th October, when all on board a Dakota of Derby Aviation had died when the aeroplane struck a mountain on its descent into Perignan, and on 16th October when the crew of four of another Dakota owned by BKS Air Transport had crashed between Leeds and Carlisle

Blue Streak came to the top of the agenda again at the end of October, when Thorneycroft opened a Conference at Lancaster House in London of nine nations involved or interested in the development of a communications satellite system based on the rocket. Australia, Belgium, the Netherlands, Italy and Spain with Great Britain and France acting as joint hosts were those involved, and Norway, Sweden and Switzerland were there as observers. By now, it was understood by all the interested parties that the British 'Blue Streak' would form the first stage of the launcher, the French Véronique rocket the second stage, and that the third stage would be the responsibility of Germany, using a rocket not yet developed. The projected cost, of which Britain would bear one third, remained at the £70 million forecast at the February meeting in Strasbourg. The objective of this meeting was to prepare a draft convention to establish an organisation to take the project forward, aiming at proving the launch vehicle in 1963 and launching the first commercial satellite into orbit in 1965. Thorneycroft underlined the significance of this first attempt at a truly multinational collaboration in a very advanced technological development which would give to the participating nations an opportunity to share in the commercial exploitation of space which they could not achieve on their own. Europe could no longer be ignored when future satellites were launched. The Lancaster House meeting achieved its objectives, and it now only remained for the participating nations to ratify the convention establishing the new European space organisation.

Almost every decision traceable to Thorneycroft up to this point in his political career had been consistent with the political philosophy he had outlined during the 1940s. On 22nd November 1961 he transgressed, announcing that he had decided to over-rule the decision of the Air Transport Licensing Board (chaired by Professor Jack) to allow a privately-owned airline, Cunard-Eagle, to compete with the state-owned British Overseas Airways Corporation on the North Atlantic route. His argument, the background to which was set out at some length in a memorandum of 31st October 1961 prepared by D.F. Allen of the Ministry of Aviation, and to be found in the National Archives (File BT 245/928), was essentially that BOAC was engaged in a massive investment of £150 million spread over five years in British built Vickers VC10 jets destined to fly the North Atlantic route, and that there was already excess capacity on the route, aggravated by a recent slump in business, which had resulted in BOAC expecting to make a loss of £10 million in its current financial year. Cunard-Eagle's proposal to fly the Boeing 707 aircraft that it was already committed to purchase would add still more capacity, with disastrous financial consequences for the airlines already flying the route with half-empty aeroplanes. The only concession he was prepared to make was to accept that Cunard-Eagle might use its new Boeings on the Bermuda route it was already permitted to fly with Britannia aircraft. Here, surely, was a classic case of a monopoly in a protected market operating inefficiently, over-investing, losing money and in dire need of a dose of competition to stimulate its management to perform better. In that context, it could be (and was) argued that the Licensing Board had correctly diagnosed the situation, and had taken a wise decision to allow Cunard-Eagle to provide that stimulus. Thorneycroft's over-ruling of that decision was contrary to his own principles and, surely, wrong.

Thorneycroft had an opportunity in February 1962 to put across his views on British accession to the European Common Market, when he was invited to speak at the inaugural meeting of the United Europe Association in Edinburgh. He was at his most convincing. He argued that Britain's decision was bound to be primarily a political, rather than an economic one; that it was unthinkable that at a time of such great danger, the nations of Western Europe should be divided; and, especially, that Britain might be isolated from Europe. The economic advantages of membership were, nevertheless, considerable and the penalties of staying out very high. He believed that the problem of Commonwealth relations could be overstated, and that it was in the common interest of Europe and the Commonwealth that trade should develop between them. He insisted that nobody was suggesting completely free trade in agricultural products. Britain supported agriculture in a different way from European practice, keeping prices to the consumer low and compensating farmers with subsidies, whereas in Europe prices in a controlled market were kept closer to the cost of production.

Thorneycroft's stay at the Ministry of Aviation was too short to bring the satellite launcher project to fruition. Indeed, he had told the House of Commons during a defence debate on 6th March 1962, that *"Ministers of Aviation very seldom live in their offices long enough to reap the fruits or otherwise of their own mistakes. They all seem to be able to rely on the mistakes of others."* What Thorneycroft had done was to prepare the ground well for future collaboration in civil space projects. Of the European states he approached, he had been able to convince France, Germany and Italy to play major roles, and Belgium and the Netherlands to take lesser parts.

32. Preparing to move in the same direction (*sketch by Peter Thorneycroft*)

Canada had resisted his advocacy, preferring to work with the Americans, but Australia was a key partner. It was not until 1964 that a later version of the European launch vehicle emerged as Europa I, also designed to use Blue Streak as its first stage, with a French second stage derived from their Coralie rocket and a German design (ASAT) as its third. The Italians provided a satellite, and Belgium and the Netherlands some of the ground equipment. Australia contributed use of the launch pad at Woomera. Although Blue Streak itself was successfully tested at every one of eleven subsequent trials between 1964 and 1970, the combined vehicle suffered successive failures of the second and third stage rockets and, finally, of the separation mechanism of the satellite. Escalating cost and lack of confidence in the design finally killed any hope of Commonwealth support. The inevitable cancellation of the Europa I project meant that there was no point in persisting with Blue Streak, which was also cancelled.

The Defence debate on 6th March had been enlivened with a statement by Harold Wilson that nobody in authority in Washington thought that Britain's hydrogen bomb (which the Labour Party wished to abandon) *"added one iota to the strength and credibility of the deterrent."* Thorneycroft thought it not very helpful to start a defence debate with an assumption that the enemy's defences were impregnable and our own weapons worthless. He pointed out that: *"Our policy is based upon the use of conventional as well as unconventional arms. It is based on volunteer rather than conscripted forces. It is based upon frontiers which are acknowledged to extend beyond the frontiers of Europe, and it is based upon alliances which are not restricted to NATO, important though NATO is, but are designed to cover the main centres of danger in the world"*. He argued that *"it must be a relevant factor in the mind of a potential enemy that a strike at Europe would also involve men and nations, or one nation, which had a deterrent held in Europe. This must add to the total of the deterrent force and its validity"*.

In what amounted to a report on his term at the Ministry of Aviation – *"a shop from which the Services buy their requirements",* as he put it - Thorneycroft reminded the House that *"The truth is that no Service can have all that it wants. All of us are, in fact, confined within the limits of the total amount of money available. In these circumstances, inevitably some things have to be cancelled."* *"We must strain every nerve to see that common requirements are achieved between the services whenever possible. Transport aircraft is [an] example of sharing between the civil and military role. Air Traffic Control is rather a good example of how both military and civil requirements have increasingly been pooled, with military and civilian personnel sitting in the same control centres".* …. *"But even sharing between the Services is not enough. We must also share on the basis of interdependence between countries. We are buying Skybolt from the United States and the AS30 air-to-ground weapon from the French".* …. *"The need is to try to co-operate, not merely in sales to one another, but in the actual making of the requirements and the research and development that goes with them. If this can be done from the start it is of immense advantage. The vertical lift aircraft P1127, in which the Americans joined in the early stages of development of the Pegasus engine or the RB162 Rolls-Royce engine, which is being developed by the Germans, the French and ourselves, are hopeful illustrations of what can be done by international collaboration. Outside the field of defence, an attempt to do this with a satellite launcher might set a pattern for the future."*

Throughout his ministerial career, Thorneycroft never failed to attend to his duties as the Member for Monmouth, nor did he allow himself to become so blinkered by his current departmental duties that he lost sight of the broader political picture.

In spite of the punishing programme of overseas visits that he had to undertake as Minister of Aviation, he regularly shared his thoughts with his constituents through his monthly letters and visits. In January 1961 he wrote:

"The opening weeks of 1961 have shown no let-up in the dangers of the tensions to which we have become accustomed. In the Far East the situation in Laos, uncertain, complicated and dangerous, has been giving anxiety to all thoughtful people. It would be easy for some struggle of this sort to blow itself up into a dangerous conflict between the great powers.

It is perhaps peculiarly the task of the British Prime Minister and the British Foreign Secretary with all the knowledge and experience that Britain has in so many parts of the world to exercise a moderating influence in situations of this kind. The moderation in itself is not enough. It must be backed by strength and by the knowledge that the West will stand together in the last resort and is not to be trifled with.

The cost of strength is very great indeed as the Defence budgets of the various Western nations show. Weapons as they become more sophisticated become more costly, and it is not possible to contract out of the struggle.

Nevertheless, costs can be saved and strength increased by seizing every opportunity of greater unity within the Western alliance. Organisations such as NATO or its corresponding body for South East Asia known as SEATO, are designed to promote this unity.

In Europe, in the Commonwealth and above all in Anglo-American relations it must be our constant aim to share our experience and knowledge and in every field of activity to back each other up. It is incidentally the absence of any understanding of this vital need which represents the principal weakness of the Labour Party today.

The United States are about to embark upon a new era with a young and new President shortly taking up what is perhaps the most responsible job in the world today. All of us who value peace must wish them well and all of us must be prepared to give them what help we can in the opening years of what is in any event likely to be a most difficult period of administration."

Minister of Defence 1962-64

On 12th July 1962, Harold Macmillan announced the third major reshuffle of his Cabinet. He kept R.A. Butler by his side as Deputy Prime Minister but, in general, his new team was seen as favouring the younger, more adventurous spirits in the Parliamentary Conservative Party. The youngest of the new ministers was the erudite Sir Edward Boyle, aged 38, who became Minister of Education. Reginald Maudling, a well prepared economist, who was 45, replaced Selwyn Lloyd as Chancellor of the Exchequer. Another of the party's intellectuals, Sir Keith Joseph (44) became Minister of Housing and Local Government. Thorneycroft's former Treasury colleague, Enoch Powell, aged 50, retaining his appointment as Minister of Health, was brought into the Cabinet. Thorneycroft himself, now relatively long in the tooth at 53, succeeded Harold Watkinson at the Ministry of Defence, replaced in his turn at the Ministry of Aviation by Julian Amery.

Thorneycroft's appointment led to the expectation in some quarters that the policy consistently espoused by Watkinson of maintaining a powerful British nuclear deterrent as independent as possible from that of the United States would now begin to shift in favour of collaboration with friendly powers in Europe aimed both at reducing the economic burden on individual states of the costly research, development and production programmes that true independence inevitably required and at reducing the risk that, if America were to use its deterrent in its own perceived interest against Russia, its European allies might be exposed to reprisals to which they would have no effective response or defence. The success that Thorneycroft had achieved as Minister of Aviation in fostering collaboration of the major European states in development of satellite communication systems, together with his persistently expressed views on the dangerously heavy economic burden of defence expenditure at the level needed to maintain an independent deterrent, certainly qualified him to promote similar policies in the military sphere.

The nuclear deterrent that Thorneycroft had at his disposal in July 1962 consisted of a fleet of 180 V-bombers armed with nuclear bombs, capable of dropping their weapons on enemy targets (on the rather heroic assumption that they would not be shot down by enemy missiles before they got anywhere near their targets). Harold Wilson had not been far wrong in asserting a few weeks before that nobody in Washington believed that the British H-bomb was of any real use. Indeed, the American Secretary of Defense, Robert McNamara, had implied as much in a recent speech in Michigan suggesting that any attempt by one of America's allies to deploy independently bombers armed with nuclear weapons would be tantamount to suicide. Review of the rationale for the policy of deterrence was clearly close to the top of the new Minister's agenda.

Macmillan also placed close to the top of Thorneycroft's agenda the task of taking forward with Admiral of the Fleet Earl Mountbatten, recently appointed Chief of Defence Staff (CDS, the further radical reform of the cumbersome and inefficient structure of Britain's defence establishment. In his masterly biography of Mountbatten (published by Collins in 1985) Philip Ziegler devoted the best part of 80 pages to a detailed and definitive history of efforts to achieve defence reorganisation from early 1957, when Macmillan had launched the process in the wake of the Suez debacle, until Mountbatten's retirement from the post of CDS in July 1965. In 1957, Macmillan had appointed Duncan Sandys as Minister of Defence and charged him to get the process moving of establishing stronger coordination of the three services. Duncan Sandys had made limited progress in this direction: in particular, he had appointed the first CDS, Marshal of the Royal Air Force Sir William Dickson. However, the structure he bequeathed to Thorneycroft was still based upon three virtually independent services, the Army, the Navy and the Air Force, each represented by a Secretary of State, and competing with each other not only for resources but also for influence in the formulation of the nation's defence policies. The three services and the government departments supporting them had, not surprisingly, proved to be intensely jealous of their prerogatives and proud of their histories, and Dickson had not been able to establish his ascendancy over the three Chiefs of Staff to the degree that Macmillan believed to be necessary. Mountbatten was the last serving officer of the war generation with direct experience (as Supreme Commander of the Allied Forces in South East Asia during the Second World War) of commanding and coordinating combined operations involving all three services. He was strongly in favour of the degree of strong central control for which Macmillan had been pressing. Thorneycroft's own experience in these lofty matters was at the more lowly level of a staff officer involved in planning the North African landings in 1942, when he had been strongly critical of the failure of the system then ruling of appointing inter-service committees to direct combined operations, a failure which he ascribed to the absence of a single commander with overall accountability. At a meeting on 2nd August 1962 of the Prime Minister with his new Minister of Defence and the CDS, Macmillan asked Mountbatten to produce firm proposals, and submit them to him via Thorneycroft, to whom the CDS reported.

Shortly afterwards, in September 1962, Thorneycroft went to Washington for his first meeting with the American Secretary of Defense, Robert McNamara, the principal proponent in the American Administration of a change in direction of United States' policy on the defence of Europe against any Soviet Bloc aggression. This had hitherto relied almost entirely on the deterrent effect of America's massive armoury of nuclear weapons, but was now to depend on maintaining large conventional forces in Europe, capable of resisting an attack on a broad front by enemy conventional forces so as to give the Allies time to decide whether, as a last resort, to use the nuclear option. A key element of this proposal was that Britain would be asked to increase significantly the number of its troops stationed in Germany, leading to concern that the deployment of British forces in sufficient strength to protect its interests in Africa and the Far East might be prejudiced. There were fears, too, that the US military were frequently rejecting weapons of British design for NATO use and insisting on American designs even when they were inferior, so as to foster the interests of the American defence industries and squeeze out British businesses. America's deployment of its naval forces was also changing. Polaris nuclear weapons were to be confined to submarines patrolling the world's oceans, leaving the surface ships of the Sixth Fleet in the Mediterranean with a non-nuclear role.

Underlying all these concerns was the British Government's desire to maintain its own independent nuclear deterrent whilst at the same time being forced to recognise that, although Britain had its own H-Bomb, it did not have a missile capable of delivering it, and had to rely on the Americans to supply an airborne missile, Skybolt, which could be armed with a British nuclear war-head and launched from Britain's fleet of V-bombers. Skybolt, however, was still under development and suffering a series of failures in trials.

The message that Thorneycroft gave to McNamara – and also directly to President Kennedy, whom he met before the end of his visit - was that Britain would be able, in an emergency, to double its forces deployed in Germany by resorting to a general mobilisation, but only at the cost of seriously weakening the country's economy and, consequently, the NATO Alliance. McNamara was well aware of the important role that British forces played in the Middle and Far East and was anxious that Britain should not strengthen its deployment in Europe by transferring troops from these sensitive areas where the United States had no presence and little influence.

Thorneycroft also argued the case for the British defence industry to receive a larger share of NATO equipment orders, and pressed for a more sensible process of reaching agreement in NATO on the specifications for new weapons before launching the ordering process, so that American and European defence companies could compete on equal terms instead of each proposing a different design. This procedure had, in the British view, led to selection of equipment on often spurious technical grounds, a recent example being the selection of the American 'Sergeant' short range missile by France and Germany for NATO deployment and the consequent abandonment of the British 'Blue Water' weapon which had a demonstrably superior performance. These arguments, it has to be said, fell on deaf ears: the Americans rather liked the procedure which resulted in orders being placed preponderantly with American firms. There was, however, one item of equipment where Britain's technical lead was acknowledged – the vertical take-off P1127 aeroplane developed by Hawker, which the Americans had agreed to evaluate by ordering a full squadron of aircraft.

Concurrently with the discussions in Washington between McNamara and Thorneycroft, the American Under-Secretary of Defense, Gilpatric, was talking in Bonn with the German Defence Minister, Strauss, who was worried by a different aspect of the American change of policy – the risk that the Americans might come to place too great a reliance on ground troops, and decide to withdraw its nuclear weapons from European territory and rely entirely on a submarine based nuclear deterrent over which Germany would have no influence.

The imminence of elections in America meant that no long-term commitments were given by McNamara on most of these issues, but Thorneycroft had presented the arguments clearly and firmly. He had to accept, realistically, that America would never rely on a single foreign supplier of any essential item of defence equipment, but he felt that he had succeeded in convincing the Americans that British research and development of weaponry was successful and must not be jeopardised.

Thorneycroft took very seriously his onerous task of merging the separate service departments into one, and he went about preparing for it in a characteristically systematic way. He began in October 1962, soon after his return from Washington, with lengthy discussions with the leaders of the land forces service, the Secretary of State for War, John Profumo, and the CIGS, General Sir Richard Hull, moving on then to the air and sea services. In each case, he asked for an assessment of the principal tasks they expected to have to carry out during the next decade and a survey of the resources already available and the reinforcements they envisaged needing in order to do so efficiently and economically, making it clear that he had no intention of allowing total defence expenditure to continue growing, and that they should not assume that currently approved budgets would be sacrosanct. On 9th October, he received Mountbatten's proposals. The paper bore the title 'Central Organisation for Defence', and there is a copy of it in the Mountbatten Papers held in the care of the Hartley Library at the University of Southampton. Drawing on his twenty years of experience of the existing organisation, he stated roundly that the present organisation suffered from an unavoidable conflict of loyalties and would not be able to cope with the demands for a consistent British defence policy which would increase with the development of NATO and future membership of the European Economic Community. His proposed solution was to abolish the service ministries with their separate accountability to Parliament leaving a single Minister of Defence responsible to the Prime Minister, the Cabinet and the Defence Committee not only for the formulation of defence policy but also for the administration and motivation of all three services, with a single defence budget. He did not go so far as to suggest merging the armed services themselves into a single Defence Force, but insisted that they must be encouraged to collaborate much more closely. He outlined provision for what he called a 'horizontal' support staff to manage common functions of Research, Development, Production, Supply, Logistics and Personnel, complemented by 'vertical' divisions responsible for those operational matters specific to a single service, but overall operational control would be exercised by the Chief of Defence Staff to whom the military heads of the three services would report. He accepted that someone would have to be responsible for production of both military and civil aircraft, for the former responsible to the Ministry of Defence, for the latter to a less senior Ministry or, perhaps, to a Minister of Transport. He recognised that such a far-reaching reorganisation would take several years to complete and should not be rushed, but urged an early decision and announcement of intention to proceed. Annexed to the paper were detailed proposals and an organisation chart, but Mountbatten was careful to leave himself flexibility in case of criticism of details, pointing out that rejection of a detail of his proposal need not prejudice the fundamental principles of his scheme.

Leaving his colleagues to digest and discuss Mountbatten's paper, in the middle of October Thorneycroft was off on his travels again, this time to Paris, where he met M. Messmer, the Armed Forces Minister, pressing him to agree that NATO forces should be equipped with the Hawker VTOL aircraft and not the French Mystère fighter.

Britain came close to having to test its readiness for war at the end of October, when the Cuban Missile Crisis broke on the 22nd of that month. A tense stand-off culminated on 28th with President Kennedy's ultimatum to Khruschev. On that Sunday morning, Thorneycroft told his Chiefs of Staff that the options available were the dispersal, ready for action, of the V-Bomber Force or general mobilisation. Fortunately Khruschev climbed down that same day.

Early November brought a diversion from the hectic but relatively predictable course of affairs, when the Shadow Minister of Defence, Patrick Gordon Walker launched a fierce attack in the Commons on the Admiralty's handling of the Vassall affair. William Vassall was a clerk in the Admiralty who, for six years, had been selling military secrets to the Russians before eventually being detected, prosecuted and committed to prison for 18 years. Labour was particularly incensed by the Government's decision that an inquiry into the affair was to be carried out by a committee of three civil servants and not by a public inquiry. Thorneycroft dismissed Labour's concerns in an ill-judged, excessively jocular manner that laid him open to strong criticism in the Press in the following days. The serious point he was making was that the job of the internal inquiry was to find out what had gone wrong with the Admiralty's security procedures, and that senior civil servants were well placed to do this. They would report to the Prime Minister, who would certainly consult the Leader of the Opposition before deciding what action should be taken. Should it be shown that the Admiralty was to blame, it would be the First Lord, Lord Carrington, who would take the responsibility. The thrust of the message was unfortunately lost in a welter of complaints that the Government was not taking the matter seriously.

Thorneycroft picked himself up and on 15th November 1962 was in Rome discussing the NATO equipment problem with the Italian Minister of Defence, Andreotti.

A month later, in mid-December, Thorneycroft was talking to McNamara again, this time in London, preparing the ground for a meeting between Macmillan and Kennedy in the Bahamas a few days before Christmas. This was a fraught discussion, Thorneycroft complaining bitterly that the USA, having promised in 1960 to supply the *Skybolt* air-borne missile on which Britain had been relying as the delivery vehicle for its nuclear deterrent, was now talking of abandoning its development in favour of a submarine-based missile, *Polaris.* A real fear was emerging in the British defence establishment that the Americans could simply not be trusted to fill gaps in the British nuclear armoury which Britain could not afford to fill on her own. Indeed, the Americans seemed to prefer that the gaps were *not* filled, and that Britain should reconcile itself to abandoning its independent nuclear deterrent altogether. In London, McNamara reinforced this impression, attempting to fob Thorneycroft off with an offer to supply an out-of-date missile called *Hound Dog* instead of *Skybolt. Hound Dog's* effective range was only 600 miles, whereas *Skybolt* was intended to have a 1000 mile reach but, as McNamara pointed out, five successive trials had been failures. McNamara knew full well that the debate about the relative merits of air-borne versus submarine-mounted missiles opened up inter-service rivalries. In Britain, Mountbatten, a naval man, in the key position of CIGS, might be inclined to favour the submarine solution, which would threaten the continued existence of the long-range bomber fleet which was a core element of the Royal Air Force.

Thorneycroft and Macmillan left for Nassau with the issue unresolved. In the Bahamas, the Americans, although willing to give Britain all the results of the research and development of *Skybolt* in accordance with the original agreement, refused to budge on US abandonment of the missile. This was a risk that Macmillan could not accept. If, in the end, *Skybolt* proved to be a failure, Britain would be left with no deterrent and no recourse to American aid in developing or supplying a new alternative. After two days of argument, Kennedy accepted that Britain would keep its "independent" nuclear capability by acquiring *Polaris* missiles, already fully developed by America in a version with a range of 1,500 miles, to equip a number of new submarines. The agreement, thrashed out in detail by

McNamara and Thorneycroft, with no escape clauses, meant that the V-bomber squadrons (175 aircraft) of the Royal Air Force would be phased out as soon as the first submarines of the Royal Navy each equipped with *Polaris* missiles were commissioned from 1967/8 onwards. The agreement included provision for America and Britain to contribute their nuclear deterrents to a NATO nuclear force. (By a malign coincidence, a test launch of *Skybolt* from a B-52 aircraft was successfully completed as Macmillan and Thorneycroft were flying home, though this was not to change the decision to scrap the project. The Americans had delayed the test until the discussions in the Bahamas were over).

At a Press conference at Heathrow on his return to London, Thorneycroft presented the arguments in favour of the agreement which was already being castigated as a British surrender to the Americans. It was Macmillan, Thorneycroft announced, who had proposed the NATO solution for deployment, the Americans having been glad to accept as an important step forward in their endeavours to emphasise the resolve of all its allies to use nuclear deterrence as a multilateral force, preventing the spread of independent nuclear weapons. President Kennedy had already sent a message to De Gaulle offering to supply *Polaris* to the French on the same terms as those agreed with the British. Thorneycroft downplayed the significance of the abandonment of *Skybolt*, saying that it would have been necessary anyway to plan for the missile's successor, and that the decision to go now for *Polaris* anticipated by seven years an inevitable decision not to build a new fleet of bombers. He was satisfied (although he revealed no figures) that *Polaris* would cost no more than the expected cost of *Skybolt*. And, to placate the protagonists of air power, he confirmed that the TSR2 bomber would proceed, and that some V-bombers with free-fall bombs were likely to be retained, with some vertical take-off aircraft.

In Europe, not for the first or the last time, a Britain asserting her commitment to European integration was adjudged, certainly by France, to be stitching up a deal with the Americans and presenting it as a *fait accompli* to its European allies. De Gaulle was not prepared to accept the American offer. France was already well advanced in the development of nuclear warheads for its own *Berenice* rocket and its own hydrogen bomb, and was determined not to become dependent on others – and certainly not on America - for its nuclear deterrent. Adenauer, the German Chancellor, was suspicious of an arrangement that would leave Germany excluded from an American–British-French nuclear grouping within NATO yet saddled with a heavy burden of providing hundreds of thousands of extra ground troops as its contribution to NATO's new policy.

The outcome was that the policy of the new American administration of denying an independent nuclear deterrent to any of its allies was compromised. Kennedy had not only conceded the right to Britain, but had been obliged to offer the same concession to France. Britain remained able to claim, however naively, that she would have nuclear weapons that, even if intended to be used only as part of a multilateral force, could as a last resort be used independently in defence of a supreme national interest. France was given yet another reason (or excuse) for suspecting British perfidy towards Europe, and Germany cause to reflect on whether, having co-operated loyally with the Americans and the British ever since the end of the war, she was really regarded by her allies as an unreservedly trusted partner

De Gaulle did not have to wait long for the occasion to show his displeasure. On 14th January 1963, he vetoed British entry into the European Economic Union.

Would this have happened had Thorneycroft been entrusted with leading the British negotiating team, rather than Heath? Probably. Both men were regarded in most European circles as strongly Europhile. Neither of them could break through De Gaulle's visceral distrust of the British. Thorneycroft might have contributed indirectly to a positive result in Europe had he been able, as Minister of Defence, to pursue (first having secured the support of the Cabinet) a policy of decisively breaking British dependence on America for nuclear know-how and committing the country irrevocably to reliance solely on its European friends. He could not do this -indeed there is no suggestion whatever that he even considered the possibility - because he judged that Britain could not rely on her principal European allies not merely to be willing to collaborate effectively, but actually to succeed, in the technically challenging and extremely costly task of developing a credible nuclear capability and subsequently keeping it up-to-date. The technical failure of the Blue Streak missile military programme and the fraught negotiations on its commercial applications when he was Minister of Aviation had been salutary experiences.

The issue of the annual Defence White Paper on 20th February 1963 was given a hot reception. It comprised only four paragraphs to support a proposed budget for 1963/4 of £1,838 million (£9m a word, the *Evening Standard* calculated), an increase of £117 million over the previous year, after transferring £117 million of works expenditure to the Ministry of Public Building and Works. The estimates for the Army, Navy and Air Force were annexed as Memoranda; the brevity so caustically criticised by the Press reflected for the first time the reorganisation which had converted the three Service ministries to subsidiary departments of the Ministry of Defence, whose previously separate budgets were now consolidated into a single Defence budget. The details were there in the Memoranda. The Army was to build up its strength to 180,000 by the end of the year, supplemented by 20,000 troops in the Gurkha regiments and the Royal Marines. The Navy, kept to 100,000 men, was to receive three guided missile ships and build two more of a more powerful version, to commission three O Class submarines, a second squadron of Buccaneer nuclear strike bombers and a number of new Wasp and Wessex helicopters, and continue design work on a new aircraft carrier. The Air Force would begin to feel the effects of transferring responsibility for the nuclear deterrent to the Navy: its only new equipment would be an early warning station for the Americans at Fylingdales in Yorkshire. The *Daily Express* pointed out somewhat gleefully that the Army would be equipped with Belgian rifles, Italian howitzers, Swedish and Australian anti-tank weapons, American heavy guns and German bridging equipment. The sharpest, and the most justified, criticism of the White Paper was that most of it had been written several weeks earlier, and was mainly a catalogue of equipment that made hardly any reference to the major impact of the Nassau agreement or, indeed, to any key aspect of defence policy.

Thorneycroft was up against the perennial problem of politicians responsible for national security, to decide how much information can safely be disclosed to the public, and how freely security issues may be publicly debated without disclosing policies, plans and the rationale for them to the enemy (or even to allies if there is a risk of subsequent leakage to the enemy). He had been strongly criticised during a Defence debate three weeks earlier for remarking that the Chiefs of Staff supported the policy of keeping an independent nuclear deterrent. What, Patrick Gordon Walker had asked, if they had not supported it? Would that have been disclosed? Having disclosed their support on this occasion, might not absence of disclosure of their views on a future policy lead to the assumption that they did not support it, whether they did or not? The Defence debate, which took place after the White Paper had been drafted but before it was published, had in fact ranged widely over the arguments for and against an independent nuclear deterrent and the Government's reasons for keeping it. The consequences of the Nassau agreement for the Air Force, the Navy and the Defence budget had also been clearly revealed.

An important absence from the White Paper was any discussion of the review of defence organisation which Macmillan had put at the top of Thorneycroft's agenda when he was appointed, and which had been under active discussion within Whitehall since Mountbatten presented his proposals in early October 1962. Mountbatten had suggested that his plan should be implemented in two phases, in the first bringing all the personnel physically together, and in the second reorganising their tasks by function – overall command, research and development and procurement - covering the requirements of all three services. In response, Macmillan had asked General Lord Ismay and Lieutenant-General Sir Ian Jacob to advise the Government on changing the structures of the Ministry of Defence and the service ministries, and their report was expected imminently. Macmillan was already convinced that Mountbatten's plan was the right way to go, and Thorneycroft needed no persuasion that the job not only could be done, but that it must be done without further procrastination. Ismay and Jacob had produced their recommendations very quickly, at the end of February, their proposals being very close to Mountbatten's first phase. On 4ᵗʰ March 1963 Thorneycroft sketched, in response to questions in a poorly attended House of Commons, the broad outline of his intention to merge the War Office, the Air Ministry and the Admiralty fully into the Ministry of Defence, with their central staffs all housed in a single building. The services themselves were not to be merged but, in future, they would be represented in the Cabinet by the Minister of Defence, their individual political heads being down-graded to Ministers of State instead of Secretaries of State, and no longer Cabinet members. The military heads of each service, the Chiefs of Staff, would keep their responsibilities for advising the Government individually or as a group. Overall defence policy would continue to be the responsibility of the Cabinet.

In May, a NATO meeting in Ottawa, attended by Mountbatten, Thorneycroft and Lord Home, the Foreign Secretary, had provided an opportunity for them to hear from their Canadian colleagues of their experience with a reorganisation of their defence service which was even more far-reaching than the British proposal, merging the army, navy and air services fully into a single defence force with joint staffs and common ranks.

Details of the proposed new structure for the Defence departments were filled in when Thorneycroft introduced a White Paper on 16ᵗʰ July 1963. This confirmed the abolition, with effect from 1ˢᵗ April 1964, of the offices of First Lord of the Admiralty and Secretaries of State for War and Air. A new Defence Council was to be established, consisting of the Minister of Defence, Ministers of State for the each of the three services, the Chief of Defence Staff (CDS), the Chiefs of Staff of the three services, the Chief Scientific Adviser and the Permanent Secretary for Defence. In the case of the Army, the Chief of Staff's title would lose the obsolete adjective 'Imperial', becoming 'Chief of the General Staff' (CGS). It was intended to set up a new Defence Operations Executive charged with organising the response to any sudden emergency, served by a permanently manned Defence Operations Centre. Most of the personnel of the Ministry of Defence were to be housed in a building in Whitehall from which the Board of Trade would have to move: the staff of the other occupant of the building, the Air Ministry, would be absorbed into the new MoD. The rationale for these drastic changes was to bring the planning of new weapons and the relevant research and development programmes under closer and better co-ordinated control. The Services themselves would retain their separate identities, recognising the importance of preserving loyalties of military personnel to their ships, regiments and squadrons, although the whole object of the new structure was to achieve much closer co-ordination between them in future. Their intelligence services would be brought together with the Joint Intelligence Bureau in a Defence Intelligence Staff. The existing Defence Scientific

Staff was to be streamlined and improved. Security of all three Services would be the responsibility of a single senior officer. The Queen would take on the ancient role, dating back to King Alfred, of Lord High Admiral. The Ministry of Aviation, responsible for civil aviation, would remain independent, but close collaboration was to be assured with the Ministry of Defence. The budget for the new Ministry would be in the region of £2 billion, and there would be 800,000 personnel in the three services and the Ministry of Defence, half of them civilians (one office wallah to every sepoy, as warriors of the old Empire would put it).

What does not appear from the White Paper's bald statement of the results of eight years planning since Macmillan first saw the need for a single Ministry of Defence in 1955 is the achievement of Thorneycroft in reaching the desired goal so speedily without a single resignation of any of the proud, high-ranking sailors, soldiers and airmen who had to be persuaded to abandon decades – in the case of the Royal Navy three centuries – of tradition in order to bring their Services under one wing. There is no doubt that Thorneycroft was possessed of a remarkable ability for persuading powerful people with disparate interests and entrenched views to accept necessary change even when it had unpleasant consequences for them, and to work together to bring it about. He was certainly unusual among politicians in his willingness to allow his colleagues, whether close to him or more remote, freely to express their opinions, to listen to them and to absorb and make his own those suggestions which he found to be well-reasoned and objectively valid. This approach had succeeded very well during his five-year tenure of the Board of Trade, as his Permanent Under-Secretary there, Sir Frank Lee, recorded in his letter of farewell quoted earlier. It had failed him in the Treasury where too many of his civil servants led by Sir Roger Makins did not expect to have their ideas challenged by mere politicians who, in their view, could hardly be expected to understand the complexities of national finance: there, it was his political colleagues who showed their trust in him to the point of joining him in resignation when they saw that the policies they believed in were to be discarded.

In the Ministry of Defence, Thorneycroft's political colleagues were of the calibre he deserved, and all of them had enough military experience to satisfy their service colleagues that they were well qualified for their jobs. Lord Carrington, First Lord of the Admiralty, had served as a Major in the Grenadier Guards in France and Germany. Hugh Fraser, Secretary of State for Air, had also been a soldier, in the Lovat Scouts and the Special Air Services. The Secretary of State for War, Joseph Godber, had only been appointed a few weeks earlier: it had been his predecessor, John Profumo, another former soldier, disgraced and forced to resign his office on 4th June for his sexual misdemeanours, but nevertheless a competent and successful politician, who had taken a valuable part in the restructuring project. The Chief of Defence Staff, Earl Mountbatten, could hardly have been better qualified or more enthusiastic for his strengthened role, for which he had written the script himself. Sir Solly Zuckerman had been Chief Defence Scientist since 1960, cultivating the fertile ground bequeathed to him by Churchill's wartime scientific mentor, Lord Cherwell. As a young man, he had been scientific adviser to Combined Operations from 1943 – 1946. Zuckerman was to take full charge of a combined defence research and development budget of over £500 million, a quarter of the total defence budget. Sir Henry Hardman, the Permanent Secretary, was a senior civil servant of the highest competence.

The White Paper was debated in the House of Commons on 31st July 1963, when Thorneycroft explained to the House the broad rationale for the major reorganisation proposed and then, in some detail, the reasons for each element of change. This was a long debate – its record occupied 113 columns of Hansard and ought to be required reading for every prospective Secretary of State for Defence – and to précis it without glossing over some important detail is a challenging task.

The broad objectives of the reorganisation outlined by Thorneycroft were:

◇ the better control of defence spending, which the existing organisation dating from 1958 had been intended, but failed, to achieve;

◇ the formulation of an integrated defence policy, overcoming the persistent tendency of the three Services to approach problems from separate points of view;

◇ the management of defence research and development to meet the needs of defence as a whole, rather than of the single Services.

The organisational measures designed to achieve those objectives were:

◇ a single Ministry under a single Secretary of State with the authority to intervene on any defence matter should he judge it to be necessary, but also able to decentralise to secure efficient administration. The Secretary of State would be supported by three Ministers of State, responsible for the whole defence field, though each would have a responsibility for a single Service. He would have three professional advisers – the Chief of Defence Staff, the Permanent Under-Secretary and the Chief Scientific Adviser. The CDS, with the three Chiefs of Staff, would lead the Naval, General [Army] and Air Staffs;

◇ a separate Ministry of Aviation, responsible for civil and military aviation. Thorneycroft acknowledged that this had been a difficult decision: there were strong arguments for bringing responsibility for aviation within the Ministry of Defence. In reaching it he had accorded great weight to the advice of Sir Frank Lee, (the senior civil servant with whom he had worked so harmoniously and successfully at the Board of Trade in the 1950s) that to include aviation would put too heavy a load on the Secretary of State. To ensure the essential close co-operation with the Ministry of Defence, the Minister of Aviation and his top staff dealing with military projects would be housed in the same building as the Secretary of State for Defence and his staff. Research and advance weapons development would be handled by two committees under the Chief Scientific Adviser, both of them with strong representation from the Ministry of Aviation;

✧ the organisation must be flexible. A Permanent Under-Secretary for the Defence Secretariat would have a specific responsibility for identifying areas of administration which might be better handled on a defence rather than single Service basis;

✧ there must be a proper balance between the military, the administrative and the scientific at all levels in the Ministry;

✧ the Secretary of State would be responsible for the Defence Estimates, and control of finance would be centralised under a Deputy Under-Secretary of State (Programmes and Budgets). However accounting was to be decentralised to four Second Permanent Under-Secretaries who would account to the Public Accounts Committee for how the money had been spent. This arrangement would permit the House to continue, if they wished, to debate separately the estimates for the Navy, Army, Air Force and centrally controlled defence projects, although Thorneycroft suggested that it might be useful to have debates on such cross-service matters as *"the deterrent, our role in Europe with all services, on what our defensive position is in those great areas of the world between Aden and Singapore – matters which merit a major debate in the House"*;

✧ the individual loyalties and traditions of the fighting men themselves must be preserved. *"Look at it how one will"*, said Thorneycroft, *"when men are on the field of battle, they do not have too high a regard even for the local staff, and very few, I am sure, are thinking about the War Office, the Board of Admiralty, or anyone else like that. Their loyalties are very much more to their ship, their regiment or their squadron. Men have done very great things for loyalties of that kind. … We should seek in every way to fortify them"*.

Thorneycroft described how the new organisation would fit into the Cabinet structure, through the creation of a single Defence and Overseas Policy Committee, in place of two separate committees, recognising that *'defence is the servant of foreign policy'*. It would have a small fixed number of Ministers under the chairmanship of the Prime Minister. Others, such as other Ministers, the CDS, the Chiefs of Staff and the Chief Scientific Adviser could be called in as required, but would not be members. The Committee would be served by officials of the Cabinet Secretariat, not from the Ministry of Defence.

Finally, Thorneycroft hoped that *"the House will not underestimate the scale of this reform. There are 25,000 men and women engaged in four Ministries and all of them are in some degree affected by this, and many of them will move. To suggest that we can turn the whole lot over by a stroke of the pen from a Service to a functional basis is utterly unrealistic"*.

The Labour Defence Spokesman, Denis Healey (himself a former Army officer who had seen active service in Italy), devoted a large part of his speech to criticism of defence failures of the past, making the perhaps rather obvious point that the re-organisation now proposed would not have been necessary had previous reforms worked as intended, and castigating the Prime Minister for failing to provide continuity of office in the Ministry of Defence during the last 12 years. *"We have had"*, Healey reminded the House, *"nine Ministers of Defence in the last 12 years. Each of them presented at least on[e] new strategic concept"*. He believed that *"behind the failure in organisation and control of our Armed Forces there is a more fundamental failure … to relate our defence policy to our foreign and colonial policy, to have the sort of integration which is required between the Foreign Office, the Ministry of Defence, the Colonial Office, and the other Departments concerned with overseas affairs"*. As examples, he mentioned the Government's decision to open negotiations for supply of the Polaris missile just when Britain's application to join the Common Market had reached a critical phase, and the withdrawal in 1956 of British proposals for general disarmament after they had been accepted by the Soviet Union when it was realised that the Chiefs of Staff had not approved them. These points were perfectly valid, but did no more than underline the need for the sort of reorganisation now presented for debate. Indeed, some twenty minutes into Healey's hour long speech, Brigadier Sir John Smyth, MP for Norwood, was moved to hope that the hon. Gentleman would say something about the White Paper before he sat down. Healey duly did so, with the preamble *"that no changes in the Civil Service are a substitute for Ministers in the Foreign Office and the Ministry of Defence who have the ability and the will to work together"*. We shall try to précis what he said:

 ◇ the new Committee on Defence and Overseas Policy should work better than the present Defence Committee because it is smaller, if it is better serviced – and the White Paper gave no hint of strengthening the Cabinet Secretariat to do this;

 ◇ the Committee should study rigorously the economic and political importance of overseas commitments and the cost of protecting them by force rather then by diplomatic means;

✧ the integration of the three Services was badly needed;

✧ in addition to integrating policies internally, British defence policy and organisation should be integrated with those of our allies;

✧ the reorganisation was a move in the right direction because it was similar to the American system, which seemed to be producing the sort of results that the Minister hoped to achieve. However, these achievements were not produced by setting up the Pentagon, but by appointing a Secretary of State of immense energy with the strength of character to impose his will on the individual services. Everything depended on whether it simply produces a new framework to which the vested interests which obstruct progress very quickly adapt themselves, and on the quality of the individuals appointed to the top jobs;

✧ the White Paper gave insufficient information about the plans for implementing the reorganisation, giving the impression not so much of integration as of creating a new organisation parallel with or on top of the existing structures. What was really needed was a switch from a Service to a functional or mission basis for the organisation and financing of our defences;

✧ Thorneycroft's recent decision to put the TSR2 aircraft into production within months was unconvincing. The Government knew it should have cancelled the project, but was frightened of the political consequences.

In his response, Thorneycroft assured the House that the points of view put forward in the debate had been helpful, and would be closely studied. He commented immediately on a few key issues. Patrick Gordon Walker had suggested that his position would be strengthened if he had the support of other Ministers of Cabinet rank – he thought that others who had held office knew that it was possible to *"have a superfluity of assistance of this character"*. He found rather curious Healey's idea that Britain should abandon the independent deterrent so as to put ourselves in exactly the same position as Germany, who might otherwise break her treaty obligations. He confirmed that the new Defence and Overseas Policy Committee would be supported not only by the Ministry of Defence, but by the Cabinet Secretariat. He agreed with Healey that *"we are talking only about a machine – what matters is the way we use it."* He also agreed that *"we should press on with rationalisation. It would be impossible to do so, however, unless we had centralised power, at least to the point we have in these proposals. I should not like anyone to think that the working out of the proposals has been a pathway of roses without any controversy whatsoever."* He confirmed the intention to seek outside advice – not only scientific and, increasingly, technological, but also administrative (about purchasing, for example). He rebutted the criticisms of the quality of equipment, retorting that constant attacks, not only on TSR2 but also on the Buccaneer project, were doing Britain's aircraft industry immense harm, and suggested that the Opposition should weigh very carefully whether any political advantage they might get was comparable to the damage it was doing to the country.

It is not surprising that the House of Lords, well stocked with ex-officers from all three services as well as by politicians with experience of senior office during the Second World War, produced a debate on the White Paper of the highest quality. Montgomery of Alamein pointed out that the Minister of Defence would have to be 'a pretty good guy', and that it would be fatal if he were changed too often. He urged that the temptation should be resisted to choose a Chief of Defence Staff from each service in turn, and insisted that the new organisation must result in fewer people at the top – a point reinforced by Earl Attlee, who saw in the new structure 'too much harness and too little horse'.

The broad conclusion to be drawn from the two very well-informed debates was that the structure proposed was sound, that it would take time to implement the complex and far-reaching changes involved, and that it would require very good people to get maximum benefit from it.

The October 1963 Conservative Party Conference in Blackpool, held without the Prime Minister (who was in the London Clinic for a prostate operation), took place at a time of vigorous debate in the country on the effectiveness of Britain's nuclear deterrent. Thorneycroft risked a negative reaction from the US Administration with a speech in which he defended robustly the policy of not relying solely on the Americans to defend Britain in the event of a nuclear attack. *"This"*, he said, *"was not vain-glory or warmongering. It is not to have a great affection for nuclear weapons. It was to possess the strength to deter an enemy. "* To those who believed that Britain should not only scrap its nuclear weapons, but also dismantle the Air Force and retreat from South East Asia, and so save a lot of money, he said that *"Of course it would be cheaper to quit but we would be doing a great deal of damage to our own great country and the world. We should be betraying our friends not only in the Commonwealth but in some of the great emerging countries such as Malaysia."*

However, discussion of serious issues like defence was now being swamped by the realisation that the Macmillan era was coming to end, and the talk in corridors, at dinner tables and in the media was about who was likely to succeed him. Thorneycroft's name was not among those most often mentioned. He was widely felt to be ruled out by his resignation from the Exchequer and, in any case, there was Rab Butler, who had been waiting in the wings for such a long time. But it was not Rab whom Macmillan picked on 18th October in a move designed to pre-empt the selection of his successor. His choice, to the consternation and anger of many of his senior colleagues, was the Earl of Home, the Foreign Secretary, who would have to renounce his peerage in order to take office. Thorneycroft remained silent, and left no clues as to his opinion. Butler was, of course, deeply hurt, not only by Macmillan's preference for Home, but by the manner in which he announced it. Home could not actually become Prime Minister until he had assured himself that he could form a Government, not a straightforward task in an atmosphere of hurt pride, dissent and even talk of rebellion within the party. Nevertheless, Home, a consummate diplomat, was able to assemble a convincing ministerial team within a couple of days. Butler, somewhat surprisingly, agreed to succeed Home at the Foreign Office; Reginald Maudling, whose name had been coupled with those of Enoch Powell, Iain Macleod and Lord Hailsham as unlikely to support Home, was appointed Chancellor of the Exchequer; and Hailsham became Lord President of the Council. Thorneycroft remained at the Ministry of Defence, perfectly happy to carry on with his job of welding the service departments together and setting the priorities for the equipment of the armed forces.

An important step forward in the equipment of the Royal Navy was the launching by Carla Thorneycroft on 3rd December 1963 of HM Submarine 'Valiant', built by Vickers Armstrong at Barrow-in-Furness. This was the first British nuclear submarine powered by a British designed and built reactor. Her sister ship, 'Dreadnought', launched in October 1962, had an American reactor.

Tour of the Middle and Far East

The early weeks of 1964 saw Thorneycroft retracing some of the steps of his 'Journey to the East' six years earlier, but this time with all the resources of the Ministry of Defence and the Foreign Office at his disposal, and he was accompanied by his wife, giving him invaluable support in a testing programme of encounters with leading politicians and rulers of the region.

Four months earlier, after a gestation period of 18 years, the Federation of Malaysia had been born, embracing a vast territory stretching from Malaya itself to the Northern part of the island of Borneo, but excluding Singapore and the enclave of Brunei on Borneo. Here, the states of Sarawak and Sabah shared an uneasy border with Indonesia, which had achieved independence from the Dutch in 1947 after a short, but bitter war fought largely by British and Indian troops on behalf of the Dutch whose army, at the end of the Second World War, barely existed. With their Eastern states of Sarawak and Sabah, the Malaysians had inherited an unresolved conflict over a border never accepted as valid by the Indonesians. One of the main purposes of Thorneycroft's 1964 visit was to re-assure the Malaysians of continued British support in their quarrel with Indonesia.

Although the need for refuelling stops still made long journeys like this rather tedious, they also provided opportunities to keep *au fait* with conditions and problems in places that would otherwise not have received a visit. This time, on the way to Kuala Lumpur, there was a brief stop in Aden for discussions with the Governor and then on to Gan for an overnight rest.

In Kuala Lumpur, intensive talks over dinner on Sunday 5th January 1964 with the Deputy Prime Minister and Minister of Defence, Tun Abdul Razak, and Lieutenant-General Tengku Osman bin Tengku Jewa, who had just succeeded General Sir Rodney Moore as Chief of the Malaysian Armed Forces, were followed the next day by a brief meeting with Tengku Abdul Rahman, the Prime Minister, and his deputy. Their discussions ranged over the tense situation on the disputed border of Sarawak and Sabah with Indonesia, where raids by armed groups were a daily occurrence; Malaysia's urgent need for arms and equipment for its military forces; the anti-piracy operations of the Royal Navy in the Straits of Malacca between the Indonesian island of Sumatra and the west coast of the Malayan Peninsula; the deployment of Malaysian and British troops and the general security situation within Malaysia's borders. The Tengku, who had just returned from a quick visit to Sabah and Sarawak, insisted that, although the border raids amounted to an undeclared war between his country and Indonesia, Malaysian troops could deal with the problem without outside help.

In the late afternoon of 6th January, Thorneycroft and his party left for Singapore, where he and his wife stayed with Admiral Sir Varyl and Lady Begg at Flagstaff House, the official residence of the C-in-C Far East. The following morning Carla Thorneycroft, paid a short visit, accompanied by Lady McGregor, wife of Air Marshal Sir Hector McGregor, Air Commander, and Lady O'Connor, wife of Lieutenant-General Sir Denis O'Connor, to the RAF base at Changi, the RAF Hospital and the transit hotel for RAF personnel and their families, meeting some of the families at the Married Families Club and being shown murals commemorating the incarceration of Empire prisoners of war at the infamous Changi gaol during the Second World War. Carla Thorneycroft was no novice in such matters, having spent many months in charge of an Italian military hospital in Rome during the war. Meanwhile, Thorneycroft was engaged with Sir Varyl Begg and other Service commanders in a review of the military situation in Borneo and the functioning of the newly unified command structure for the Far East. Later in the day, he met Lee Kuan Yeu, the Prime Minister of Singapore for general talks on the worsening political situation in the region. In the evening of 7th January, there was another formal dinner, this time at Admiralty House with Admiral Sir Desmond Dreyer, Flag Officer Commanding-in-Chief Far East Fleet. The following morning, Carla Thorneycroft continued her programme of visits to Service families with a tour of the Naval Base Asian Kindergarten. These were not examples of a Minister's wife enjoying herself while her husband carried on with his official duties: the visits were of real value in conveying to families, far from home, the comforting realisation that they were not forgotten by the powers-that-be and, indeed, of helping the Minister and his staff to understand the problems that Service families face. Thorneycroft, at the end of another long day improving his understanding of the military situation, completed his talks with Far East Command with a dinner at Air House hosted by the McGregors and attended also by the Deputy Prime Minister of Singapore, Toh Chin Chye, Dato Loke Wan Toh, the Chairman of the Cathay Organisation, and Mr R L G Challis, the Commissioner for New Zealand.

Early the next morning, Thursday 9th January, Thorneycroft and his party left for Kuching, the capital of Sarawak, where only a couple of hours before their arrival, information had surfaced of an impending major assault by Indonesian forces, which the garrison from 40 Royal Marine Commando was preparing to resist. Thorneycroft was not put off by the threat. He was flown by an RAF Whirlwind helicopter to a camouflaged defensive post near the border where he talked to some of the marines before touring other positions of British and Malaysian forces in Sarawak and Sabah, with Hunter jets escorting him as close to the Indonesian border as possible. The local commander, Brigadier Patterson, announced later in the day that the reports of a major build-up of Indonesian troops were false, but the alarm had given Thorneycroft a clear picture of the ability of the troops to respond rapidly to a threat and, by the end of the tour, he was satisfied that the British, Gurkha and Malaysian troops were completely in control, with no need for immediate reinforcements, although more troops would be sent if necessary. Returning to Kuching for lunch with the Chief Minister at the Istana (the beautiful palace built for himself by the erstwhile 'White Rajah' of Sarawak, Sir James Brooke, whose descendants had ruled the State until the Japanese invasion in 1942), Thorneycroft left in the early afternoon for Brunei, touching down briefly on the little island of Labuan. After an audience with the Sultan, he had dinner with the High Commissioner for Brunei, and was then allowed a day's rest before flying, on 11th January, to Jesselton, the capital of Sabah, where he called upon the Ruler, H E the Yang di-Pertuan Negara, and then the Chief Minister of Sabah. Thorneycroft made a brief visit to Tawau, on the East coast of Sabah, close to another area where Indonesian incursions had occurred, and then returned for the night to Brunei. The following morning, 12th January, he spent a couple of hours visiting British troops in Brunei, bringing his visit to a close before returning via Labuan to Singapore, and an overnight flight from Changi to London in one of the early Comet jets.

Thorneycroft's original intention had been to go on from Brunei to Hong Kong, but he had been obliged to return to London early for an important Defence debate, leaving his wife to carry on to Hong Kong and complete her parallel programme of visits to welfare and hospital facilities in the Far East. In Hong Kong, these included the NAAFI Shop and Junior Ranks Club at Victoria Barracks, the military hospital at Mount Kellett and the Infants' School at Headquarters Land Forces.

This had clearly been a punishing tour for Thorneycroft, still suffering from back problems which made air travel often excruciatingly painful, and for his wife. When one considers that the salary for a Minister at the time was only £5,750 per annum, and that those wives who were prepared to shoulder the burden of giving their husbands active support received no recognition, their dedication to duty can only be described as quite remarkable.

The load on the British armed services, already heavy enough in the Far East, had been exacerbated just after Christmas, a few days before Thorneycroft's departure for Malaysia, by a sharp increase in tension between the Greek and Turkish communities in Cyprus in reaction to a proposal by President Makarios to grant the Turkish minority constitutional rights in the public service and legislature. This had been opposed by armed groups of Greek Cypriots and an armed response by Turkish Cypriots. On 27th December 1963 an advance party (one company) of 1st Battalion, The Foresters' Regiment flew from their base at Lyneham to Cyprus to reinforce a joint British-Greek-Turkish force assembled to police a cease-fire. A squadron of 14/24 Hussars with scout cars also moved from Libya to Cyprus. On Thorneycroft's return from the Far East, there were immediate questions from the Press about the ability of the Forces to do everything that was being asked of them, and whether the Government was contemplating restoring conscription, given the poor performance in recruitment of volunteers since compulsory National Service was abandoned a few months earlier. Thorneycroft rejected the idea. He no doubt had in mind that a General Election was approaching, and that the general public had an intense dislike of conscription, especially after the call-up of reservists for the Suez campaign, but he was also convinced that the Forces still had enough reserves to cope efficiently with their tasks. His discussions with commanders in the Far East had reinforced that conviction. Nevertheless, he told the Press that, if he found conscription necessary to deal with a new situation, he would go straight ahead with it. He was also considering making Hong Kong a base for reinforcing troops in the Far East, rather than relying on reserves based in Britain.

It was not only the British and Malaysian Governments who were concerned about the belligerent policies of Indonesia towards the new Malaysia. The American Attorney-General, Robert Kennedy, was due to arrive in Tokyo on 16th January for discussions aimed at deterring the Indonesian President, Sukarno, from military action. Not for the first time, there was concern that American and British armaments supplied to the government of a newly independent state to enable it to build up its defence forces were being used for aggression against a neighbouring country. The Americans, here, were engaged in a balancing act, trying to calm down a recalcitrant Sukarno whilst keeping the Indonesian military onside.

Secretary of State for Defence 1964

On 1st April 1964, the merger of the former Service Departments into a unified Ministry of Defence was brought into effect, only 18 months after Mountbatten submitted his plan. Thorneycroft now became Secretary of State for Defence and the only representative of the Armed Forces in the Cabinet. For practical purposes, his role changed very little, having been evolving with generally constructive support from most of his political and military colleagues for well over a year – although there still remained some disquiet, and even opposition, in the upper ranks. In the Thorneycroft Papers at the University of Southampton, there is a hand-written letter, marked 'Private', from Montgomery of Alamein dated 15 April 1964 which drew Thorneycroft's attention to remarks, which Montgomery felt to be disloyal, made by Dick Hull (Lieutenant-General Sir Richard Hull, the Chief of the General Staff) after an Army Council dinner a few days earlier. Montgomery described Hull as *"reactionary, single service minded"*, and advised against his appointment as Chief of the Defence Staff in the new structure. (This was not an immediate issue, as Mountbatten was expecting to stay in post for at least another year. Hull, promoted to Field Marshal, was eventually appointed by Denis Healey to succeed Mountbatten as Chief of the Defence Staff in July 1965 - as Healey records in his autobiography, *The Time of my Life*, overruling Mountbatten).

Mountbatten and Thorneycroft soon got down to discussing how to move on to the second, 'functionalisation' phase of Mountbatten's plan. Thorneycroft saw no reason for delay. He appointed a committee led by Sir Ronald Melville to produce detailed proposals for its implementation, asking that the report be submitted by January 1965.

Thorneycroft was not granted much longer in office – not long enough to achieve his objectives. Six months later, in the General Election of 15th October 1964, he retained his Monmouth seat with a majority reduced from 6,259 to only 714, but in the country as a whole Labour won a tiny overall majority of five seats. The independent nuclear deterrent policy was a significant issue in the campaign, and Thorneycroft robustly defended the policy. His arguments were consistent: that Britain's island home could no longer be defended by the Royal Navy and Fighter Command; and that the nuclear deterrent ensured that an enemy would know that there was *"no prize that he could ever win which would compensate him for the damage he would suffer"*. In response to Harold Wilson's assertion that *"these weapons were a pretence and would not deter"* he pointed out that *"a single V-bomber on a solitary mission can drop in destructive power more than was dropped by the whole of the RAF in the whole of the last war"*. He refrained from pointing out - it was election time after all - that the single bomber had first to reach its target. He dismissed Wilson's wish to abandon nuclear weapons as an internal party political matter. *"Always"*, he said, *"the leader of the party has found it difficult to bring the Left wing and the pacifist element with him"*. However, the electorate had issues other than nuclear deterrence on its mind, and these arguments were not enough to sway the national electorate. The ex-Minister of Defence would now have to press his case from the Opposition benches. Denis Healey, certainly well-qualified for the task, was appointed by Wilson as the new Secretary of State for Defence, and Thorneycroft would be his 'shadow'. (Healey, in a letter to the author of 15th September 2006, recalls that he found in his desk some good watercolour sketches by Thorneycroft - they were both keen amateur artists).

On the day following the Election, Thorneycroft received two letters, one from Mountbatten, the Chief of the Defence Staff, the other from Solly Zuckerman, Scientific Adviser to the Ministry of Defence. Mountbatten wrote *"Working with you has not only been a privilege, but a pleasure and, if I may say so, an inspiration, and I, and all the military members of this Ministry are going to miss you very much"*, and Zuckerman, *"Your determination to get things done just suited my temperament. Once before I told you that in a year you'd achieved more than any Minister of Defence before you. I don't imagine I shall see your record touched"*. Ministers departing after an Election often receive valedictory letters, but they are more usually perfunctory than truly appreciative. When Thorneycroft was first appointed, Mountbatten was not sure of him. By the time the Minister left office, he had earned the full confidence of his Chief of Defence Staff.

Speaking of his own slender victory in a letter to his constituents, Thorneycroft told them that Monmouth was a constituency that could only be won by Labour if enough voters switched from the Conservatives to the Liberals. He did not complain of this. It was, for him, an inevitable consequence of the British electoral system, which could not safely be changed by any reform of the system. (His wife was Italian, they had many Italian friends and acquaintances, and he had seen the damage that one of the alternative forms of voting (proportional representation with party lists) had done to the governance of that country, keeping the old guard of Christian Democrats in effectively permanent control, switching the top ministries between themselves as each in turn lost votes of confidence).

Opposition 1964-66

Thorneycroft soon found himself in action again, frustrated because he was no longer in charge of defence policy, but determined to fight any Labour move that he judged to be against the national interest. The Melville Committee's report would now be submitted to Denis Healey, and Thorneycroft could only wait until Healey's conclusions on it were presented to Parliament.

In a Foreign Affairs Debate on 17th December 1964, Prime Minister Harold Wilson asserted that Polaris missile warheads could not be made or tested in Britain: the 'independent' deterrent was dependent on America. Thorneycroft was quickly on his feet retorting that this was false.

Two months later, on 9th February 1965, an Aerospace Industries Debate was enlivened by a sharp clash between Thorneycroft and Wilson that led to the Prime Minister walking out of the Chamber. The debate was on a Conservative motion of censure of the Government's handling of Aviation policy, the Minister of Aviation, Roy Jenkins having announced a purchase of American F-4 *Phantom* fighter-bombers and C-130 *Hercules* transport aircraft, American built, although to be fitted with British engines and ejector seats. He had decided also to cancel two major British aircraft projects, the Hawker Siddeley P1154 vertical take off and landing supersonic fighter and the same company's HS681 freighter, and had implied also a severe slash in the TSR2 aircraft project. Thorneycroft taunted Labour by reading from a pre-election report in the *Daily Express* that Wilson had promised workers on the TSR2 project at Preston that their jobs would be guaranteed under Labour. Wilson insisted that the next few words should also be read out. Thorneycroft refused to do this and, in an undignified exchange, a copy of the newspaper was flung back and forth between the two men until Wilson eventually read out the passage himself, *"Our position on the TSR2 is exactly the same as the Government's. If it works and does what is expected of it and at reasonable cost, we shall want it, though not for a nuclear role."* – and threw the paper back again. Jenkins had also announced the intention to make renewed efforts to reach agreements with the USA and France on air projects, including a study with the French of an 'aero bus' designed for cheap travel by large numbers of people. Jenkins made it clear that any new development of an all-British aircraft designed solely for the British market was out of the question. Thorneycroft reminded him of the abortive attempts made by the Conservatives to collaborate with the Americans on a supersonic airliner and the subsequent agreement with France to develop *Concord,* and how Labour had sneered at that project and tried to cancel it. Thorneycroft accepted that these problems had no easy solution. He had no qualms about buying foreign aircraft, and he did not regard the structure of the aircraft industry as sacrosanct, or argue that no project should ever be cancelled, but he believed that to cancel these three major projects simultaneously would be a grave technological blunder that would not only seriously damage the British aircraft industry but also result in almost complete reliance on the Americans for our defence. Even to cancel two would mean the end of Hawker Siddeley. The C-130 transport aeroplane would be cheaper because it would not have the operational capabilities of the Hawker Siddeley HS681. If those capabilities were not required, Hawker Siddeley had a cheaper design, the HS802 – faster than the C-130 - ready to offer. In the case of the P1154, Britain had a two-year lead over the Americans in vertical take off and landing research. Why make a present of this to the Americans? The only alternative to the TSR2 was the American TFX. He had no doubt that the Americans had offered an attractive package deal: it would pay them to give us the TFX free to put us out of business. Jenkins was not to be moved. He described the British aircraft industry as different from any other in its dependence on Government funding of research and development and military production. It was misplaced chauvinism, Jenkins averred, to insist on building, at enormous expense, British aircraft designed solely for the British market. Neither the HS681 nor the P1154 would be ready before the aircraft they were intended to replace - the *Hastings* and *Beverley* and the *Hunter* - were due to go out of service. The only reason for delaying a decision on the TSR2 (which would cost 25 times as much as the *Canberra* it was due to replace) was that it, at least, should be ready in time. The P1157, which was being evaluated by a joint British, German and American group, had a better chance of sales to our European allies than the P1154. It was the drama of Wilson's storming out of the Chamber that captured the headlines of the popular Press the following day, but the more serious organs of the media recognised that this was a fine example of parliamentary debate involving a number of very well informed protagonists from all three parties deeply engaged with the substance of the discussion, even if they also enjoyed the Party games and repartee. The Liberals were not convinced by Jenkins' plan to collaborate with both the Americans and the French. They felt that effectively complete American control of aircraft design could only be combated by creating a European aircraft agency capable of developing later into a unified European industry able to compete with the Americans on equal terms. The Government won the day, with a majority of five, perhaps rather lucky that news of a detailed American announcement of the terms of the contract, which had not been disclosed to Parliament during the debate, reached London only after the House had divided. The Government's excuse, that they had not wanted to disclose the terms because other countries might expect similar treatment, was really rather lame.

Only a week after the Aerospace Industries censure debate, Sir Alec Douglas-

Home took most observers by surprise when, in the wake of R A Butler's decision to retire from active politics, he announced a reshuffle of his Shadow Cabinet much more far-reaching than expected. Thorneycroft was moved to Home affairs, succeeding Sir Edward Boyle, and ceding his Defence responsibilities to Christopher Soames, although Thorneycroft would lead for the Opposition in the debate on the Defence White Paper due to be published within a few days. Edward Heath took over Treasury affairs from Reginald Maudling, who would now shadow Foreign Affairs. Although he was not given the formal title of Deputy Leader, Maudling was to preside at meetings of the Leader's committee in the event of Sir Alec's absence. Boyle's move was seen as a convenient way of stifling his somewhat embarrassing 'softness' on immigration policy and capital punishment. Sir Alec seems to have felt that Thorneycroft was the man to take a tougher line. There is no record of what Thorneycroft himself felt about the move. He had certainly been thoroughly at home in the Ministry of Defence.

His Parliamentary début as Shadow Home Secretary came on 25th February 1965, when his opposite number, Sir Frank Soskice, had to face a censure motion after he had intervened against the recommendation of the Commissioner to alter the ward boundaries in Nottingham, apparently swayed by a complaint from the city council that the proposed change would favour the Conservatives. Thorneycroft did not impugn the Home Secretary's personal integrity, but argued that his judgement had been seriously at fault in giving way to political pressure, putting at risk the whole procedure for examining boundary changes as well as the reputation of the Home Office. Labour's slender majority enabled poor Sir Frank, a kind and gentle man, to survive the onslaught, to everyone's relief.

On 3rd March 1965, Thorneycroft rounded off his defence efforts when he led the Opposition attack on Denis Healey's first exposition as Defence Minister of Labour's defence policy. Healey's was a hard-hitting speech of high quality in which he questioned in great detail every essential aspect of his predecessor's approach, based as it had been on the fundamental principle of maintaining an independent nuclear deterrent. He argued that this was unsustainable. The speed of development of new weapons and their high costs, added to the expense of keeping a large army in Germany made it impossible for Britain to sustain the economic burden, which had run out of control in recent years. Taking over responsibility for defence last October had been like being *"pitch-forked into the cab of a runaway train"*. There had been times when there had been no battalions available for duty overseas in the strategic reserve without breaking the rules on family separations which were essential if voluntary recruitment was to be kept at an adequate level. The Navy was short of technical personnel to keep all its weapons serviceable. He had been forced to buy aircraft abroad because the previous Government's procurement programmes had failed to order replacements in time. He rejected, however, the proposal espoused by his back-benchers of speeding up the withdrawal of troops from overseas deployment. Britain could not just walk away from commitments without consulting its allies: there was a grave risk that some areas outside Europe would dissolve into violence and chaos. The presence of our forces in Malaysia had prevented major warfare. His most important conclusion had been that Britain could not go it alone in a nuclear age. If, as he proposed, Britain's nuclear weapons were pooled with those of its allies in an Atlantic Nuclear Force there was a chance of discouraging the spread of such weapons. The best answer would be a security guarantee from all the existing nuclear powers to all others. He saw no point in planning to resist a premeditated attack by massive ground forces. Instead we should concentrate on dealing with a 'war by mistake', due to a political or military misunderstanding. We should make the most of our existing forces to deal with dangers that are likely, not those that are inconceivable.

Thorneycroft's response was equally robust. He condemned the opening words of the White Paper on the note that our forces were overstretched and under manned as 'political slapstick' which would give much greater comfort to an enemy than any political satisfaction it could give. He welcomed the recognition of the importance of a powerful nuclear capability. He thought it essential that defence problems should be subjected to scientific analysis not just for the individual services but on a unified defence basis. Unless this were done, the Government's hopes of making sensible savings in the future would be frustrated. He urged that the rationalisation almost accomplished when he left office be completed: he had been nervous, when he read the White Paper, that the instructions he had left for this to be done might not have been properly carried out by the present Government. Healey retorted that the Tories had left behind no model of what they meant by the functional organisation they were seeking, and this was now being studied. *"My suspicions were justified"*, said Thorneycroft. *"The rats did get at it. All the impetus, drive, absolute determination that we go forward to a functional approach has in fact been lost. It is indeed a disappointment"*. He had also given instructions, he said, that much more information should be given to Parliament about plans for major equipment. He recognised that the Minister was studying a range of equipment problems and might not yet have all the answers, but he felt that there ought to be another White Paper in the summer when the Minister was ready. Healey replied that when dealing with forces seriously under-equipped and undermanned, information would reveal weaknesses, not strength. He would try to give more information within the limits of not damaging our security or weakening morale. To this, Thorneycroft retorted that British forces had earned the admiration and envy of the whole world for the way they had carried out their duties in the past twelve months, and it would be better to cut out the political slapstick and spend more time praising the men who discharged these functions. Turning to the Atlantic Nuclear Force, he said that the Minister's military advisers would explain to him that this new nuclear force with a United States veto would be a complete waste of time and money. It was an extraordinarily misbegotten creature, bristling with safety catches, and would never happen. Among the Labour back-benchers who contributed to the debate, Mr Reginald Paget, the member for Northampton, probably summed up their mood best. He said that he had been waiting for an explanation as to why the Labour Party defence policy, worked out over many years, had been abandoned and the Conservative policy adopted in its stead. It was a good debate, both Healey and Thorneycroft distinguishing themselves. Faced with the realities of office, Healey's subsequent actions were not too dissimilar from those that Thorneycroft would have taken had he remained in post.

Now, however, Thorneycroft had to leave defence policy to others and concentrate his attention on the issues awaiting him as Shadow Home Secretary, and we must follow him, interesting though it would be to explore more thoroughly what his successors would do with his defence legacy.

Shadow Home Secretary

Thorneycroft's first foray in his new role was into the sensitive question of immigration policy, following up a speech made by Sir Alec Douglas-Home a few weeks earlier, when Sir Alec had suggested stricter controls on entry of immigrants and greater emphasis on measures to help existing immigrants to adjust to life in Britain. Thorneycroft, responding to a debate on a motion at a conference of the Central Council of his party on 5th March which called for cessation of mass immigration and complete integration of existing Commonwealth immigrants into the political, social and economic life of the country, highlighted two principal areas of concern about what he described as *"one of the most important and human social problems of our time"*. These were: the rate of flow into Britain of immigrants' relatives, often of remote kinship, and the need to locate and return to their countries of origin people who had entered the country illegally, especially those who had committed crimes. He argued that there was a pressing need for developing central policies and providing finance to deal with areas where immigrants had exacerbated housing shortages and local authorities did not have the resources to cope with the burden placed upon them. For example, he suggested *"special action of a non-discriminatory character"* to speed the building of new homes, *"not tied to immigrants, but for the whole of the community, including immigrants"*. The wide range of views within the party revealed during this debate led to further discussion in the party's Home Affairs Committee to try to reach a consensus before a debate in the Commons on 23rd March. The resulting view put to Parliament by Thorneycroft was that there should be a drastic reduction in the number of male immigrants allowed to enter the country, but that no obstacles should be put in the way of wives and young dependants wishing to join men already in the country. This stricter control should be accompanied by positive measures to help immigrants become British citizens in the fullest sense, for example in facilities to teach English to immigrants from India and Pakistan. There were, nevertheless, many Conservative MPs remaining in favour of a more drastic approach – a complete ban on further immigration until those already arrived were sufficiently integrated into their local communities. The concern of the party leadership, shared by the majority, was to prevent the party moving to such an extreme position.

On 3rd May 1965, Thorneycroft led the Tory response to a Race Relations Bill introduced by the Government that would, for the first time, make it a criminal offence to indulge in racial discrimination. In a most unusual move, the Home Secretary, Sir Frank Soskice, had offered before the debate began to amend the bill in the Committee stage to allow for some form of conciliation, almost as though he was not happy with his own Department's drafting of the bill. Thorneycroft found this offer extraordinary, and vowed that the Opposition would fight by every method open to them this attempt to criminalise the *"kindly, just and wise"* British people. The kindly, just and wise Sir Frank took this quietly, and proceeded with a lengthy and rather boring lawyer's lecture explaining that the Bill, after all, would not apply to cases of discrimination in housing or employment or private clubs. It was intended merely to implement a promise in the Labour Manifesto to outlaw discrimination in public places and incitement. Ordinary people would have nothing to fear. Thorneycroft was not interested in legal niceties, but in something more fundamental. He reminded Sir Frank that the history of the loss of free speech was studded with examples of Governments *"twisting some statute or other to catch some wretched creature. This is the way to lose your freedom"*. He recognised that there may have been incidents in some pub or other, but Sir Frank had produced precious little evidence of widespread incitement to justify an important change in the criminal law. The idea of trying to define words or behaviour that stir up racial hatred was *"frocked with difficulty"*. He quoted classical phrases like *"Taffy was a Welshman, Taffy was a thief"* and *"Yanks go home"* as examples that could present difficulty. Thorneycroft's colleague Selwyn Lloyd agreed. *"The Bill is as full of holes as a sieve"*, he said. But this was a Manifesto commitment and, however controversial the commitment, and however flawed the Bill, it had to go through. The Government won the day with a majority of 12, the Liberals voting for the Bill.

One of Sir Alec Douglas–Home's early initiatives when he became Leader of the Conservative Party in 1963 had been to devise what he felt was a better system for the election of Leader. He had opted for a ballot of the Party's Members of Parliament to replace the opaque and much-criticised selection by Party elders that had brought him to power. On 22nd July 1965, he announced his decision to resign the Leadership and to set in motion the process for a ballot to elect his successor, so that the Party could prepare for the next general election under a new Leader. He would not stand himself. Sir Alec's recent Cabinet reshuffle had prompted a good deal of speculation as to which of his colleagues he was preparing for future leadership: was Maudling being given fresh experience at the Foreign Office to complement his economic expertise? what about Heath, with his formidable record in economic and European affairs? and was Thorneycroft being moved only to give a tougher lead to Home Affairs than Boyle or to bring himself up-to-date on domestic issues after his long stint at Defence? Maudling and Heath were the names most frequently mentioned in the hours after Sir Alec's announcement. Iain Macleod, who might well have been a candidate, quickly ruled himself out of the race to be Sir Alec's successor. Enoch Powell had not made up his mind, but was under strong pressure to stand from a small group of Right-wingers. Thorneycroft made no comment. By the time that nominations closed on 26th July, there were three candidates – Heath, Maudling and Powell. Thorneycroft decided not to intervene. A hand-written note found among his papers (one of very few records he left of key moments in his career) read, *"that he was satisfied that the approaches made to him represented a respectable body of support within the Conservative Party. Nevertheless, he had decided not to accept nomination in the first ballot. He took this decision in the belief that the public and Party interest would best be served by a quick and clear decision on the leadership and he would not wish his intervention to be the cause of deadlock. In the event, however, of no clear decision being reached in the first ballot he reserved his position as to accepting a nomination in the second"*. The first vote was not, in fact, decisive. Heath received 150 votes, Maudling 133 and Powell 15, an overall majority for Heath, but not the 178 votes he needed under the rules to avoid a second ballot. Nevertheless, Thorneycroft's advice to go for a quick and clear decision had not fallen on deaf ears. There was no second ballot – Maudling and Powell both withdrew their candidature. Heath would now be the Leader of the Conservative Party. Thorneycroft remained Shadow Home Secretary in Heath's first Shadow Cabinet.

In an article published in the July-September 1965 issue of *"Crossbow"*, Thorneycroft discussed with great sensitivity the problem of how to reconcile the desire for social reform with the need to keep law and order. He began with a definition of Freedom redolent of the theme of his 1947 *"Design for Freedom"*. *"Freedom is a condition hard to gain but easily abandoned"*. *"The essence of Freedom is that it knows no frontiers save those hallowed by tradition, good manners, and the narrow, jealously guarded area of the criminal law"*. He was concerned by the extent to which areas traditionally regarded as of personal responsibility had already been abandoned to the State, quoting as an example how the extension of the Welfare State to cover some of the requirements of sickness and old age had narrowed the obligations of the individual. *"Visit any old people's home"*, he wrote, *"enquire as to the frequency of visits by their younger relatives and one will come away with a sharp realisation that for many the Welfare State has come to represent a substitute rather than a reinforcement of what were once regarded as normal family obligations"*. *"Rights have been emphasised at the expense of duties"*. Parallel to these developments, there had grown up a new approach to crime, that virtually all conduct inimical to the well-being of society stemmed from psychological or physiological causes that were capable of remedy. *"Sympathy is extended more readily to the criminal than to the victim"*. He did not argue against social services: *"their benefits were not lightly to be dismissed; but the wise reformer should stand back from time to time and study them in the context of the world in which we live"*. He acknowledged that defects of conduct might be influenced by the size of institutions (large factories or comprehensive schools); by the complexity of life which may lead to a sense of failure; by the bewildering pace of change. Certainly, an ever increasing supply of criminals was drawn from youths who felt inadequate, sometimes physically, sometimes emotionally and often intellectually. He did not, however, *"proceed from this point in the argument to the view that crime is non-existent or that punishment is irrelevant or retribution wrong*. He saw the need to extend responsibility for making good criminal damage; for recognition of the role of parents of juveniles engaged in criminal activities; and for strengthening of police forces. He recognised that the absence of relevant statistics made the identification of the causes and sources of crime *"not particularly easy"*, but he believed that it could be demonstrated that there was more crime in town than in country and in some parts of some towns more than in others. He was also concerned with the broader picture *"of traditional freedoms deteriorating into licence; of a trend towards playing down the idea of punishment and discounting the idea of crime"*. He referred to a recent *"remarkably partisan"* pamphlet by Lord Longford, proposing that perpetrators of crime be assumed to be incapable of criminal intent; that juvenile courts should be abandoned *"on the somewhat surprising ground that they were aimed at the working classes"*. The distinction between right and wrong was being *"steadily obscured under a haze of amiable intention and largely inept proposals"*. He urged a concentrated drive to improve the lower strata of the educational system. *"We concentrate on the A stream and the university entrants, but the greatest public good might be served by a drive to improve conditions in the D stream"*. He asked whether more could be done to build up appreciation of school achievement in humbler fields that were not accorded academic merit, and to identify potential delinquents at an early stage so that remedial education could be provided. He acknowledged that these were questions to which no one knew all the answers, and that the nature of the world in which citizens grew up could not be dramatically changed. Prison reform and remedial treatment claimed a high priority, but *"compassion was not enough. What was needed was a considerable toughness in the treatment of offenders with some revolutionary ideas for dealing with the evil at its source".*

Just before Christmas 1965, Harold Wilson announced a reshuffle of his Cabinet which brought Thorneycroft up against a more formidable opponent than Sir Frank Soskice, now appointed to the less exposed post of Lord Privy Seal, whose main role was to chair Cabinet committees. Roy Jenkins became the new Home Secretary, joining the Cabinet for the first time.

Thorneycroft did not give his opponent much time to settle down in his new office. He went onto the attack early in the New Year, tabling a question challenging the new Home Secretary to inform the House how many murders and violent crimes had been committed in 1965. It was time, Thorneycroft said, to treat the increase in crime as a grave social problem, and to choose between the two possible approaches, the liberal one of bringing the criminal back to normal life or the authoritarian one of catching the criminal and punishing him. Labour, he averred, had been dealing with crime as if it were an extension of the Welfare State. In a second question, Thorneycroft picked on a currently sore point, asking Jenkins to explain how he could reconcile the difficulties of recruitment to the police with the Government's rejection of their recent claim for a pay increase of £5 a week.

On 19th January 1966, Thorneycroft introduced a report, "Crime knows no boundaries" prepared by his colleagues of the Conservative Political Centre, which questioned whether the current organisation of the police - the Metropolitan Police and 126 other forces controlled by counties and county boroughs – was capable of coping with criminal gangs which recognised no boundaries. Although they did not propose a national police force, the authors of the report argued that faster amalgamation of forces was needed, and that the Home Office should take on a strategic role, providing centrally funded resources for intelligence, research and co-ordination of operations. Research into the causes, prevention and treatment of crime should be sponsored by the Home Office in universities and elsewhere. They were not in favour of a separate traffic police corps, but suggested that more use should be made of automatic fines for motoring offences so as to make better use of police time. They recommended a significant increase in police numbers, work and methods study aimed at reducing the excessive amount of police time spent on paperwork and measures to attract more university graduates into police careers. Many detailed recommendations were made, such as making much less use of short prison sentences which they judged to be ineffective and more recourse to fines for less serious offences, the provision of a small number of secure prisons for the minority of offenders who ought to be kept in custody and, in the case of juvenile crime, more emphasis on the responsibility of parents for their children's behaviour, and on investigating the role of television programmes as a cause of juvenile crime. Thorneycroft's aim was to encourage debate on the issues raised rather than to present them as settled Party policy but, as he had chaired the study group responsible for the report the recommendations undoubtedly reflected closely his own views. His emphasis was on the need to ensure detection and conviction as the best deterrent to criminal activities, and for giving the Home Office a much stronger role in the organisation and supervision of the police.

The publication of the Tory report was soon followed by a debate in the House of Commons on 2nd February 1966 on a motion of censure moved by Thorneycroft, citing grave public concern at the mounting wave of crime and the falling rate of detection. He said that the two approaches to crime – punishment and deterrence, and seeking out its origins – were both needed, but the Government's actions raised doubts about their commitment to either of them. He considered the recent decisions to release prisoners who had completed a third of their sentences and to abolish juvenile courts to be *"remarkably undistinguished"*. He urged the Home Secretary to stop increasing the range of criminal offences – it would break the back of the police. He pressed for the appointment of somebody in charge, with a clear chain of command – a 'chief of staff' on the police side of the Home Office – and for faster amalgamation of police forces, with the Home Office taking on more of the financial responsibility. He criticised a recent decision to allow the train robbers to be interviewed by the media in Durham Gaol: *"Some people must have recalled the poor man who was battered. We must not forget the victims of these crimes"*, he said. He regarded the idea of taking young people out of juvenile courts and treating them as an extension of the welfare service as a grave error of judgement. *"Human liberty is a matter for a judge, not for a welfare officer, and the liberty of a child is just as important as the liberty of anyone else. To have the liberty of a child a bargain struck between parents and welfare officers will not easily be forgiven"*. Replying, Jenkins noted that Thorneycroft had not moved the motion in terms appropriate to a vote of censure, and he appreciated that. *"Crime was a most unsuitable subject for party conflict. Passion and emotion were bad counsellors"*. He was in no doubt about the magnitude of the problem. The main emphasis should be on detection and conviction, and detection was primarily a question of police efficiency. He defended the Government's attitude to police pay, which he believed was not ungenerous, and not a prime question in the problem of police manpower. The past year had been a good one for police recruitment. He had set up three working parties to look at manpower, operational organisation, and equipment, assisted by outside experts. Five small police forces would merge voluntarily into a single new force in the West Midlands, and he was urgently considering how far and how fast further amalgamations should go. He revealed that research was under way to find an automatic process for identifying a single fingerprint found at the scene of a crime, and other programmes to obtain information from glass, blood or explosives. The Criminal Law Revision Committee was considering the law of evidence in criminal cases: if significant changes were recommended, the Government would have to be convinced that individual rights and liberties were protected. However, he insisted that *"We should not defeat ourselves by archaic, elaborate and highly formalised rules which may give undue advantage to the enemy because it is with enemies that we are dealing"*. All in all, there was not much difference between Thorneycroft and Jenkins on this complex issue, except in their approach to juvenile crime.

Thorneycroft's stint in Home Affairs came to an abrupt end in March 1966. Harold Wilson, his tiny majority eroded to zero by deaths and by-elections, had judged very well the right moment to call a General Election. On 31st March he was returned to power with an overall majority of over one hundred, taking fifty-one seats from the Tories and two from the Liberals. The electors of Monmouth, whom Thorneycroft had served loyally and very well for twenty-one years, rejected him in favour of a twenty-six year old Labour candidate, Donald Anderson, a university lecturer, who won the seat in a straight fight by 2,965 votes. William Deedes, writing in the *Sunday Telegraph* the following weekend, lamented the loss of Thorneycroft who, he said, *"contrived better than almost any other senior Conservative to blend new talent with experience. Young men learned fast from him."* Forty years later, Lord Deedes, in a letter to the author, set his earlier remark in context, recalling that *"in 1950 there was a huge intake of Tory MPs, full of enthusiasm, but not always well-versed in parliamentary ways"* and that *"the two people he remembered as being of most help to newcomers were Harold Macmillan and Peter Thorneycroft"*, adding that *"of all the parliamentary figures I encountered in my 25 years as MP, he [Thorneycroft] stands out as a powerful speaker, who mixed a sardonic style with wit better than anyone else"*.

Marking time

Thorneycroft took his time in deciding what he should do next. On 10th May 1967, he asked his Monmouth supporters to accept his resignation as their prospective candidate so that he could fight a constituency elsewhere should the opportunity arise. He dismissed the idea that he might be elevated to the House of Lords as a working peer, telling the *Western Mail* that, *"My home is in the Commons where I fought my battles and where I hope to fight my battles again."*

Thorneycroft's role in his time at the Ministry of Aviation came under critical scrutiny in June 1968 when the Government announced its intention of withdrawing from the European Launcher Development Organisation (ELDO), which had been formed in April 1962 to develop a satellite launch vehicle powered by a three-stage rocket system of which the first stage was to be the British *Blue Streak* missile. Thorneycroft had seen this project as an opportunity for a sustained effort by European countries to work together on a technologically advanced project which none of them could afford to carry out alone. The alternative had seemed to be to leave such costly developments to the Americans and the Russians, leaving Europe reliant on America to supply the equipment and technical know-how required not only for their military, but also for their civilian needs.

In July, Thorneycroft and his wife were invited to attend the Service for the Blessing of HMS *Valiant"*, the nuclear submarine which Carla Thorneycroft had launched in 1963.

July 1966 was also the month of Harold Wilson's dramatic admission that the country was in a very serious economic crisis, announcing a draconian freeze of prices and incomes for six months, to be followed by another six months of severe restrictions. Thorneycroft described the proposed remedy as *"rather like putting a patient suffering from a grave disease into a refrigerator in the hope that if we leave him there long enough someone will think of a cure."* His own cure was the same one he had prescribed in 1958 – get the Government's own expenditure under control – adding a few more suggestions appropriate to a Socialist Government: treat transport as a commercial concern, not a social service; restore prescription charges as a way of discouraging profligate use of medicines; treat restrictive practices by trade unions as severely as those of companies; leave the steel industry alone.

But giving unsought (and largely ignored) advice to the Socialists through Press articles was not a productive way for a person of Thorneycroft's ability to spend his time.

In December 1966, the death of the MP for Honiton, Robert Mathew, had seemed, briefly, to create an opportunity for Thorneycroft to return to Parliament and, for a while, he and Christopher Soames stood out in the list of candidates for the seat. However, the Honiton Conservative Association decided to insist that whoever was adopted must undertake to move to the constituency and make it his home. This was a condition that neither Soames nor Thorneycroft was prepared to accept, and Honiton eventually adopted Peter Emery, a former MP for Reading, a member of the Bow Group and a strong supporter of the Party Leader, Edward Heath. There was no encouragement here for Thorneycroft to believe that he could soon return to a rewarding political life.

Thorneycroft had established many contacts in the business world during his twenty years of active politics, and some of the people who knew him well began to press him to make better use of his qualities in their companies. He decided to do so, and a new phase of his career, as a businessman, began.

On 16th November 1967, the country's dire economic situation could no longer be disguised. The Chancellor of the Exchequer, James Callaghan, had found himself forced to negotiate a loan of $3 billion, $1.4 billion from the International Monetary Fund and $1.6 billion from central banks of other countries, and news of the negotiations had leaked into the market. Callaghan's response of *"No comment"* to questions from the media had, inevitably, been interpreted as confirmation, and the pound suffered a few jerky hours on the exchanges before the details of the arrangement and of the consequent economic measures were announced. These included an increase in the Bank Rate from 6.5 to 8 per cent, a devaluation of the pound from $2.80 to $2.40, sharp cuts in public expenditure, including defence, and a series of tax increases and other measures. Having done his duty, Callaghan resigned saying that he had been forced to give assurances to overseas countries that the parity of the pound would be defended, and had been unable to respect those assurances. Thorneycroft, interviewed by the journalist Calder Dunn, expressed sympathy for Callaghan, *"A man of considerable character, for whom I have great respect."* He hoped that this might be a lesson for future cabinets not to impose on their Chancellor policies that were bound to lead to financial crisis. In his own case, he had resigned rather than support policies he believed to be wrong. Callaghan had stayed, and then took the blame for the inevitable failure.

House of Lords 1967-94

Thorneycroft's subsequent business career is the subject of a later chapter but, for the present, we continue with the story of his parallel political career as it developed in the new role of elder statesman with his elevation to a life peerage in November 1967. Three other life peerages announced by Harold Wilson went to senior Liberals, and there was conjecture at the time that Wilson was reacting to criticism that his patronage had been too often used to fill the House of Lords with his minions, and hoped that his appointment on this occasion only of peers from Opposition parties would be seen as a demonstration of

33. Thorneycroft's introduction to the House of Lords

his support for balanced membership of the second chamber. Whether this was so or not, it seems likely that the nomination of Thorneycroft owed as much to Wilson's recognition of the contribution that this particular Tory could make to the Lords, as to Edward Heath's own somewhat ambivalent support for it: for Heath, it seems that Thorneycroft's resignation from the Treasury almost a decade earlier still rankled. Thorneycroft took his seat in the Lords on 6th December 1967, introduced by Toby Aldington and Hugh Molson, who had been one of the authors of pamphlets in the *Forward - By the Right* and *Design for Freedom* series twenty years before.

A biography, a story of a life, is almost by definition a record of a chronological sequence of events from birth to death. However, when the subject is a politician acting in a democratic regime, whose successive appointments tend to follow a random course dictated by the accidents of success or failure in elections and the wishes and whims of a Prime Minister or Party Leader, chronological treatment tends to obscure the way in which his ideas on distinct political themes develop. A peer who has no official, ministerial or shadow ministerial job to do is inclined to intervene in debates only on subjects of great interest to him, and a thematic account of his contributions may be more appropriate and more informative, as well as more congenial, and this is certainly so for Thorneycroft. There are peers who make a speech so rarely that their biographers may indulge in quoting the whole of the one or two interventions they have made. Thorneycroft was not one of those. He had something to say on many subjects, and his peers recognised that what he had to say was always worth listening to. Because the topics that interested him were the great topics of politics, the debates were usually lengthy, attracted many other distinguished speakers and are so full of interest that one has been strongly tempted to expand the story of our protagonist into a general history of his lifetime. Reluctantly, we have resisted the temptation. That territory belongs to historians and especially, for this period, to Peter Hennessy, whose masterly surveys are unlikely to be surpassed. Instead we have tried to concentrate on the core themes of Thorneycroft's interventions and the reactions to them, with some indication of the context in which they were made. The narrative that follows is therefore a partial one, and no more than a sample of the many speeches that Thorneycroft delivered in the Lords.

The Economy

In the weeks that followed Thorneycroft's presentation in the Lords, the consequences of the latest economic crisis in which the country had been landed by years of excessive public spending became clearer. In November 1967, the Government had been forced to accept yet another devaluation of sterling, triggered this time by a series of moves out of sterling by Sterling Area countries. With the support of the IMF an agreement was reached – the Basle Agreement – to provide earmarked resources to enable Britain to bring to an end the reserve role of sterling. On 16th January 1968, Harold Wilson delivered a major speech in the House of Commons spelling out the conclusions of the Government's latest review of public spending, which had been one of the conditions of IMF support. Much of what he had to say echoed the message that Thorneycroft had tried and failed to put across ten years earlier: the need to keep public expenditure within the resources available; to avoid unacceptable restrictions on private consumption; recognition that military strength had to be firmly founded on economic strength; and that Britain's security lay in Europe and NATO. Wilson's domestic savings were to be achieved by re-introducing prescription charges; postponing for two years the raising of the school-leaving age from 15 to 16; and suspending or reducing university building projects. On defence, Wilson announced some drastic intentions: withdrawal of British forces from the Far East by the end of 1971; cancellation of a large order for American F111 aircraft; phasing out of aircraft carriers after the withdrawal from Singapore, Malaysia and the Persian Gulf had been completed. *"Defence"*, he said, *"must be related to the demands of foreign policy, but it must not be asked in the name of foreign policy to undertake commitments beyond its capability. It is not only at home in these past years that we have been living beyond our means."*

A back bench Thorneycroft would have been in his element in the ensuing Commons debate. Instead, Wilson's crisis measures provided the opportunity for a brilliant maiden speech in 'the other place' on 23rd January 1968. Thorneycroft delivered it, as he so often did, without obvious notes. He would have a piece of paper tucked away out of sight of his audience bearing a few words written mainly in capitals with a thick pen. This gave him all the prompting he needed to keep his discourse on track, relying on his extraordinary ability to master a brief on almost any subject and to deliver a fluent, cohesive argument dosed every now and then, as he judged appropriate from the reaction of his listeners, by a witty aside, a hesitation to encourage an intervention, or a determinedly unquenched flow of words when he had no intention of giving way to someone he thought might try to push him off course. The notes he made for his speech on this occasion are reproduced below. (It might be interesting to ask a group of budding politicians to compare them with the Hansard record of the speech, or even – without looking at Hansard - to try to reproduce the gist of the speech from the notes.)

Exactly ten years had passed since his resignation as Chancellor of the Exchequer and, recalling that day, he said, *"If the Macmillan Government had stood then, as I think they should have done, though the Conservative Party might well have lost the next Election, this country would not have been in the state of humiliation that it is today." "Mr Macmillan, who had great qualities … and who will take a great place in history, found it exciting to live on the edge of bankruptcy. My Lords, I found it very exciting too. So did my other colleagues in the Treasury. But we found it was an excitement scarcely consistent with our responsibilities for the national Exchequer, and so we parted company."*

34. An example of Thorneycroft's notes for a major speech

He had a word of praise for the courage shown by the Wilson Government in applying its cuts. (A peer has the luxury of not always having to adopt a partisan stance). He singled out for approval the decisions to cancel the order for the F111 aircraft, which he felt had no conceivable role of any use, and to keep the nuclear deterrent, but expressed serious doubts about withdrawing from the Far East. He urged instead urgent action to cut the cost of the extravagant bases in Singapore – a huge naval base, a huge air base, a huge Army base, and the Ministry of Defence - reducing them to a single base. He said that the answer to demands for wage increases should be not "3½%", but "No", otherwise all the benefits of devaluation would be lost within 12 months. He recommended a radical look at the social services, *"not simply in the interests of the economy, but in the interests of the poor and the afflicted as well."*

Just over eight years later, on 4th October 1976, there was a virtual replay of the 1968 debate. In the intervening years, the world had suffered the oil crisis of 1973-4 and the consequent international economic recession and leap in the rate of inflation which, in Britain, had peaked at 26.9% in August 1975. (In Argentina and Brazil it reached the dizzy height of 1,000% and sometimes even more). Measures, including a 'Social Contract' with the Trade Unions taken by the Labour Government under Harold Wilson, had helped to bring inflation down, but many Trade Union members and back-bench MPs of the Labour Party had not taken kindly to the wage restraint asked of them. In September 1976, the Government had decided, *in extremis,* to ask the IMF for a loan, an episode admirably analysed by the first Thorneycroft Scholar at the University of Southampton, Kevin Hickson, in his doctoral thesis and subsequent book, *The IMF Crisis of 1976 and British Politics* (Tauris Academic Studies, 2005). Yet in spite of the clearly precarious economic situation, with Sterling sliding on the exchange markets and the IMF poised to examine a plea for help from the Government, the annual Labour Party Conference in September had insouciantly asked its leaders to nationalise the banking and insurance industries and abandon free trade. Opening for the Opposition in the House of Lords debate, Thorneycroft, now the Conservative Party Chairman, acknowledged that, in his speech to the Labour Party Conference, *"The Prime Minister was speaking against a heavy tide"*. (Callaghan had told his coldly unreceptive audience that *"We had lived for too long on borrowed time, borrowed money and borrowed ideas",* reminding them that *"Over the last three years, ... while our domestic product has risen by 2 per cent, the increase in our public expenditures .... has increased by 18 per cent"*). Thorneycroft told the Lords that this was a brave speech to make. Not much had changed since Thorneycroft, Powell and Birch had preached an almost identical message to a Conservative Government almost twenty years earlier, except in one very important respect. In 1958, the people had been prepared, following the crisis of the previous summer, to accept the sacrifice that Thorneycroft (but not Macmillan) wished to ask of them: in 1976, they were much less receptive. Reinforcing what Callaghan had told his Conference, Thorneycroft pointed out that *"We are borrowing £35 million a day. There are many families in this country who cannot afford to live on their income of £3.50 a week"*. *"My Lords"*, said Thorneycroft, *"oddly enough, it is fairly easy to know what it is right to do; it is harder to say what it is right to do, and it is hardest of all to do it"*. *"What is needed is to try fairly quickly to live within our means"*. He urged the Government not to opt out by putting up taxes, which were already too high, or to listen to those pressing for a closed economy. *"Stop the world and let me get off"*, he said, *"reads rather attractively ….. but it will not work"*. This was a measured and responsible debate in which almost all the speakers clearly intended to make constructive suggestions to a Government which had to take decisions of national, not just party, importance, and were received by the Government representatives present in that spirit.

On 11th March, 1987, the House of Lords was concerned about the decline of the manufacturing industry in Britain, and its effect on the economic prosperity of the country. A reader of reports of debates in the House of Lords cannot help being impressed by the depth of knowledge which Peers reveal, and by the quality of their debates. This debate was no exception. Their Lordships recognised that manufacturing is no more intrinsically virtuous than services, but that there was more overseas demand for manufactured goods than for services; that improvement in productivity, and therefore in education, training, research and investment, was essential to competitiveness in world markets, but at the same time inevitably reduced the number of employees needed for a given level of output; and that the design of products, as well as their cost, was important for their success. Thorneycroft on this occasion was brief and to the point, concentrating his attention on the degree to which Government might usefully intervene to support manufacturing industry. He described himself as a very cautious interventionist, reminding the House that *"if any single man was responsible for the introduction of Concorde through the British Cabinet and past the Treasury, it was me"* – and having said that, he drew attention to the *"absence of cheers for me on this side of the house"*. He concluded that some intervention was desirable, but that *"the future of industry depends more than anything on itself"*, and that *"The balance between manufacturing industry and service activities ... depends on what standard of life those who are engaged in manufacturing industry demand for themselves. If they demand ... a very high standard of life, you will find that they are in some difficulties and that there are a lot of service industries too"*.

On 2nd December 1987, Thorneycroft opened a debate on his own motion to call attention to the state of the world economy and its effect on the United Kingdom. A few weeks before, in October, the American stock market had suddenly collapsed, the reverberations rapidly being felt throughout the world. Britain had not escaped. The question now was, what could be done about it? Thorneycroft had three suggestions: *"First, we shall not solve America's problems by adopting the very policies which caused it; …… It would be folly to do that. We need to pursue the policy of sound money, prudent finance and living within our income. Where can we have heard those words before?"* Secondly, *"our aim should … remain to secure wider trade. We sell enormous quantities of goods to Europe, but the ideal of the common market in Europe has hardly got off the ground. It is marked by a massive misuse of resources in agriculture and, in many cases, a closed shop in telecommunications and high-technology products. At any time, but especially at this time, it would be of immense help, not only to us but to the rest of the world, if we could open up those markets. My third point relates to exchange rates. I ask the House to fasten its seat belts while I talk about exchange rates. ……I do not think one should try too hard to support the dollar unless one is certain that one knows whether the Americans wish it to move up or down. The central bankers have just put in 500 million dollars to support the dollar. It is absolute peanuts!"* One risks becoming too repetitive. This was another excellent debate. As Thorneycroft said in his response, *"There is no assembly in the world which equals your Lordship's House, with its range of experience and knowledge of different disciplines and which can conduct a discussion on such a difficult subject"*. And the debating chamber achieving this level of excellence was, we must remember, an unreformed House of Lords. Will a reformed House be able to keep up the standard? Probably not, unless both it and the House of Commons know exactly what it is there for, and its members are of the calibre and have the experience appropriate to that purpose.

In 1991, the latest of the rounds of the General Agreement on Tariffs and Trade (GATT), the Uruguay Round, was approaching yet another of its crises, in danger of being stalled as the Americans approached a presidential election. The principal issues were agricultural subsidies, the liberalisation of the rapidly developing trade in services and the rather esoteric problem of the Multi-Fibre Arrangement – one of those unwise 'temporary exceptions' to the rules which was proving difficult to get rid of. In a speech on 4th December 1991, Thorneycroft recalled how he had found himself involved in a similar position of stalemate at the Beau Rivage Hotel in Geneva when the hotel keepers were on the verge of kicking all the delegates out. He thought that the same principle might be applied in Uruguay. He recalled that his efforts in Geneva had not been universally popular. *"It is only fair to point out,"* he said, *"in a House united about these matters, that 30 years ago the Conservative Party was not in favour of GATT. …. It favoured Imperial Preference. When I returned I remember going to the Cabinet in November to find, as a young President of the Board of Trade, that the distinguished gentlemen there assembled did not think that I had been up to much good while passing my time at the Beau Rivage. They argued passionately against me and suggested, when a motion against GATT was put down at the party conference, that we should accept it. I argued that we should fight our corner and said that I believed we could win. Of all the delightful things that I remember in my life, I remember Winston Churchill saying at the end of it, 'Let him try'. He was a remarkable man to serve under. At any rate we went to Blackpool, we argued the case and we won. That was the last time imperial preference was argued as a main principle for the Conservative Party."* As he so often did, he wanted to stress principles. *"Every day I read new ideas for trade, but I hardly ever hear an interesting discussion about what is the main strategy of trade. The GATT is the main strategy. The GATT lays down the rules. .... It ensures that .... we treat each other the same. If the world turned into one in which one group was in Japan, another was in Europe and a third somewhere in the Americas and there was no overruling law such as we have today about the way trade goes on, it would be a disaster. ... We should turn the opportunities we have enjoyed and are enjoying today into something narrow and protectionist. I am delighted to hear not from one side of the House but from all sides that it is seen with absolute clarity that to turn back now to that narrower world would be the worst course we could adopt."*

Defence

In a speech on a Defence White Paper in the House of Lords on 13th March 1968, Thorneycroft trenchantly expressed his disquiet at what he saw as confusion in the Labour Government's judgement on the range of British foreign policy. *"The foreign policy of the Prime Minister ... has at times rested our frontiers upon the Himalayas and at times upon the South Downs, and at the moment they are resting, rather uneasily, and perhaps impermanently on the Rhine. ... it is not very easy to devise defence policies which fit fluctuations quite as rapid and as wide as that."* He reminded his peers that the defence of the British islands could not be guaranteed by conventional means. It was on the deterrent and the network of alliances – NATO, CENTO, SEATO and the United States – that their defences relied, and their effectiveness depended on *"the belief in the mind of an enemy that we should all stick together."* *"Defence is not really about the Northern plains of Germany. [It] is about Vietnam, South Africa, the Gulf, the sealanes of the world upon which are to be found an increasing number of Russian naval forces."* He could not understand why, at a moment when our most important ally was in a difficult situation in Vietnam, we should choose to walk out of East Asia altogether. He gave some advice on equipment and economy. *"Whenever an emergency arises, the question the Secretary of State asks is, "Where is the nearest carrier?" ... "We should certainly keep the carriers. ... I recognise that anyone who says these things has to study methods of economy. For example, I would fly the Royal Air Force off the carriers. There is no reason why one should not substitute the Fleet Air Arm by the Royal Air Force." "What else do you spend money on in defence? Most important of all you spend money on men. I would rather see this country with 100,000 men who were really trained and capable of being moved about the world, efficient commando-*

trained, properly equipped, flexible and mobile than with 140,000 men sitting in Northern Germany." … *"The Singapore base today has more men on its headquarters staff than it had at the very peak of confrontation. Why cannot economies be made? Why wait until 1971? Why face us with the situation of saying, 'We cannot afford these massive bases, and therefore we have to get out of the Far East', when that base could be cut by half within six months? … The noble Lord, Lord Shackleton, asks, 'What is the answer to the question about economy?' The answer is to get on and do some economising."*

Eighteen years later, opening a debate in the Lords on 3rd December 1986, Thorneycroft once again called attention to the state of the nation's defences. This was at a time when the Labour Government was proposing to scrap the country's nuclear missiles and not replace them, relying on the current talks between President Reagan and Mr Gorbachev on nuclear disarmament being successful. Thorneycroft urged the House not to forget the horrors of conventional war recalling that when, 40 years earlier, the atom bomb had been dropped on Japan it had ended a war and begun 40 years of peace in Europe, but it had also dimmed the memory of Passchendaele, Okinawa, the bombing of Coventry, London and Dresden. *"During all that time"*, he said, *"and all my active life in politics, this country has been broadly united about defence – Mr Attlee, Mr Churchill, Hugh Gaitskell, Mr Callaghan, Mr Macmillan, Mr Healey – all of them"*. They had all supported NATO and its strategy of a mix of nuclear and conventional weapons capable of a flexible response to any attack. He referred to a report of the Institute for Strategic Studies, which Lord Chedwyn had recently interpreted as showing that *"we are outgunned and outmanned"*. Thorneycroft agreed that this was so, but asked that the difference in conventional weapons should not be exaggerated, adding, *"I should not like it to go out from any part of this House that the Russians would expect a walkover in a conventional struggle in Europe"*. He said that the first question he had asked when he arrived at the Ministry of Defence was whether we should possess Polaris at all. He had asked the Chiefs of Staff to ignore the fact that he was a Conservative and anything that the Conservative Party or any other party had said. *"The Chiefs of Staff would do that, for the advice of such men … is not based on party politics: it is dispassionate, determined and very bluntly put"*. The advice he received from them and from the Chief Scientific Adviser, was overwhelming, that we should. *"The reason"*, said Thorneycroft, *"is not often stated. It is that if a situation arose in which the American Government distanced themselves a little from the British Government, if they became a little more isolationist, if they became disappointed with the activities and the loyalty of the British to the alliance, it is conceivable – or it might be just conceivable in Russian eyes, and it is Russian eyes that we must consider – that if the Russians limited the war to Europe the Americans might stand aside. At such a moment the presence in Europe, and in European hands, of a nuclear deterrent is absolutely vital. That has been recognised by one chief of staff after another, by one government after another and by the*

Americans as well as ourselves. We should therefore be slow to change it". He believed that the Labour policy of scrapping Trident and expelling the United States from British bases was fraught with danger and would leave us wide open – singled out for attack.

Europe

In December 1991, the Prime Minister John Major had signed the Maastricht Treaty, whose purpose was to delineate areas where, first, powers already ceded to the European institutions should continue to apply, and Community action continue to be decided by those institutions in accordance with established procedures; secondly, areas where the Governments of Member States would co-operate to determine whether a common policy was appropriate and, if so, what that policy should be (foreign and security policy, and justice and home affairs); and thirdly, a provision for the principle of 'subsidiarity', allowing the Community to act only where the member states are unable to achieve the desired result alone. It might, perhaps, have been better had the Maastricht Treaty been confined to a simple statement of those three objectives, and even better if the existing body of European law had been reviewed and pruned of the many measures which conflicted with them and, especially, with the principle of subsidiarity. However, the Bill providing for ratification of the Treaty which the Lords were invited to examine on its Second Reading on 7th and 8th June 1993, although itself a short measure with only seven clauses, was the result of a year and a half of frequently bitter discussion in the Commons during which virtually every word of the Treaty had been scrutinised and dissected by a House divided – often bitterly divided - into shifting cross-party alliances of more or less Europhile and more or less Eurosceptic members. The debate in the Lords was just as passionate. Thorneycroft had been engaged in problems of relations with Europe since his days in the Board of Trade in the 1950s and, several years before that, had contributed to the relevant discussions of the Tory Reform Committee. His speech on 7th June 1993 drew upon his half-century of involvement. It reflects the mood of an old warrior recalling past battles won and lost, but also of a statesman putting his finger unerringly on the key issues facing the nation. It is Thorneycroft at his very best and it calls for reproduction in full:

> *"My Lords, I rise for a very few moments to support the Government and the Prime Minister and to express my hope that the Bill will find its way on to the statute book in the foreseeable future.*
>
> *I do not pretend that the Bill is ideal. I do not believe that anyone who has had the privilege of listening to my noble friend, Lady Thatcher, could have doubted that there were some drawbacks in the Bill. That is not altogether the point. The noble Lord, Lord Carrington, made an absolutely admirable*

speech and struck the right note. We are entering into a Europe that is developing and changing all the time. The question is: can we play a part in shaping that growth and development? I was encouraged by the speech of the noble and learned Lord, Lord Wilberforce. He gave an admirable, practical, commonsense view to some of the legal provisions. We are not yet defeated on all those points. It is not the time to quit; it is the time to go on. It is the time to see whether we can find friends in Europe, skills in this country, and ways in which we can make it a Europe far closer to the organisation we want.

I recognise that we are divided. We have been divided all my life. I have lived through parliaments in which great divisions have taken place on foreign and trade policy. I have known all the time that this country wanted to protect its own personal, individual interest, and its pride in its parliament, its rights and authority, as the noble Viscount, Lord Tonypandy, once said. At the same time, as a small island, its people have wanted to look beyond these shores and to achieve some method for finding markets, trade and investment. If we cease to look beyond these shores, half the public in this country would have to leave. They would have no jobs. Winston Churchill once remarked, 'There would be an awful lot of altercation as to which half.' We have therefore to look outside this island; we have to look somewhere.

The noble Lord, Lord Carrington, referred to this matter in his speech. In my youth the Conservative Party in particular was attached to the concept of imperial preference. It wanted to find the answer there. Leo Amery used to fight a great battle. I remember that, having just returned from a General Agreement on Tariffs and Trade meeting – I was its first chairman – I attended a Cabinet meeting. I was told that Leo was moving such a resolution. I was asked what I intended to do. I said I thought we should oppose it. The Cabinet believed unanimously that I would be defeated, all except Winston, who said, 'Let him try'. He was a very great man and a very brave one. My noble friend Lord Aldington and I fought it out in Blackpool and we won. Imperial preference was effectively buried. We moved over to a system of wider trade and payments, and the General Agreement on Tariffs and Trade – with all the enormous benefits that that has brought. I was very proud to have played a part.

Then in Europe we had the Schuman Plan. I was present, although I do not believe that I played a very distinguished part. However, I was brilliantly served by Sir Frank Lee, the Permanent Secretary. He was one of the greatest permanent secretaries a man could ever wish to have. I wanted to take him with me to the Treasury. I believe that history would have been a little different if I had managed that. However, I was not allowed to do so. There was a young man whose name ought to be mentioned because it is never known now. He was very young and junior, and was treated with not too great respect. I refer to Russell Bretherton. He was a brilliant civil servant. In so far as the light of European union was carried at all during that period, it was due to him.

I do not say that I was the only man at that time who stood for Europe. I dare say that one could find members of the Foreign Office now who favoured union with Europe. There was, after all, a massive case for such union on foreign policy. In my generation there had been two wars. As several speakers have mentioned in the debate, at least the thought of war in Europe has now disappeared. There was also a great case for trade.

We had those opportunities, but I failed completely. The forces against me were too strong. Under Anthony Eden, the Foreign Office was absolutely determined that we should not go into Europe. The noble Baroness is a Euro-enthusiast compared with Anthony Eden. We have the Single European Act and many other matters which Anthony Eden would not have touched. We could hardly get a hearing in the Cabinet at that time. I therefore make no apology: I failed miserably. I was a young, rather over-promoted (some people thought) President of the Board of Trade and Anthony Eden was at the peak of his powers. He was assumed to be, and was, the heir apparent to Winston Churchill. Therefore I could not achieve such a union.

Harold Macmillan played a magnificent part. He argued the case for Europe. In the early days he was Minister of Housing, and one cannot do much about Europe as Minister of Housing. However he was promoted to Chancellor of the Exchequer and eventually became Prime Minister. In so far as we had a European policy, it was due to Harold Macmillan; but he arrived too late. Europe was already being formed on terms which were rather more provincial and more bureaucratic than we would have wished. However, he did the best he could and we managed to achieve a Europe of some kind with us on the fringes. But the Europe we wanted was not provincial and bureaucratic. The Europe that we want today, as we wanted then, is outward looking and pledged to the General Agreement on Tariffs and Trade – and we must fight as we always have. We have not lost the battle yet. The only way in which we could lose the battle is to lose this Bill. We must make an effort with it; we must pull ourselves together and steel the forces that we have. We are not without friends in Europe or new allies coming in. I believe we stand a chance. If we fail, we shall do our best without it, but we may yet succeed.

I only wish to say one thing in conclusion. We are not dealing with a lot of Committee points. Underneath and behind all this there is an enormous issue of principle. People talk on public platforms sometimes about unemployment and the recession; they are the terrible, great problems which confront us at present with the young men who cannot get jobs and young men who are losing jobs. I sometimes listen and wonder what people will do about them.

There are only two things that can do anything about it, one of which is the General Agreement on Tariffs and Trade, to maximise the trade between us and other countries. The other is the huge area of Europe which may not have been as successful as it might have been in the past – and the noble Baroness is perfectly right – but it is still an enormous potential market force. We cannot throw it away, we cannot abandon it at this moment. Therefore I move that we accept the Bill.

Trade Unions

29th April 1987 was the occasion of a debate on a Green Paper *Trade Unions and their Powers* (Cmnd 95), published two months earlier, whose consultation period was approaching its end. The Green Paper proposed a number of detailed changes to trade union law, including provision for minorities in a ballot in favour of industrial action not to take part in the action. Thorneycroft had been preceded in the debate by the newly created Peer, Lord Basnett, a former General Secretary of the General and Municipal Workers Union making what he described as a non-controversial maiden speech asking who wanted the proposed changes and who would benefit from them, and by Lord Murray, a former General Secretary of the TUC, who had strongly attacked the proposal on dissident minority rights. Thorneycroft, showing little interest in the proposals for further detailed changes, was more concerned to underline the principles on which the Conservative Party had based its approach to trade union law: *"It wanted a free society. It wanted to get the unions back to a position where there could be free collective bargaining. .... How did we set about that? ... First, we had to lower inflationary expectations. .... That was one leg of the policy. The other leg was to reduce a little the immunities and powers of the trade union movement."* He reiterated a principle that he had expressed many times before. *"The purpose of the trade unions is not to help a government. .... The job of trade unions is to help their members."* He finished with a confession: *"Years and years ago when I was a young and innocent President of the Board of Trade, I introduced something called 'Three wise men' under Lord Cohen, who sat up all night thinking about what people should be paid. I confess this blushingly to the noble Lord, Lord Murray. That is the sort of thing I did. I was not alone. That is the type of rubbish that every party has done."* 'Free collective bargaining', for Thorneycroft, did not include the notion of a prices and incomes policy or anything resembling one.

Education

Thorneycroft did not in the course of his long career bear any direct responsibility for education policy. His speeches contain few references to the subject. His intervention in a debate on 3rd May 1988 in the Committee Stage of the Education Reform Bill was an exception, and was the result of strong pressure put upon him by Baroness Cox (who was well aware of his strong Christian faith) to support an amendment she had tabled which would require religious education in maintained schools to be predominantly Christian, except in schools established as denominational schools where the religious education should be of that denomination. In his brief speech, Thorneycroft asked *"What is the alternative? .... The amendment tabled by the noble Baroness, Lady Cox, goes to the root of the alternative, which is some kind of multi-faith education. I beg the Committee to think carefully before going too far along that road. The Chief Rabbi called it a 'kind of religious cocktail'. The right reverend Prelate the Bishop of London said that he is nervous of compulsion. So am I. I would be most nervous of compelling people to have a multi-faith education. Of course there is room for the teaching of comparative religion in a pluralist society. It is a fascinating subject when dealt with by men of great ability before intelligent audiences. However, for amateurs to try to teach it to kids of 12 and 13 is asking rather much."* This was a spirited – and predominantly spiritual – debate. In the end, Baroness Cox withdrew her amendment after the Bishop of London offered to try to draft a proposal that might be acceptable to all.

The Bill was a long one, and the Committee Stage stretched into a fourth day, when Thorneycroft himself moved an amendment to a provision for a daily act of collective worship, asking for the word 'Christian' to be inserted after 'collective'. He argued that *"we should not introduce clauses on religious worship and leave the question of what is being worshipped entirely in a vacuum. One does not worship in a vacuum. One either worships humbly and devoutly or one should not worship at all."* He insisted that *"we do not ask the Moslims and the Buddhists and other faiths to join together with the Jews and have an act of collective worship. We are saying that if there are a lot of children of other faiths in the school and the parents want it, each of them should have an act of worship which applies to their own religion. .... It comes to all of us: moments of darkness, moments when we lose loved ones or find ourselves abandoned by friends and moments of defeat. In those moments, some men find their way back to their religion. Through the great prayers of the Church and the beauty of the English and Welsh liturgy, they find the ability to worship again. But they will never again find it if they have never experienced it. The purpose of the amendments is not to deny children that important part of life."* Kenneth Baker, who was Secretary of State for Education at the time, thought (as he records in his autobiography, *The Turbulent Years*), that Thorneycroft's amendment was going too far. It was also against the wishes of the Bishop of London, Graham Leonard, who wanted more time to come up with alternatives to the amendments proposed by Baroness Cox and Lord Thorneycroft. The motion was pressed to a division which was carried by 17 votes to 2, but ruled as 'not decided' because fewer than 30 peers had voted.

Health

Thorneycroft was an admirer of the National Health Service, and said so very clearly in a debate in the House of Lords on 23rd March 1988, describing it as *"a triumphant contribution to the welfare of the nation"*, ... *"always coupled with the name of Aneurin Bevan."* He thought that *"everyone agrees, even if we do not agree about anything else, that the great centrepiece of the health service is that no man should be denied access to medical skills through his own lack of means. Whatever happens, we should hold firmly to that principle."* And he spelled out the consequences of this principle: *"If one has a service, free at the point of sale, with people getting older, new diseases developing and new cures developed, I can see no possibility of avoiding some measure of underfunding. I think it much better to accept that. It would be a pity if we were all to spend the rest of the century belabouring each other because a very obvious situation exists."* He ended with a word of advice that those who ask for money should make sure that it was well spent. *"It is no good striking because there is not enough money for the health service and then striking because you don't like contracting out."*

These, necessarily brief quotations and summaries of a few of Thorneycroft's many speeches in the House of Lords can hardly do justice to a man whose musings and pronouncements are a fount of so much political wisdom ranging over a vast range of subjects. They leave many loose ends untied, but they may be enough to give a clear idea of the quality of his character, his judgement and his humanity. Even as he aged, he tried always to ensure that his remarks were relevant to the world as it is, not as it might be.

Conservative Party Chairman 1975-81

The election of Margaret Thatcher as Leader of the Conservative Party in 1975 brought Thorneycroft back into active politics. Thatcher had admired Thorneycroft since her Oxford days. He had given her his support on the occasion of her political début as Secretary of the University's Conservative Association when he spoke at her first meeting in her new role. To the surprise of many political commentators at the time, it was to Thorneycroft that she turned in 1975 as Chairman of the Party.

The post of Party Chairman is not always of particular importance, but at that time it certainly was. Labour had been returned to power in 1974 with a tiny majority in the House of Commons and, although it managed to survive, it was throughout its life exposed to the risk of having to call a General Election at almost any time. The other parties had also to be ready to fight an election at short notice, so that the party organisations had to be kept on their toes not just for the short burst of activity which normally precedes an election, but for several years. It fell to the Party Chairman to keep the party machine ready for action.

Thorneycroft, by now, had accumulated fifteen years or so of business experience in the private sector, and it was business method that he applied from the moment that he took up his post as Party Chairman. He saw immediately the potential for friction at the top of the organisation arising from the existence of a Director General with the authority of a chief executive reporting to an executive chairman. Such an arrangement can sometimes work, although rarely without difficulty, if distinct, non-conflicting executive roles are unambiguously defined and rigorously respected by both parties, but Michael Wolff had been appointed in August 1974 with the title of Director General and the all-embracing role of 'Chief Executive of the Party Organisation, directly responsible to the Chairman for overseeing and co-ordinating the work of the publicity, research and organisation departments'. Thorneycroft knew that there had been some friction before he took over as Chairman from his cousin, William Whitelaw, between Wolff and Lord Chelmer, one of the Treasurers, who complained to Wolff on 1st August 1974 of a serious misunderstanding about the handling of funds intended for spending on critical seats, to which Wolff had reacted, not by dealing with the issue or responding to Chelmer, but by writing to the Chairman the following day that he really did not know what to make of Chelmer's letter. On 28th November 1974, Wolff had complained in a letter to Whitelaw that a proposal made by the Chairman in a meeting with the Treasurers to set up a high-powered committee to discuss Party Organisation had taken him somewhat by surprise, implying that the Chairman should not have made such a proposal without first consulting him. Thorneycroft wanted there to be no doubt about who was to be the boss. He explained to Wolff what he wanted to do and why and, on 6th March 1975, wrote to confirm that he wished Wolff to leave his post on terms to be agreed. Commenting on Wolff's dismissal Robert Blake mentions, in his masterly history of the Conservative Party, that Wolff, who had been appointed as Director General by Edward Heath, was inevitably regarded as a committed Heathite and could hardly have expected to survive for long. This could be construed as implying that Wolff was dismissed by Thorneycroft because he was a Heathite, but there is no evidence to suggest that this was the case. Thorneycroft's decision was reached on managerial, not political grounds. Indeed, Thorneycroft made this clear in explaining his approach to his task in a speech that he made to the Central Council of the Party in Harrogate on 14th March 1975:

> "The Conservative Party has a vital role. We cannot of course win an election by organisation alone but we certainly cannot win it without it.

> "When I was asked to take on the Chairmanship of the Party, I realised that my first task would be to make a close study of the top direction of the Central Office. I make no reflection whatever upon the able men I found there. The fact is, however, that the Conservative Party has had seven Chairmen in ten years.

> "Each added bits to suit his taste and not all the bits were entirely relevant to one another. I found a central organisation which resembled nothing so much as one of those charming country houses where wings and annexes have been added at various periods to suit the whim of successive owners. Some of them have services, some have staircases and some are devoid of most facilities. But whatever else Central Office appeared to be, it did not look like battle headquarters, and it is a battle that the Conservative Party has got to fight.

> "There are, in my judgement, two essentials for any organisation – clear lines of command and responsibility at the top, and effective financial and budgetary control throughout. It seems to me that both were lacking. I am therefore in the process of introducing these requisites, and I will not be deflected from this course. I am not in the least concerned with who previously appointed whom; nor am I concerned with whether administrators are judged to be of the right or the left of the Party, whatever those terms may mean. The function of the Central Office is to provide organisation and communications to link together the different elements of the Party; to assist Conservatives to develop their ideas within the broad framework of Conservative principles; and to link the Party with the electorate.

*"The Central Office organisation is now being shaped to take account of
these objectives."*

*"Lastly, of money. I have separated fund-raising from financial control.
Lord Chelmer and Lord Ashdown [Treasurers] will be responsible for the
former. Financial control will be the responsibility of William Clark [Deputy
Chairman]. I regard those arrangements as a more businesslike approach.
However hard I try, I cannot run the Conservative Party organisation
without substantial central funds. I thank those who have helped and are
helping us, but the truth is that a subscription which works out at a few
pence per Conservative voter is not enough. We are going to have to bring
ourselves to think in terms of new pounds rather then new pence.*

*"As to industry, I am an industrialist and I know something of their
problems. We need to persuade people of the vital importance of wealth
creation. Without it policies cannot prosper and compassion is reduced to
an empty slogan. The hard fact is that there will be no halt in the advance
of Marxism and the grave damage that results to the economic and social
fabric of this country until there is a majority of Conservatives in the
House of Commons. Our job is to achieve this and to back the clarity and
courage and devotion to principle which our Leader, Margaret Thatcher,
has been showing.*

*"I would say only this to you in conclusion – in the course of a long career
in the Conservative Party it is impossible not to suffer defeats. No one
can get through a political career without some wounds. Now, however, is
surely the time to put old squabbles aside, and certainly not to create new
ones over the administration of the Party.*

"It is a moment to unite and stand up and be counted."

That speech was delivered only a fortnight after Thorneycroft took up his office,
and implies that he had been following the activities of Conservative Central
Office for some time, and was already well aware of its problems.

Thorneycroft appointed no replacement for Wolff as Director General, but took
on his own shoulders the supervision and co-ordination of the departments of
Central Office, whose Directors now reported directly to him. Before considering
further changes, Thorneycroft wanted to encourage his colleagues (and not only
those who reported directly to him) to give him their views – a practice he had
admired in his business assignments and adopted as his own. Some of those
views did not make comfortable reading.

Alan Howarth, Thorneycroft's Personal Assistant, kicked off on 23rd May 1975
with a brief paper, promising to produce a more substantial document later
(although there is no trace of such a document). He listed the Party's principal

failings: thin support among young voters; decline in the share of the working class vote; loss of votes to Labour in the North, and to the Nationalists in Scotland and in Wales; allowing opponents to dictate the themes of political discussion; demoralisation and distrust within the Party, resulting in members talking to themselves rather than trying to engage with the uncommitted; the perception that Central Office gave poor service and bad value for money. Howarth made some tentative suggestions for corrective action; greater attention to local government; engagement with pressure groups, including ethnic groups and, most especially, trade unions, and with schools and universities; a more relevant Research effort with better contacts outside Westminster, aiming to anticipate strategic problems, such as the immigrant and youth votes, the demand for devolution, electoral reform, elections to the European Parliament; training of agents, candidates, councillors and MPs.

On 10th July, Joan Varley, Director of Local Government and responsible also for the Women's Organisation, revealed in a memorandum addressed to Alan Howarth her misgivings about the effectiveness of the chain of command and of communications both within the office and with agents in the field, and emphasising how important it was that the Chairman should act and be recognised as not only the titular but also the executive head of Central Office. A few weeks later, on 12th September 1975, Joan Varley sent her own assessment to Thorneycroft himself, apparently in response to a specific request from him. She described a party divided between 'traditionalists' and 'reformers', naming those whom she saw as the principal supporters of each of these two diametrically opposed schools of thought, and she expressed reservations about the wisdom of recent efforts by Sir Richard Webster, the Director of Organisation, to phase out centrally employed agents and to delay providing resources for a campaign aimed at winning critical seats (those where opposition majorities were slim), the topic on which Wolff and Chelmer had been at variance a year or so earlier.

At the Party's National Conference in Blackpool in October, Thorneycroft presented to Conference a clear picture of the obstacles that the Party had to overcome if it was to win the next election. He began with an up-beat assessment of the Party's strengths, especially the qualities of its Leader, Margaret Thatcher, *"a woman of principle and courage in a world in which both these qualities appear to be sadly lacking."* He informed Conference that he had appointed a Working Party under Reginald Eyre MP (a Vice-Chairman and one of the 'reformers' named by Joan Varley) to examine all the ideas on Party organisation and report back by Christmas. He wanted to hear the views of constituency party leaders during his proposed tour of areas planned for the coming months. He would then discuss the recommendations with the Agents, the 1922 Committee and the National Union.

Compared with the swift and decisive action he had taken within a week of taking office to remove the potential clash between Director General and Chairman, the measured pace at which he moved to resolve other weaknesses in the Central Office organisation seems remarkably cautious. His concern was almost certainly to carry with him the people who would be affected by any reorganisation, recognising that complex changes will not succeed if they are imposed on people who have the power to frustrate them. The ability to frustrate the intentions of the leadership is, perhaps, especially strong in a democratic political party, where the balance of power between the leader, his committed senior supporters, his senior opponents, the party members, the national executive, the constituency parties and their activists, and the MPs, individually and in like-minded groups, is so confused and constantly shifting.

A few other important changes were, however, made quickly. One was the appointment of Saatchi and Saatchi as public relations advisers, a selection which appears to have been made by hunch, relying on the judgement of Gordon Reece, the Director of Publicity, with no formal selection process and, according to a note written to Thorneycroft much later (on 12th August 1983) by Michael Spicer, MP, with inadequate controls that had led to excessive expenditure.

Another change was the appointment of Alistair McAlpine as a Treasurer, with particular responsibility for fund-raising, initially joining the two others, Lord Ashdown (who had been appointed by Heath) and Lord Chelmer. It seems that in the case of the Treasurers, Thorneycroft was not initially too worried about having a plethora of bosses. Indeed when, in April 1976, Chelmer indicated that he wished to resign because of the increasing pressure of other work, Thorneycroft wrote to Thatcher that *"this was a pity. He is on very good terms with all of us and is well liked everywhere."* However, both he and McAlpine were worried that Chelmer's resignation would leave Ashdown as the longest serving and, by implication, the senior Treasurer. In the same message to his Leader he said of Ashdown that *"he lacks all Chelmer's gifts of pouring oil on troubled waters, and he will be generally obstructionist everywhere."* adding *"My own judgment is that the most satisfactory situation would be to have Alistair McAlpine as the single Treasurer of the Conservative Party. …. If we cannot manage to part with Ashdown and I see all the difficulties of it then we will have to resign ourselves to Ashdown and Alistair working in harness but neither senior to the other."* *"In any event at this stage I would not recommend the appointment of an additional third Treasurer which would only complicate the situation further."*

A further change in Central Office resulted from the ostensibly unforced resignation in January 1976 of Sir Richard Webster, who had been Director of Organisation for the past ten years and therefore must have been largely responsible for the poor state of Central Office that Thorneycroft found when he took up his post. Webster was not replaced, his responsibilities being re-allocated amongst the existing senior officers.

The report of Reginald Eyre's working party was presented in December 1975, and its recommendations dealt mainly with the Party's organisation in the field, in particular, that Area status should be conferred on five metropolitan counties where the Party had performed badly at the last General Election, with several other recommendations aimed at making better use of Constituency Agents and reducing the work-load on local officers. Thorneycroft referred the report to the Constituency Chairmen, the 1922 Committee and others for consultation and comment. By the beginning of April, most of the recommendations were accepted, although with modifications. Area status was not conferred on metropolitan counties which, instead, were to be supervised by Deputy Agents of Central Office.

Whilst his primary responsibility was for Party organisation, Thorneycroft also contributed in a number of ways to policy formulation. He was a member of a number of groups and committees so engaged:

- the Strategy Group, which Margaret Thatcher set up in 1976;

- the Strategy and Tactics Committee which, in addition to the Party Leader and the Chairman, included other Shadow Cabinet members and some Central Office staff;

- the Campaign Committee, established in January 1978, which was concerned with planning for the four plebiscites which took place during 1979 – the two votes on Welsh and Scottish Devolution, the General Election and the election for the European Parliament;

- an *ad hoc* Education Project Group which Thatcher asked Thorneycroft to chair. (The performance of Norman St John Stevas in shadowing Shirley Williams seems not to have satisfied Thatcher);

- the Competition Policy Group, in which Thorneycroft had to mediate in a disagreement between John Nott and Sally Oppenheim;

- the Office for Closer Liaison with Industry;

- the Leader's Consultative Committee and its Policy Sub-Committee.

A strategy paper of 20th June 1978 prepared by Thorneycroft was directed at maximising the number of votes for the Party in the General Election widely expected to be called in the Autumn of 1978, (although Prime Minister Callaghan confounded the pundits by delaying it until the following year). Thorneycroft proposed:

- targeting those who had voted Liberal in 1974, voters in constituencies where Labour was vulnerable, skilled workers;

- concentrating on issues of prevailing public concern – unemployment, rising prices, controlling immigration, law and order;

- ✧ cautious handling of sensitive issues – Trade Union attitudes, reduction of civil service numbers, breaking up the public sector, ending special measures to create employment. – on which public comment should be cleared in advance with the Shadow Cabinet;

- ✧ refraining from direct attacks on Trade Unions, and concentrating on industrial policy issues – productivity, high wages/high production, capital investment.

In a further paper of 24ᵗʰ July, Thorneycroft suggested draft answers on economic issues likely to be raised at daily press conferences – inflation, incomes policy, taxes, unemployment, Trade Unions. On 7ᵗʰ August, when most of the country thought that a General Election was imminent, he suggested to Thatcher that she should consider *"how the Labour Party would try to present to the public the broad issue between the Parties in general and between herself and Mr Callaghan in particular,"* and also that *"the public as a whole and to some extent our own backbenchers probably do not understand [our] economic policy."* He advised her that, in her Leader's message, she should not attempt to cover every department, nor make pledges, but make it *"short, blunt, comprehensible, confident and given the staggering complexities of some of the difficulties rather cautious."*

On 21ˢᵗ November 1978, (by which time it was clear that the Election would not be held that year) he revealed that he had misgivings concerning the Party's policy on pay:

> *"[The Party] would do well to ponder deeply the present state of public opinion before we finally decide upon either [the policy's] nature or its timing. ---- I am, I must admit, to some extent suspect myself [being] not confident that any of the solutions put forward are likely to succeed [including] full and responsible bargaining without Government interference."*

He followed this up on 4ᵗʰ December with a draft note to Sir Keith Joseph for a statement on incomes policy and the Unions, with which Joseph told him he was happy.

In December 1978, Margaret was to give a speech to the constituency party in Paddington, which was intended to set the keynote for a series continuing into the New Year which would outline Conservative policies, and she asked Thorneycroft for ideas. He sent her a brief note on 12ᵗʰ December suggesting that its main theme should be the country's potential greatness, that a second speech should deal with *"the real heart of the economic problem – how are we to compete?",* and be followed by a third talking about the kind of country we want to live in: *"Men are moved by more than material things,"* he said. He followed up a day later with a longer memorandum, (copied to Humphrey Atkins, Sir Geoffrey Howe,

Lord Carrington, Sir Keith Joseph, Jim Prior, Francis Pym and Willie Whitelaw):

1. *"You have it in mind to make a series of speeches in the New Year …*

2. *"You will probably find it of advantage to discuss the general theme of these speeches with some of your colleagues not only to ensure agreement on a common approach but to ensure that their speeches and our public relations generally coincide with the line that you are taking. The purpose of this note is to provide you with a possible basis for that discussion.*

3. *"A sensible starting point for such discussions might be provided, at least in part, by a study of public opinion as it appears to stand …The key of rising prices, level of taxation and controlling immigration …On the key question of incomes policy, no matter how the idea of the present Government's pay policy is put to the electorate, support for it tends to be fairly strong. The vast majority of the electorate …think that the Trade Unions have too much power … [The] public is not yet fully aware of our commitments in the taxation field and still sees us as the Party of the rich …[On] defence, the electorate does not see this as a key problem … On housing, we do not have any significant lead …*

4. *"What all this … amounts to is that voters are in many cases tired or disillusioned with … Labour … but far from being yet convinced that we are an obvious or very attractive alternative. The objectives of the New Year campaign must be to heighten the sense of disillusionment … while presenting [us] in positive and simple terms and in a general tone of voice with which voters find it congenial to identify.*

5. *"Perhaps the first strategic decision to make is …. which of these tasks is undertaken by whom. You will probably think it right to concentrate yourself on the positive lines of a Conservative approach [and] leave the main attack on Labour to others. We need however to discuss which others and what lines …*

6. *"What matters most is the tone of voice and the general attitude of our approach and I personally believe that these may prove even more important than the details of any policy that we may lay down …*

7. *"First as to the nature and problems facing an incoming Government. There is the obvious and usual choice between claiming that we know exactly what to do about everything and emphasising that we shall want to look long and hard at the books before we act. Wise oppositions generally lean towards the latter …*

8. *[On] pace and timing, Mr Callaghan and Mr Benn don't really differ in their support of Labour Party policy. They do differ about pace and timing. Mr Callaghan is a real threat in the Election. Mr Benn would lose it. Whatever the policy the truth about Government is that good Government does not consist in trying to change everything in the twinkle of an eye. Good Government consists in the gradual*

slowing down of mistaken trends – the edging of the ship a few points at a time in the right direction and the quiet introduction of trends more favourable to the nation.

9. *"We need to discuss how much of this truth we are prepared to tell. In terms of winning votes, the pace at which we propose to do things may be just as important as the things we propose to do … You cannot eliminate swiftly huge blocks of Government expenditure; you can make a start by not increasing it and then begin to spend less. You cannot revolutionise the law on Trade Unions; you can stop legislating to strengthen the militants even more. A note of moderation and quietness … would help greatly …*

10. *"We need also in the presentation of our case to talk and act like a National Party … We shall be saying tough things about [the Trade Unions] but we should be careful to praise the institutions. A hard line on immigration needs to be matched by a very forthcoming one on race relations.*

11. *"None of the above involves any real alteration in Conservative policy. It is concerned with attitudes, with tone of voice, with the pace of advance. It is however just in these factors that elections are won and lost. If the Labour Party do well in the election it will not be because the public believe in Socialism: it will be because Mr Callaghan has created the illusion that he has been talking commonsense with which the ordinary man and woman can identify.*

12. *"The last general point I would make is that in the presentation of our case we should not spend much time arguing with the public …*

13. *"We need then to present ourselves as a prospective Government capable of taking over … "*

A clearer, more comprehensive yet concise plan for an election campaign can hardly be imagined.

The speech that Thatcher delivered in Paddington on 18ᵗʰ December embraced the first two of Thorneycroft's suggested themes, but with emphases different from his. In speaking of the country's potential greatness, her stress was on the damage done to it by Labour: *"But where are we under Labour? Balefully bringing up the rear. Today, our status as a second-class country is all but confirmed."* (She evidently had not accepted Thorneycroft's advice that she should concentrate on the positive lines of a Conservative approach and leave attacks on Labour to her colleagues). On economic policy she wanted to leave no doubt about the actions that the Conservative Party would take in Government and, listing them, she emphasised that these were policies clearly set out a year before and were unchanged. (There was no hint here of 'taking a long, hard look at the books before we act'). She pointed out that if national economic recovery was to be achieved a responsible

Trade Union movement was essential, and she rehearsed the measures, including a review of recent legislation, which would be taken to encourage this. She was, however, careful to add, *"We shall invite the Unions to join with us in building the new and prosperous Britain we all want. We shall not 'bash' the Unions. Neither shall we bow to them."* At the end of the speech, there was a brief reference to the social climate and the economic climate: *"These will be our guidelines. 'Free for all' – No. "Freedom for all under the law' – Yes."* Her speech was a fine one. She knew it. She wanted to be sure that everyone else acknowledged it as the careful exposition of the Conservative policies on which the election would be fought. There is, perhaps, a hint of tetchiness in a confidential letter she wrote to Thorneycroft on 5th January 1979 complaining that copies of her Paddington speech had not been distributed quickly enough, and that only two Shadow Ministers had followed it up. It must be remembered that throughout this unusually protracted pre-election period, Saatchi and Saatchi and Gordon Reece, as well as Shadow Cabinet members and many others, were also proffering their advice on content and presentation of the Party message, but the Party Leader always – and rightly - had the final say. Thatcher's concern was that the media and the public should be left in no doubt that the policy she announced was supported by everyone in the Party. She emphasised this in her letter to Thorneycroft:

> *"A letter from you in the next weekly envelope setting out the importance of the Paddington speech might be the answer if there remain those who believe we are not at one on this issue. Judging from my correspondence there are constituencies who are still confused. One can hardly blame them for this if the marketing operation through press, media and our own distribution network has not achieved the measure of success we were all hoping for."*

Thorneycroft did as he was asked, and refrained from reminding his Leader that he had foreseen the problem in his memorandum of 13th December, when he had advised her to discuss the general theme of her speeches with colleagues before delivering them so as to ensure agreement on a common approach. Thatcher was not that sort of Leader. However she had, at least to a degree, listened to his advice to *'adopt a tone of voice with which voters find it congenial to identify'*.

Thatcher gave a number of further speeches during January, but events dictated that they did not really form a logically developing series of policy presentations, because they were delivered against the background of a national transport strike which was seriously disrupting the lives of the general public, and the content and tone of the speeches had, perforce, to register the Party's reaction to this serious – however transitory - state of affairs.

On 15th January 1979, Thorneycroft sent Thatcher a *"mere skeleton of a speech. It may help in putting some order into the argument. It is important that a national rather than a Party line is struck. I am confident that it is the national approach which will appeal to the country and to Conservatives inside and outside the House of Commons."* Thorneycroft repeated his advice to open on a non-controversial note and then outline national problems but not saying in detail what the Conservatives would do about them. As Thatcher had already set out the Conservative stall in her Paddington speech this advice may have been a bit tardy, but it does seem to have influenced the tone of later speeches.

During the Summer of 1978, when the date of the Election was still uncertain, Central Office under the guidance of Baroness Young, a Deputy Chairman, had prepared a plan for the election campaign in quite meticulous detail, down to making sure that the Leader's time schedule would allow time for make-up and hair. As the Election approached this plan was reviewed and revised and, by the end of March 1979, Thorneycroft was able to inform the Management Group that *'the organisation was now in a state of readiness to fight an Election'*. Callaghan announced on 4th April 1979 that the Election would take place on 3rd May.

During the campaign, unlike most of his predecessors, Thorneycroft stayed in London, making sure that Central Office was ready to respond swiftly and efficiently to whatever the ebb and flow of events in the field threw at it. Every day at 8 am he attended the daily press conference accompanied by Adam Ridley, the acting head of the Research Department, Tim Bell of Saatchi and Saatchi and those Shadow Ministers called for duty that day according to the issues that were exercising the media and the public. There usually followed a brief meeting with Thatcher before she set off on her round of speaking engagements, a working lunch at St Stephen's Club with as many senior members of Central Office as were available, and a 9 pm meeting with Department Heads to review the day's events and prepare for the next day. Throughout the campaign Thorneycroft was supported in Central Office by one of the Deputy Chairmen, Angus Maude, whilst Baroness Young, whom he held in very high regard, travelled with Margaret Thatcher with the responsibility to keep in regular touch with Party HQ. Thorneycroft kept up a flow of guidance to candidates and Shadow Ministers on the issues they should be concentrating on in their speeches. On 20th April, the list of topics included sale of council houses, cutting taxes, law and order, and help for the elderly – and candidates were advised to ignore the opinion polls and Labour smears. On 25th he was urging members of the Front Bench to allay public anxieties on public expenditure cuts, privatisation, unemployment and regional aid. On 30th April he issued a warning that the MORI poll showed a narrowing of the Party's lead to only 3 points, and told candidates to rebut Labour lies about Tory intentions (*"putting VAT on food, charging for doctors' visits"*) and suggested some Labour weak spots that could usefully be attacked (*"under Labour, one man has been put out of work every four minutes"*).

A post-election analysis of the campaign concluded that the Conservative machine had operated exceptionally smoothly and without rancour. Thorneycroft had done his job very well. Margaret Thatcher was the new Prime Minister. In 1980, Thorneycroft was made a Companion of Honour in recognition of his services.

The story of the early years of the Thatcher government has been told in great detail in so many books, not least those written by Thatcher herself, that it would be superfluous to add further comment. Thorneycroft remained in the post of Chairman of the Party for a further two years, engaging in a steady flow of highly effective representation of Party policy in television, radio and press interviews, in discussion programmes, and in the House of Lords. As time went on, it became fashionable to discern schools of Conservative politicians as 'dry' – those who gave Margaret Thatcher their unequivocal support – or 'wet' – those who believed that the 'dry' side of the face of Toryism was becoming less acceptable to many Conservative supporters in the country at large. Thorneycroft who, throughout his political career, had consistently been a 'one-nation Tory' put the dilemma rather well during a Press Conference on 1st August 1981, two years into Margaret Thatcher's first Government, saying that he felt *"a little rising damp"*, a gentle enough hint to the Prime Minister, but seemingly enough - together with some more serious remarks he made about the severity of the economic recession, and a comment (clearly straying into the Prime Minister's own territory) that a Cabinet reshuffle seemed unnecessary - to bring their six-year partnership to a close. On 25th August, Thorneycroft sent a letter to the Prime Minister which read:

My dear Margaret,

You appointed me as Chairman of the Conservative Party six and a half years ago. Under your leadership, our Party won a momentous victory in May 1979. Since then, despite the upsurge in oil prices and the world recession the Government has made significant progress in the massive task of halting and reversing the long years of decline.

After the Election you asked me to stay on as Party Chairman and I was glad to do so. I have enjoyed the last six and a half years enormously. During nearly half a century of politics they have been the most rewarding.

About a year ago however I reminded you that by the time of the next Election your Party Chairman would be around seventy five years of age and that if a new Chairman was to be appointed it would be sensible to do so in time for him to assume responsibility for the Party Organisation in time for the run up to that event. My advice to you now is that you should appoint a younger man to undertake this task.

I would like to take this opportunity to thank you for having given me the opportunity to serve the Party during such an important period and also for many kindnesses in rough times as well as smooth.

For my part I have always sought to present the collective view of the Government and of the Party on many platforms throughout the country. I attach as part of this letter the final message which I sent to constituency Chairmen, to Agents and to others at the beginning of this month which I hope illustrates the determined, undogmatic and caring party which we have always been and will under your leadership I know remain.

Yours ever

     Peter

Margaret Thatcher's reply of 7th September, delayed by her absence abroad, was equally warm in tone, with no hint of the recent emergence of differences of view. It read:

My dear Peter,

Thank you so much for your letter of 25th August.

You know how greatly I have relied upon your advice since I became Leader of the Party in February 1975.

You know, too, how enormously I have valued your untiring work as Chairman of the Party over the past six and a half years.

The Conservative Party has had many distinguished Chairman. You have served in this post for longer than any of your predecessors with the single exception of Lord Woolton. Your contribution to the advancement of the Conservative cause has been unique and it is typical of your magnanimity that you should advise that I should now appoint a younger successor.

I remember that you first entered the House of Commons in 1938, and that you first became a Minister in 1945. I remember, too, your long service as a member of the Cabinet. You say, generously, that your time as Chairman of our Party has been the most rewarding of your long career. I have enjoyed, so much, working with you. I hope that the Party and I may continue to have your advice in the years that lie ahead.

I send to you – and to Carla – who has always supported you magnificently – my warmest gratitude and that of the whole Party for all that you have both done for our Party and for our country.

Yours ever

     Margaret

Had there really been a serious rift between the Chairman and his Leader, or had Thorneycroft's retirement and its timing already been agreed between them?

The 'rising damp' remark which gave rise to so much fuss may well have been no more than one of those flashes of wry humour, typical of Thorneycroft, made to lighten the atmosphere at what had been a rather dismal press conference about unemployment, recession, inflation and low productivity. Only a few weeks before, on 8th July, Thorneycroft had spoken very warmly about Margaret Thatcher's courage and determination in dealing with these problems. There is no doubt that he believed, as he had made clear in 1979, that to win elections it was wise to *adopt a tone of voice with which voters find it congenial to identify*. If that advice was 'wet' it was also perennially sound. In any case, it related to tactics, not to strategy, and was just the sort of advice that a highly competent and confident leader should expect - and hope - to receive from a wise and robust chairman. All the evidence that the author has seen or heard indicates that, in the summer of 1981, Thorneycroft's faith in and support for Margaret Thatcher's political strategy was undimmed, and that he ceased to be Party Chairman at that time because it was the right time for the change to be made.

~ 5 ~

Business

Apolitician's life in a democracy is inherently hazardous, subject to the mood of the electorate who can launch a career in one election and destroy it in another, to the state of personal relations with the Party Leader (when in office, the Prime Minister) and to events, foreseeable and unforeseeable. On the positive side, the experience, especially of ministerial office, can be a remarkably effective training for alternative careers if the political one is broken or interrupted. Thorneycroft, faced with a period in the political wilderness after his resignation as Chancellor of the Exchequer in 1958, needed a new source of income. He found it in business, first with the Pirelli Group. Return to office as Minister of Aviation in 1960 obliged him to suspend his business activities, but he rejoined Pirelli in 1967 and soon afterwards was invited by the Philips Group to chair their newly acquired British subsidiary, Pye of Cambridge. In 1969 he joined Trust House Forte Limited as Chairman and, in the 1980s, added to his portfolio of directorships the British Reserve Insurance Co Ltd, Gil, Carvajal and Partners Ltd (the British arm of a Spanish legal firm, of which he was Chairman from 1981-1989) and the Italian Banca Nazionale di Lavoro (1984 until his death). He also served as Chairman of two business related Government agencies, SITPRO (Simplification of International Trade Procedures), from 1968 until 1975, and the British Overseas Trade Board, from 1972 to 1975.

Unfortunately, information about some of these appointments is rather sparse, partly because neither commercial firms nor Government agencies are particularly interested in keeping archives of relevance or are reluctant to give access to their records before they have to. However, enough information is available to give a flavour of the sort of contribution Thorneycroft was able to make to some of these organisations.

The Pirelli Group

It was Dr Alberto Pirelli who first 'discovered' Peter Thorneycroft, an up and coming young British politician, when he was President of the Board of Trade between 1951 and 1957. Alberto Pirelli who, with his brother Piero, took charge of the Pirelli Group on the retirement of their father, was firmly convinced that the executives of the operating companies of the Group and the management of the Group as a whole could derive great benefit from the advice of first class people drawn from the upper ranks of the business and political communities in the countries where the Group had industrial operations. He therefore devoted a great deal of effort to identifying and recruiting such people as chairmen or non-executive directors of Pirelli subsidiaries.

Peter Thorneycroft was invited to join the Board of the UK tyre subsidiary, Pirelli Limited, in 1958, after his resignation as Chancellor of the Exchequer. His appointment as Minister of Aviation in 1960 and then as Minister of Defence in 1962 interrupted his Pirelli board membership, but he returned as a non-executive director of Pirelli Limited in 1965, when he also joined the Board of the cable subsidiary, Pirelli General. He was appointed Chairman of both companies in 1967.

He soon revealed an outstanding competence in the sensitive role of advisor to the managers of subsidiaries of a multinational group, whose loyalties lay both to the national companies for which, and to the Group management to which, they were responsible.

There are many ways in which the relationship between a chairman of such high profile and his managing director can develop. Thorneycroft saw his role as not unlike that of Bagehot's Monarch to his Prime Minister. This was the role that he described in one of the seemingly off-the-cuff, but deeply perceptive and incisive speeches at which he was so adept, that he made to a gathering of all the Group's national chairmen and chief executives in Basle in 1986, concluding with Bagehot's pithy *'to advise, to be consulted and* (in that booming voice which so often struck terror into the hearts of lesser folk on the Opposition benches) *to WARN!.'*

That was very much like the relationship developed over a period of four years with the present author who, from 1967 to 1971, was the managing director of Pirelli General. In July 1967, we were both new in our jobs. Within the first five minutes of our first meeting, Thorneycroft realised that I was a little unsure of protocol in talking to a recently created Peer of the Realm. "Look! Call me Peter." he said, "Much more friendly than My Lord". So I shall call him 'Peter' in this chapter instead of the formal 'Thorneycroft' used in most of the book.

We found it useful, at first, to meet once a fortnight for a quite informal chat

INTERIOR

Drawing Room, Eaton Square

Plate 9

Venetian doorway, Rio degli Ognissanti

Plate 10

INDUSTRY
Peter Thorneycroft was also an industrialist, and this is reflected in his art

a. An Industrial Scene painted in acrylic and crayon

b. Watercolour of an industrial landscape near Leeds

Plate 11

STILL LIFE

a. Chrysanthemums in a black vase

b. Still life with fruit

Plate 12

PETER LOVED VENICE
His sketchbooks are full of images like these

a. Canal bridge

b. Traghetto

c. Isola San Giorgio

Plate 13

285

DOMESTIC ARTISTRY

Peter Thorneycroft's talents extended to the kitchen. He enjoyed preparing meals for his family and favoured guests, and had a wide repertoire of Italian dishes.

a. Peter Pieman

... and he was a patient and loveable Grandfather.

b. Peter with Alexander and Daniel - a study in concentration

Plate 14

PETER'S GRANDCHILDREN WERE A SOURCE OF PRIDE
AND ENDLESS PLEASURE TO HIM

a. When they lived at Northbourne Court in the 1980s, Peter and Carla were able to invite all of their grandchildren to visit them together

Alessandra Richard Daniel Eleanor

Peter Carla

Susannah Alexander

b. Here John Ward visits the Thorneycrofts at Northbourne Court to discuss painting, and finds Carla and Peter with their grandchildren, Susannah, Daniel and Alexander (Victoria's children)

1985

Plate 15   287

THE ENJOYMENT OF PAINTING LASTS FOREVER

a. Peter continued to paint until close to the end of his life, setting up his easel or painting kit whenever he saw a suitable subject, or making a sketch in the little book he always had with him ...

b. ... even when he had to rely on a wheel chair to get him to a suitable spot.

lasting a couple of hours or so about what had been happening. I soon realised that the best way to spend the time was to concentrate, not on the detail (which the chairman could find in the board papers), but on the few major issues of current importance, especially when there were problems to which the solution, for me, was not clear-cut. Peter had an extraordinary knack of listening, often without saying a word. At a crucial point there would be a mere flick of an eyelid or an especially intense look, and I would find that I suddenly knew what the answer was. If the problem was particularly complex Peter would ask for an explanation of what alternative courses of action might be taken and how I judged each of them. He would then probe key aspects of my reasoning, or sometimes suggest an avenue that I had not explored. We did not always arrive at a solution, but I would always go away with fresh insights. Sometimes he would telephone me a day or two later to tell me of some further thought that had come to him.

As we came to know each other better, and trust developed, our meetings became less frequent. I would meet him for dinner the evening before each board meeting to go through the agenda or, if I had a difficult matter to discuss, arrange to see him specially.

One major initiative in which the Company was engaged was a project for changing the organisation from one based on functions – research, development, production, sales, finance, personnel – to a decentralised structure of product divisions – power cables, telecommunication cables, building wires, magnet wires and cable installation, with only finance, research and key elements of personnel policy remaining centralised. The way we went about this was of special interest to Peter. He was a strong believer in the principle of delegating authority to the lowest level at which it could be efficiently exercised without, in so doing, losing control of crucial policies. He found it encouraging that this was exactly what we were trying to achieve in an industrial setting. Of particular interest to him was the approach we had taken to win and maintain the support of the employees. We had arranged for parallel studies to be carried out by the top management team, by a junior board of up-and-coming executives, (whose proposed solutions proved to be almost identical), and by the Group Organisation and Methods Department based in Milan who, initially, were very sceptical but were converted by their own analysis to a proposal which differed in no significant respect from our own. This process was accompanied by a series of meetings with representatives of all the major groups of employees – middle managers, staff employees and shop stewards from the three factories - to explain the rationale of the new structure and how we intended to implement it.

It was clearly understood that the chairman had no executive authority, but Peter had no wish to be merely a figurehead remote from and unknown to the employees. We already had a well-established system of consultation with employees, and we arranged for him to have frequent opportunities to meet senior and middle managers by chairing our regular discussions of operating results and management plans. He loved the job of making annual presentations of long-service awards to employees, when we saw to it that he also met union representatives, usually placing the most combative shop steward at his table – although he always had the longest serving employee on his right. The twenty-year period of his chairmanship embraced a long spell of rapid development of both the tyre and cable companies, with inaugurations of several major factory projects – a new tyre plant in Carlisle; a telecommunications cable factory at Bishopstoke; the acquisition of a small competitor, Aberdare Cables Limited, and its subsequent conversion from a worn-out power cable factory to a computer integrated factory of advanced design making building wires (our simplest product); and a submarine power cable factory at Southampton with facilities for loading 50 km lengths of high voltage cable directly into cable-laying ships. Peter was always able to ensure that a leading national figure was available to cut the ribbon – a Postmaster-General, a President of the Board of Trade, the Prince of Wales – and his own short speeches on these occasions were cameos of well-judged emphasis and perceptive insight laced with good humour.

When, in 1971, I moved into Group management, I encouraged other chief executives of the subsidiaries for which I was responsible to develop similar relationships with their chairmen. I am firmly convinced that those who succeeded in doing so were the most successful in managing their companies. Peter had created a role model for non-executive chairmanship, demonstrating how a person of high calibre, socially, politically, culturally and intellectually, in harmony with the Group ethos, and with just the right touch in advising (and even warning) his executive colleagues - without interfering - could add great weight to the running of the subsidiaries. It was a model that we implemented throughout the Group.

Although Peter was not directly concerned with the Pirelli companies outside the UK, I often found it helpful during the years when I had responsibility for them to consult him when I faced a problem in the international business and felt the need of wise counsel, rather than just another opinion (never in short supply). One such occasion was in 1975, when we wanted to set up a new cablemaking venture in Australia. We had been given permission to do so by the Federal Government the previous year but, following intensive lobbying by competitors, this had been withdrawn. Peter was very familiar with the Australian political scene and also had business contacts there through his similar role in Pye of Cambridge, a subsidiary of the Philips Group. In fact, three years earlier, when we had first considered an Australian venture, he had helped me to find a first-class Sydney lawyer, John Holman, of Holman, Webb & Partners, to look after our interests. He now happened to mention that he was about to visit Australia on Philips Group business, and I thought that he might be able to give me some ideas on how best to try to persuade the Government to restore our licence. He suggested that I prepare a memorandum for him explaining the history of the negotiations and, when he had read this and discussed it with me, he felt that we had a very strong case. However, he thought that the prospects of persuading any Government to change its mind for a second time were rather slim and that, in the case of a Labor Government in Australia, the Prime Minister himself was probably the only person who would risk taking such a politically sensitive decision. He was going to meet Prime Minister Gough Whitlam during his trip, and he said that he would keep his ears and eyes open in case an opportunity should present itself to raise the issue. He told me on his return that I had come very close to spoiling a very pleasant dinner in Canberra for him, but that he had managed to broach the topic and get the Prime Minister to agree that we should be invited to present our case to his Minister for Industry. The rest was up to John Holman and me, but Peter had opened a door that we would probably have been quite unable to open on our own.

Peter's ability to give sound advice and assistance in such cases was nourished by the deep mutual respect and friendship which had developed between himself and Leopoldo Pirelli. This had enabled him to gain a thorough understanding of the Group's business and its managerial style and approach, so that he could view the problems of the UK subsidiaries of which he was Chairman in the context of overall Group policy, and frame his advice appropriately. For example, in the late 1970s, an opportunity arose to bid for a contract to manufacture and install for the Central Electricity Generating Board two submarine power cables across the English Channel to link the British and French high voltage grid systems, in parallel with a similar pair of cables which would be the responsibility of Electricité de France. At the time, the Group's Italian subsidiary had sufficient capacity in its well-established submarine cable factory near Naples to undertake the contract, whereas Pirelli General would have to build a new factory. The logical business solution would have been for the Italian company to bid for the contract with marketing support from its British colleagues. However, the management of the UK company was convinced that the CEGB wanted to give its share of the business to a British firm, just as Electricité de France was determined to give its contract to a French cablemaker. We asked Peter for his opinion and, a few days later, he told us that his judgement was that the relationship between the British and French authorities at the time was such that only a UK based company had any real hope of securing a contract from the CEGB. The European Common Market was not yet functioning as it should. We decided that, in the circumstances, the best way to exploit the Group's resources and provide a technically sound solution for the customer would be for Pirelli General to bid, including in its tender the full cost of building a new factory using the technology and relying on the experience of the Italian company. Pirelli General's bid was successful. A new factory was built at Southampton and opened by Cecil Parkinson, the Secretary of State for Trade and Industry, in July 1983. The cables were successfully installed and are still operating in 2007.

In another case, the situation was not so clear-cut. Pirelli General had decided to close an old factory at Southampton, difficult to modernise economically, and whose location close to the city centre had become an obstacle to the city's development. Manufacture of its products would have to be moved to other sites or, if this was not economically feasible, abandoned altogether. The most important product line was building wire, technically very simple and serving a highly competitive market. One solution was to stop manufacture in Britain and import supplies from subsidiaries in Brazil, Peru or Mexico, with lower labour costs (but with high costs of transport to the British market): another was to use the rapidly developing technology of computer control of manufacture and distribution to sharply reduce the labour content and facilitate a much better service to customers. We chose the more challenging solution, not just to preserve - perhaps only for a few years - the British company's competitiveness, but also to develop a model which could be adopted later elsewhere in the Cable Sector of the Group, even in countries where labour cost was currently low, but rising as their own countries' economies developed. The question was then, where the new computer controlled factory should be located, one possible site being an old and obsolete factory at Aberdare, in a deprived area of Wales, which would otherwise have to close. Other possibilities were sites in other development areas to which the Government was endeavouring to direct new investment. Recalling Peter's experience in such matters at the Board of Trade, we sought his opinion. This was very clear: that we should by all means look carefully at development areas, including Aberdare, but not allow ourselves to be persuaded to accept a solution which was economically unsound. Our final decision was to use the Aberdare site, replacing the old building and collaborating with the local technical college to devise training programmes for the new breed of computer-literate employees we would need to operate the new factory.

During the period of our business relationship, Peter and I rarely discussed politics unless some political issue was particularly relevant to our business but, occasionally, he would ask whether I had any strong opinion on some topic that he was due to debate. He liked to prepare for debates by canvassing the views of any of his friends and acquaintances he believed to have thought deeply about the matters under consideration, and he was very good at sensing what their interests were and making a mental note for future reference. He knew, for instance, that I had strong views on education, and asked me once to jot down for him the reasons why I was so opposed to the narrow academic focus and early specialisation inherent in the A-level system that Margaret Thatcher, then Education Secretary, was espousing. (I had two principal concerns: first that the more academically inclined students entering university should have a broad intellectual foundation not confined to the specialist subjects they were about to study in depth – historians should know something of science and engineers of literature, and all would benefit from some appreciation of other cultures acquired from foreign language studies; secondly, that an exaggerated emphasis on the 'Gold Standard' of A-levels tended to devalue and, worse, divert resources from vocational education).

Knowing of my wartime experience in the Far East, he was interested to know what I thought of pursuing aged war criminals to the end of their lives. (I was in favour of leniency).

He once asked me what I thought about how politicians should approach the privatisation of the nationalised industries. (I felt that the Coal Board could be privatised as separate pits or groups of pits competing with each other; the steel and telecommunications industries broken down into competing units; that the railways should revert to regional companies owning their own tracks, competing with road and air transport. In the case of gas and electricity supply, I considered generation and distribution could be provided by competing units and the transmission systems operated as 'common carriers', but would have to be regulated to ensure that adequate capacity was always assured. There was widespread concern at the time about the control of nuclear generation facilities, and my recommendation was to split the small number of nuclear plants between the projected generating companies so that they would each be able to make their own strictly commercial - and competitive - judgements on the economic and technical viability of nuclear compared with fossil fuelled plants, finding their own solutions to the difficult problems of waste disposal and eventual decommissioning costs.)

In 1983, the two UK operating companies of the Pirelli Group were brought, for the first time since their formation in 1910 and 1914, within the embrace of a single holding company, Pirelli UK plc, of which Peter became Chairman, retaining the chairmanships of the operating companies until 1987. He remained Chairman of Pirelli UK until 1989 when, in recognition of the exceptional contribution he had made, he was appointed President for life of all three companies. This was a purely honorary appointment, but it entitled him to attend board meetings if he wished, and he continued to do so for several years, until failing health forced him to give up. Just as he had understood perfectly the role of a non-executive chairman, he was a model 'retired chairman' and, whilst always ready to give advice or an opinion if asked, never intervened in any way that could embarrass his successors, to whom he gave his complete loyalty and support.

Pye of Cambridge

Early in 1967, the Philips Group of Eindhoven acquired Pye of Cambridge, an electronics company controlled for forty years by C O Stanley, a British entrepreneur whose remarkable ability to divine the impact which technological developments would have on the demand for electronic products had served his company very well for four decades but was unfortunately offset by an equally remarkable financial incompetence. This combination had led to a series of hazardous acquisitions and risky investments which eventually resulted in economic collapse of the business. The Philips Group had given Pye a great deal of technical and business support for many years and, anxious not to allow its protégé to fall into the hands of a competitor, had little choice but to acquire the company when it could no longer sustain its independence. A spoiling bid by Thorn Industries had to be beaten off, raising the cost of the transaction to Philips. Although Philips had a very good understanding of what it was buying, there is no doubt that it acquired not only a considerable financial mess, but also a major problem which had built up in recent years of bitter discord among senior executives, the effects of which remained even after both C O Stanley and his son John had been forced out of office by a boardroom rebellion in the final stages of the company's financial collapse. Thorneycroft was called in to chair the Board of Pye Holdings, a UK financial company formed by Philips to control the operating company, which was to retain the name Pye of Cambridge, and would continue for the time being to be chaired by F B Duncan, one of the senior Pye directors deeply involved in the collapse. In addition to his chairmanship of the holding company, Thorneycroft was initially appointed as deputy to Duncan in the operating company, and would succeed him as Chairman in due course.

As in the case of his role in Pirelli, Thorneycroft was the non-executive chairman of a national subsidiary of a multi-national group. However Pye of Cambridge had, until the takeover, been an independent UK quoted company, itself a multi-national with a network of overseas subsidiaries mainly in territories of the British Commonwealth. Furthermore, it was the practice of Philips to allow its national subsidiaries a substantial degree of autonomy, and the Group was content to accept at first that Pye should retain a substantial minority of other shareholders and its quotation on the London Stock Exchange. Indeed, Philips had agreed to a demand by Anthony Wedgwood Benn, the Minister for Industry, that Pye be run as an independent public company.

In this context, Philips accepted a recommendation from the Pye Board that an established Pye executive, Peter Threlfall, should be appointed as Managing Director of Pye of Cambridge, reporting to Thorneycroft and the Board of Pye

Holdings, but also with a strong link to the Philips Group management in Holland. Threlfall had been the chief executive of Pye in Australia, appointed to that post by the *ancien régime* of the Stanley family. He did not take easily to the new set up, bridling at the supervisory systems which Philips used to monitor the activities of their subsidiaries and at the role of Pye Holdings, interposed between the operating company for which he was responsible and the ultimate controlling shareholder, Philips. Personality clashes developed and it was not long before Threlfall was asked to leave. This time his successor was chosen by Philips from one of their wholly owned subsidiaries, Philips Electrical Limited, which ran the electrical consumer goods business of Philips in the UK. This was Jack Stewart-Clark, a Briton, who had been recruited by Philips five years earlier when he had been in charge of the Dutch subsidiary of the well known British textile firm, J & P Coats. He and Thorneycroft, in Stewart-Clark's own words (in a letter to the author), *"hit it off well from the start. I liked him enormously for his ability to grasp a complex situation quickly and unfailingly to assist me with good advice and to give me support when I needed it. He had an incredible ability to grasp the essentials of a complicated problem and to recommend a wise course of action and when necessary to bat on one's behalf. He had a rich sense of humour which, with his intelligence and wisdom, often helped him to defuse a problem. He was also a very good listener and able to assimilate detail with rapidity. These qualities made him an excellent non-executive chairman"*.

Because of the international reach of Pye of Cambridge, Thorneycroft, although clearly non-executive, found himself to a much greater extent than in the Pirelli Group using his political and diplomatic contacts to further the interests of Pye and its shareholders, not only in Britain, but in all the countries where Pye had operations. To do this effectively, Thorneycroft needed to make himself thoroughly familiar with the complex activities of the parent Philips Group, as well as of Pye of Cambridge itself.

He began in April 1968 with a comprehensive tour of the Philips Research Laboratories at Eindhoven, where he was shown some of their work on integrated circuits and ceramics and applications of other research in electron microscopy and analytical equipment and was introduced to applications of closed-circuit television. He was taken to see the principal factories in Nijmegen and the Telecommunications factory at Hilversum and, perhaps the most important aspect of the visit, met the Group Chairman Frits Philips, the Group Chief Executive P H le Clercq and some of their senior colleagues to learn from them what the Group's intentions were for the development of Pye of Cambridge following the acquisition, and what sort of contribution they were looking for from him.

This visit prepared Thorneycroft very well for a lengthy familiarisation tour of most of the Pye subsidiaries overseas in the Autumn of 1968. The tour was to start in Hong Kong and proceed to New Zealand, Australia and South Africa , and Thorneycroft decided to take the opportunity to introduce his wife and daughter to the world in which he moved, for much of the way retracing the steps of his journey to the East ten years before. On the way to Hong Kong they were able to visit Beirut, Baalbek, Angkor Wat and Bangkok. They had friends everywhere, especially in the embassies, to greet them, introduce them to local dignitaries and show them the sights.

The serious business of the tour started with a visit to the factory in Kowloon of a small company, Coronet Industries Limited, which had been manufacturing radio sets for Pye for several years. Thorneycroft also took the opportunity to look at some of the social consequences of the explosion in the population of Hong Kong during the past few years, visiting one of the Colony's resettlement estates in which immigrants from mainland China were housed while they looked for work and permanent accommodation. In a meeting with the Rotary Club of Hong Kong, Thorneycroft used a technique he had employed long ago when he was President of the Board of Trade: instead of making a formal speech, he asked his audience to fire questions at him. He told them that *"this will assure you that I am speaking on a subject in which at least one person present will have a faint interest."* It is a technique that can only safely be used by a person able to make a pretty good judgement in advance as to the questions he is likely to be asked, and confident of his ability to respond to them convincingly and fluently. Although he reminded them that he was not a politician any more, but *"a normal, respectable businessman"* the first question was on the Labour Government's decision to pull out of the Far East, diplomatically fielded with *"a hunch that the most likely thing to happen is that there will be a rundown (of forces) and that the timing will be fixed in consultation with men like Mr Lee Quan Yeu, in Singapore, or with Mr Tungku Abdul Rahman, in Kuala Lumpur, whose interests will, I think, be very well matched in this."* Asked about Hong Kong's role in the electronics industry, he foresaw that it would develop towards more sophisticated products, and so it would be in the interests of Hong Kong to concentrate on improving the quality of what is made, as well as the amount sold, so as to be better prepared to compete with others, especially the Japanese, who were interested in selling to the same markets. On the prospects for sterling, he had no doubts that the present parity could be sustained following the recent devaluation, but drew attention to the longer-term question of whether sterling could continue to be an international currency given its relatively narrow trading base. Would Britain join the Common Market? Yes. It was a question of time, but it would not happen while 'our dear friend, Charles de Gaulle' was there. One questioner asked why Britain was not contributing more to Hong Kong's technical education and industrial investment rather than helping Singapore to compete with Hong Kong, drawing the response that there was no sign of a shortage of capital in the colony, and the fact that Hong Kong was managing so well should be a reason for pride, not despair. The UK was at present hard pressed to invest abroad. This was a fact of life, and there was no point in saying this was a pity, and ought to be reversed. It could not be reversed. So Hong Kong should look for capital wherever it could, just as Britain would. He believed in a free flow of investment for the development of a prosperous world. Was Britain in an economic mess? No. It had an unpopular Government. All Governments were unpopular –a very good feature of democracies - and we change them from time to time. But to be fair to the present Government, it had been making considerable efforts to get its balance of payments into better shape and improve exports. Would the Conservatives win the next election? This was an academic point: there wasn't going to be an election within two years. Labour had been returned with broad-based support, genuine support by people who wanted an alternative Government, and were able to get what they wanted because the democratic system of the UK was based upon the possibility of having an alternative Government. This inevitably prompted the response that Hong Kong did not have democracy – it's just a branch of London dictating to Hong Kong - so what did Thorneycroft have to say about that? (He had to waffle a bit here). In a strange way, Hong Kong had managed, under this curious, almost archaic system, to generate success. We know you could change it, but if you've got a method which over the years had given a certain stability in a situation which many people would regard as inherently unstable, he would be slow to change it, or change it too much, or in too much of a hurry. So could Thorneycroft say anything to dispel the illusion that a Conservative Government would act in its own interests, rather than those of Hong Kong? Not too much – he did not like dispelling illusions. He rather thought that people should be willing to help themselves and make contributions to (solving) their own problems. He did not have to argue this very hard in Hong Kong of all places. He did <u>not</u> think that the attitude of any British Government, under any political party, would be a narrow and self-seeking one. If Britain entered the Common Market, what would happen to Hong Kong's money held in the British reserves? It would not be affected, Thorneycroft assured them. "*Sterling remains a world currency. London remains a world banking centre and the reserves remain in London. You must understand that the UK system of banking is like a shopkeeper who is banking out of the till. They are trading and banking on the same account and it works, it works frightfully well. It's a question of confidence. It does mean that any slight disturbance on the trading account would have a remarkable effect on the banking account as well. So there have been some people who say it would be better if it was based on something wider. In the last resort, these things are based not really on gold; they are based upon the productive capacity of the area which is seeking to generate this confidence. Some people think it wouldn't be a bad thing, in the longer term, if we could get a European currency, or a system in which balances were held on a European account. But that is quite a long way ahead. For the moment, Hong Kong needn't, I hope, rush to withdraw the Hong Kong sterling balances this afternoon. I can assure you, with reasonable safety, that you can hold on to them for a bit longer."* The *South China Morning Post* the following day quoted one of its journalists who had been present at the Rotary Club, *"You have to like him. He doesn't skitter away from the curly questions. Although a dyed-in-the-wool Tory, he does give credit where due to them 'damned Socialists' for the way they are trying to keep Britain out of the red. And when he praises Hong Kong, he's not just being mellifluous."*

Towards the end of their stay in Hong Kong, the Thorneycrofts lunched with the Acting Governor and then, on 4th November, left for New Zealand, where their Pye hosts had the good sense to leave them free of engagements for one evening. During the next few days, Thorneycroft gave a Press Conference in Auckland and then visited the Ultimate Ekco factory before a dinner with Pye Directors. The next day was taken up with a tour of Akrad factories at Waihi, followed by a peaceful break at Rotorua, fishing and walking. On Sunday, 10th November, they flew to Wellington for supper at Government House and the following day, after a discussion with the High Commissioner and Pye executives, another Press Conference, a dinner with Wellington dignitaries and lunch with the Prime Minister, moved on to Sydney.

On arrival in Sydney, Thorneycroft was greeted by another Press Conference before calling on the Prime Minister, Mr John Gorton, and later dining with the Governor of New South Wales, Sir Roden Cutler, VC, whose other guests that evening included Lt-Gen Sir Frank Berryman, Maj-Gen Sir James Harrison, Rear Admiral D C Wells, The Hon Mr Justice Jenkyn and The Hon Sir Howard Beale (who was the Chairman of Pye in Australia). Sir Howard had arranged a board meeting the following day to give Thorneycroft the opportunity to meet the local directors and executives and get a feel for the problems they were facing. Later he visited some of the subsidiaries in the Sydney area, Vincent Bros at Ryde, Gemco in North Sydney, Pye Business Machines at Crows Nest, Franks & Levitt at St Peters, and TMC at Erskineville. A private meeting with the Governor-General and Lady Casey took place over lunch at Admiralty House, and afterwards he even managed to squeeze in, (at the author's request) a brief meeting with Ken Ryder of Pirelli Construction Company, who was managing a number of major high voltage cable contracts in Australia. There was a further factory visit, to Pye Industries at Wollongong, and a lunch with the Australian-British Trade Association before leaving Sydney for Canberra Here, he was met by the UK High Commissioner to Australia, Sir Charles Johnston, who accompanied him to a meeting and lunch with the Prime Minister. At dinner that evening he met The Hon David Fairbairn, Minister of National Development and the Italian

Ambassador, Sig Majoli. The next stop after Canberra was Melbourne, where Thorneycroft visited the Managing Director of Pye Pty Limited, Roger Threlfall at his headquarters, and later dined at Government House with Sir Henry Bolte, who had been Premier of Victoria since 1955, longer than any previous holder of the office. Then on to Adelaide to visit Dunlite (another Pye subsidiary) and a Philips valves factory at Hendon, and to meet the Press, whose main interventions concerned Britain's intention to withdraw its Forces from the Far East by 1971, the recent speech by Enoch Powell on immigration to the UK and the reports that the Labour Government wanted to limit membership of the House of Lords to life peers only. On defence, Thorneycroft believed that it would be sensible for the governments of Britain, Malaysia, Singapore, Australia, New Zealand and America to agree on a lasting arrangement for a joint garrison in Singapore. On immigration, he recommended critics to read the full text of Enoch Powell's speech, which they would find a carefully reasoned statement of the problem and not the racist diatribe that the media had depicted. He thought if the House of Lords were to be reformed, restriction to life peers was as good a way as any of doing it. The final stage of this marathon journey took the Thorneycrofts to Perth, where they arrived on 3rd December 1968. Very hot - 98°F – Carla Thorneycroft noted in her press-cuttings' album. There was another press conference, picking up most of the points raised in earlier meetings with the Press, adding a comment that the new world monetary institution being discussed would be no substitute for countries living sensibly and frugally, and a dinner with the Governor of Western Australia, Sir Douglas Kendrew, preceded by a visit to the Pye facilities in Perth, before the Thorneycrofts departed on 6th December for Johannesburg.

Once again, there was a Press Conference shortly after arrival, this time, not unexpectedly, more interested in the British embargo on the supply of arms to South Africa. Thorneycroft believed that South Africa had an important role to play in Western defence, especially after Suez and the recent increase in Soviet naval activity in international waters. He also questioned whether the aura of secrecy about developments in armaments could really be justified, saying that when he was Minister of Defence he had come across cases where British exports of arms to friendly countries was hampered through withholding information from potential buyers that had already leaked to the Russians. Asked about a recent suggestion by Enoch Powell that Britain should recognise rebellious Southern Rhodesia as an independent state, Thorneycroft thought that it might be a good way out: after all there was the precedent of acceptance of the successful American Revolution. The rest of the stay in South Africa followed a pattern similar to the tour in Australia – visits to Pye and Philips facilities and talks with local dignitaries and business organisations (but not, this time, with Government leaders or officials). Once again, Thorneycroft managed to fit in short meetings with representatives of Pirelli General, R J Smith, the Export Sales Manager on a visit from Britain, and the resident representative, Mr Allen.

Chairmen and senior executives of multinational companies will certainly recognise this description of a tour of facilities. The travelling schedule is punishing. One tends to arrive with a body clock hours adrift from the local time, having to cope with an important engagement immediately after a quick wash and brush-up. One meets dozens of people, many of them important local dignitaries and others who expect the visitor to recognise them straight away and remember how and when they had met before. In factory visits and business discussions, one is expected to have all the facts – financial ratios, productivity indices, investment programmes – at one's fingertips. In spite of a congenitally painful back which made long air and car journeys very unpleasant, Thorneycroft managed to pass these tests with remarkable aplomb, and at the same time seize every opportunity to look up political personalities with whom he wished to nurture old contacts or make new ones.

Thorneycroft made at least one more lengthy tour of Pye facilities in March and April 1975, following a similar pattern. On this occasion he was accompanied by his wife, Carla, and by Stewart-Clark, and visited Australia and South Africa, but arranged for their New Zealand colleagues to join them in Sydney.

On the home front, the Pye of Cambridge board of directors met monthly under Thorneycroft's chairmanship. By modern standards of governance it was a well-composed board. There were three other non-executives: Jan Bosch, the Financial Director of Philips UK; John Baring, a Senior Partner of Baring Brothers, the bankers; and Sir Arthur Knight, the Chairman of Courtaulds; and two executives, Stewart-Clark and F E Jones, a senior Pye director of long standing. Stewart-Clark recalls that board meetings never took more than two hours and that, at the end of a meeting, Thorneycroft would leave his papers on the table. *"He was"*, says Stewart-Clark, *"a master of avoiding any clutter and, as far as I could see, held all the knowledge he needed in his head"*.

Stewart-Clark mentions another strong feature of Thorneycroft's personality, *"complete compartmentalisation. Whilst he was on Pye business, he was entirely focussed on Pye, whilst dealing with political affairs the total politician, whilst on holiday, dedicated to his painting and social conversation. On one occasion we both found ourselves with our wives on Corfu. Full of good humour and wit, it was almost an intrusion to mention the business with which we were so closely involved. This was Peter's way of completely relaxing and doing what so many of us do so badly – that is, forgetting about the burdens of public and business life"*.

In 1979, an opportunity arose for Stewart-Clark to present himself as a candidate for the European Parliament, a task for which he felt well qualified, having a Dutch wife, a good knowledge of several European languages and wide experience of international business. He sought Thorneycroft's advice, and recalls that *"I thought he might say, 'Jack, stick to your last'. But he said, without much hesitation, 'I would give the European Parliament a go, if I were you. After all, I was a successful politician and went into business and why shouldn't you be the same but the other way round?' And then he continued, 'I'll see you right by Philips but don't count on me to help you with the Conservative Party, as that would be the kiss of death.'"* The Philips Group were, in fact very supportive, and Stewart-Clark went on to be an MEP for twenty years, five of them as a Vice-President of the European Parliament.

Stewart-Clark recounts that his last few months with Thorneycroft in 1979 were spent arranging for Philips to buy out the remaining minority shareholders in Pye of Cambridge, to give them full control, and that they selected 'a brilliant young man' named George Magan of the merchant bankers, Morgan Grenfell, to negotiate the terms. The transaction was completed after Stewart-Clark left for the European Parliament, and Thorneycroft ceased to be Chairman on completion of the deal, although he was retained by Philips as a consultant for several more years.

Trusthouse Forte

The background to Thorneycroft's recruitment to the Board of Trust Houses Forte is described in frank and engaging style by Charles Forte in his autobiography published by Sidgwick & Jackson in 1986. The company had been formed in 1970 by the merger of Trust Houses Group Ltd and Forte Holdings Limited, chaired respectively by two strong characters, Lord Crowther and Sir Charles Forte. Crowther was a Cambridge economics graduate whose early career had been in financial journalism with the *Economist*, which he had rescued from decline. He then built up a portfolio of directorships of important companies, one of them Trust Houses, of which he became Chairman. Charles Forte was a formidable entrepreneur, a self-made man who had built up his business from a single milk bar in Regent Street to an international restaurant and hotels group ranging from coffee shops all over Britain to the Plaza Athénée in Paris.

Unusually for a merger between firms in the same industry, there was hardly any overlap in their operations. No merchant banking advisers were appointed by either side, but both were agreed that the merger should be one of equals, on terms which they arranged to be drafted for them by a mutually trusted businessman and accountant Sir Charles Hardie, at the time Chairman of Metropolitan Estates (who had also, some years earlier, been a director of Forte). It was agreed by both sides that Crowther should be the first chairman with Charles Forte as his deputy, it being understood that Crowther would resign after one year and be succeeded by Charles Forte. Each partner would have the right to nominate nine members of the new board of directors, although initially Forte had only eight nominations to put forward. The initial team of executives was to be headed by people from Trust Houses', the Chief Executive, Michael Pickard, the Financial Director, George Hendrie and the Company Secretary, Donald Durban, all being appointed to the corresponding posts in the new company, Trust House Forte. At the operating level, Forte people predominated, two of them having the title of Deputy Managing Director. This allocation of senior positions doubtless reflected the fact that all of the Forte directors had direct operating experience in their industry, whereas the Trust Houses' directors came mainly from financial or accounting backgrounds but, though the numbers may have been almost equal, influence on the future conduct of business was not.

Although Crowther, in tentative discussions with Charles Forte several months before the merger negotiations began in earnest, had expressed reservations about the possibility of two such different companies being able to work together he seems, during the very short period – only three weeks – of active negotiations, to have overcome his early doubts, and concluded that the two groups were complementary to each other and would fit well together.

With the merger completed, the differences began to emerge. These had nothing to do with the business structures. They arose, as so often happens when large groups merge, from their contrasting management styles. In his autobiography, Charles Forte sets out succinctly what those contrasts were. He believed that the way to manage a large group was to rely on *"human contacts, discussion, and personal supervision, with paper work reduced to a minimum"*, and he had run his Forte Group that way. He described Trust Houses as *"run on bureaucratic lines, accompanied by mountains of paper and bulging files"*. These, indeed, are descriptions of management styles which are utterly incompatible. This does not imply that the merger, which had a sound industrial logic, should not have been attempted, but it does mean that its implementation had been inadequately thought through. A large, complex organisation cannot easily support more than one management style. Crowther's early misgivings were soundly based and should have led him to insist on a choice of the future management style being made before the merger, and an implementation plan prepared to create the decision making structure appropriate to the chosen style. The arrangement of giving the two camps equal numbers of directors for reasons of 'fairness' could only have worked if all the directors had then adopted a rigorously objective approach to every important post-merger decision, especially on the style of management to be adopted, with no regard to their previous loyalties, a saintly approach that normal human beings find virtually impossible to achieve. In its absence, the 'balanced' board became a board split between two opposing camps.

It is not, therefore, surprising that difficulties soon arose in the conduct of the merged group. An early, rather petty, example concerned the allocation of an office to Charles Forte. Highly centralised organisations tend to provide their leaders with large and imposing head offices, and Trust Houses was no exception. To run his decentralised group, Charles Forte made do with a penthouse on top of the Café Royal which had no room to accommodate an influx of senior staff from Trust Houses. It was therefore decided that the Trust Houses' offices in High Holborn would become the headquarters of the merged group, and that Charles Forte, would have his Vice-chairman's office there. For reasons which can only be described as either inexcusably insensitive or gratuitously offensive, he was initially offered a small office which could not even accommodate his secretary. Of much more importance were instances of major transactions being approved by the top management team of former Trust Houses' directors either ignoring the views of their Forte colleagues or not consulting them at all. Forte mentions a decision not to complete an acquisition the Forte Group had intended to make of the Sonesta Tower Hotel in London, and the purchase of the Apollo Hotel in

Amsterdam at a price which Charles Forte considered much too high. Of even greater importance was a failure to implement an agreement that, to balance the appointment of Trust Houses' people as Chairman, Chief Executive, Financial Director and Company Secretary, Charles Forte should become the Chairman of the Finance Committee. The final straw for Charles Forte came when Crowther showed no sign of handing over the Chairmanship at the end of the first year, arguing that the agreement for him to do so was not legally enforceable.

It must be remembered that this description of the merged group's first year is one-sided, and may therefore be biased, but there seems to be no reason to doubt the accuracy of Charles Forte's account. It may be argued that Forte and his colleagues had been somewhat naïve in assuming that they would have an equal say in major decisions in a management structure so heavily weighted in favour of Trust Houses' directors, but there is little doubt that they were being treated in a most cavalier fashion. The disagreements were descending into damaging personal animosity, and Charles Forte decided that he had to take action to secure respect for the original intentions.

The approach he took was, first, to exercise his right to appoint an additional director, to bring the number of his appointees to nine. He already had on his team plenty of people with experience of the industry. What he needed now was someone of great integrity capable of drawing out of his colleagues the objective, non-partisan approach to running the business that the initial, 'fairly balanced' board of directors had failed to achieve. The person he turned to was Peter Thorneycroft, a friend of many years standing to whom he had been introduced by Thorneycroft's Italian wife, Carla, when she was fashion editor of *Vogue* just after the war. This would secure parity of the Trust Houses and Forte nominees (although voting parity would depend upon the rather unlikely assumption that a person of Thorneycroft's calibre and values would allow himself to support a Forte stance with which he did not agree). The appointment was clearly not enough on its own to break a deadlock if the Trust Houses' camp chose to continue to take a partisan approach. Charles Forte, however, had no right to nominate more than his quota of nine directors, and the only way in which he could secure the appointment of another director was to persuade a majority of the board to approve it. He now approached Sir Charles Hardie, the man who had made the initial valuation of the two businesses, initially only seeking his advice on what he might do, but pleasantly surprised when Hardie offered himself as a candidate arguing that, although he might be regarded as too close to Forte, Crowther would find it very difficult to reject him. This proved to be the case, and Hardie joined the board, adding a second independent voice to its deliberations.

Charles Forte now had sufficient confidence in his ability to influence decisions for him to seize an unexpected opportunity to make a crucial change in the executive ranks. In July 1971, the Chief Executive, Michael Pickard, was strongly criticised in a Board of Trade report on a company with which he had become involved in a previous appointment. The report was given wide publicity, inflicting serious damage on Pickard's reputation. Pickard was later able to refute the allegations but, at the time, the mud stuck and, aided by the absence of one of the Trust Houses directors from a board meeting, Forte was able to persuade eight of the sixteen directors present, including Thorneycroft, to vote for Pickard's dismissal, although his other recent nominee, Hardie, voted against the motion. Pickard himself was not allowed to vote on an issue touching upon his own position.

It was a narrow and fortuitous victory for Charles Forte, secured in a somewhat opportunistic manner of which Forte himself was a little bit ashamed, but it was not a Pyrrhic one. It gave the new Group a chance to achieve its full potential which would certainly have eluded it had the running conflict not been resolved. In the absence of an obvious successor the Board decided that, until one could be found, Crowther and Forte would act as joint Managing Directors. A little later, the Board drew up a job description for a new MD and set up a committee to conduct the search for candidates. Although deprived of his Chief Executive role, Pickard was still a board member, clearly an uncomfortable position to be in. He soon decided that he should resign, posing two conditions: that he should receive appropriate compensation, and that his successor should be acceptable to the remaining Trust Houses' nominees. His compensation condition presented no problem, but the second condition was kicked into touch, and remained unresolved when Pickard left in January 1972.

Before then, in August 1971, the Forte supporters on the Board had proposed the appointment of Charles Forte as Group Managing Director. This was immediately rejected by the Trust Houses side, as it would have meant that the three top executive posts would have been occupied by Forte people. This issue was eventually resolved by the appointment of Michael Matthews, ex-Trust Houses, in place of one of the Forte Deputy Managing Directors, Eric Hartwell, who relinquished his post.

The Trust Houses' people were determined not to give up easily. They fought back by persuading a competitor, Allied Breweries Limited, to launch a takeover bid, which was submitted on 18th October 1971. Charles Forte was not short of friends to weigh in with their support in crises such as this and, with the full support of Hardie, Thorneycroft and his old Forte colleagues, managed to get Lord Robens, who was about to retire from the chair of the National Coal Board, appointed to the Board as a third non-executive of recognised stature, Crowther failing in an attempt to persuade Robens to withdraw his nomination. In a bizarre sequence of events, Allied withdrew their bid only ten days after launching it, but returned with a new one on 23rd November, the ground having been prepared by a public denunciation by Crowther of his Forte colleagues in an article in the *Sunday Times* two days earlier. Crowther's position was clearly unsustainable after this extraordinary attack by a public company chairman on his own company. At an emergency meeting of the Board, Hartwell proposed his removal from all his offices in the Group. After a conciliatory proposal by Hardie that he should resign was rejected by Crowther, the motion was carried, and Thorneycroft was elected as Chairman in his place, on the proposal of Charles Forte. The Board could now proceed with their consideration of the Allied bid which, after a battle graphically described, stroke by stroke, by Charles Forte in his autobiography, was defeated.

This is not the place to rehearse how Charles Forte turned the opportunity he had created into achievement. His own account is complete – and contains so much practical advice that many budding entrepreneurs would find it much more rewarding as a manual than the glib precepts of most 'gurus'.

35. The Thorneycrofts with the Fortes at the Café Royal 1984
(The occasion was an exhibition of Peter Thorneycroft's paintings.) (*photo: from the family albums*)

Thorneycroft would certainly not have claimed that his role in these exciting events had been decisive. Charles Forte was always the leading actor. In his own words, *"After all that had happened, I thought it would be invidious for me to step immediately into Crowther's shoes. It would have smacked too much of triumph. I knew Peter Thorneycroft would make a first-rate chairman, and I wanted to be completely free to reorganise the company and to get on with running the business."* Thorneycroft did play a very important part in helping Charles Forte to sort out the imbroglio of conflicting ideas and tortured personalities which had impeded the business in its early years. He went on, in fact, to "make a first-rate chairman" who not only understood perfectly the relationship that Charles Forte wished them to have, but was wholly convinced that this was exactly the relationship which any first-rate non-executive chairman should seek to build with a chief executive who was also the controlling shareholder and in whose competence to run the business he had complete confidence. The two men worked harmoniously and effectively together in these roles for another ten years. George Proctor, who was Legal and Commercial Director of the Group for many years, says that *"Lord Thorneycroft was liked and respected by all members of the THF Board. He had a way of always quietly bringing matters into perspective, and contributed substantially to what became the long running and frustrating Savoy saga"*, the fascinating story of which is colourfully told in Forte's book. In 1981, when Charles Forte was ready to hand over his chief executive role to his son Rocco and take on the chairmanship himself, he asked Thorneycroft to become honorary President of the Group, a position he held until 1992, when Rocco Forte became Chairman as well as Chief Executive, and Charles Forte succeeded Thorneycroft as President.

SITPRO

SITPRO is one of those dreadful acronyms for agencies with impractically long titles, in this case "Simplification of International Trade Procedures". Thorneycroft had been unfavourably impressed during his time at the Board of Trade in the 1950s by the volume of paperwork impeding the efficiency of the nation's export efforts, which he at first assumed to be a relic of wartime controls, but found when he delved into the matter that some of the practices had been around since the Nineteenth Century. SITPRO was set up by the Government in 1970, following publication of a report by a committee of the National Economic Development Council, formed in 1968 with the same name. SITPRO was charged with the task of studying international trade documents and procedures and recommending changes to assist the flow of trade. Thorneycroft, who had chaired the NEDC committee since 1968, was appointed Chairman of SITPRO, serving until 1975.

Thorneycroft was a very good choice as its first Chairman. He already knew a good deal about trade procedures and understood well from his early work at the Board of Trade in dismantling wartime regulations how tangled is the web of a long-established system, so that breaking a single strand of the web may unintentionally rupture another, sometimes with catastrophic consequences. It took, to take just one of hundreds of examples, almost two decades for SITPRO to design a 'Single Administrative Document' to cover the movement of goods within the European Common Market, enabling over a hundred Customs documents to be scrapped. During Thorneycroft's term of office, the main emphasis was on finding out how other trading nations dealt with similar problems and arranging collaboration with them, and gaining an understanding of the role that electronic data processing and telecommunication systems might play in speeding up procedures and reducing paper work.

The scale of SITPRO's task was huge and, it seems, never-ending, as it continues its work until the present day, with a heavy programme of work still before it.

~ 6 ~
Painting

How better to capture Peter's introduction to the tranquil pastime of painting than in his own words. In his book, *The Amateur*, published by Sidgwick & Jackson in 1985, he tells us that:

"I started more or less by accident. In the summer of 1951 I was on holiday in Brittany with my wife and four children ranging from a stepson then aged fourteen down to our daughter Victoria who had only been borne that June. It rained as it often does in that north-western, misty, beautiful area of France. My wife took herself off to Lannion to buy watercolours and we embarked on an intensive portrayal of the local scenery. We had exhibitions in our rooms each evening and, as in the modern system, prizes were awarded to all. It was to be the first of many painting holidays which I was to enjoy. Did I but know it, those first rather clumsy attempts at drawing and watercolour were to trigger an interest which would drive me to spend many hours in mastering the art and occupy great stretches of any spare time that I was to have in the years to come. All my family remember that holiday. What fun we had and how laughter echoes down the years! I remember that hotel if only from the fact that it only cost £1 per head per day full pension. When we left the proprietor enquired whether he could have a painting, not, he explained, necessarily by the master, but by one of the others. As we were turning out paintings in a quantity, though not perhaps of the quality, of an Italian Renaissance workshop there was no difficulty in this. In years to come, if any art historian, researching in that area, comes across a painting of La Chapelle de la Bonne Nouvelle rather weakly drawn, he should therefore attribute it to one of the younger artists, though not to the youngest and later the best watercolourist, who was, of course, still in her cradle."

A short while after that holiday, Peter was appointed President of the Board of Trade and for many years had to fit his painting into the gaps, some planned, but the majority of them unexpected opportunities, seized in the crowded life of a cabinet minister. That his painting skills improved at all in those busy years is something of a miracle, but they developed so well that his friend Lord Clark, no mean judge of an artist, would write of him:

"There are plenty of VIPs who happen to paint. Peter is a painter who happens to be a VIP."

It was not only among friends that his artistic talents were noticed. On 9th February 1961 the *Evening Standard* could quip:

"We take it Mr Peter Thorneycroft will remain in the Cabinet until the urge to paint again becomes too strong. The fruits of his last self-imposed sabbatical can be seen at the Trafford Gallery from the end of this month until Easter. There are some 30 landscapes, flower-pieces and still lifes and they are unashamedly for sale."

Although he described *The Amateur* as *"not primarily about how to paint. It is about how to enjoy painting."*, a budding artist would be well on the way to a first drawing or painting of an acceptable quality were he to follow Peter's short, pithy recommendations on how to go about it:

"What is needed for a beginner is minimal. You buy, beg or borrow:

1. A sketchbook which will fit in your pocket, 6" x 8".

2. A Biro indelible pen. (Later, you will try more sophisticated pens, but this does well for a start).

3. A small brush, No 6 or 7. Get a good quality one, but you need not at this stage buy a sable one as they are expensive.

4. A cake or tube of paint of some neutral colour. Brown, black or Paynes Grey will do.

5. A small container for water, such as the bottom half of a plastic soap container.

6. A small dish or saucer on which to mix the wet paint.

"Having so equipped yourself, you open the book and draw anything you like, however badly'. …. At this stage the accuracy of the shapes doesn't matter – just draw and go on drawing. Forget about pencils and rubbers and whether the lines are in the right place – if you don't like one line, draw another."

"The tendency for an amateur is to try to draw too much of the scene in front of him and to try to draw too fast. Select a small area and try to draw that rather slowly and well."

"A sketchbook should be kept. It becomes a kind of diary of one's travels. Draw everything and draw every day."

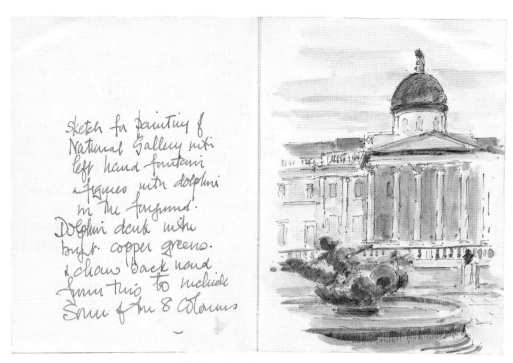

36. A page from Peter's sketchbooks

When ready to move from sketching to painting:

"My advice is this. Don't use lightweight papers. They can be very lovely but when wet swell into a kind of mountain range. Instead, buy some proper paper, by which I mean paper graded at a weight of not less than 175 lbs, which means a pretty thick one."

About the board; you will find that 12" x 17" is a convenient size. There is, however, a snag. The ordinary art shop sells beautiful boards, but they are designed to stretch paper on and are thick, inconvenient and remarkably heavy. You need a light, thin board. Hardboard will do, but hard wood is better, because if hardboard gets very wet it will warp."

You will need a paintbox. I have come around to using a fairly large box with full-size pans for the paint and deepish hollows for mixing the wash. Finally, your brush. I'm afraid that a brush suitable for anything more than small sketches will set you back a bit. You need a large (at least No 11 or No 12) sable brush. Nothing else is capable of the clear, brave strokes you ought to bring yourself to make. With this equipment you can really paint."

As to the artist himself – (and, Reader, please note in passing that, for Peter, the masculine used in this sort of context always implies also the feminine. He really believed male and female to be unequivocally of equal value, and his use of the all embracing masculine was simply for brevity, avoiding the clumsiness of 'he/she' and the grammatical absurdity of 'they' as a singular pronoun):

> *"There are, I think, three things necessary to make a good painter. He must love it, he must look closely at the paintings done by others and he must learn all he can about it."*

These brief extracts from *The Amateur* give a flavour of the essential practicality of Peter's advice on <u>how</u> to paint, but to convey an adequate picture of his thoughts on how to <u>enjoy</u> painting, one can only advise our reader to 'buy, beg or borrow' the original book and read it from cover to cover. It will be a most enjoyable experience, because Peter writes an elegant, attractive prose, informed by a deep knowledge and love of his subject, and with a witty touch that leaves the reader chuckling away as he almost unconsciously learns a very great deal from the master. Unfortunately, the book is out of print but, following another gem of practical advice from *The Amateur*, go to your public library and ask them to find you a copy (and, if they can't, keep on asking until they get on to the publishers and coerce them into producing what might well be a highly profitable reprint).

Peter's own enjoyment of his painting began as a shared experience with his wife and four young members of his family during that damp holiday in France, and a great deal of the pleasure he derived from it for the rest of his life was in company with one or more members of his family. Victoria, the baby of the group on that first occasion, and probably more interested at the time in studying her toes than in the diligent artistic exercises going on around her, later became first Peter's pupil, then his companion on many a happy occasion and, finally, a considerable painter in her own right.

Victoria recounts that *"when she was growing up [her father] was often away in the constituency or abroad, but always kept in touch by letter and, as he was just discovering his talent and love for painting, these were illustrated with delightful little sketches."* A charming example from Victoria's collection of her father's letters is reproduced in (Plate 7).

Peter's son John recalls the quiet pleasure of taking out his prep school drawing kit and finding his father leaning over his shoulder as he sketched some detail of a church building, saying nothing, but giving quiet encouragement just by being there. In *The Amateur*, Peter writes of John:

> *"Painting is, after all, a means of communication. It records a kind of vision that one person has of something and seeks to transmit to another. My son is an architect and when at school used to draw in ink and wash a long series of strange, beautiful baroque buildings. Just who should live in the impressive towers, courtyards, terraces and so forth was not defined. They were for him a kind of dream world and he sought to record it for*

himself. It was his drawing master [this was Wilfred Blunt at Eton] *who suggested that others might be interested to see these drawings and that they could be pinned up for exhibition. My son at first regarded this idea with surprise – almost with awe. He had thought of his paintings as a means of communicating with himself and not with others. He accepted the suggestion, however, and began the process of communicating ideas with a pencil – which in his work he, of course, does very well today."*

37. One of John Thorneycroft's early architectural fantasies

John was to become a leading architect in the Department of the Environment (later English Heritage) team responsible for looking after the Royal palaces and other monuments and ancient buildings. The wrought iron gates erected to close Downing Street to the public are an example of his work, and he had a major role in the restoration of Windsor Castle after the disastrous fire.

Carla Thorneycroft's participation in the artistic life of her family was less direct, but she shared her husband's delight in seizing every opportunity presented during their extensive travels together to visit art galleries and museums and to meet artists at work, and her sterling work in organising the British contribution to restoration of Florentine art treasures severely damaged by the Arno floods of 1966 and in the Venice in Peril campaign was a striking manifestation of the same family spirit. Both Peter and Carla had an extensive knowledge of the masterpieces, ancient and modern, they had seen in collections all over the world, from London to Melbourne, from Glasgow to Vancouver, and their albums are so full of photographs of the paintings they had seen that they could almost serve as an anthology of the world's art treasures.

Victoria describes the strong bond that developed between herself and her father in these words:

"We shared a great love of painting which must have been partly inherited from his mother Dorothy Franklyn whose early sketchbook shows great sensitivity. We could talk for hours about various techniques and, during

the summer holidays, especially in Italy, we would have great fun trying these out together. He loved Italy and felt very at home there and, of course, the Italians loved him. When staying in my grandfather's house in the Republic of San Marino we would take off to paint the surrounding countryside or go as far as Arezzo, San Sepolcro and Monterchi to see Piero della Francesca's great frescoes. Another summer when we went to Mallorca to stay with a dear friend called Kitty Miller he hired a motor scooter so that he and I could easily get into the olive groves to paint.

"We also painted on board an old river cruiser which we would hire from Banham's boatyard in Cambridge. From here we would explore Ely, the old west river, Wiken fen, St Ives and Huntingdon. This was an ideal way to paint and study the landscape. Father enjoyed being the Captain on these expeditions and of course had the best cabin."

38. Peter the Captain Boating on the Fens (*photo: from the family albums*)

"It was on these holidays that he taught me to cook. Usually there was my brother John, his girl friend, Delia, and me. We each had to take it in turns to produce the evening meal in the small galley.

39. Boating on the Fens: Victoria in the galley (*sketch by Peter Thorneycroft*)

"Later, when I was married, I left my family for a week to join him at Plumpton Agricultural College for a week's painting. This was a very special time. We painted all day. Dinner was at 6.30 and afterwards we would continue until the light went (and Father would work on his book, 'The Amateur'). By 11 we were starving, so we ended up having a midnight feast.

"After I left home, I was living in North London as a teacher. The job had its challenges, and I remember coming home late one evening after a difficult day to find an encouraging letter left by Father under the milk bottle.

"When I was cooking, I would often ask his advice and, one day, I rang him *at his office when he was Chairman of the Conservative Party. I wanted to know how to make a bollito. He gave me the necessary instructions. Unknown to me, he had actually been in a meeting and so the entire office had a lesson as well. Apparently, when he put the phone down, they all applauded.*

"I think of him often. Sometimes when I am in difficulty, but also at happy moments when I am mixing a colour or trying to paint the light on a cloud.

"Above all, I remember his humour and his humility, his compassion and his love for all things."

It was not only the company of his family that Peter found to be enriched by his painting hobby. He also loved the broader companionship of the world of art. He was immediately at home amongst the disparate groups of people taking part in the art courses and sessions he attended from time to time, whether at the Chelsea under the tutelage of Vivien Pitchforth or at the Heatherly colleges of art or an occasional painting holiday. (There is a much later connection between the Thorneycroft family and the Heatherly School of Art - Peter's grandson Richard now works with John Walton, himself a portrait painter of note, in running the Heatherley)

Peter had many friends who painted. In *The Amateur*, he mentions Derek Hill, Lady Bessborough and the Australian painter Judy Cassab as among those with whom he had spent happy hours painting side by side, but there were many others. It was Carla Thorneycroft who first met John Ward, when he came to see her in her office at *Vogue* magazine, where she was Fashion Editor, and left with a commission for a series of fashion sketches which helped to launch him on his long career. He and his wife Alison became affectionate and long-standing friends of the whole family, marking every important event in Peter's and Carla's lives with delightfully illustrated messages. Indeed it was John Ward's example that prompted both Peter and Victoria to illustrate so many of their own letters. John Ward encouraged Peter in his painting in many other ways, from inspiring him to experiment and develop his technique, to sending him rolls of a special caramel-coloured paper that he so enjoyed working on. Peter also shared a close companionship rooted in their mutual passion for art and politics with Christopher Northbourne, and they attended the Byam Shaw art school together. Christopher's home, Northbourne Court in Kent, is a beautiful house surrounded by a lovely old garden enclosed in a Tudor wall. The two friends often set up their easels and painted together in the delightful Kentish landscape nearby.

Over the years, Peter built up an *oeuvre* of several hundred paintings, attracting the attention of the art world from quite early on. Indeed, only two years had passed since Peter's first essays into drawing before, in the Spring of 1953, one of his early paintings was included in an exhibition, *Painting is a Pleasure*, at the Trafford

Gallery in London. This was *Flower Market, Covent Garden.* Other notable amateur exhibitors on that occasion included the American Ambassador, Winthrop W. Aldrich, Field-Marshal Sir Claude Auchinlek and Miss Freya Stark, and all of the proceeds were donated to Toc H. In the Summer of 1955, at another *Painting is a Pleasure* exhibition at the Trafford Gallery, Peter showed his *Venetian Sketch,* one of very many drawings and paintings which he produced during holiday visits over the next forty years to that still lovely city. This time, he exhibited in the company of King Feisal II of Iraq, Douglas Fairbanks Jnr and Miss Beatrice Lillie.

40. Venetian Sketch PeterThorneycroft, 1955

The years 1957 to 1961 when he was first Chancellor of the Exchequer and then Minister of Aviation were busy enough for Peter the Politician but, somehow, Peter the Painter managed to complete 35 paintings, often painted late in the evening, which were judged worthy of a solo exhibition at the Trafford Gallery in March 1961: as all but six were sold that judgement was evidently sound. The works ranged from landscapes to flowers. One of the paintings, *A Child's Dream,* was his interpretation of a dream described to him by Victoria, then nine years old, an early example of the artistic collaboration between father and daughter.

The next one-man exhibition took place at Chichester Antiques in July 1963, in aid of the King George's Fund for Sailors, and Admiral of the Fleet Earl Mountbatten was 'told off', as he put it, to open his political boss's display. On that occasion fifty-five paintings were shown, and this time, Peter had extended his range to include eleven nude studies.

There were several more exhibitions in later years, to make sixteen in all, one of the last being at the Lichfield Festival in July 1989, displayed in the Chapter House of the Cathedral under the title 'The Pursuit of Excellence'. The forty-three watercolours in the Lichfield exhibition included several landscapes painted mainly in Kent, a number of Venetian buildings, *"The Library of the House of Lords"*, and some light-hearted subjects such as *"His and Hers – Hats"* and *"Beach Hat and Towels"* (which brightens the back dust cover of this book).

Peter was primarily a watercolourist, but he was quite prepared to experiment in other media from time to time. Victoria talks of a period when he was trying his hand with acrylics and crayon, preparing a background with broad, bold strokes of colour on canvas or board of much larger dimensions than his usual watercolours, on top of which he painted his image in whichever medium suited the subject. They would often sit side by side, sharing ideas as they tried different techniques.

41. Peter and Victoria sketching together (*photo: by Terence Daum*)

42. 'Mona Monkey' From a painting by Victoria Thorneycroft-Nathanson

Peter and Carla liked to stay sometimes at the Calabash Hotel on the island of Grenada, where they became such welcome visitors that the owners, Leo and Lilian Garbutt, named a suite after them. After Peter's death, Victoria accompanied her mother on a recuperative stay at the Calabash and, whilst there, painted a set of murals depicting local flora and fauna, including 'Mona Monkey', striking enough in black and white as shown above, although the original is in the gayest of colour with a vibrant green background of leaves.

In 1985, Christopher and Marie-Sygne Northbourne lent their house, Northbourne Court, to the Thorneycrofts, enabling Peter and Carla to gather their many grandchildren around them at weekends in the delightful house and garden. It was here that, in 1989, Peter celebrated his 80th birthday in the company of his family and many friends from home and abroad, amongst them Margaret Thatcher, the Prime Minister, whose warm tribute to his achievements, his friendship and his loyalty gave Peter enormous pleasure.

43. Peter's 80th Birthday Celebration, 29th July 1989, Northbourne Court, Kent.
Carla (who had almost lost her voice) wishes Peter a Happy Birthday (*photo: from the family albums*)

44. Prime Minister Margaret Thatcher's Tribute to Peter (*photo: from the family albums*)

After mentioning that Peter had just told her in a confidential tone that he had been in the same Parliament as Lloyd George (not something, she thought, to boast about!), Margaret Thatcher said that he could certainly boast of having served three great Prime Ministers - Winston Churchill, Anthony Eden and Harold Macmillan - a remarkable record of service. She had chosen Peter as Party Chairman because of what he stood for (and insisted that she had only learnt afterwards that he was related to Willie Whitelaw, his predecessor.). As a young man, he had stood for the 'Dash for Freedom' school. Under Macmillan, he had stood for sound money. He belonged to a generation of politicians which knew how to debate in Parliament with courtesy and clarity. As Party Chairman she remembered vividly his injunction to delegates at a Party Conference, *"You will save your firepower for the enemy, won't you?"* In the House of Lords, up he would get and make three straightforward points which could unlock the whole argument and so often win the vote. She had valued his friendship and his loyalty.

45. Peter responds (*photo: from the family albums*)

Peter began with his thanks to Carly. It was 60 years ago that he had proposed to her: he was 21, she 17 - and he thanked God that she had not lost her voice that day! They had separated, come together again and married, and what a marriage it had been. His family was a great, great joy to him. He also thanked the Northbournes, Christopher and Mariecyne (who were celebrating their 20th wedding anniversary) for allowing them to live in their lovely house, with its originally Tudor garden, lovingly redesigned and planted - and painted - by Christopher's father, Walter.

He said that he was basically a politician and, in some ways, an industrialist, but he was also a painter - a man must have something else to do when he comes down from the mountain tops and into the valleys. A man is a reflection of his friends and of the times he lives in. He was very happy to see John Ward, who had given him so much with his painting. He had learnt what he knew of manufacturing industry from Pirelli, from Alberto and Leopoldo, members of that great, Northern Italian family. From them he had learnt how to behave in business. It was Charles Forte who had taught him about the service industry that he had built up from small beginnings to one of the great companies in the land.

But of all the jobs he had done, he was most proud of being Chairman of Margaret Thatcher's party, under her, particularly in the years of opposition. Those were very happy years, and he looked back on them with pride and gratefulness. He remembered Margaret when she was an undergraduate and he was a young MP and, he said, *"To tell you the truth, Margaret, you don't look any different today."* She had changed the history of this country, she had changed the mould of political life, and she had done things for the country that could never be undone. He remembered her for her energy, her compassion and the pride a man could have in serving under her.

Peter continued to paint almost to the end of his life, taking his sketchbook with him everywhere, and setting up his easel wherever he could, very often in the Venice he loved so much.

46. Peter sketching in Venice, 1989 (*photo: from the family albums*)

~ 7 ~
Retrospective

The career path that Thorneycroft trod was not a straight one between a clear starting point and a recognisable finishing post. It was only after trials with the Army and the Law that he settled upon a political career and, in his later years, he extended his range and achieved a considerable success in a number of business appointments. Nevertheless, despite the pragmatic adjustments which had to be made from time to time to take account of contemporary realities, the fundamental principles with which he set off remained with him to the end of his life. He left few clues as to his own judgement on the degree of success he had achieved in applying those principles except, occasionally, in personal and unrecorded conversations with trusted friends towards the end of his life. Any attempt to summarise on his behalf what he would consider to be the achievements of such a complex life, or the lessons that might be drawn from them, calls for humility and circumspection. One important general lesson that may certainly be drawn from his career is that a competent minister of state who has the wisdom to develop a deep understanding of his brief and a productive working relationship with his civil servants will be able to achieve much better results if he is permitted to remain in office in one department, ideally for the lifetime of a Government. His long and highly effective spells at the Board of Trade, in Defence and as Party Chairman demonstrate this very clearly.

At the heart of everything that Thorneycroft believed and did was the conviction he expressed in *Design for Living* that *"the State is the most imperfect guardian of the public interest, and that British history had been a long struggle to protect the individual against central authority, devising one check after another to this end."* The crucial test that he applied to any policy was the extent to which it protected or infringed the freedom of the individual.

Secondly, *"since no one person can enjoy more than a certain amount of wisdom, experience or knowledge, it is necessary, in politics as elsewhere, to delegate responsibility. Decentralisation is preferable not only for reasons of efficiency, but also because it is good for people to make up their own minds and take their own decisions."*

On these two commandments, it might be said, hang all the law and the prophets.

One key element of Thorneycroft's practical advice of 1949 remains as valid today as it was then - that political parties should make good use of their periods in opposition to analyse and review their policies because, once elected, they inevitably find themselves under pressure to understand and deal urgently with the realities of the day, with little opportunity for quiet reflection.

He held the firm belief that the delicate and dearly-won constitutional balance between the executive, the legislature and the judiciary must not be put at risk by an overweening executive, especially one with a large majority in the House of Commons but lesser support in the country. He was quick to see through schemes called 'modernisation' which resulted only in change and not in improvement. Although inclined to leave well alone a system that was working quite well, he was not against reform of the House of Lords provided that its crucial role of improving the quality of legislation was not weakened.

He believed that capitalism is the best way to give consumers freedom of choice, whilst recognising its imperfections. He knew that capitalists like to control markets rather than be controlled by them but considered that Government could deal with such defects by rigorous monitoring of monopolies and restrictive practices.

He abhorred State ownership of an industry or service precisely because it deprives consumers of freedom of choice. It also severely limits the negotiating freedom and choice of jobs of its employees; and the monopoly it creates is often unmanageably large, with no inherent incentive to operate efficiently in the public interest. Thorneycroft, however, regarded the National Health Service as an exception, not as a matter of principle, but for the practical reason that its essential rationale of providing access to its services at no charge, to sick people who were not free to choose whether to be ill or not, made the normal disciplines of the market inappropriate. He recognised that there could never be enough money in such a situation to provide free of charge all the health services that its users might like, and would certainly insist that the funds allocated to the NHS should be used to meet the essential health needs of the people, not their inessential desires; and that they be spent efficiently and wisely. Applying his principle of decentralisation, he would urge the maximum delegation of responsibility to ensure that the nationally approved treatments and services were delivered in the way best suited to local conditions. His industrial experience would have made him wary of nationally imposed performance targets, knowing the risk that concentration of attention on a target related to one aspect of performance was almost bound to lead to neglect or even directly consequential deterioration of performance elsewhere.

His criterion for determining what public expenditure was 'affordable' was very simple: the State's books must balance. Expenditure must not exceed income; and borrowing should normally be resorted to only to finance investment. He saw the management of the nation's accounts not as a technical issue, but as one of attitude. Since some public expenditure is unavoidable (principally on defence), expenditure on discretionary items – even when fervently desired by the electorate - must be reduced if necessary not only to ensure that total expenditure does not exceed income, but also to keep the taxation which is the principal source of that income at a bearable level. The level of direct taxation must not create a disincentive to earning, nor indirect taxation unduly distort the freedom of consumers' choice. He recognised that it was a duty of Government to ensure the provision of an adequate infrastructure of essential services, such as transport, energy, communications, health, police, prisons, etc, but generally by regulation of private provision, not by direct ownership or management.

He was convinced that the security and defence of the realm must never be put at risk, but that this did not mean that expenditure on defence could not be controlled. It must be spent efficiently and effectively, without waste. This was a major consideration in persuading him that the military, procurement and administrative activities of the three armed services should be controlled by a single defence staff reporting to a single Ministry of Defence, an exception to his general predilection for decentralisation. He believed also in the scope for reducing some major items of military expenditure by sharing the cost of development with reliable allies, and he devoted a great deal of effort during his career to pursuing possibilities of collaboration to this end with European allies. He was conscious of the risks involved in relying on the sometimes overbearing Americans to supply or provide access to the technology for key weapons, but accepted realistically that Britain had perforce to do so, because it could not afford to develop them on its own.

For Thorneycroft, Britain's place in the world order was largely determined by security considerations. In his era, the United Nations had been rendered impotent by the Soviet Union, and he had no doubt that Britain must join the USA and the free nations of Europe against any attempted aggression by the Soviets and their satellites. Britain must therefore be part both of Europe and of a transatlantic alliance of Europe and the USA. He was a Europhile in that sense, as well as in the context of encouraging free trade and economic growth. He had deeply regretted the failure of the pre-war League of Nations, and the post-war emasculation of the United Nations, and it seems certain that, when the Soviet empire collapsed, he would have wanted the UN to take up at last the role for which it had been designed - the resolution of international disagreements and rapid suppression of conflicts - with the full support of all its members. He supported the Suez Campaign in 1956, and the first Gulf War in 1991 as the correct reaction to the Iraqi invasion of Kuwait. It is not so clear that he would have supported the 2003 pre-emptive invasion of Iraq in the absence of an undeniable aggressive act. He would surely have been strongly against the decision of the US Administration to set up the Guantanamo Bay detention centre outside the reach of the law, on the ground that the world leader – above all the world leader

- must rigorously and unequivocally respect the law. He would have been deeply suspicious of the motives of any Government for resorting to lengthy detention of suspects without trial. Whether he would have supported the replacement of the independent nuclear deterrent (the submarine-mounted *Trident*) it is impossible to guess. When he bore personal responsibility for deterrence as Minister and Secretary of State for Defence in the 1960s, he had been concerned about its high cost, but accepted that it was an expense that had to be borne to ensure that Britain would be able to retaliate if Russia should launch a direct attack or react against an American attack on Russia by a punitive strike on America's loyal ally. He certainly had no love for nuclear weapons, and would have wanted to be sure that any replacement for *Trident* was the most appropriate available weapon to deter the quite different kinds of enemy who might think of attacking Britain in the 21st Century. He regarded the aircraft carrier, transporting properly trained and equipped ground troops to trouble spots, as the best way to deal with local uprisings and minor wars when recourse to nuclear weapons or massive air strikes was not appropriate. He supported the policy of seeking to secure by diplomatic means the effective and reliable implementation of progressive nuclear disarmament by all nuclear powers, accompanied by strict enforcement of non-proliferation. He was also a realist. He knew that diplomatic efforts to resolve such matters could succeed only if there were a readiness to reach agreement on the part of all the protagonists, and that force should not be ruled out if that readiness did not exist. Nevertheless, he was not one to take an action without considering what the consequences of that action might be, and having a viable plan for dealing with those consequences.

He believed that, for the economic benefit of all, the European market, including the British market, must be enthusiastically committed to the international system of free trade. Because he believed so fervently in decentralisation, it seems unlikely that he would have thought very highly of the appetite of the European Commission for detailed regulation of so many aspects of everyday life. He would almost certainly have argued that, if the European Union was to have a constitution, it should be a very short document setting out unambiguously the few key functions of the Commission and leaving everything else to the member states. The principles of 'decentralisation' and 'subsidiarity' are not so far apart. One might expect that his brief list of key functions would have included close co-operation in foreign policy and defence between those member states prepared to provide the resources required to implement the agreed policies; the lightest possible regulation, informed by commonsense, to ensure that the Common Market was truly 'common', including unrestricted access to transport and utility infrastructures and to financial institutions; regulation of such supranational issues as pollution of the environment and cross-border crime – and very little else.

Although he never had the opportunity to put them into effect, Thorneycroft showed during his brief spell as Shadow Home Secretary that he had clear views on crime and punishment. Crime must be quickly detected and punished with toughness to discourage repetition, but its roots must also be analysed, understood and dealt with. Whilst accepting that there were no easy answers and that remedial actions would be slow to take effect, he thought it already clear that the education of young people who were not academically inclined, and who so often felt inadequate, needed drastic improvement. He saw a strong case for merging some small police forces to cope with criminal gangs operating without regard to boundaries. He was deeply worried by the tendency to increase the range of criminal offences, placing unmanageable demands on the police and on prison accommodation. He asked, as Montaigne had done four centuries earlier, *"What have our legislators gained by picking out a hundred thousand particular cases and deeds, and attaching to them a hundred thousand laws?"* He believed that imprisonment should be reserved for serious offences. Prison sentences should be of the severity considered by the judge to be appropriate to the criminal and his crime, and there should be no automatic early release.

With regard to the education system as a whole, he was concerned at what he saw as a common tendency to devote too much attention to the narrow fields of A levels and university education and to undervalue the importance of practical education for those not academically inclined – who are the source of the skilled craftsmen and technicians just as vital to the economy as graduates. His view was that the State should fund as an essential item of public expenditure all primary and secondary education and training; and also ensure that further and higher education and training was available without financial constraint to all who were capable of benefiting from it, to the extent that this could be afforded within overall public spending constraints. He was comfortable with the concept of asking university graduates to pay back, later in life, part of the cost of the State's investment in their higher education, to contribute towards keeping public expenditure within reasonable bounds, to ease the grip which Government funding exerts on the universities and to encourage young people to choose their courses carefully and to appreciate better the value of the educational opportunities available to them.

Finally, Peter Thorneycroft was a man of faith, a committed Christian, who deeply regretted the steady erosion that he had observed during the course of his life of the Christian ethic in British society. His advocacy at the time of the 1988 Education Act of Christian religious teaching in State schools reflected his earnest desire for recovery of that ethic, whilst accepting without reservation the right of other faiths to provision for the religious upbringing of their own children in their own faith. His family life was of the utmost importance to him, and a model of mutual love and support embracing four generations.

Peter Thorneycroft died at his home in Eaton Square, London, on 4th June 1994, devotedly nursed through a distressing final illness by Carla. A Funeral Eucharist for Peter was held at St Peter's, Eaton Square, on Thursday, 9th June, and a Memorial Service at St Margaret's, Westminster, on 26th October 1994. The addresses of The Revd D B Tillyer at the Funeral Eucharist and of Lord Carrington at the Memorial Service, recalling Peter's life of great endeavour always strengthened by his faith, add fitting final brush strokes to this sketch of a great man.

Address of The Revd D B Tillyer
St Peter's, Eaton Square
9th June 1994

We have come to the funeral of one we have all known and loved. I cannot by myself express the fullness of what Peter means to each one of us. I can only speak out of my own personal relationship with him as a parishioner and good friend. My hope is that my words will help each of you to express in his heart to God those personal thanksgivings for all that Peter means to us so that, by gathering up the broken fragments of our individual gratitude, nothing is lost, and to place him with confidence in God's hands.

Today, the preacher's predicament is compounded by the many full and generous obituaries which have appeared in the media, revealing the extent to which the public figure has contributed to our national life. Therefore I want to spend the rest of this address speaking more personally of Peter as a man of faith and a wonderful human being. And in order to do so, I shall take as my framework that fact that he was baptised with three great saints' names, George Edward Peter. In a strange way his life was already present in his name.

First, St George, Patron of England.

Peter was born in the heart of England, an Englishman to his fingertips and a devoted son of the Church of England. He once said to me, "I am a one nation Tory because I am a member of the Church of England", and again, on another occasion, "I hold fast in difficult times to the Church of England because I am a one nation Tory."

But he was never a "little Englander", but very much a European, with a special love for Italy and, particularly, Venice. How would it be otherwise, married to Carla? And before Sister Wendy let out the secret on television, I am sure that many of you already knew the hidden treasure in Venice, the Schola di San Giorgio, with its exquisite sequence of paintings of the life of St George by Carpaccio, that painter who captured the essence of Venice long before Canaletto. Peter himself was a water-colourist of note, and he loved to capture the beauty of Venice in his paintings, and my future visits to Venice will be touched by the recollection of how much Peter loved the city.

At the climax of Carpaccio's sequence is, of course, St George slaying the dragon, reminding us that as a man and as a politician Peter was a man of principle and therefore a slayer of dragons. Appropriately, he entered Parliament as an MP for Stafford on this very day, 9th June, 1938, as a young man of 29, with vision and integrity, setting out on the road of public service. His resignation 20 years later as Chancellor of the Exchequer was but the most spectacular example of his placing of principle before expediency but, of course, like all slayers of dragons he carried in his struggle the marks of the dragon's teeth.

Which brings me to his second patron saint, St Edward the Confessor, Patron of Westminster..

Peter was a great lover of Parliament, both as an MP and as a member of the House of Lords. To the end, his desire was to be in the House. Interestingly, his surname, Thorneycroft, with an 'e', prefigured Thorney Island where the Palace of Westminster is built, and he certainly earned for himself a "croft", a cultivated part, in the hearts and affections of politicians of all parties. His last official engagement shortly before he died was the photograph taken at No 11 of the former Chancellors of the Exchequer.

But St Edward built another house on Thorney Island, long before the Palace of Westminster was built, the Collegiate Church of St Peter, commonly called Westminster Abbey, which brings us to Peter's third and greater patron and the patron of this church.

St Peter was the leader of the apostles. All except for him, and later St Paul, are fairly anonymous characters. Indeed Peter and Paul make an interesting contrast.

Paul was a born again Christian, single-minded, running the straight race, a perfectionist.

Peter was a flawed Rock, loveable, fumbling, bold in vision, aware of his sins and backsliding, fallible, human and generous with the faults of others.

Our Peter was also a loveable person. He knew himself to be a sinner, and was troubled at times by the sense of his sins even though he believed himself forgiven. He was a person of joy, he radiated fun, he was good company, with a lively sense of humour. But he could also be impractical and exasperate those who loved him.

This is the Peter we knew and loved, loved because he was so loveable, the hidden Peter who was husband to Carla, father, stepfather, family man, fellow politician and business man. This is the Peter for whom we give thanks to God today. Like St Peter, he was universal in his outlook, comprehensive in his thinking, able to live with his own contradictions.

- *a monetarist with rising damp;*
- *a fun person with a sense of social concern;*
- *demanding of affection and love, yet so loveable and attentive;*
- *a leader but without ambition;*
- *a disciple but not subservient.*

When Peter was made a Companion of Honour we rejoiced that he was counted worthy to be a companion of honour to an earthly crown. Today we pray that he will be made a Companion of Honour to the Eternal King and be granted a place with the saints and angels in heaven.

Lord Carrington's Tribute to Lord Thorneycroft
Memorial Service
St Margaret's, Westminster
Wednesday 26th October 1994

In the nature of things, however well we here think we knew Peter Thorneycroft, we only knew a part of his life. Barrister, soldier, business man, politician, statesman, painter, none of us except his immediate family have known him in all these different capacities.

To those of my generation who were interested in politics, our first memory of him, though almost certainly we did not know him personally, was of a debonair young Conservative MP elected just before the War, and already making a name for himself as representative of a new and up and coming generation of young Conservatives.

The war years intervened, and it was not until the short-lived caretaker Conservative Government of 1945 that he was given office as Parliamentary Secretary at the Ministry of War Transport followed by six years in Opposition. It was a period in which he became well-known as the Chairman of the Tory Reform Committee, author of a pamphlet called Design for Freedom, a cogent argument against Socialism and centralisation and a forerunner of policies subsequently adopted, and Opposition Spokesman for Transport in which position his already growing reputation was confirmed.

But at that time something else happened and it changed his life. In 1949, Carly, whom he had met and from whom he had been parted, he met again, and they were married. A fairy tale and, as in all good fairy tales, they lived happily ever after, sharing together the successes and setbacks of political life, each contributing to a contented and fruitful partnership

In 1951, he was appointed President of the Board of Trade, a job he remained in for six years, a round peg in a round hole. Also, in 1951, he was on holiday in Brittany with the family and it rained, it was cold and it blew. Carly suggested that they go to Lannion, the nearest town, and buy paints and brushes. The rest you all know, and know too what talent Peter had and what pleasure his painting gave to him and to others, and incidentally he wrote an excellent book about it. Never was a better day spent.

His time at the Board of Trade was rewarded by his appointment as Chancellor of the Exchequer at a critical time in the aftermath of Suez. A year later, he resigned.

He had, of course, suffered some political setbacks before, notably his defeat in 1945 at Stafford; but the decision to leave office must have been the most difficult decision he ever had to take. All resignations are painful, but a resignation on an issue of principle is the hardest. It implied disagreement not only with the Prime Minister, but most of your colleagues as well. It takes a man of courage and principle to hold an opinion so firmly in the face of his friends and colleagues and to sacrifice his career, as also did his two colleagues. Whatever view his friends took as to whether he was right or wrong, none failed to admire his integrity.

It also says much about a man's character subsequently to conduct yourself as Peter Thorneycroft did; there was no bitterness, no recrimination, no malice and no thought of leaving politics. It is clear, too, that those qualities and his outstanding ability caused Mr Macmillan two-and-a-half years later to ask him to rejoin the Government, first as Minister of Aviation, and subsequently as Secretary for Defence.

It was at that time I first got to know him well. It had been decided that the three Service Ministers of whom I was one, should be amalgamated into the Ministry of Defence and lose their Headquarters, and their status, and their age-old independence. We did not really much like it. We were disgruntled princelings, deprived by the emperor of our Castles and Duchies, and rather sensitive. A lesser man than Peter would have found us difficult to handle, but he behaved with tact and generosity whilst at the same time firmly carrying out the policy of unifying our diffuse defence arrangements.

The task of amalgamating the three Service Ministers into one was not an easy one, and the fact that it was successful and that we all got on so well together was due to his outgoing personality and his very astute handling of quite difficult people.

His spokesman in the House of Lords when he was Minister of Aviation told me that, on their first meeting, Peter had said to him, "Don't worry if you make a mistake and get it wrong. I will support you". And what is more, he did, through thick and thin in all our many troubles.

During that time, I was in bad trouble due to a spy in the Admiralty. A critical debate took place in the House of Commons in which Peter defended me. He went far beyond the sort of routine defence which would have been normal and adequate and, in the process, was heavily criticised. Loyalty of that kind is not all that common. This is not something which I will ever forget.

He was, of course, a formidable debator, trenchant and lucid. Sometimes scornful but never unkind; courteous and modest as he always was, and never let political differences interfere with his personal friendships which stretched across the party political divide.

A year or two after the election of 1964, Peter was created a Life Peer, and from then took an active part in the House of Lords; and did so until the very end of his life, coming to the House in a wheelchair, listening to the debates and commenting as actively and as forward looking as ever.

After 1964, he devoted himself to business in various capacities and was as much a success as he was in politics. But in 1975, rather unexpectedly I think, he was asked by Lady Thatcher who had just become the Leader of the Conservative Party, to become its Chairman, a position in opposition only second in importance to the Leader.

Those who have held that position will perhaps agree that it could not be called a bed of roses. It is physically demanding, it entails endless travelling around the constituencies, countless evening meetings, digestively arduous – as the Chairman is expected to drink and eat both heartily and appreciatively; mentally exhausting as there is nothing more tiring than affability and politeness 24 hours a day whilst parrying extremely acute questions; and of course the need to deal with political activists who very properly expect instant results, whilst the reality may be rather more delayed. I do not think that any Chairman and his wife – because Carly was as important as he was – have ever been more successful in that post. He led, he inspired and he calmed.

Their reward, and I hope they knew it, was the respect and the undying affection of all those who met them during that period. We his colleagues know – and I am certain that I speak for Lady Thatcher as well – how much his wise counsel and common sense contributed to the success of the Party at the election of 1979 and afterwards.

In later years, he remained as always a good friend, full of sound advice to those wise enough to ask him for it; the most enjoyable of companions.

It is now commonly supposed that all or most of those in public life are venal and selfish with unworthy motives, men of straw unfit for the positions they hold or seek to hold. Let those who believe that look at the record of Peter Thorneycroft, his courage, convictions, principles and integrity. A good man and a great public servant.

Notes

General

We have endeavoured to provide within the text sufficient information on sources for general readers. Additional information for academic readers is given below. Books referred to in the text are listed in the Bibliography.

Frontispiece

Page iii - Illustration 1: copyright Pirelli UK Limited

1. Preparing for Service

Thorneycroft Family personal papers, including Record of Service of GEP Thorneycroft (Army Personnel Centre).
Page 14 - Illustration 13: copyright National Portrait Gallery

2. Politics

When speeches recorded in Hansard are directly quoted, the date is given in the text. The relevant references are given below in the approved standard format.

MP for Stafford
10.11.38   HC/OF/S5/341 cols 362-365

MP for Monmouth
Page 39 - Illustration 17: copyright Associated Newspapers Limited

President of the Board of Trade
10.02.54   HC/OF/S5/523 cols 1309-1314
Page 57 - Extract from *Vancouver News*: copyright Vancouver News
Page 61 - Extract from *Manchester Guardian*: copyright Guardian News & Media Ltd 1954
Page 63 - Extract from *Punch*: copyright Punch Limited 1955
Page 70 - Cartoon: copyright Punch Library
Page 77 - Letter from Anthony Eden: courtesy of The Countess of Avon

Chancellor of the Exchequer
24.02.57   NA/PREM 11/1768
23.01.58   HC/OF/S5/580 cols 1294-1297
Page 82 - Extract from *Evening Standard*: copyright Associated Newspapers Ltd
Page 85 - Extract from *Evening Standard*: copyright Associated Newspapers Ltd
Page 86 - Illustration 26: copyright Getty Images
Pages 93-94, 97, 103 - Extracts from Edward Heath's autobiography: copyright Estate of Sir Edward Heath (Literary Agent CFD)

Page 97 - Extract from *The Times*: copyright News International Syndication
        - Extract from *Daily Telegraph*: copyright Telegraph Media Group
Page 98 - Extract from *Investors' Chronicle*: copyright Investor's Chronicle

3. Gap Years and World Tour

Peter Thorneycroft's own diary of his 'Journey to the East'.
Page 104 - Extract from *Daily Mail*: copyright Associated Newspapers Ltd
Page 140 - Illustration 30: copyright BAPCO

4. Return to Politics

23.02.60   HC/OF/S5/618 cols 200-206
06.04.60   HC/OF/S5/621
Page 201-2 Extracts from *Financial Times*: copyright The Financial Times

Minister of Aviation
31.07.61   HC/OF/S5/645 cols 928-942
02.08.61   HC/OF/S5/645 col 1485
31.10.61   NA/BT 245/928
06.03.62   HC/OF/S5/655 cols 238-250

Minister of Defence
31.07.63   HC/OF/S5/682 Debate cols 465-478;
                      Quotations cols 472, 477, 479, 484, 488, 569, 573, 575
15.04.64   Letter Montgomery to Thorneycroft
16.10.64   Letter Mountbatten to Thorneycroft
            Letter Zuckerman to Thorneycroft
Page 219 - 'Central Organisation for Defence': Mountbatten Papers Ref MB1
K96, Hartley Library, University of Southampton
Page 223 - Reference to *Evening Standard*: copyright Associated Newpapers Ltd
Opposition
17.12.64   HC/OF/S5/704 cols 702-703
09.02.65   HC/OF/S5/706 cols 213-336
25.02.65   HC/OF/S5/705
03.03.65   HC/OF/S5/707 Debate cols 1327-1452 Quotation cols 1328, 1352
03.05.65   HC/OF/S5/711
02.02.66   HC/OF/S5/723
Pages 244-246 Extracts from *Crossbow*: copyright The Bow Group

House of Lords

Page 251 - Illustration 33: copyright UPPA

Economy

16.01.68   HC/OF/S5/756
23.01.68   HL/PO/OF/S5/288 cols 168-178
04.10.76   HL/PO/OF/S5/374 cols 833-840
11.03.87   HL/PO/OF/S5/485 cols 1066-1067
02.12.87   HL/PO/OF/S5/490 cols 1062-1133
04.12.91   HL/PO/OF/S5/533 cols 231-289

Defence

13.03.68   HL/PO/OF/S5/290 cols 253-261
03.12.86   HL/PO/OF/S5/482 cols 822-823

Europe

07.06.93   HL/PO/OF/S5/546 cols 578-580

Trade Unions

29.04.87   HL/PO/OF/S5/486 cols 1512-1515

Education

03.05.88   HL/PO/OF/S5/496 cols 514-515
12.05.88   HL/PO/OF/S5/496 cols 1343-1344

Health

23.03.88   HL/PO/OF/S5/495 cols 204-205

Conservative Party Chairman

This chapter draws heavily on the Conservative Party Archives in the Bodleian Library, reproduced with the permission of Conservative Central Office.

5 Business

Trust House Forte

pp 302-307 Extracts from *Forte - The Autobiography of Charles Forte*: copyright Charles Forte 1986: courtesy of Pan Macmillan

6. Painting

Pages 309-322 Extracts from *The Amateur*: copyright Lord Thorneycroft 1985: courtesy of Pan Macmillan
Page 310 - Extract from *Evening Standard*: copyright Associated Newspapers Ltd
Page 318 - Illustration 41: copyright Terence Daum

Bibliography

Forward - By the Right: (Tory Reform Group, 1943)

Design for Living: Peter Thorneycroft (The Falcon Press, 1949)

Not Unanimous (A rival verdict to Radciffe's on money: Peter Thorneycroft et al; ed. Arthur Seldon (Institute of Economic Affairs, 1960)

"Hinch" – A Celebration of Viscount Hinchingbrooke, MP, 1906-1995: ed Andrew Best and John Sandwich (Mapperton Estate, 1997)

Macmillan 1891-1956: Alistair Horne (Macmillan, 1988)

Macmillan Diaries – The Cabinet Years 1950-57: Peter Catterall (Macmillan, 2003)

Like the Roman – The Life of Enoch Powell: Simon Heffer (Weidenfeld & Nicolson, 1998)

The Course of my Life: Edward Heath (Hodder & Stoughton, 1988)

A Sparrow's Flight: Lord Hailsham (Fontana, 1991)

The Turbulent Years – My Life in Politics: Kenneth Baker (Faber and Faber, 1993)

Conflict of Loyalty – Geoffrey Howe (Macmillan, 1994)

The Path to Power: Margaret Thatcher (HarperCollins, 1996)

The Conservative Party – From Peel to Major: Robert Blake (William Heinemann, 1997)

The IMF Crisis of 1976 and British Politics: Kevin HIckson (Tauris Academic Studies, 2005)

The Time of my Life: Denis Healey (Politico's, 2006)

Radio Man – The remarkable rise and fall of C O Stanley: Mark Frankland (IEE, 2002)

Forte – The Autobiography of Charles Forte: (Pan Books, 1997)

The Amateur: Lord Thorneycroft (Sedgwick & Jackson, 1985)

Peter Thorneycroft' 80th Birthday Celebration: Video-recording (DEL Video Services, 1989)

Mountbatten: Philip Ziegler (Collins, 1985)

Having it so good - Britain in the Fifties: Peter Hennessy (Penguin Allen Lane, 2006)

Index

Symbols

10 Corps 18
11 Downing Street 80
12 Corps 18
1912 Club, Bucklersbury 17
1941 Committee 20
3rd Field Brigade RA 10
5th Field Regiment, Royal
    Artillery 182

A

Abadan 107, 137, 138
Aberdare Cables 290
ability to worship 263
Acland, Richard 20
Acre 130
acrylic 318
Adelaide 299
Adenauer, Konrad 73, 222
Agra 149
agriculture 28, 75, 212
agriculture (India) 148
aircraft carrier 224, 252
aircraft industry 231
Air Ministry 225
air transport 29
Air Transport Licensing Board
    212
Air Transport Policy 29
Alam, General Igo 129
Aldington, Lord (Toby) 251, 260
Aldrich, Winthrop W (American
    Ambassador in London) 317
Algeria 201
Allen, DF, Ministry of Aviation
    212
American Sixth Fleet 104
Amery, Julian 216
Amery, Leo 54, 61, 260
Amman 124
Analgesia in Childbirth 40
Anderson, Donald (Labour
    candidate, Monmouth* 248
Andreotti, Giulio 221
Angkor Wat 296
Anglican Church 36
Anglo-American Financial and
    Commercial Agreement
    1945 51

Anglo-Japanese Trade
    Agreement 55
Anschluss of Austria 15
Antonius, Tuto 109
Approved Societies 21
Arab Union 104, 107
Arab world 106
Argentina 57, 254
Argyll and Sutherland
    Highlanders 65
Arif, Deputy PM Iraq 111
Army Personnel Centre 9
Arno floods, 1966 313
AS30 missile 214
Asahi Evening News 55
ASAT rocket 213
Ashdown, Lord 267, 269
Assembly, Indonesia 164
Astor, Nancy 26
Aswan Dam 110, 112
Athabaska tar sands 72
Atkins, Humphrey 271
Atlantic Charter 1941 51
atomic energy 82
Attlee, Clement 38
Attlee, Earl 231
Auchinlek, Field-Marshal Sir
    Claude 317
Auckland 298
Auckland Harbour bridge 178
Australia 53, 62, 74, 208, 296
Australian-British Trade
    Association, Sydney 298
Austria 65, 81
Autolycus 13
Ayub Khan, Muhammad
    (President of Pakistan) 136,
    142, 148
A levels 327
a little local difficulty 96
A National Policy for Coal 27

B

Baalbek 108, 296
Bagehot 280
Baggi, Swedish Minister to Iraq
    111
Baghdad 111
Baghdad Pact 133, 136

Bahrain 139
Baker, Lord (Kenneth) 263
Bali 165
Banca Nazionale di Lavoro 279
Bandaranaike, Mrs Sirinavo
    (Prime Minister of Ceylon)
    209
Bandaranaike, Solomon (Prime
    Minister of Ceylon) 154
Bangkok 296
Bank of England 84, 86
Bank of Indonesia. 163
Bank of Japan 185
bank rate 81, 88, 90, 91, 203, 250
Bank Rate (Pakistan) 142
bank rate tribunal 1957 91
Bareau, Mr 91
Baring, John (non-executive
    Director, Pye of Cambridge)
    300
Barnes, Alfred 43
Basle Agreement 252
Basnett, Lord 262
Basra 123
BBC 'Any Questions' 42
Beale, The Hon Sir Howard
    (Chairman, Pye in Australia)
    298
Bedford, Bill (chief test pilot,
    Hawker) 211
Bedouin 127, 131
Beersheba 130, 131
Beirut 106, 107, 296
Bell, Lord (Tim) 275
Ben Gurion (Prime Minister of
    Israel) 128, 160
Berenice rocket 222
Beria 77
Berryman, Lt-Gen Sir Frank 298
Bessborough, Lady 316
betterment 24
Bevan, Aneurin 43, 264
Beveridge Report 20, 21
Biblos 110
Birch, Nigel 69, 79, 86, 94, 96
birthrate 26
Bishop of London 263
BKS Air Transport 211
Black Knight missile 204, 206
Blair, Tony xii, 97

Blake, Robert (historian) 266
blood sports 36
Blue Streak missile 204, 205, 206, 207, 211, 213, 249
Blunt, Wilfred (drawing master at Eton) 313
BOAC 29
Board of Trade 64, 67, 69, 76, 225
Bodleian Library xiii
Boeing 707 aircraft 212
Bolte, Sir Henry (Premier of Victoria) 299
Bombay 151
Bosch, Jan (Financial Director, Philips Group) 300
Botanical Gardens, Djakarta 163
Botanical Gardens, Kandy 158
Botanical Gardens, Nikko, Japan 187
Boyle, Sir Edward 216
Brabazon, Lord 29
Brazil 73, 254
breaking the sound barrier 211
Bretherton, Russell (civil servant) 261
Britannia aircraft 212
British Bank of the Middle East 106
British Institute of Management 54
British National Committee for Space Research, 207
British Overseas Airways Corporation 212
British Overseas Trade Board 279
British people 23
British Productivity Council 54
British Reserve Insurance 279
British Road Services 45
British Transport Commission 200
Brookeborough, Lord 207
Brown, George 100
Brown, Gordon 22, 97
Bruce, Mr (High Commissioner, NSW) 166
Buccaneer aircraft 224, 231
Budget 1957 81, 82, 84, 85
Budget 1958 100
Bulganin 56, 77
Bunker, Rev (Head of American Mission, Jaffna) 156
Burma Oil Company 143
Butler, RA 46, 61, 64, 66, 68, 79, 83, 216, 231

Buto, Zulficar (Pakistani Minister of Commerce) 141

C

Cabinet 24
Cabinet Defence Committee 219
Cabinet Government, Ceylon 154
Cabinet Secretariat 23, 229, 230
cablemaking venture, Australia 290
Cairo 107
Caledonian Ball 143
calico printing industry 63
Callaghan, James 250, 270, 272
Campbell, Dorothy 91
Canada 57, 58, 72, 75, 208, 225
Canadian Manufacturers Association 58
canal waters, Punjab 141, 143, 145, 146, 148, 149
Canberra 171, 298
Canton 188
capitalism 38, 324
Careno, David (Spanish Ambassador to Jordan) 124
Carrington, Lord (Peter) 167, 221, 226, 259, 272, 328
Carrington, Professor 172
Casey, Dick (Australian Foreign Minister) 170
Cassab, Judy (Australian painter) 168, 171, 316
caste system, India 148
Cementation Ltd 137
CENTO 257
Central Statistical Office 23
Centro Internazionale delle Arti e del Costume 60
Ceylon 53, 105, 153, 157, 208
Chamberlain, Neville 16, 17
Chamoun 104
Chamoun, President 109
Chancellor of the Exchequer x, 36, 61, 64, 76, 79, 81, 84, 90, 97, 99, 201, 202, 216, 232, 250, 253
Chedwyn, Lord 258
Chehab, General 109
Chelmer, Lord 265, 269
Cherwell, Lord 227
Chichester Antiques 317
Chiefs of Staff 217, 224, 225, 258
Chief Defence Scientist 227
Chief of Defence Staff 217, 220, 225, 226, 227, 231

Chief of the General Staff' (CGS 225
Chief Rabbi 263
Chief Scientific Adviser 225, 258
China 41, 60, 73, 151, 161, 162, 171, 197
Chinese Airlines 189
Christian Arab wedding 130
Christian ethic 327
Christian religious teaching 327
Churchill, Randolph 54
Churchill, Winston xi, 19, 30, 33, 41, 45, 60, 64, 73, 78, 79, 227, 257, 258, 260, 261
Church liturgy 263
Cinematograph Film Bill 82
civil aviation 226
Civil Defence Bill, 1937 18
Clark, Lord 309
Clark, William (Deputy Chairman Conservative Party) 267
coal 27
coal crisis 1972 100
coal mines 20
coal supplies to Denmark 66
Cohen, Lord 262
collective bargaining' 262
Colombo Plan 177
Comet aircraft 211
Committee on Defence and Overseas Policy 229
Commonwealth 50, 104, 231
Commonwealth Bank of Australia 167
Commonwealth Conference 1959 105, 173
Commonwealth Finance Ministers 72
Commonwealth Finance Ministers' Conference 1957 89
Commonwealth Relations Office 178
Common Wealth Party 20
communications satellite 205
communications satellite system 211
communism, Malaya 159
Communist Party of India 149
Companion of Honour 276
comprehensive schools 245
computer integrated factory, Aberdare 290
Concorde aircraft 255
Congress Party, India 148

Congress Party (India) 146
Conscription 18
Conservative Central Office xiii, 266, 267, 275
Conservative Party 1922 Committee 199, 268
Conservative Party Chairman 265
Conservative Party Conference 1947 34
Conservative Party Conference 1953 54
Conservative Party Conference 1954 61
Conservative Party Conference 1955 66
Conservative Party Conference 1957 90
Conservative Party Conference 1963 231
Conservative Party Conference 1975 268
Conservative Party Leader 265
Conservative Party organisation 267
Consortium, The (Iran) 138
Constitution of Ceylon 154
consultation with employees 290
conventional war 258
Coralie rocket 213
Coronet Industries Limited, Kowloon 296
Cotton Board 62, 63, 67
Cotton Board Conference 1952 52
Cotton Mill No. 2, Peking 190
Council of Europe 73, 75
Coventry 258
Cox, Baroness 263
crayon 318
cricket 170
crime 245
Criminal Law Revision 248
criminal offences 247
cross-border crime 326
Crossbow 244
Crosthwaite, Moore 108
Crown Prince Abdul Illah 104
Crowther, Lord (Geoffrey) 302, 304
Cuban Missile Crisis 220
Cunard-Eagle Airways 211, 212
Cutler, Sir Roden, VC 298
Czechoslovakia 17

D

Daily Express 224
Daily Mail 104
Daily Telegraph 85, 97
Daily Worker 85
Dakota aircraft 211
Dalgleish, Wing Commander (Pilot of King of Jordan) 125
Dalton, Hugh 82
Darius the Great 135
Darwin 179
Dead Sea 127
Death Grants 21
Debré, M (French Prime Minister) 206
decentralisation 37, 323, 326
decentralised organisation 289
Deedes, Lord (Bill) 248
defence 83
Defence and Overseas Policy Committee 228, 230
defence commitments 252
defence expenditure 324
Defence Intelligence Staff 225
defence reorganisation 217, 219, 225, 230
defence research and development 83, 227
Defence Scientific Staff 226
Delhi 145
democracy 37
Denmark 65
Denny, Admiral Sir Michael 66
denominational schools 263
Derby Aviation 211
Desai , Morarji (Indian statesman) 148
Design for Europe 32
Design for Freedom 32, 93
Design for Living 32, 35, 37, 323
Design for Recovery 32
Design for Wages 32
devaluation 250, 252
de Gaulle, General Charles 68, 222, 296
De Havilland 204, 205
De Zoysa, Mr (Minister of Finance, Ceylon) 154
Dickson, Marshal of the Royal Air Force Sir William 217
Dictionary of National Biography 9
Diet, Japan 185
dissident minority rights 262
Djakarta 163
docks 20

Donoughmore Report 154
Douglas Aircraft 204
Downing Street 313
Dresden 258
Drew, Richard 77
Drogheda, Lord 91
Duke of Edinburgh 66
Dulles, John Foster 74, 191
dumping 192
Duncan, FB (a Director of Pye) 294
Dunston Hall 1
Duplessis 58
Durban, Donald 302
Dytrik, Mr (Polish Minister of Finance) 196

E

early warning station, Fylingdales, Yorkshire 224
Eastern Bank 107
Eastern Europe 26, 31
Eccles, Sir David 81, 82, 85, 87, 89
Economic Commission for Africa. 177
economic cycle 98
Economic Survey 1949 and 1951 91
Eden, Sir Anthony 64, 65, 67, 68, 72, 76, 77, 261
education 20, 82, 263, 327
educational system 245
Education Act 1988 327
Education Reform Bill 1988 263
EEC 87
Egg Scheme, Gambia 42
Egypt 71
Eisenhower, Dwight D 60, 74, 76
Elephant Island, Bombay 152
Elizabeth II 77
Emery, Peter, MP 249
Empire Club of Canada 58
employers 89
employment 20, 25
English Church, Karachi 144
English Heritage 313
Epstein, Jacob 78
Eshkol, Israeli Finance Minister 128
ethnic groups 268
Eton 9, 313
Euratom 73
Euro 22
Europa I (European space vehicle) 213

Europe 33, 46, 72, 81, 104, 252, 260, 261, 325
Europe, German occupation 27
European air traffic control 206
European Association of Ceylon 155
European Coal and Steel Community 68
European Commission 326
European Common Market 81, 174, 201, 205, 208, 210, 212, 296, 308, 326
European currency 298
European defence policy 326
European Economic Community 219
European financial institutions 326
European foreign policy 326
European Free Trade Area 73, 81, 87, 201, 205, 208
European infrastructures 326
European Iron & Steel Community 75
European Launcher Development Organisation (ELDO) 248
European Parliament 268, 270, 301
European Recovery Programme 88
European Space Research Organisation 206, 207
European Union 326
European Union constitution 326
Evening Standard 82, 85, 223, 310
Everybody's 34
exchange rate 88, 256
Eyre, Reginald MP 268

F

F111 aircraft 252, 254
factory projects 290
Fairbairn, The Hon David (Minister of National Development, Australia) 298
Fairbanks, Douglas Jnr 317
family obligations 245
Fargeallah, Maud 109
Far East 218, 252, 296
fashion industry 59
Faure, Maurice 87
Fauteux, Gaspard 58

Federation of British Industries 76
Finance Minister, Indonesia 164
First Lord of the Admiralty 225, 226
Flatow, Mr (Polish Ambassador to China) 189
Fleet Air Arm 257
Foot, Hugh 106
Forbes, Sir Archibald 68
Forbidden City, Peking 189
Foreign Minister, Indonesia 164
Foreign Office 261
Forte, Lord (Charles) 304, 306
Forte, Sir Rocco 307
Forte Group acquisition projects 303
Forward – By the Right 22
Forward by the Right 30, 31, 93
Foster Dulles, John 73
France 53, 56, 74
Franklyn, Dorothy (Mrs Mervyn Thorneycroft) 1, 313
Fraser, Hugh 226
freedom 244
Freeman, John 43
free trade 32, 326
Fry, Mr 91
functional organisation 289

G

Gaitskell, Hugh 43, 64, 89, 91, 97, 210, 258
Galilee 129
Gampel, Mr 91
Garuda Airways 163
Gath 130
GATT 50, 52, 55, 61, 66, 72, 260, 261
GATT Round, Torquay 52
GATT Round Annecy 52
GATT Round Geneva 1953 53
GATT Uruguay Round 1991 256
General and Municipal Workers Union 262
General Election 1945 30
General Election 1950 40
General Election 1955 64
General Election 1959 199
General Election 1979 275
General Election 1951 43
General Electric Company, Singapore 163
Germany 57, 74, 198, 218, 257
German Navy 206
Ghana 208

Gil, Carvajal and Partners 279
Glasgow Chamber of Commerce 60
Glaves-Smith, F W 57
Glentoran, Lord (Northeren Ireland Minister of Commerce) 207
Godber, Joseph 226
Gogogovsky, Jan (Petroleum Institute, Cracow 195
Gold Standard 1931 91
Gorbachev, Mikhail 258
Gordon (Chief Engineer Water Supply, Gath) 130
Gordon Highlanders 65
Gordon Walker, Patrick 220, 224, 230
Great Wall of China 189
Gregg, Milton (UNO representative in Iraq) 112
Grenadier Guards 226
Gronvold, Mr (Norwegian Ambassador to Poland 197
Groundnuts Scheme 42
Group management 290
Guantanamo Bay 325
guided missile ship 223
Guillebaud Committee 201
Gurkha regiments 223

H

Habbaniyah RAF Base, Iraq 123
Haifa 107, 130
Hailsham, Lord 96, 232
Haley, Sir William 91
Hall, Sir Robert 92
Hammarskjöld, Dag (Secretary General of United Nations) 211
Hansard 35, 253
Hansen, HC 66
Hantsbourne Manor, Watford 18
Hardie, Sir Charles 302, 304
Hardman, Sir Henry 227
Hare, John (Minister of Labour) 208
Harlech, Lord 15
Harrison, Maj-Gen Sir James 298
Hartley Library, University of Southampton 219
Hartwell, Eric (Deputy Managing Director of Forte) 305
Hawker Hunter aircraft 211
Hawker P1127 VTOL aircraft 206
Hawker Siddeley 205

Healey, Lord (Denis) 230, 258
Heath, Sir Edward 93, 97, 103, 208, 210, 249, 251, 269
Heathcoat Amory, Derick 96, 100, 202
Heffer, Simon 9, 93
Hendrie, George 302
Hicks-Beach, Beatrice 91
Hickson, Dr Kevin 254
Hinchingbrooke, Lord 20
Hindu welcome 156
Hitler, Adolf 15
HMS Apollo 66
HMS Valiant 232, 249
Hogg, Quintin 27
Holman, John (Sydney lawyer) 290
Holt, Harold (Australian Finance Minister) 169
Holy Land 124
Holy Sepulchre 127
Home, Lord 83, 225, 231
Home Office 246, 247
Home Secretary 246
Hong Kong 180, 296, 298
Hong Kong Chamber of Commerce 181
Hong Kong Shanghai Bank 185
Honiton Conservative Association 249
Hot Springs Conference 28
Houldsworth, Sir Hubert 68
Hound Dog missile 221
Household Cavalry 80
House of Lords reform 299
Howard, Peter 1
Howarth, Alan 267
Howe CD 57
Howe, General Richard (C-in-C Far East) 160, 163
Howe, Sir Geoffrey 100, 271
HRH the Prince of Wales 290
Hull, General Sir Richard 219
Humphrey, Mr (Secretary to Treasury, Malaya) 160
Hungary 76, 198
hydrogen bomb 65, 214, 222

I

Iengar, Mr (Governor, Reserve Bank of India) 151
Ilangaratne, Mr (Minister of Trade and Commerce of Ceylon) 209
IMF 67, 84, 89

immigrants resettlement area, Kowloon 183
immigration 26
Imperial Preference 32, 50, 61, 74, 256
Incorporated Society of Fashion Designers 60
India 53, 62, 73, 105, 141, 208, 209
Indian Airways 145
individual freedom 37
Indonesia 53, 105, 163, 167, 170
Industrial Assurance 21
industrial relations 27
inflation 141, 254
Inner Temple 13
Institute for Strategic Studies 258
insurgents 104
integrated defence policy 227
Intercontinental Ballistic Missile (ICBM) 204
International Monetary Fund 61, 72, 250
international relations 23
International Trade Organisation 33, 51
Investors' Chronicle 98
Iran 134
Iraq 53, 104, 107, 136
Iraqi invasion of Kuwait 325
Iraq Petroleum Company 121
Iron and Steel Board 68
Isfahan 134
Ismay, General Lord 224
Israel 76, 111, 112, 125, 132
Israeli defence system 129
Istituto per lo Studio della Politica Internazionale 56
Italy 36

J

Jacob, Lt Gen Sir Ian 224
Jaffna 155
Japan 53, 56, 62, 184
Java 164
Jay, Douglas 71
Jenkins, Roy 246
Jenkyn, The Hon Mr Justice 298
Jericho 127
Jerusalem 127, 131
Johannesburg 299
Johnston, Sir Charles (UK High Commissioner to Australia) 298
Jordan 104, 125, 126, 132

Jordan Valley Scheme 125
Joseph, Sir Keith 216, 271, 272
Journey to the East 105
Jowitt, Sir William 21
Jumah, Said (of Jordanian Foreign Office) 124
junior board 289
juvenile courts 245
juvenile crime 247
juvenile unemployment 104

K

Kaberry, Donald 67
Kaldor, Nicholas (economist) 154
Kandy 157
Karachi 140
Kariv, Charles (Israeli Ministry of Foreign Affairs 128
Kashmir 142
Kassim, Brig Abdul Karim (Prime Minister of Iraq) 104, 111, 121, 132, 136, 143
Keep Left Group 43
Kendrew, Sir Douglas (Governor of Western Australia) 299
Kennedy, John F 205, 218, 220, 221, 222
Kerala 149
Khan, Ayub 108
Kharami, Rashid 110
Khruschev 56, 77, 103, 220
kibbutz (kubuz) 129
Kilmuir, Lord 89
King David Hotel 128
King Feisal 104
King Feisal II of Iraq 317
King George's Fund for Sailors 317
King George VI 77
King Hussein 104, 123, 132
Knight, Sir Arthur (non-executive Director, Pye of Cambridge) 300
Koramshah 137
Korean War 41, 64
Kowloon 183, 188
Kremlin Museum, Moscow 194
Kuala Lumpur 159
Kubba, Ibrahim (Iraqi Minister of Economics) 121
Kurdistan 112, 133
Kuwait 138

L

Labour Believes in Britain 35
Labour Party 34, 154
Labour Party, New Zealand 172
Labour Party Conference 1976
  254
Lamont, Norman 100
Lancashire textile industry 47
Lancaster House Conference
  1961 211
Land Use 24
Lannion, Brittany 309
Laos 215
La Chapelle de la Bonne
  Nouvelle 309
Lawson, Nigel 100
League of Nations 17, 325
Leathers, Lord 30
Lebanon 104, 106
Lee, Sir Frank 52, 79, 226, 227,
  260
Lee Quan Yeu 296
Lee Quan Yeu 162, 209
Legislative Assembly, Singapore
  162
Lend-Lease Agreement 51
level tendering 71
le Clercq, PH (Chief Executive,
  Philips Group) 295
Le Mayeur, Mme (widow of
  Belgian painter) 166
Liberal Party 31
Lichfield Festival 1989 318
Life Guards 65
Life magazine 64
Like the Roman 93
Lillie, Beatrice 317
Lim Yen Hook 161
Liverpool Cotton Exchange 47
Llandogo 42
Lloyd, FG 15
Lloyd, Geoffrey 68
Lloyd, Selwyn 69, 83, 209, 216
Lloyd George, David 15
Lloyd Oakley, AB 31
local government 268
Longford, Lord 245
Lord, Cyril 67
Lord's Day Observance Society
  84
Lord High Admiral. 226
Lord Mayor's Banquet 1957 90
Lovat Scouts 226

M

Maastricht Treaty 1991 259
MacArthur, General Douglas 42
MacDonald, Malcolm 145, 146,
  149, 151
Macleod, Iain 69, 232
Macmillan, Harold x, 68, 72, 76,
  79, 81, 82, 90, 92, 93, 95, 97,
  103, 156, 203, 204, 205, 208,
  210, 216, 217, 221, 224, 226,
  231, 248, 253, 255, 258, 261
Madame Tussauds 201
Magan, George (of Morgan
  Grenfell) 301
Majoli, Sig (Italian Ambassador
  to Australia) 299
Major, John 100, 259
Makins, Sir Roger 80, 92, 226
Malaya 159, 161, 208
Malaysia 231, 252
Malenkov 56, 77
Malery, Mahmoud (Iranian
  Ambassador to Iraq 111
Mallaby, George 172
management style 303
Manchester Engineering Council
  70
Manchester Guardian 61
Manifesto, Conservative Party,
  1945 28
manufacturing industry 255
Margesson, Capt, MP 17
Marsden, Ernest 41
Marshall Aid 40
Marshall Plan 33, 87
Martinelli, Mario 56
Massey, Sir Harry (Head of
  British National Committee
  for Space Research) 207
Mathew, Theobald 13
Maude, Angus 167, 171, 275
Maudling, Reginald 208, 216,
  232
Maxwell Fyfe, Sir David 41
Mayer, René 68
McAlpine, Lord (Alistair) 269
McIlwaine, Jeremy xiii
McNamara, Robert (US Secretary
  of Defense) 216, 217, 221
McVee, Sir Daniel (Head of
  Metal Industries, Australia)
  171
Medium Range Ballistic Missile
  (MRBM) 204
Meir, Golda (Israeli Foreign
  Minister) 132

Melbourne 299
Melbourne Art Gallery 171
Melbourne Cricket Ground 169
Menzies, Sir Robert 167, 170, 172
Merchandise Marks Act 1953 56
Messina Conference 72
Messmer, M (French Armed
  Forces Minister) 220
Middle East 105, 107
Mikardo, Ian 43
Milner, Major 41
Ming Tombs, Peking 189
Minister of Aviation 210
Minister of Defence 219, 225, 231
Minister of Education 216
Minister of Fuel and Power 68
Minister of Health 216
Minister of Housing and Local
  Government 216
Ministry of Aviation 204, 214,
  216, 226, 227
Ministry of Defence xi, xiii, 69,
  216, 220, 223, 224, 225, 226,
  227, 229, 230, 232, 236, 237,
  240, 254, 258, 325
Ministry of Fuel and Power 28
Ministry of Information 23
Ministry of Public Building and
  Works 223
Ministry of War Transport 30
Minsk 195
missile 258
Moab, Hill of 128
Mohammed, Jamal (Sudanese
  Ambassador to Iraq) 112
Molson, Lord (Hugh) 20, 25, 251
Monckton, Sir Walter 69
Monmouth xi, 31, 40, 42, 43, 64,
  98, 103, 104, 199, 214, 236,
  237, 248
Monnet, Jean 73
Monopolies Commission 62, 65
monopoly 324
Montgomery of Alamein 231
Morley, Mr (British High
  Commissioner in Ceylon)
  153
Moscow 188, 194
Moslem religion 133
Mountbatten, Admiral of the
  Fleet Earl 217, 219, 224, 225,
  226, 317
Mountbatten Papers 219
Mount of Olives 128
multi-faith education 263
Multi-Fibre Arrangement 256

multinational collaboration 211
Munich Conference 17
Murray, Lord 262
Mystère fighter 220

N

Nabarro, Gerald (Conservative MP) 201
Nash, Walter (Prime Minister of New Zealand 172
Nassau 221
Nassau agreement 224
Nasser, Abdel Gamal 71, 76, 107, 110, 111, 123, 125, 126, 139
Nasser (Finance Minister, Iran) 133
Nathanson, Victoria (*vide* Thorneycroft, Victoria)
nationalisation 27, 34, 36, 50, 90
National Coal Board 35, 68
National Economic Development Council 308
National Health Service 43, 264, 324
National Insurance 82
National Iranian Oil Company 137
National Plan 1964 100
National Production Advisory Council for Industry 88
National Publicity Office 23
national security 224
National Society of Pottery Workers 69
National Union of Railwaymen 199
Native Products Export Corporation, China 192
NATO 56, 81, 178, 214, 215, 218, 219, 222, 225, 252, 257, 258
Nazareth 129
Nehru, Pandit Jawaharlal (Prime Minister of India) 146, 170
News Chronicle 85
News of the World 104
New Labour 22, 98
New Territories 182
New Zealand 53, 74, 172, 208, 296, 298
New Zealand Trade Mission 107
NHS 82
Nigeria 208
Nikko, Japan 186
non-proliferation of nuclear weapons 326

Northern Territories, Australia 180
Northumberland Division. 19
North African landings 217
North Korea 60
nuclear bomb 216
nuclear deterrent 205, 216, 219, 221, 224, 231, 254, 257, 326
nuclear deterrent. 224
nuclear disarmament 258, 326
nuclear weapons 204, 217
nylon trade 70

O

OEEC 67, 72, 73, 75, 81, 87
Okinawa 258
Ormsby-Gore, WGA 15
Ottawa Agreement 1932 51, 62
Otter Hounds 4
Ottoman Bank 122, 126
Overseas Trade Corporation, China 190
Oxford University Conservative Association 265
O Class submarine 223

P

P1127 aircraft 214, 219
Paget, Reginald (MP for Northampton) 242
Pakistan 53, 105, 136, 148, 208
Pakistan Petroleum Company 141, 144
Panorama (TV programme) 200
Parker, Lord Justice 91
Parliamentary privilege 90
Parry, Gordon (Labour Candidate, Monmouth) 199
Passchendaele 258
patronage 251
Peace Through Strength Initiative 46
Pegasus engine 214
Peking 189, 190
Pentagon 230
Perera, Mr (Trotskyist Opposition Leader of Ceylon) 154
Permanent Secretary for Defence 225
Persepolis 134
Perth, Australia 299
petrol duty 85
Philips' factories, Nijmegen 295
Philips' factory, Hilversum 295

Philips, Frits (Philips Group Chairman) 295
Philips Group 279, 294
Philips Research Laboratories, Eindhoven 295
Phillips, Sir Thomas 21
Pickard, Michael 302, 305
Picture Post 34
Piero della Francesca 314
Pirelli 181
Pirelli, Dr Alberto 56, 280
Pirelli, Ing Piero 280
Pirelli Group 279
Pirelli UK plc 293
Pitchforth, Vivien 316
planning 20, 24
Plumpton Agricultural College 315
Poland 198
Polaris missile 205, 218, 221, 229
police 246
police forces, amalgamation 247
pollution 326
Poole, Oliver 67, 90
population 26, 27
pottery industry 69
Powell, Enoch 79, 84, 86, 89, 93, 94, 149, 200, 203, 216, 232, 299
practical education 327
pre-emptive invasion 325
prescription charges 249
President of the Board xi, 45, 48, 61, 81, 89, 208, 256, 261, 262, 280, 309
Press, British 23
Press Conference TV programme 54
Price, Brigadier RA 18
price-fixing 65
prices and incomes freeze 1966 249
price control 141
Priestley, JB 20
Princess Maria Pia of Savoy 78
Prince Alexander of Jugoslavia 78
Prior, Lord (Jim) 272
prisoners, release of 247
privatisation 50
Proctor, George 307
productivity 26, 28, 46, 88
Profumo, John 219, 226
Profumo prize 13
Propaganda 23
public expenditure 82, 84, 201
Punch 63

Punjab Regiment 65
Purchase Tax 64, 69, 85, 86
Pye facilities, South Africa 299
Pye factories, New Zealand 298
Pye of Cambridge 279, 294
Pye subsidiaries, Australia 298
Pym, Francis 272
Pym, LR 31

Q

Quadir, Mr (Pakistani Minister of
    Foreign Affairs 142
Queen Mary 77
Queen Soraya 77

R

Radcliffe Commission 86, 92
RAF Aldergrove 207
RAF Bishopscourt radar station
    207
Rahman, Halfizur (Pakistani
    Minister of Commerce) 209
Raikes, Sir Victor 61
railways 20
Rangernathan, Mr (Secretary,
    Indian Ministry of Commerce
    and Industry) 147
Rapacki Plan 197
RB162 Rolls-Royce engine 214
Reagan, Ronald 258
Reconstruction Problems,
    Committee on 21
Reece, Gordon (Director of
    Publicity, Conservative Party)
    269, 274
refugees 127
religion 263
religious education 263
Remorino, Jeronimo 57
Renolds Chain 70
Republic of San Marino 314
resettlement estates, Kowloon
    296
resignation 94, 96, 98, 99, 167
restrictive practices 25, 249
restrictive trade practices 65,
    70, 324
Restrictive Trade Practices Court
    70
Rhodesia/Nyasaland 208
Richardson, Josephine 43, 200
Ridley, Adam (Research
    Department, Conservative
    Party) 275
road transport 35

Robbins, Lionel 92
Robens, Lord (Alf) 305
Roi, Mr (Secretary, Indian
    Ministry of Finance) 147
Roosevelt, Franklin D 51
Rootes Group, Australia 168
Rotary Club of Hong Kong 296
Rotary Club of Montreal 58
Rowlatt, Mr Justice 13
Roy, Mr (Indian Ambassador to
    Poland) 198
Royal Air Force 73, 205, 221,
    231, 257
Royal Artillery 10, 21
Royal Institute of International
    Affairs 105
Royal Marines 223
Royal Military Academy,
    Woolwich 9
Royal Navy 205, 223
Royal Yacht Britannia 66
rubber-growing, Ceylon 158
Russian paintings 195
Ryder, Ken (Pirelli Australia)
    298

S

Saar 73
Saatchi and Saatchi 269, 274, 275
Salisbury, Marquess of 83
Sandys, Duncan 83, 208, 217
Sanshal, (Minister of Guidance,
    Iraq 122
Sato, Mr (Japanese Minister of
    Finance) 184
SC1 VTOL aircraft 207
Schuman, Robert 46, 68
Schumann, Maurice 56, 60
Schuman Plan 260
Scott, Mr and Mrs 110
Scott, Sir Robert (Commissioner-
    General, Malaya) 160
Scottish Devolution 270
Scott Report 20, 24
Seacat missile 206
SEATO 178, 215, 257
Second World War 20, 27
Secretary of State for Air 225,
    226
Secretary of State for Defence
    227
Secretary of State for War 225,
    226
Selkirk, Lord (Commissioner-
    General for South East Asia)
    208

Sergeant missile 218
Shackleton, Lord 258
Shadow Home Secretary 244
Shadow Minister of Transport
    35
Shaeb, Mr (Pakistani Minister of
    Finance) 141
Shah, Manubai (Indian Minister
    of Industry) 147
Shahanshah of Persia 77
Shiraz 135
Shiva 152
Short Brothers 206, 207
Sierra Leone 208
Signorini, Renato 60
Sikri 150
Singapore 105, 160, 161, 252,
    254, 258
Single European Act 261
SITPRO 279, 308
Sitwell, Sacheverell 136
Skion Kop, Battle of 2
Skybolt missile 205, 214, 221
Smith, RJ (Export Sales Manager,
    Pirelli General) 300
Smuts, Jan Christian 19, 78
Smyth, Brigadier Sir John, MP
    229
Soames, Christopher 249
Social Contract 254
social security 21
Soskice, Sir Frank 246
Southern Rhodesia 299
South Africa 257, 296
South China Morning Post 298
South East Asia 154, 231
South Sea Cotton Mill, Hong
    Kong 182
Soviet bloc 56, 61
Soviet Congress 194
Soviet naval activity 299
Spaak, Paul-Henri 81
Spadeadam 207
Special Air Services 226
Spicer, Michael, MP 269
spin 23
Stafford 1, 15, 16, 17, 18, 30, 36
Staff College, Camberley 19
Stalin 56
Stanislavsky Ballet Company,
    Moscow 194
Stanley, CO (entrepreneur) 294
Stark, Freya 317
Stassen, Harold 56, 60
State ownership of industry 324
steel industry 249

Sterling Area 121, 175, 252
sterling convertibility 58, 61
sterling devaluation 1967 100
Stewart-Clark, Sir Jack 300, 301
Stewart-Clark, Sir Jack 295
stock market 255
Strasbourg Conference 1961 207
Strauss, Franz-Josef (German
    Defence Minister) 219
Strauss, H 64
St George's Ball, Hong Kong 187
St James's, Spanish Place. 42
St Laurent, Yves 57
St Lawrence Seaway 57
submarine power cable factory,
    Southampton 290
subsidiary 259, 326
Sudan 112
Suez 299
Suez Canal 71, 76, 83
Sumatra 163, 165
Summer Palace, Peking 189
Sunday Pictorial 85
Sun Yat Sen 188
supply of arms to South Africa
    299
surtax 84
Swindell, Archdeacon 16
Swingler, Stephen 30
Sydney 179
Sydney Art Gallery 168
Symon, Alec (British High
    Commissioner in Pakistan)
    140
Syria 123, 126

T

Taj Mahal 150
Tamils 156
Tang, PY 182
technical university, Peking 191
Teheran 132
telecommunications cable
    factory, Bishopstoke 290
television 200
Telling the World 23
Tel Aviv 128
Temple of Jupiter 108
Temple of the Tooth, Kandy 158
Terms of Trade 202
Tettenhall Towers 2, 16
Thatcher, Baroness (Margaret)
    ix, x, xi, 100, 259, 265, 267,
    268, 269, 270, 271, 273, 274,
    275, 276, 278, 293, 334
the 'Six' 81

The Amateur xii, 309, 310, 312
The Economy 252
The Husbandman Waiteth 28
the Six 72, 74, 87
The Sunday Times 202
The Times 97
The Vancouver News 57
Thomas, Graham 40
Thorneycroft, Carla x, xi, xiii, 13,
    39, 42, 45, 57, 59, 78, 80, 87,
    199, 232, 233, 249, 277, 300,
    304, 313, 328
Thorneycroft, Delia 314
Thorneycroft, Dorothy 2
Thorneycroft, Elizabeth 1, 57,
    164
Thorneycroft, George Benjamin
    2
Thorneycroft, John xiii, 18, 312
Thorneycroft, Maj-Gen
    Alexander Whitelaw 19
Thorneycroft, Mervyn 1, 5, 10
Thorneycroft, Victoria xii, xiii,
    42, 59, 80, 103, 127, 190, 309,
    312
Thorneycroft Benefaction 2
Thorneycroft Light Horse
    Regiment 2
Thorneycroft Scholar 254
Thornicrofte, Hamo de 2
Thorn Industries 294
Threlfall, Peter (Managing
    Director, Pye of Cambridge)
    294
Threlfall, Roger (Managing
    Director, Pye Pty, Australia)
    299
Tiberias 129
tied garage system 71
Tillyer, Revd DB 328
To-morrow's Children 26
tobacco duty 87
Tokyo 184
Tonypandy, Viscount 260
Tory Reform Committee x, 20,
    30, 47, 79, 259, 332
Town and Country Planning 25
Trade 32
trade agreements, bilateral 32
trade unions 27, 32, 43, 89, 262,
    268
trade union law 262
trading practices, French 171
traffic police 246
Trafford Gallery 310, 317
train robbers 247

Transport Commission 41, 199
transport policy 42
Transport Users' Consultative
    Committee 104
Treaty of Rome 87
Triad Societies 183
Trident missile 259, 326
Trucial States. 112
Trust House Forte 279, 302
TSR2 aircraft 222, 230, 231, 238
TUC 262
TUC Conference 1948 36
Tungku Abdul Rahman 296
Tyerman, Mr 91
tyre factory, Carlisle 290

U

unemployment 25, 262
United Europe Association 212
United Nations 33, 41
United Nations Organisation
    104, 325
university education 327
University of Kandy 158
UNO 108, 109, 197
UNRRA 127
urban areas, rebuilding 25
USA 23, 32, 33, 53, 56, 58, 75, 104,
    204, 206, 216, 221, 231, 257,
    259, 325
USSR 23, 31, 56, 103, 106, 110,
    216, 220, 258, 325
US Congress 34
Uthwatt Report (1942) 20, 25
Utility Scheme 50

V

V-bombers 216, 218, 222
Varley, Joan 268
Vassall, William (spy) 220
Venice 60
Venice in Peril 313
Véronique rocket 206, 211
Vickers Armstrong 61, 232
Vickers VC10 aircraft 212
Vietnam 257
Viking aircraft 211
Vineyvitch, Mr (Polish Vice-
    Minister of Foreign Affairs)
    197
Viscount aircraft 61
Vogue 59
Vulcan bomber 205

W

wages policy 20
wage bargaining 88
wage restraint 254
Walker-Smith, Derek 71
Wallace, Clarence 57
Ward, John (painter) 316
Warsaw 196
wartime controls 41
War Office 19
watercolour 318
Waterhouse, Capt, MP 17
Watkinson, Harold 216
Webster, Sir Richard, (Director of Organisation, Conservative Party) 269
Wedgwood Benn, Tony 272, 294
welfare milk 82
Welfare State 245
Wells, Rear Admiral DC 298
Wells Page, Sheila 16, 39
Welsh Devolution 270
Wessex helicopter 224
Western European Union 73
Western Mail 248
Western Mail and South Wales News 64
Westlake, Sheridan xiii
West Germany 56
White, Irene 57
White, Mr 107
Whitelaw, Maj-Gen Alexander 2
Whitelaw, Viscount (Willie) 79, 265, 272
Whitlam, Gough (Prime Minister of Australia) 291
Who goes next? (TV programme) 200
Wilberforce, Lord 260
Wilson, Harold xi, 43, 63, 71, 86, 89, 90, 100, 214, 216, 236, 237, 238, 239, 246, 248, 249, 251, 252, 253, 254
Wincott, Harold (Financial Times columnist) 98, 201
Wolff, Michael (Director General Conservative Party) 265
Wood, Alan 85
Woolgar, Dr Chris xiii
Woolton, Lord 67
Woomera firing range, Australia 204, 206
works councils 20
Work or Want 36
World Bank 72, 89

Y

Yamajiwa, Masamachi (Governor, Bank of Japan 185
Yay, Mr (Chinese Minister for Foreign Trade) 192
Yorkshire Evening Post 41
Young, Baroness 275

Z

Ziegler, Philip 217
Zotoff, Mr, GOSPLAN, USSR 194
Zuckerman, Sir Solly 227